# SALT & LIGHT

## The Complete Jesus

*Inlaid marble panel of Jesus from the 300s CE. Discovered in 1959
in the ruins of an unfinished mansion in Imperial Rome's port city of Ostia.*

## JONATHAN GEOFFREY DEAN

ISBN
978-1-7782504-2-2 (Hardcover)
978-1-7782504-0-8 (Paperback)
978-1-7782504-1-5 (eBook)

Front cover image by Alexander Awerin. The image shows a portion of one of the doors of the unfinished Sagrada Familia basilica in Barcelona, Spain.

Genres: Nonfiction, History, Historical Jesus, Christianity, Biography

RELIGION / Biblical Criticism & Interpretation / New Testament
RELIGION / Biblical Commentary / New Testament / Jesus, the Gospels & Acts
RELIGION / Biblical Studies / New Testament / Jesus, the Gospels & Acts
RELIGION / Christian Theology / Christology
BIOGRAPHY & AUTOBIOGRAPHY / Religious

Keywords: Popular non-fiction, historical non-fiction, Jesus, historical Jesus, religion & spirituality, New Testament studies, Christology, Christian books, ancient history.

#jesus #christ #christianity #christian #bible #atheism #jesuschrist #gospel

Distributed to the trade by The Ingram Book Company

Visit www.saltandlight.ca

THIS BOOK IS DEDICATED TO ALL THOSE WHO ARE SEARCHING—EVEN IF THEY'RE NOT SURE WHAT THEY'RE SEARCHING FOR—IN THE HOPE THAT THEY MAY FIND SOME MEASURE OF TRUTH, KNOWLEDGE, AND PEACE THROUGH THIS BOOK.

# TABLE OF CONTENTS

# PREFACE AND WELCOME

I have written *Salt & Light* for those, like myself, who want to learn about the authentic Jesus. This work is intended to be of interest to all people of any and no religious background. I welcome both the New Testament academic and the person on the street who has never had exposure to Jesus in any form. I assume no prior knowledge of the sources about Jesus and no special training, just an open mind and common sense.

This book, the first in a two-book series, has been built using widely disparate research from the academic world. However, I have unified this information into a straightforward and easy to grasp form. I provide all the references for further reading and appendices with side discussions if the gentle reader wishes to dig deeper into any topic.

*Salt & Light* is the product of more than ten years of reading and thinking on my part. Why did I write it? Because I am interested in Western Civilization. I am indeed a product of it, part of it, living in it. And I am thus, albeit in a modest way, contributing to its politics, history, arts, literature, and culture. Western culture is staggeringly rich, but the most influential work it produced is undeniably the Christian Bible.

I have read the entire Christian Bible numerous times, and, despite being completely overwhelmed by the scope of its contents, for me the most compelling part is the stories about Jesus, namely the four Gospels'[1] accounts in the New Testament section of the Bible. Jesus, incredibly, is the single most important influencer of Western civilization, and perhaps the world. He was a poor man who taught for a few years in a backwater of the Roman Empire and was then killed for sedition 2,000 years ago. However, Jesus started the world's largest movement, and to billions of people now and in the past, somehow he has served in some form or other as a model for our humanity. He is compelling and allusive, so, indeed, time spent studying Jesus is time well spent. After putting the Bible down, I came away wanting to know everything about him, to get to the complete Jesus once and for all—and this book is the result. I hope you come along with me on this fascinating journey to discover the Complete Jesus.

# ACKNOWLEDGEMENTS

> "If I have seen further, it is by standing on the shoulders of Giants."
>
> – Sir Isaac Newton, *Letter to Robert Hooke*

I gratefully acknowledge the unwavering patience of my wife, Lynn, who has always been "in my corner" and supportive throughout the creation of this book. I also gratefully acknowledge the tremendous work of editor-extraordinaire Ariane Magny, whose comments and suggestions I accepted without hesitation (almost) all the time. I thank those volunteers, including my mother, Shirley, who read the manuscript in various forms and provided me with vital feedback. I want to thank all the scholars

---

1   The Gospel of Mark, the Gospel of John, the Gospel of Luke, and the Gospel of Matthew. The word "gospel" was ultimately derived from the ancient Greek word euángélion, which means "good news." It translates into Latin as bonus nuntius (or evangelium), and to old English as gōdspel, a portmanteau of "good" (god) and "story" (spel). Originally, the expression "the good news" applied to the Christian message, but over time, it came to mean the major works describing Jesus' life and deeds. As we shall see, there are, in fact, more than four gospels.

and researchers in this field, as their diligent work is the bedrock upon which this book stands. We are lucky to live in a time of rational and free inquiry into matters of faith. Also, I acknowledge those people and institutions who gave their permissions freely so I could include certain images for the benefit of the reader.

I have made every effort to attribute works. Any factual errors, errors in attribution, or uncritical thinking are my fault. You are free to disagree, of course, in whole or in part with anything I say!

## A FEW PRELIMINARIES

- I will use CE (Common Era) and BCE (Before Common Era) for date eras, as they are more commonly used and therefore less religiously charged, instead of the older AD (Anno Domini = "in the year of the Lord") and BC (= Before Christ).

- I will try to use actual dates versus century designations. For instance, instead of saying "mid-second century CE," I will write "around 150 CE" or "c. 150 CE."[2] It is less confusing, although, for the first century CE (years 1–99), I will use the phrase "first century."[3]

- I place the death of Jesus on April 1, 33 CE.[4]

- I will use the traditional names for sources. For instance, I will use the title Gospel of Peter for that source, even though the disciple Peter did not write the work. I also will refer to John the Baptist as "the Baptist" to distinguish him from other Johns.

- When it is clear, I will refer to gospels by their traditionally attributed name, for instance, Mark for the Gospel of Mark.

- I often quote from the New Testament (NT) section of the Christian Bible.[5] The New Testament was written initially in koine Greek, the ancient world's English. Since then, there have been many translations of the Bible into most modern and ancient languages (over 2,000 languages!). And within any one language, there are various versions, because a translation is also an interpretation. This is especially true in modern English, as there are over 100 major versions of the Bible, all the way from the American Standard Version (ASV) to the Young Literal Translation (YLT). These include Wycliffe's Bible (WYC), the first English version from 1388, the famous King James Version (KJV) of 1611, and The Message (MSG,) a modern paraphrase in contemporary English from 2002. I will be quoting from the best seller New International Version (NIV) unless otherwise noted. The NIV is a popular and scholarly version first published in 1978. I will follow its chapter and verse notations. There are also many online Bible resources available, including free downloadable copies of the NIV. As you read through this book, you will find it helpful to have a copy of the New Testament handy to look up the context and specifics of NT references.

- I will avoid the term "Jesus Christ," since it relies on assumptions yet to be examined, for instance, that Jesus is the Jewish Messiah[6]. For that same reason, I will use "he" or "him" to refer to Jesus instead of "He" or "Him." "Christ" is from the Greek *Christos,* meaning "the anointed," which in Hebrew is *masiah,* or "messiah." The expressions "Jesus the

---

2    "c." stands for "circa," which is the Latin for "approximately."

3    Although I use the Chicago Manual of Style 17, I have deviated from it in a number of areas to improve clarity.

4    I will thoroughly discuss the reasoning for this date in the Chapter 26.

5    I will use the title New Testament (NT) for clarity, although I will argue this is a misnomer, as it implies a previous "Testament."

6    In the Jewish religion the Messiah was an ill-defined liberator descended from King David, either a political or religious leader, who would free the Jews and rule them according to God's laws. For more information see (The Editors of Encyclopaedia Britannica, Messiah 2020).

Anointed" and "Jesus the Messiah" will also be avoided. Jesus' actual Aramaic[7] name was Yeshua, or Yahushua, meaning "God's deliverance." The name was transliterated into Greek as Iēsous, since Greek masculine names did not end with a vowel. In the 400s CE, scribes transliterated the Greek into the Latin equivalent, Iesous (Eel-ay-sous). In 1526 CE, William Tyndale's translation of the Bible from Latin into English used the English-Germanic "J" to render the name "Jesus." However, it was still pronounced "Eel-ay-sous." Later pronunciation in English changed to "jay-sous" and then the current "jee-zuz." I will stick with the English name "Jesus" or "Jesus of Nazareth."[8]

- In a few cases, where noted, I use images made available under the Creative Commons Licence, via Wikimedia Commons. For example, "CC BY-SA 3.0" means the Creative Commons Attribution-ShareAlike Licence version 3.0. I thank the original images contributors for making the images available. Here is the link to the various licenses used, https://creativecommons.org/licenses/, and a link to Wikimedia Commons https://commons.wikimedia.org/wiki/Main_Page.

---

7    Aramaic was the language that Jesus and his followers primarily spoke. Greek and Hebrew also existed, the former being the common language of non-Jews and the primary written language, while the latter was more the preserve of the religious establishment. For more information see (The Editors of Encyclopaedia Britannica, Aramaic language 2018).

8    (Weyler 2008, 54).

# INTRODUCTION

*Figure 1 **Jesus Obscured.***

*This detail is from a damaged wall painting depicting the story of Jesus (right) and his follower Peter (left) walking on water. Peter steps out of a boat onto the water with Jesus, but then Peter starts to sink—one can indeed see the waves starting to come up over him, and he is reaching out to Jesus to save him. This is a crude picture, taken from the house church in Dura-Europos, Syria; it could be the oldest datable depiction of Jesus. Archaeologists have dated the work to 233–256 CE, painted a mere 200 years after the alleged event took place. Image courtesy of Yale University Art Gallery.*

I think this is a very appropriate picture to start the book. We see a story about Jesus, yet the figure of Jesus is shadowy, incomplete and ill-defined. It sums up the starting point—*Jesus obscured*.

This book is a definitive and complete inquiry into the authentic Jesus. This Jesus is based on rational thinking, the simplest conjectures, and the best available sources of information. This project's building blocks are ideas derived from the critical method of inquiry, often inspired by academic sources. The critical method is concerned with avoiding, in the case of religious writings, religious doctrine and human bias by applying a non-sectarian, reason-based approach to arrive at reasonable conclusions. As Christopher Hitchens put it: "That which can be asserted without evidence, can be dismissed without evidence."[1] I do not want *Salt & Light* to be so easily dismissed.

---

1    (Hitchens 2009, 258)

# THE THREE QUESTIONS

As with any journey, it is essential to be clear on the destination to keep us on course, so in the interest of clarity and brevity, I propose the Three Questions to be our guide. The purpose, then, of this book is to answer, as best as possible, the following simple questions:

1.   What did Jesus do?

2.   What did Jesus say?

3.   Who was Jesus?

But first things first. Do we need to engage in this project at all? The fastest way to read a book is to discover that you do not need to read it. Two scenarios need investigation before going any further, for if either is correct, then there is no need for this book.

First, I must tackle the minority scholarly view that Jesus never existed … that is, he is a myth. If this is true, this will be a very short book, and we need not proceed any further. So I must review this fascinating idea first before proceeding.

Second, if Jesus did exist, the next step is to review current opinions on Jesus to see if others have already completed this project. In other words, have the Three Questions been answered and are these answers reasonable and widely held? If there are excellent existing answers, *Salt & Light* is not needed, and I will not proceed any further other than to repeat the answers to the questions. Suppose there is general confusion within current opinions about Jesus? In that case, I will need to embark on this project by starting from ground zero, casting a wide net and examining everything about Jesus without bias, and then proceed to answer the Three Questions.

# CHAPTER 1

# DID JESUS EXIST?

"Something that doesn't actually exist can still be useful."

—Ian Stewart, *Infinity: A Very Short Introduction*

The idea that Jesus is merely a myth certainly stands as a minority position in the academic arena; however, I do think I should examine it first, since if Jesus did not exist, there is nothing to investigate. Perhaps I can save myself (and you) a lot of work by making this project pointless. And it is always a good thing to challenge the majority view!

Perhaps the most compelling and complete Jesus-as-myth argument has been put forward by Richard Carrier in a fascinating work entitled *On the Historicity of Jesus: Why We Might Have Reason for Doubt*. In this book, Carrier explains how myths can become intertwined with reality:

"In 1945 Betty Crocker was rated in a national survey as the second most admired woman in America, and to this day a street is named after her in Golden Valley, Minnesota, where she still lives. Her father was William Crocker, a successful corporate executive in the food industry, and she started her career answering letters on cooking questions for her father's company, then acquired her own national radio show where she delivered cooking advice for twenty-four years. Later she had her own television show, while making appearances on other TV shows and in TV commercials to promote her products. I've seen actual videotapes of her cooking and speaking, and her picture still adorns various General Mills baking products. She has published several cookbooks, and now has her own website. All of this is 100% percent true. And yet she doesn't exist."[1]

Betty Crocker is a myth, yet many people, Carrier argues, believe she is just as real as Jesus. Other widely circulating myths include the 1947 Roswell UFO crash, the notion that Sherlock Holmes was a real detective, the idea that the US government destroyed the Twin Towers on September 11, 2001, the cargo cults on Pacific islands,[2] and the Mormon Church founder Joseph Smith's story of the golden plates.[3] These all illustrate how quickly people can come to believe unexpected things, even in the face of overwhelming evidence to the contrary.

Carrier does an excellent job presenting evidence to show how unsurprising it would be if Jesus were only a myth. For instance, he points out how the Apostle Paul[4] in his letters stresses a celestial divine Jesus and ignores any physical Jesus, a view known as Pauline Christianity. According to Carrier, Christianity started as a merging of pagan and Jewish salvation theologies (called syncretism) that took the form of a mystery cult. It arose in Palestine during a time of fevered and imminent

---

1   (Carrier 2014, 11947).

2   For more information on the cargo cult phenomena see (The Editors of Encyclopaedia Britannica, Cargo cult 2017).

3   For more information see (Bushman 2020).

4   Also called Saint Paul and Saul of Tarsus (c. 5 CE–c. 62 CE), a noted early missionary and letter writer. For a background on Paul please see (Sanders, St. Paul the Apostle 2020).

Messiah expectation. At the time, many Jews searched the body of Jewish religious literature[5] for secret meanings to "prove" various religious ideas, such as the identity of the Messiah or how mediation between Heaven and Earth would be carried out.

An ancient mystery cult, according to Carrier, was a religious system that kept its precepts hidden from outsiders; these were only slowly revealed to initiates as they progressed through their conversion. Most of these cults included the following elements: an initiation; ritual sacrifices, meals, and purification; a mystical and revelatory experience; a back story of the death and rebirth/resurrection of a hero or god who accomplishes some tasks; and the promise of rewards in this life and the next.

Mystery cults were widespread at the time in the free-wheeling religious environment of the Roman Empire. The main ones we know of were the Eleusinian Mysteries, the Dionysian Mysteries, the Orphic Mysteries, Mithraism, the Romulus/Quirinus cult, and the cult of Isis.

According to Carrier, a Christian cult arose out of this milieu, with Jesus Christ as a Jewish celestial deity who communicated with followers through dreams, visions, and hidden meanings in the Jewish Scriptures (JS) or written prophecy. Like deities from other mystery cults, for instance Romulus, celestial Jesus endured an ordeal involving "incarnation, death, burial and resurrection"[6] in the supernatural realm. Over time, as the search for converts became more competitive with other cults, the proto-Christians did as other cults were doing—namely, they composed allegorical stories (the Gospels) around a physical Jesus who had taught and healed in Palestine, a process called historicization. Therefore, they placed a fictional character in history. Carrier notes how closely the Jesus story matches other cults' stories. For example, in the main story from the Romulus cult, the hero, Romulus, the legendary founder of Rome, was a god's son, born of a virgin. He later became a shepherd. He was then hailed as a king and killed by the elite. Finally, he rose from the dead, appeared to his friends to tell them the good news, and eventually ascended into heaven.

Carrier further explains that the upheavals of the First Jewish-Roman War,[7] a rebellion by the Jews against Rome (66–70 CE), which resulted in the destruction of Jerusalem, created a thirty-year "gap" from 65 CE to 95 CE in the history of Christianity, where the original proto-Christians died out and were replaced by new converts who took the allegorical stories about Jesus as fact. To them, Jesus was an actual historical figure.

Finally, Carrier argues that the later Church then aggressively put down many alternative Christian groups, and their works, that questioned Jesus' physical existence, so what remained were the original allegorical stories, the Gospels, detailing a physical but made-up Jesus. Christianity was thus born despite Jesus never existing.

I admire Carrier's project, and I do concur with him on specific issues. He correctly makes much of the fact that many of the earliest Christian works, such as Paul's letters, belay little or no knowledge of a physical Jesus. If we only had the very early texts of the first letter of Clement of Rome,[8] the letters of Apostle Paul, disciple John, James the Just, and disciple Peter[9] as sources, all we would know of Jesus would be a mainly spiritual Jesus in Heaven, who communicates with people through visions, prophecy, and reading "between the lines" of JS.

However, Carrier fails in his overall argument for a variety of reasons. To believe that Jesus never existed, one must assume that *all* the information from inside and outside Christianity about a physical Jesus, namely, a complex set of sayings and

---

5    Judaism's sacred texts can be divided into two groups: those from before the destruction of the Jewish Temple in Jerusalem in 70 CE and those from after. The destruction of the Temple destroyed the temple-sacrifice model of Judaism and initiated the current Rabbinic version of Judaism. The pre-70 sacred texts correspond to the Jewish Scripture (JS), also called the Hebrew Bible or the *Tanakh*, the canonical collection of sacred Jewish literature. It includes the Torah (The Law or the Five Books of Moses), the books of the Prophets, and other books of poetry, law, wisdom, prophecy, songs, folklore, teachings, history, and theological and royal propaganda. The Christian Old Testament is drawn from the JS and contains essentially the same information, although there are some differences in books included and ordering. See also (The Editors of Encyclopaedia Britannica, Hebrew Bible 2020).

6    (Carrier 2014, 2109).

7    For more information (The Editors of Encyclopaedia Britannica, First Jewish Revolt 2020) and (Mattis 1995).

8    Fourth Bishop of Rome, (c. 35–99 CE). Please see (The Editors of Encyclopaedia Britannica, Saint Clement I 2013).

9    Early followers of Jesus.

doings, as well as incidental information and reactions, set in an accurate historical time and place, were complete fabrications with symbolic meanings. That is extremely unlikely.

Carrier, therefore, must portray all the sources that include a physical Jesus as fabrications written by untrustworthy authors. According to him, the important early Christian author Papias,[10] who discusses information about the followers of a physical Jesus, is dismissed out of hand; "the things he tells us are ridiculous."[11] Carrier states that the book of Acts of the Apostles, an early history of the Church in the NT, is "not really to be trusted."[12] Similarly, the four Gospels are "primarily and pervasively mythical."[13] For instance, the Gospel of Mark is a "fictional, symbolic construct, from beginning to end,"[14] and so on. This position is only possible if all these sources were composed after 100 CE, allowing the authors the creative freedom to make everything up and not be challenged by eyewitnesses who would have all passed away by the 90s. However, when I examine these sources, I will show that they are much earlier works written during the lifetime of eyewitnesses; therefore, no such creative freedom existed.

Richard Carrier must also show that all the passages presenting physical evidence of Jesus are allegorical or metaphorical. For example, when Simon of Cyrene helped carry Jesus' cross (Mark 15:21), this simple extraneous detail is explained away by Richard Carrier in a complicated, esoteric allegory requiring four pages of explanation! Indeed, the simpler explanation that a real Simon helped a real Jesus makes better sense.

Therefore, for these reasons, it is safe to dismiss Carrier's argument that Jesus never existed and move forward to the next topic: Do reasonable and widely held answers exist already for the Three Questions?

---

10  Papias was a bishop and author (c. 60–163 CE) who lived in the ancient city of Hierapolis in the Roman province of Asia (western Turkey). For more information see (The Editors of Encyclopaedia Britannica, Papias 2020).

11  (Carrier 2014, 17055)

12  (Carrier 2014, 21931).

13  (Carrier 2014, 23439).

14  (Carrier 2014, 24212).

# CHAPTER 2

# VIEWS OF JESUS

*Figure 2 **The Deesis Mosaic from the Hagia Sophia Holy Grand Mosque in Istanbul***

*This is a detail of an eye-popping mosaic from the mid-1200s. The mosque was initially built as a Christian church called the Hagia Sophia (or "Holy Wisdom") Basilica; it was the largest building in the world when built in 537 CE by Roman emperor Justinian I, as it was the main Imperial church. It replaced an earlier church built by Emperor Constantius II that had burned down under Justinian. When Constantinople was conquered in 1453 by the Turks, it was converted into a mosque; the mosaics were plastered over, and all the crosses chipped off. The building was converted into a museum in 1931, and the above mosaic was restored. However, Turkey's current government has re-designated the museum as a mosque, and it is unclear what the mosaics' fate will be. Image courtesy of engin akyurt.*

"If you're not confused, you're not paying attention."

—Tom Peters, *Thriving on Chaos: Handbook for a Management Revolution*

## CURRENT VIEWS

The world's most popular religions each bring their own set of answers, usually contradictory, to the Three Questions.

Judaism teaches that Jesus was a false prophet, not the Messiah expected by the people of Israel. The Rabbinic tradition (called the Talmud, stories and opinions of ancient rabbis added to Judaism's literature), in turn, claims that he asked followers to worship him as divine, denounces him as a sorcerer, and says he "led Israel astray" and, as a result, he was "hanged on Passover Eve."[1]

Islam, however, views Jesus as belonging to the long line of biblical prophets and as a teacher of "the Children of Israel" sent by the Muslim God, Allah. Jesus is thus the second last prophet before Muhammad, and Allah saved him from death at the very last moment.[2]

On the other hand, Buddhism considers Jesus to have lived many previous lives, and his teachings, although good, are still subject to Karma, his actions in his previous lives. Jesus' crucifixion is a non-event, and Jesus' teachings about a Father-God are incorrect.

The Baha'i faith considers Jesus as having both a physical and divine nature. He was a messenger sent from God to teach salvation and was born of a virgin, but Jesus was not bodily resurrected from death.

Mainstream Christianity, however, believes, for the most part, that Jesus was born of a virgin. He was both human and divine and came into the world as the son of only one earthly parent, Mary. He was also sinless, unjustly tried, and killed by the Romans, then buried in a tomb. He then returned to life on the third day after his death, when various people saw him. He eventually ascended back to God the Father and will come back again to Earth at a time called the Second Coming. He is/ was some combination of Son of Man, Son of God, Preexistent, Lord, Prophet, Messiah, Messenger, Teacher, Servant, Saviour, Apostle, High Priest, and is also one part of a Trinity consisting of God, the Holy Spirit, and God's Son, Jesus. Finally, he is the only way to salvation, and by dying, he atoned for the sins of the world in a cosmic, salvific event, thereby "saving" it.

Although these are the core beliefs of Christianity, there are additional variations amongst Christian denominations. Current, non-orthodox Christian views include a bewildering array of substantive, variant beliefs, from Monophysitism, Mormonism, Unitarianism, to Christian Science, to name a few. And this excludes fringe points of view with unique versions of Jesus' identity, for example, the theory claiming a connection between UFOs and Jesus.[3]

In short, the answers to the Three Questions depend on the faith system that one adopts, because each system provides very different interpretations of Jesus' life and deeds. For example, each major religion has a different take on the death of Jesus. Therefore, I find it confusing and hard to reconcile all the various views proposed by traditional faith systems.

But perhaps this confusion is just a recent phenomenon. If we go back in time closer to the time of Jesus, should things not be more straightforward? Well, not really; the confusion gets worse.

---

1    (Sanhedrin. Translated into English with Notes, Glossary and Indices n.d., Folio 43a 34–35).

2    (Ali 1998, 4:157).

3    (Twichell 2000).

# ANCIENT VIEWS

---

> "Before I came here I was confused about this subject.
> Having listened to your lecture I am still confused. But on a higher level."
>
> —Enrico Fermi

---

There was a profound disagreement even amongst his earliest adherents about Jesus' identity, the facts surrounding his person, and the theological interpretation of him and his teachings. For example:

## IDENTITY OF JESUS

According to the Gospel of Matthew, Jesus was the divine Jewish Messiah by birth and was the only correct Jewish interpreter of the Torah laws. As for the Gospel of Mark, it shows Jesus as a heroic emissary from God whose teachings were not connected with Judaism. The Gospel of Luke, in turn, portrays Jesus as the saviour of the world and the Jewish Messiah. Finally, the Gospel of John has Jesus as divine, preexistent, and identifies him with God. Even within the Four Gospels' stories, there is an almost comical confusion over people's thoughts on Jesus. He is characterized, in turn, as a prophet, a zealot, a Son of David, the King of Israel, the King of the Jews, a demon-possessed man, a charlatan, a crazy person, a magician, the re-incarnated Prophet Elijah or John the Baptist, the Jewish Messiah, the Son of God, and a heretic.

## BASIC FACTS

Both Matthew and Luke have Jesus born in Bethlehem but under conflicting circumstances, while John and Mark allude to Jesus being born in Nazareth, while never mentioning Bethlehem. Also, the three Gospel writers—Matthew, Luke, and Mark—have Jesus' mission length of about one year, while John documents at least a three-year mission.

## THEOLOGICAL OPINIONS

Different texts have their own opinions on when Jesus became the Son of God/Lord/Messiah. According to the Apostle Paul, it happened on the day of the Resurrection (Acts 13:34). The Acts of the Apostles seem in agreement with Paul when they relate Peter's speech at Pentecost; Jesus was a "man" whom God then freed from death at the resurrection (Acts 2:34). Luke, however, has it either at Jesus' birth (Luke 2:11) or at his baptism (Luke 3:22). In turn, John seems to believe that he eternally held that position (John 1:2), whereas Mark alludes to it occurring upon his baptism (Mark 1:11).

## TEACHINGS

The Gospel of Matthew and the Letter of James[4] claim that followers of Jesus must observe the laws of the Torah—that is, the Jewish laws. However, for the Apostle Paul, the teachings of Jesus were not important. Still, Paul claimed that the new Christian Gentiles (non-Jewish adherents, typically pagan Greeks and Romans) did not need to follow the Torah. However, the Gospel of Mark seems to stand in the middle and has Jesus abrogating at least some of the Torah, while John, in turn, has no mention of Torah-related teachings.

Given these conflicting views, it is hardly surprising that after Jesus' death, many strange groups abounded, all arguing about who Jesus was, what he said, and what he did. Amongst some of the better-known ancient Christian sects —or "Christianities"— were: Pauline Christianity, which put Jesus the Christ at the centre of worship; the Torah observant Jewish-faction-Christianity

---

4    Also known as James the Just and a probable brother of Jesus, he was an Early Church leader. For more information, please see (The Editors of the New World Encyclopedia, James the Just 2016).

of the early Jerusalem Church led by Peter and James; Docetism, which taught that Jesus was a phantom rather than a real person; Arianism, which said that Jesus was created at a point in time and not pre-existent; the Ebionites, Jews who thought Jesus was the Messiah, albeit not divine; Marcionism, which believed that Jesus was not a material person but, rather, a spiritual entity sent by the true God, not the Jewish God; the Nazarenes, who were Jews who accepted Jesus' virginal birth; Nestorianism, which taught that Jesus was distinctly a man and God at once; and many variants of Gnosticism, a synthesis of Greek philosophy and elements of Christianity that flourished from the 100s to 300s CE, in which Jesus taught a liberating but secret knowledge that allowed the follower to escape the evil part of the world, but he was never resurrected.[5] These are some of the ones we know of; there were probably many others.

Most of the Early Church's writings, councils, and creeds were a response to the critics who pointed out the inconsistencies and confusion around Jesus. Eventually, a canonical version of Christianity was proclaimed in the Nicene Creed of 325 CE to combat the chaos, and it is this version, as well as its later elaborations, which define Christianity today.[6]

In summary, faith systems present me, the person in the street, with a bewildering set of opinions on Jesus. Still, it remains unclear to me which, if any, I should embrace … say, the Baha'i or the Nazarene faith. Should I adhere to the Catholic Church, or become a particular brand of Gnostic? Or should I mix and match different opinions and create something unique just for myself?

So rather than spend a considerable amount of time sifting through all these opinions on Jesus, it seems to me that the better route is to return to the facts and see what I can establish. I will, therefore, leave faith-based opinions behind and turn to the information as presented by academics in my own "Quest of the Historical Jesus."

## SCHOLARLY VIEWS. THE QUEST OF THE HISTORICAL JESUS

"What is important is to spread confusion, not eliminate it."

—Salvador Dalí

Over the last 200 years, one of NT scholars' main interests has been the Quest of the Historical Jesus (the title is taken from Albert Schweitzer's work of that name).[7] The quest began in the late 1700s, as scholars started to apply the new scientific method to what had been, up until then, shrouded in religious opinion—or dogma. But to what extent was it possible to apply unbiased, critical inquiry to research a historical Jesus?

This "quest" has made immense progress over time. Since its inception, many new facts have been uncovered, either through archaeological finds or textual discoveries. These have been coupled with a much better understanding and interpretation of the manuscript tradition and a better historical and cultural understanding of Jesus' time, which includes contemporary first-century Rome and Palestine. Also, new types of literary analysis have been developed, for instance, the Criteria of Authenticity, which I discuss next. The result is a vast body of academic research built up over two centuries of non-religious inquiry into the life and times of Jesus.

---

5     (Williams 2019).

6     It is interesting to note that this foundational statement of Christian belief contains almost nothing to aid in the Three Questions, simply that Jesus was born, was crucified by Pilate, and died. Also, the Creed's insistent statement of Jesus being "begotten, not made" was in direct response to Arianism. For more information, please see (The Editors of Encyclopaedia Britannica, Nicene Creed 2020).

7     (Schweitzer, *The Quest of the Historical Jesus* 1906).

# THE CURRENT MINIMALIST CONSENSUS ON JESUS

Many of the works I initially reviewed are from the Minimalist scholarly consensus—a body of opinions developed over the last 100 years. According to this consensus, the answer to the question of how much we can know about Jesus is, in short, "very little." Here are the central tenets of the Minimalist consensus on the four Gospels:

- They are not eyewitness accounts; that is, they were written long after the events that they record. For example, some scholars argue that the Gospel of John— usually thought to be the last Gospel written—was composed more than a century after the events it purports to relate.

- They record oral traditions passed down over time. As a result, the information from those traditions has drifted, become embellished or obscured, mixed with preexisting folklore, or it may even be made up. According to Randel Helms: "Oral tradition is by definition unstable, notoriously open to mythical, legendary and fictional embellishment …"[8]

- The Gospels were composed within disparate communities that had different issues and needs, which each Gospel text attempted to address.

- Numerous anonymous editors worked on the Gospels over time, adding layers to the texts.

- The Gospels are not so concerned about actual history but more concerned with relating the opinions of their authors.

While it may be possible to tease out a few basic facts about Jesus, everything else is a hopeless mess; most of it is so distorted or made up to be useless to anyone seeking the facts. It is like a broken chain of custody for evidence in a trial; anything achieved from further analysis is built on sand, a very disheartening point of view.

Gleaning information on Jesus from the Gospels is, therefore, a challenging task. According to Ed Parish Sanders, we know only of eight "almost indisputable facts" about Jesus: that he was baptized by John the Baptist; that he was a Galilean who preached and healed; that he called "disciples," his followers, and spoke of there being twelve; that he confined his activity to Israel; that he engaged in a controversy with the Jews about the Temple of Jerusalem; that he was crucified outside Jerusalem by the Roman authorities; that, after his death, his followers continued to abide by his teachings as an identifiable movement; and that certain Jews persecuted some members of the new movement, and this persecution may have endured until the end of Paul's career.[9] Nothing more. There exist other, equally minimalist lists of facts about Jesus, all just as brief as Sanders'.

To overcome this frustrating view of Jesus, other scholarship has focused on the Criteria for Authenticity, how to identify "authentic" information in the Gospels while leaving behind the "inauthentic" information. Once completed, the "authentic" bedrock material will lead us to the real Jesus.

To accomplish this, a myriad of methods have been proposed. For instance, some have developed the Criterion of Embarrassment, which states that if a portion of the text is contrary to the author's purpose, it is probably authentic. In the Gospel of Mark, for example, there is a story of Jesus' family showing up to take him away because they said he was "out of his mind" (Mark 3:21). This story would be considered against the author's intent of aggrandizing Jesus and therefore authentic. Another example is the Criterion of Semitisms. If some dialogue in the Greek text suggests Aramaic or Hebrew grammar, then the passage should be deemed more authentic. In the Gospel of Matthew, Jesus uses the Aramaic term "Raca" for "empty-headedness," which suggests it may be an original bit of dialogue (Matthew 5:22). There is also the Criterion of Multiple Attestation. If a story is repeated across different sources, such as Mark, Matthew, and Luke stating Jesus was baptized, then that material is more likely to be authentic.

---

8    (Helms 1988, 32).

9    (Stanton 1997, 146).

However, there is increasing scholarly agreement that the search for authenticity by academics has failed—the problem being that each criterion requires a set of assumptions; for instance, the Criterion of Embarrassment assumes the author would be embarrassed by a story. As Dale C. Allison Jr. puts it:

"Our criteria have not led us into the promised land of scholarly consensus, so if they were designed to overcome subjectivity and bring order to our discipline, then they have failed; the hopelessly confusing parade of different Jesuses goes on."[10]

I can attest personally to this "hopelessly confusing parade," as I have come across many conflicting speculations on the identity of Jesus arising from this methodology. Was he a zealot or the leader of a zealot faction? Or an eschatological prophet? A Jewish cynic or rabbi? A wandering apocalyptic preacher? A sage? Or a Messiah poser? Some kind of "spirit person"? A Hillelite? Or a proto-Pharisee? An Essene aesthetic? An ordinary man? Or an ordinary man with schizotypal traits? A religious reformer? A spiritual magi-cian? Or perhaps he is simply unknowable to us?[11]

As for myself, early on I rejected the Minimalist view on the Gospels. I also dismissed the Authenticity project, as many of its criteria seemed hopelessly complex, subjective, and requiring too many assumptions, rendering any conclusions reached using them useless. Instead, I agree with the newest strand of scholarship that views the gospels as "coherent artefacts of social memory designed for first-century performance"[12] based on my experience in reading them. Indeed, I did not find that the Gospels read the way the Minimalists say they do, and I was confused by their immediate scepticism of the texts. According to my initial careful yet non-expert reading, the Gospels instead come across as coherent. It also seems to me that a single author wrote each Gospel. The authors appeared to be almost always correct on the details of the environs, history, and practices of the place and time they describe. They are also a version (not a transcript) of events and interpretations told by each author, who wants to influence the reader's reactions and beliefs. They also contain seemingly eyewitness information, "inside" information, or extraneous details unlikely to have been added by someone not "on the ground" or far-removed and writing decades later. Finally, the Gospels were meant to be read carefully and plainly, and not be subjected to complex analysis.

To me, therefore, the Gospels read naturally and seem to be, on first reading, what they claim to be—namely, records of Jesus' life and teachings written soon after the events they relate by a trustworthy author who believed the events as described, even if fantastical. It is important to remember that each author of the Gospels had their agenda for composition, and that what we get is their "take" on events, not a modern biography or an exact transcript of all events; Craig Keener calls the Gospels' genre "ancient biography," as it is concerned with the facts.[13] The authors of the Gospels also passed on their personal theological opinions. Still, these are recognizable, for instance, when an author inserts a scriptural reference to explain something—this is the author expressing an opinion that can be assessed separately.

So various scholars have been moving forward toward a "post-minimalist" approach.[14] As Gerd Theissen puts it, "literary critics have demonstrated that in their present form, the Gospels are relatively polished and intricate works."[15] He also argues that "our starting assumption should be that the disciples of Jesus would have learned and transmitted his teachings no less carefully than most ancient disciples transmitted the wisdom of their mentors."[16]

In short, the best approach (and my approach) should be to *trust the information we are given until we have a good reason not to*. As Morna D. Hooker stated, "I suggest that it is time to throw away the tools altogether and opt for plain common sense."[17]

---

10    (Keith and Le Donne 2012, 195).

11    For more information on theories about Jesus see (Kirby, Historical Jesus Theories n.d.).

12    (Keith and Le Donne 2012, 20).

13    (Keener 2009, 2336).

14    A term coined by historian Gerd Theissen.

15    (Keener 2009, 2076).

16    (Keener 2009, 3953).

17    (Keith and Le Donne 2012, xvii).

I will return to square one and assemble the facts as I see them, and with the support of the newer "post-minimalist post-authenticity common sense" build a new alternative Jesus hypothesis. I will thus follow Nicholas Thomas Wright's rule, which is based on the research he conducted on the identity of Jesus, namely, that "the offering of an alternative hypothesis that actually does the job that a successful hypothesis must: make sense of the data, do so with an essential simplicity, and shed light on other areas."[18] This is the goal of *Salt & Light*.

18     (Wright 1999, 28).

# CHAPTER 3

# THE ROAD MAP

"I know of no society in human history that ever suffered because its
people became too desirous of evidence in support of their core beliefs."

—Sam Harris, *Letter to a Christian Nation*

While the Three Questions positively state this project's goals, it is essential to note what, by implication, is excluded. This project is not concerned with opinions about Jesus, either theological or historical, old or new. This project is not about the Early Church and its members, or a particular denomination or Christianity as a whole. Instead, as the Three Questions state, this is about finding the real Jesus' complete story.

However, the complete story of the real Jesus can never be uncovered with absolute confidence; at best, my goal is "a most probable" Jesus because the historical Jesus is lost to us in a strict sense. He lived about 2,000 years ago in a vastly different time and place. Jesus left us no written records, whether in the form of writings, speeches, notes, poetry, or books. We also have no direct physical evidence of Jesus, such as dwellings, belongings, portraits, or inscriptions.[1] Any indirect records of him or his family—such as birth records, census records, deeds, receipts, or wills—are all long gone.

What we do have are stories about Jesus and his teachings, including the Gospels, left to us in texts claimed to have been written either by eyewitnesses or other people who said they had heard and recorded stories about Jesus. Although the original copies of these stories are lost, they were copied and recopied over 2,000 years to create the manuscript tradition we have today. There currently exist about 5,500 handwritten manuscripts, either complete or incomplete, of the Greek NT alone, and more are still being discovered. While much has been made of variations between the texts, there are extremely few significant variations, all of which are well documented and researched; for example, the Longer Ending to the Gospel of Mark, the *Testimonium Flavianum*, and the *Pericope Adulterae*, all of which I will cover. All the other variations are small copyist mistakes that can be accounted for. So we can have confidence that the texts we do have accurately reflect the original texts written by their authors.[2]

Answering my Three Questions is a simple two-part process:

Part 1. I will compile the list of useful sources about Jesus, which I call my Source List.

Part 2. Using my Source List, I will answer the Three Questions.

---

1    I will discuss some alleged relics when I cover Jesus' last week in Chapter 28.

2    (Stanton 1997, 37–48).

# CHAPTER 4

# COMPILING MY SOURCE LIST

"It is a capital mistake to theorize before one has data. Insensibly one begins to twist facts to suit theories, instead of theories to suit facts."

—Sir Arthur Conan Doyle, *A Scandal in Bohemia*

While the Three Questions are quite simple, finding the best texts to use for my Source List has, surprisingly, been a complicated but fascinating step. I say surprising since I had assumed that the list of best sources of information about the real Jesus had been settled long ago, given the vast current literature on Jesus. I have never encountered a discussion on which sources to use in any books on Jesus; instead, the standard approach uses a small set of sources, typically those in the NT or just the four Gospels, and treats them all uncritically, as equally valuable.

So I must deal with this issue because I do not want to use the uncritical "normal approach." Instead, I want to cast the broadest net possible for sources. Why? By ensuring that nothing useful for answering the Three Questions is missed, the best possible conclusions will be possible. In addition, this gives the gentle reader context for these conclusions through an excellent introduction to the sources themselves, even if some (or most) prove not to be useful in the end. I want to examine all the relevant information in the primary religious texts of the major faith traditions that mention Jesus, that is, Islam, Judaism, and Christianity, in addition to pagan writers. However, this is a massive task, as there are hundreds of sources to consider. Are there any shortcuts or rules that can be applied to efficiently "filter out" useless sources? Absolutely!

In the coming chapters I will define and apply four rules to filter the many hundreds of potential sources, namely:

1. The Date Rule.

2. The Credible Facts Rule.

3. The Repetition Rule.

4. The Custody Rule.

I will apply each of these rules to the pool of potential sources and derive my surprisingly short Source List, summarized in Chapter 24 (Appendix 7 summarizes the before and after effect of applying the four rules). This will conclude Part 1 of this book. Then in Part 2 I will use my Source List to answer the Three Questions.

# CHAPTER 5

# THE DATE RULE

I want sources that are as "close" to Jesus as possible. Every time information is retold, either orally or in writing, there is a risk of embellishment, distortion, error, and omission. All things being equal, a source created closer to Jesus' in time is better than, say, one from 300 years later, since the latter's information has the potential for many retellings and hence more opportunity for changes during transmission.[1] This gives us our first rule for assessing sources for their usefulness:

## THE DATE RULE

Two hard dates will help determine usefulness: 1 CE and 100 CE; any sources composed on these dates or outside this date range shall be eliminated. But why these two dates?

### THE 1 CE CUT-OFF

I am excluding any sources that have their latest composition dates occurring before Jesus' birth, which was between 6 BCE and 1 CE, according to most scholars. This may sound like mere common sense, but the case of Jesus is different. Indeed, some Christians believe that there was information about him circulating even before he was born, specifically in JS prophecies. This was and still is a major project for some Christians—to decipher specific passages using Christian doctrine and read them as foreknowledge of Jesus or prophecies of the First (or Second) Coming of Christ, the Virgin Birth, Jesus as the sacrificial Lamb of God, the Jewish Messiah, or the Suffering Servant in the book of Isaiah (Isaiah 42:1–4, 49:1-6, 50:4–7, 52:13–53:12). This allows pronouncements of "as predicted in the Scripture" to raise Jesus' legitimacy. Given this project's historical aims, I cannot accept such texts as reliable sources to study the figure of Jesus, for they are not "accounts" per se. I am making this an explicit rule, since it eliminates almost all the JS (including the Christian Old Testament) from consideration, which may be controversial to some readers.

### THE 100 CE CUT-OFF

Let us assume that you witnessed Jesus early enough in life to remember important information about him, such as what he did and what he said. You then went on to live an extraordinarily long life for that time in history, retained your memories accurately, and passed them on orally, in writing, or through dictation at the very end of your long life. How late could the "publishing" of your eyewitness testimony be?

Jesus died in 33 CE. Let us assume that 20 years of age is a reasonable age to have accurate memories of Jesus. Twenty years old in 33 CE means that the person was born in 13 CE. Now let us assume that our witness lived to the age of 80, which happened to only 1 in 100 people at that time.[2] So this elderly eyewitness would die around 93 CE. It

---

1    There is another important benefit to early information; if it is within the lifetime of eyewitnesses, then they act as guarantors of the accuracy of the information.

2    (Fried 2000, 789).

is, therefore, safe to say that by the 90s CE, we would be on the cusp of losing the remaining contemporaries of Jesus (if any still lived), and indeed, by 100 CE, all eyewitnesses would have died.

Thus, 100 CE is my cut-off; all sources with their earliest possible composition dates on or past 100 CE will be excluded from my Source List. This approach may seem overly minimalist, but I consider it better to discard a potentially informative source rather than let an erroneous or spurious work "under the wire" sow confusion. Any source composed in 100 CE or after cannot be eyewitness testimony; either it has no source(s) behind it (it was created), or it must be retelling information from an earlier source(s).

Using the Date Rule has a dramatic impact on the number of potential sources, as we shall see in the following three chapters.

# CHAPTER 6

# JEWISH SOURCES

*Figure 3* **Destruction of the Temple in 70 CE.**

*A picture of the debris from the Temple at the foot of the Temple Mount retaining wall in Jerusalem exactly where it fell when it tumbled from overhead as the Temple was destroyed. This occurred on or around August 2, 70 CE, during the Roman siege led by Roman General Titus.*

---

"On the eve of Passover Yeshu was hanged."

— *The Talmud*[1]

---

Almost all the books making up the JS were finalized before 1 CE, so I can exclude the JS in its entirety (including the Christian Old Testament since it is derived from the JS) from consideration using my Date Rule.[2] However, despite the JS never mentioning Jesus, it is still crucial for my argument to survey it.

---

1    Babylonian Talmud Folio 43a 34–35.

2    The two books, the Wisdom of Solomon and 4 Maccabees, included in the JS, were probably written after 1 CE, so I will evaluate them in a later chapter 11.

After the Temple's destruction, Judaism developed into Rabbinic Judaism, with its main sacred text being the Talmud. This is about 6,200 pages long and made up of numerous rabbis' teachings on all aspects of Jewish life. There may be some brief and challenging-to-interpret mentions of Jesus in the Talmud.[3] However, I can set it aside, since recording the Talmud was started by Rabbi Judah around 200 CE, and work continued for centuries after. Therefore, this puts it beyond my Date Rule cut-off of 100 CE, and I need not consider it a potential source.

## THE JEWISH SCRIPTURE

Many of the Christian sources have quotations from the JS, usually either on the lips of Jesus or proposing that some incident in the JS somehow foreshadows Jesus in some way. For example, in the Gospel of John, we can find the following quote: "These things happened so that the scripture would be fulfilled: 'Not one of his bones will be broken.'"[4] In the Gospel of Mark, there are JS references reportedly uttered by Jesus: "For Moses said, 'Honour your father and your mother,' and, 'Anyone who curses his father or mother must be put to death.'"[5]

In Appendix 1, I briefly look at the JS and conclude almost all the JS "history," that is, the stories of Creation, Adam and Eve, the Exodus, the Flood, the glittering Davidic kingship, the Covenant, the Promised Land, the conquests, and so on are myths, and its central figures—Moses, Abraham, Isaac, and Jacob—are mythical.[6] The Jewish elites created this ancient narrative to serve as a history to support the day's religious and political agendas. Thus, the JS is to the Jews what the *Iliad* was to the Greeks and the *Aeneid* to the Romans: a literary pseudo-history creating a grand mythical past and a sense of national superiority.

However, it is essential to remember that the JS was considered the irrefutable truth for the Jews of Jesus' time. We will see this has implications for answering the Three Questions. As I will show, Jesus had little to do with Judaism, and his death resulted from his opposition to the religious system supported by the JS.

---

3    Joseph Klausner, a Jewish researcher, sums up some of the conclusions that can be drawn from the Talmudic theories about Jesus: "The references in the Talmud (this applies of course only to the old editions or manuscripts which have escaped the hand of the Christian censorship) to Jesus are very few; and even these have little historical value, since they partake rather of the nature of vituperation and polemic against the founder of the hated party, than of objective accounts of historical value." (Klausner 2020, 18–19).

4    John 19:36 drawing on JS verses Exodus 12:46, Numbers 9:12, and Psalm 34:20.

5    Mark 7:10 drawing on JS verses Exodus 20:12 and 21:17.

6    A King David probably did exist, as a "house of David" is mentioned on the Mesha monument of about 840 BCE, but the extent of his "kingdom" is wildly exaggerated in the JS. See also (The Editors of the New World Encyclopedia, Mesha Stele 2018).

# CHAPTER 7

# MUSLIM SOURCES

"That they said (in boast), 'We killed Christ Jesus the son of Mary, the Messenger of Allah';
but they killed him not, nor crucified him, but so it was made to appear to them, and those who
differ therein are full of doubts, with no (certain) knowledge, but only conjecture to follow,
for of a surety they killed him not:"

—*The Qur'an* 4:157

Islam's primary religious texts are the Quran and the sayings from the companions of Muhammed, called the Hadith,[1] which run into the thousands of pages in many texts. Jesus—or *Isa* in Arabic—is mentioned directly 93 times in the Quran (versus just four for Muhammed) and is a significant figure in Islam. However, the Quran and subsequent Hadith were composed after 600 CE, centuries after my Date Rule cut off of 100 CE, so they must be based on preexisting sources.[2] I will thus set aside Muslim sources.

---

1   (Cragg 2020).

2   Pre-existing Christian sources detected in the Quran include the four Gospels, the *Infancy Gospel of James*, the *Infancy Gospel of Thomas*, and the *Coptic Apocalypse of Peter*.

# CHAPTER 8

# CHRISTIAN SOURCES

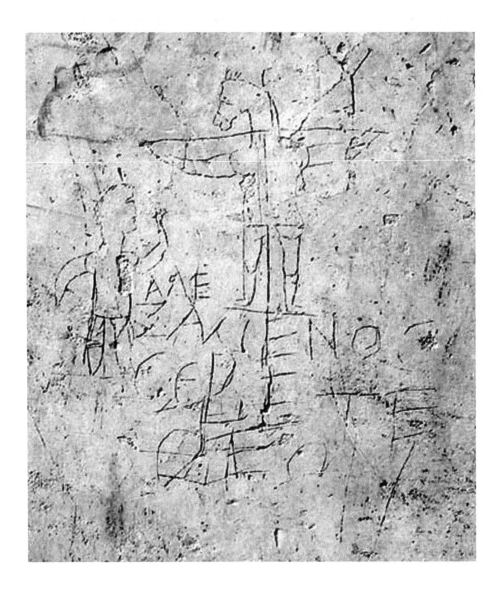

*Figure 4 **Mocking graffiti scratched into a plaster wall.***

*This was unearthed in a room near the Palatine Hill in Rome; dating could be from the 70s to the late 200s CE. Although hard to see, it shows a man saluting a naked, crucified, donkey-headed figure on a cross, with a caption in elementary Greek reading: "Alexamenos worships his God," obviously someone poking fun at Alexamenos. Early (mid-100s CE) pagan rumours suggested that Christians did indeed worship a donkey. This image may be the earliest depiction of the crucifixion, albeit a derogatory one in intention. Interestingly, in the next room, someone else had written, "Alexamenos is faithful!"*

"The proposition that the Sun is the center of the world and does not move from its place is absurd and false philosophically and formally heretical, because it is expressly contrary to Holy Scripture."

—*Papal condemnation of Galileo*, 1633

I will be using the comprehensive Early Christian Writings (ECW) site created and owned by Peter Kirby as my universe for Christian sources.[1] The purpose of the site is "to set out all of the Christian writings that are believed to have been written in the first and second centuries, as well as a few selected from the early third."[2] The cut off is just before the Council of Nicaea in 325 CE, which is sensible for two reasons:

- In 325 CE, the first major council of the Christian Church, ordered by the Roman emperor Constantine the Great (272–337 CE), convened in the ancient Greek city of Nicaea. Its purpose was to provide the Roman Empire with a consensus on Christian orthodoxy, encapsulated in the Nicene Creed.[3] Thus, the sayings and activities of Jesus were no longer up for further investigation.

- It was 300 years after the death of Jesus, so it is inconceivable that any new substantive and unadulterated information on Jesus was not by this time written down and still circulating orally. Indeed, whatever written sources were available in 325 CE, we can be confident that they contained all the existing information about Jesus, whether in the form of a primary source or other sources.

The ECW site includes a composition date range for each source based on majority scholarly opinion, for example, 50–140 CE for the Gospel of Thomas, meaning composition is most likely between 50 and 140 CE. I will use the earliest date in the range to maximize the writings for consideration. The site has 226 separate sources arranged chronologically, from the Passion Narrative (30–60 CE) to the Pseudo-Clementine Recognitions (320–380 CE). However, applying the Date Rule pares this down dramatically to just 44 sources: from the Passion Narrative to Flavius Josephus (93 CE).

The books of the NT are included in the ECW list, and as the NT, the Christian portion of the Christian Bible, is the primary source of information on Jesus, I will do a brief review of the NT.[4]

## THE NEW TESTAMENT

The NT is a collection of Christian texts written at different times and places, by various writers, in the first and second centuries CE, in the common (koine) Greek language, the lingua franca at the time.

The NT currently consists of the following works:

- The four Gospels (Matthew, Mark, Luke and John); narratives of the life, teachings, and death of Jesus.

- A narrative of the first 30 years of Church history, called the Acts of the Apostles, or just Acts, with special attention given to the Apostle Paul's journeys. The author of the Gospel of Luke almost certainly wrote Acts; it indeed reads like a second part of one whole work. As a result, the two are frequently lumped together as Luke-Acts.

- Twenty letters—called "epistles," from the Greek *epistole*, meaning "letters"— written by various authors and containing Christian doctrine, counsel, argumentation, encouragement, instruction, and conflict resolution. They are divided

---

1     (Kirby, *Early Christian Writings* 2021).   Website www.earlychristianwritings.com

2     Ibid, Introduction.

3     (The Editors of Encyclopaedia Britannica, Nicene Creed 2020).

4     The rest of the Bible, the Christian Old Testament, is not mentioned here, as it is drawn from the books of the JS, which have been excluded, being composed before 1 CE.

according to their traditional ascriptions: thirteen letters ascribed to Paul, called the Pauline Epistles collectively; the Epistle of James, written by an author named "James" and often identified with James, the brother of Jesus; the First Peter and Second Peter, ascribed to the disciple Peter; the First John, Second John, and Third John, ascribed to disciple John; the Epistle of Jude, written under the name of Jude, who is traditionally identified as the brother of Jesus and James;

- An example of apocalyptic literature, the Book of Revelation, assumed to have been written by the disciple John.

It took a while for the NT to achieve its current form; different books were used in different locations, and there was no central authority yet to finalize a list. While there was agreement amongst Early Church leaders on the core books that should be included by the middle of the 100s CE, the discussion of a formal list (the Canon) continued for another 200 years. Some disputed books, such as the Book of Revelation and the Minor Catholic (General) Epistles, were introduced into the Canon quite late in the process, in the late 100s and early 200s CE. Other works earlier held to be canonical, such as *1 Clement*, *The Shepherd of Hermas*, and *The Diatessaron*, were eventually excluded from the NT.

Despite the First Council of Nicaea in 325 CE, the final NT list was not agreed upon until the end of the 300s CE. In his Easter letter to Christians in which he announces the date of Easter for that year, 367 CE, Athanasius, Bishop of Alexandria, lists the books that would formally form the New Testament canon, using the word "canonized" (*kanonizomena*) concerning them. The contents of the NT seem to have been considered as final by the 400s CE. However, differing opinions have persisted over time, particularly with the rise of the Reformation (Protestant) movement in the 1500s. As Ben Witherington III states:

"In short, none of the major Bible translations that emerged during the German, Swiss, or English reformations produced a Bible of simply 66 [the traditional number] books."[5]

For instance, Martin Luther, the leader of the German Reformation, tinkered with the canon in his German translation of the Bible; he dropped what he considered to be non-canonical books, including Revelation and the Epistle of James, claiming it was "an epistle of straw."[6] However, most Reformation groups have since reverted to the original canon of 66 books.

---

5    (Witherington III 2017).

6    (Luther 1960, 362).

# CHAPTER 9

# WHAT MAKES A SOURCE "USEFUL"?

"Even though there are no ways of knowing for sure, there are ways of knowing for pretty sure."

— Daniel Handler, *The Vile Village*

The Date Rule application has had the dramatic effect of eliminating the literature of Judaism (except for 4 Maccabees and the Wisdom of Solomon) and Islam from consideration. Also, my Christian sources have been reduced to 44 in number (with pagan sources still to be examined). The next step is to assess each remaining source for usefulness.

## THE CREDIBLE FACTS RULE

So what makes a source "useful"? For a source to be deserving of time and attention, it must say something factual about Jesus that aids in answering the Three Questions. Many sources discuss Christianity and Jesus, but surprisingly few offer any facts about Jesus and his teachings. For instance, some texts may have a solid Christian theme but never mention anything specific about Jesus, for example, 3 John is a Christian letter but does not mention Jesus, or other sources mention Jesus but only in metaphorical or theological terms, such as the Epistle of James, which only refers to Jesus as "Jesus Christ," a term from Christian doctrine. Neither of these sources is useful in answering the Three Questions.

A source may have facts about Jesus but still not be useful. How? If the facts lack credibility since they seem contrived to serve some obvious purpose. An example is the Gospel of Thomas. In Thomas, Jesus allegedly expounds Gnostic teachings, which are out step with his other teachings, and given the propensity of the Gnostics to plagiarize existing Jesus sources and blend in Gnostic teachings, this means the Gospel of Thomas has poor credibility and is not usable. The facts may also seem very unlikely. The Gospel of Luke's narrative of Jesus' birth includes grand speeches, talking angels, a fantastical worldwide census, and heavenly hosts, which all seems doubtful. So these facts of Jesus' birth have a credibility problem (as does the author who relates them), impacting their usefulness.

All of this gives us a rule, the Credible Facts Rule. Unless a source contains credible, factual information about Jesus, it can be discarded from consideration.

## THE REPETITION RULE

A source may pass the Credible Facts Rule but still be useless. How? If the source's information is simply a repetition of information from a source known to be earlier and already in the Source List, the source is redundant and can be discarded.

# THE CUSTODY RULE

Quadratus was a shadowy figure. He is said to have been the Bishop of Athens from about 124 to 129 CE. Church tradition states that in 124 CE, Roman Emperor Hadrian was staying in Athens, and Quadratus sent him a letter explaining Christianity. Eusebius,[1] an Early Church historian, quotes Quadratus:

> "He [Quadratus] himself reveals the early date at which he lived in the following words: 'But the works of our Saviour were always present, for they were genuine:— those that were healed, and those that were raised from the dead, who were seen not only when they were healed and when they were raised, but were also always present; and not merely while the Saviour was on earth, but also after his death, they were alive for quite a while, so that some of them lived even to our day.' Such then was Quadratus."[2]

Thus, Quadratus was in touch with early followers of Jesus, who were healed and raised from the dead. This is evidence that people were meeting with and inquiring of those who had met Jesus personally. However, apart from this snippet, nothing of Quadratus' writings survived, but he does pass on facts about Jesus: he healed and raised people from the dead. He is a prime example of eyewitnesses of Jesus passing on their information to a later person, who then wrote down the information in a text after 100 CE. My criteria for including such an after-100 CE source are that this link must be documented somewhere, like a chain of custody. For instance, "So-and-So" had access to an authoritative source, such as an elderly eyewitness of Jesus, and then created some work that includes information about Jesus, which we have in Quadratus' case. In such a case, I am willing to retain the source for further consideration, even if it was written after 100 CE. This Custody Rule is the only exception to the Date Rule.

What remains, then, is to apply these rules to the remaining Christian and pagan sources to find sources with useful content. This means critically assessing each source by asking the following questions:

- When was the text composed?

- Is the factual content rationally credible?

- Is the information contained already available in an earlier source?

- Who was the author?

I will apply these criteria ruthlessly to cut down on the number of sources. Any source without useful information as defined above will be dropped without further consideration. This process will eliminate sources that are too allegorical, too speculative, too incredible, too late or irrelevant for the Questions. I will also eliminate sources that have information repeated in earlier sources and are inconsistent with other sources whose authors are deemed more reliable. Notice that this novel approach does not guarantee that the traditional pool of sources used by searches for the historical Jesus will be reproduced. Instead, as we shall see, this process will yield a small set of high-quality sources, my Source List.

Equipped with these new rules, I will review the remaining Christian and pagan sources, starting with the pagan sources.

---

1    Eusebius (c. 260–c. 340 CE) was an early Christian bishop who wrote many works, including a comprehensive *Church History* and a biography of Emperor Constantine. See also (The Editors of Encyclopaedia Britannica, Eusebius of Caesarea 2019).

2    Eusebius, *Church History*, 4.3.2.

# CHAPTER 10

# PAGAN SOURCES

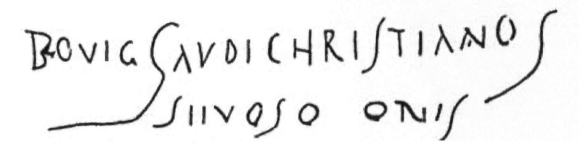

*Figure 5 **Christianity in Pompeii?***

*In 1862, archaeologists working in Pompeii excavated a large inn. They found on an atrium wall a charcoal graffito that seemed to use the word Christianos ("Christians"). Pompeii was buried in ash following the 79 CE eruption of nearby Mount Vesuvius, thus providing a snapshot of a Roman city. Scholars have often searched for physical evidence indicating whether Christianity had a presence in the city; however, most arguments are unconvincing, except for this graffito. When it was uncovered, archaeologist Giuseppe Fiorelli made this line drawing. However, the inscription started to fade after a few days of exposure and has since disappeared. While scholars have debated the reading of the whole sentence (it either means "Bovios is listening to the Christians" or "rejoice in the fire, Christian!"), the meaning of the word Christianos is not disputed. Therefore, it appears as if a Christian, or someone who knew of Christians, was at the inn in 79 CE. This inscription would make it the earliest physical evidence of Christianity. Image reproduced by permission from Tuccinardi (Tuccinardi 2016, 63).*

The Greco-Roman world had a rich history of historical writings. The ancient Greek writers Herodotus and Thucydides are considered the first historians, so it is not surprising that there are a few interesting references to Jesus and Christians in general in Roman and Greek literature. I have dropped several famous sources mentioning Christians as potential sources: Satirist Lucian's *The Passing of Peregrinus*, Pliny the Younger's *Letter to Trajan*, historian Suetonius' *The Twelve Caesars*, and Emperor Marcus Aurelius' *Meditations* are all sources from after the Date Rule's 100 CE cut-off. And apart from Lucian, they have nothing specific to say about Jesus. Three sources do provide some facts about Jesus: Tacitus, The Letter of Mara Bar-Serapion, and Josephus.

## TACITUS

Publius Cornelius Tacitus (56–120 CE) wrote two major historical works covering Roman history between c. 14 and 70 CE.[1] He is generally considered the most reliable source for the political history of that period, as he was a Senator and had access to, and used, the official archives, reports of the Roman government and public records such as memoirs. He was in direct contact with known experts, whom he names on occasion, such as Lucius Vipstanus Messalla, an influential military leader during

---

1    (McDonald 2021).

the tumultuous Year of the Four Emperors in 69 CE. Tacitus reports that after the Great Fire of 64 CE that destroyed Rome, Emperor Nero scapegoated the Christians because he was accused of starting or abetting the fire:

> "… to get rid of the report [of starting or abetting the fire], Nero fastened the guilt and inflicted the most exquisite tortures on a class hated for their abominations, called Christians by the populace. Christus, from whom the name had its origin, suffered the extreme penalty during the reign of Tiberius at the hands of one of our procurators, Pontius Pilatus, and a most mischievous superstition, thus checked for the moment, again broke out not only in Judaea, the first source of the evil, but even in Rome, where all things hideous and shameful from every part of the world find their centre and become popular."[2]

Tacitus is not explicit about this passage's source, but we can be confident he got the information on Jesus from official records. So even though Tacitus started writing his *Annals* after 100 CE (probably in the early 110s), the Custody Rule applies, so I will add this account to my Source List.

## THE LETTER OF MARA BAR-SERAPION

This is a rather touching letter written in Syriac by a Stoic philosopher named Mara bar Serapion to his son, Serapion, who appears to be studying abroad. Mara lived in Samosata, a city in southern Turkey (then the Roman province of Syria). In 72 CE, the Romans conquered the city, and Mara was taken prisoner. His letter is full of paternal advice, as he encourages his son to pursue learning over accumulating riches. In a passage about God punishing oppressors who target wise men, in this case the philosopher Socrates, the mathematician and philosopher Pythagoras, and apparently Jesus, Mara writes:

> "For what benefit did the Athenians obtain by putting Socrates to death, seeing that they received as retribution for it famine and pestilence? Or the people of Samos by the burning of Pythagoras, seeing that in one hour the whole of their country was covered with sand? Or the Jews by the murder of their Wise King, seeing that from that very time their kingdom was driven away from them? For with justice did god grant a recompense to the wisdom of all three of them. For the Athenians died by famine; and the people of Samos were covered by the sea without remedy; and the Jews, brought to desolation and expelled from their kingdom, are driven away into every land. Nay, Socrates did 'not' die, because of Plato; nor yet Pythagoras, because of the statue of Hera; nor yet the Wise King, because of the new laws which he enacted."[3]

In 72 CE, the First Jewish-Roman War had just ended, and the Romans had catastrophically destroyed Jerusalem and its Temple in 70 CE. They ended the short-lived Judean Free Government and dispersed the Jews throughout the empire, creating the Jewish diaspora. Most certainly, this is the "desolation" and expulsion to which Mara refers.

The "Wise King" would appear to be Jesus. Indeed, there were no murdered Jewish kings during that period, and all five Herodian kings, including Herod the Great, had met natural deaths. No other figure (that we know of) fits the bill. Furthermore, the expression "King of the Jews" was applied to Jesus by his accusers and posted on a plaque above his corpse (John 19:19). And Jesus' teachings—or "new laws"—lived on in the region's growing Christian communities.[4] Finally, Mara was not a Christian, and no other Christian themes appear in the letter; we can deduce, therefore, that the story of Jesus' death was circulating in the area at the time and was thus common knowledge.

---

2    Tacitus *Annals* 15.44.

3    (Mara n.d.).

4    After the destruction of Jerusalem (70 CE), the centre of Christianity moved north to the region of modern-day Syria and western Turkey near Samosata.

Dating would indicate some time just after 72 CE, since Mara is talking of his capture as if in the immediate past, perhaps within a year or two. This source passes the Date Rule, and although the source of the information Mara relates is unknown, this reasonably seems to be a snippet of information about Jesus. And it will be included in my Source List.

## JOSEPHUS

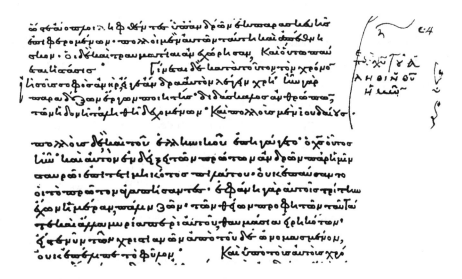

*Figure 6* **The Testimonium Flavianum**

*This is the oldest extant copy of Josephus' Testimonium Flavianum (TF), discernible between the two blanks: one on the fourth line and the second on the last line. This is from the Codex Ambrosianus (Mediolanensis) F. 128, dated to the 1000s CE, there are earlier fragments of Josephus, but this is the first to contain the TF. The name Jesus, Ἰησοῦς, can be seen at the beginning end of the second line with the large downstroke.*

Titus Flavius Josephus (c. 37–c. 100 CE), born Yosef ben Matityahu, is the most important historian of Jewish history in Antiquity.[5] He provides us with vital, contemporary mentions of Jesus outside Christian literature. A high-born Jew, he fought against the Romans in the First Jewish-Roman War, during which he was captured; he later defected to the Romans. He was then freed by Emperor Vespasian, granted Roman citizenship, and, in return, adopted a Roman name. The Emperor and his sons, Titus and Domitian, became his patrons. He went on to publish *The Jewish War*, a history of the war between Jews and Romans, and *Antiquities of the Jews*, a history of the world from a Jewish point of view. *Antiquities* was written around 93–94 CE, just inside my 100 CE-time cut off. The work mentions many important figures from first-century Judea, including John the Baptist, Pontius Pilate, and James. More importantly, it appears to mention Jesus twice. If historically reliable, those passages would constitute the most essential non-Christian references to Jesus.

The first reference to Jesus in Josephus has been the focus of intense debate for so long that it has been given its own title, the *Testimonium Flavianum* (TF):

> "Now there was about this time Jesus, a wise man, if it be lawful to call him a man, for he was a doer of
> wonderful works, a teacher of such men as receive the truth with pleasure. He drew over to him both many
> of the Jews, and many of the Gentiles. He was the Christ; and when Pilate, at the suggestion of the principal
> men amongst us, had condemned him to the cross, those that loved him at the first did not forsake him, for
> he appeared to them alive again the third day, as the divine prophets had foretold these and ten thousand

---

5    Josephus was Jewish, but I have placed his works under pagan sources since they were written for a pagan audience. For more information on Josephus see (Poole 2020).

other wonderful things concerning him; and the tribe of Christians, so named from him, are not extinct to this day."[6]

There is no scholarly consensus on the TF. It is, in turn, viewed as a later Christian fabrication, a genuine passage from Josephus, and an original entry that was later altered.[7] Geza Vermes argues that depicting Jesus as a "wise man" and "performer of paradoxical deeds" is entirely consistent with Josephus's writing style, so the complete passage is unlikely to be a later Christian fabrication. It would, therefore, represent popular and primitive views of Jesus.

I doubt that Josephus, a Jew, would declare a person to be the "Christ" or the "anointed Messiah." If he is proclaiming Jesus the Messiah, he would not do so in such a casual and passing statement unless the text is meant to be read as a satire; after all, there were many phony Messiahs in Josephus' time. Furthermore, to declare that someone came back to life but not expound on this at length makes no sense; in the section just after the TF, Josephus goes into the details of King Agrippa's building program, which seemed to be his primary focus, not a person who came back from death. Part of Josephus' intent in writing *Antiquities* was to explain Jewish history and culture to a Graeco-Roman audience. Yet here he is casually proposing a significant historical and theological event—a son of God coming back to life. He also uses the term "Christ" without defining it; his audience would not understand the meaning of the term. Therefore, John P. Meier amended the TF as follows:

> "At this time there appeared Jesus, a wise man. For he was a doer of startling [or paradoxical] deeds, a teacher of people who receive the truth with pleasure. And he gained a following among many Jews and among many of Gentile origin. And when Pilate, because of an accusation made by the leading men among us, condemned him to the cross, those who had loved him previously did not cease to do so. And up until this very day the tribe of Christians (named after him) had not died out."[8]

This amended TF version drops the three blatant Christian additions: "if it be lawful to call him a man," "He was the Christ," and "for he appeared to them alive again the third day, as the divine prophets had foretold these and ten thousand other wonderful things concerning him." These additions probably came from including notes made in the margin, called glosses, the equivalent in early manuscripts of our footnotes; these were eventually inserted into later manuscript copies in error. This amended TF theory seems the most probable solution to me for six reasons. First, a substantial majority of scholars accept some form of "partial authenticity" TF. Second, Meier's version reads reasonably and naturally without the awkward (and incredible) brief inserts. Third, Josephus was writing a history of the Jewish people. It would seem odd not to mention Jesus, for he was an interesting person who started a religious sect that still existed when Josephus was writing. Fourth, the existing Greek manuscripts and Latin, Syriac, and Arabic translations contain no significant TF variants. Fifth, we need to consider the mechanics of a complete Christian fabrication of the TF. There must have been many copies of *Antiquities* circulating all over the Roman Empire; to insert an entire paragraph about Jesus (as opposed to the simple insertion of small helpful glosses) would mean making either a messy and obvious insert job or recopying many or most of the copies in circulation. The alternative would be to produce a few altered documents and hope your version would become prominent over time. Lastly, the second reference to Jesus later in Josephus' text seems to assume Jesus had already been mentioned.

The second reference to Jesus is further on in Book 20 of *Antiquities* and concerns the shady actions of one newly minted high priest of the Temple in Jerusalem, Ananus. It is 62 CE, the Roman governor of Judea has just died, and the newly appointed governor is travelling to Jerusalem to take up his post. During this time, Ananus used the power vacuum to get rid of some opponents, as the following citation shows:

---

6    Josephus, *Antiquities of the Jews*, 18.63–64.

7    Peter Kirby and Christopher Price both give outlines of the arguments put forward by scholars. (Kirby, *Josephus and Jesus: The Testimonium Flavianum Question* n.d.) and (Price 2004).

8    (Meier 1991, 61).

"… so he [Ananus] assembled the Sanhedrim of judges, and brought before them the brother of Jesus, who was called Christ, whose name was James, and some others, [or, some of his companions]; and when he had formed an accusation against them as breakers of the law, he delivered them to be stoned …"[9]

Some scholars have argued that this whole James reference was inserted later by Christian copyists, or more likely, the phrase "who was called Christ" was a later insert. However, Graham Stanton argues convincingly that a Christian would not have said "was called Christ," but rather "was the Lord" or "was the Christ"—not the hesitant "was called by some."[10] But there are three additional reasons why this passage is probably authentic. First, there is an almost unanimous scholarly consensus on the authenticity of this reference. Second, given the existence of some form of TF, this second reference to Jesus as the brother of James seems to make sense. Having told his readers who Jesus is, he then uses this information to help disambiguate James in the passing reference on Ananus. James was a widespread name, so when Josephus mentions James, he needs to tell us which one he means—in this case, the "brother of Jesus." However, Jesus was also a common name; for instance, immediately following sections of Book 20, two more Jesuses are mentioned: Jesus the son of Gamaliel, and Jesus the son of Damneus, being distinguished by their father's name.[11] "Who was called Christ"—or, as we find in some translations, "the so-called Christ"—may have been, therefore, a neutral term used to help differentiate between numerous Jesuses. Third, Josephus' emphasis in this section is not on Jesus or James but on Ananus; if this were a Christian insertion, this would not be the case.

Josephus' *Antiquities* passes the Date Rule, as it was written just before the 100 CE cut-off. The two amended references to Jesus provide useful information; therefore, I will include them in my Source List.

My Source List now contains three useful sources: the passage from Tacitus, The Letter of Mara Bar-Serapion, and Josephus. The number of remaining pre-100 CE sources to examine are 42 (as Tacitus is post-100 CE).

---

9    Josephus, *Antiquities of the Jews* 20.9.1. The Sanhedrin was a tribunal of elders, the Great Sanhedrin in Jerusalem was traditionally comprised of 71 judges.

10   (Stanton 1997, 125–126).

11   There are at least 12 people named Jesus mentioned by Josephus.

# CHAPTER 11

# APPLYING THE DATE RULE

*Figure 7 **A Jewish War year 5 (70 CE) shekel***

*When the Jews revolted against the Romans in 66 CE, they immediately took over the mint and silver supply in Jerusalem and started minting coins. Shekels minted in 66 CE are referred to as year one shekels, while this one is a year five shekel, minted in 70 CE, just before the Romans re-conquered Jerusalem, perhaps in the months while the Romans were besieging the city (April to August). Shekels were still being minted until the last minute so Jews could pay the temple tax. After the war, the revolt coinage was not allowed, so many were melted down, making revolt shekels rare while the year 5 shekel is very rare. Image reproduced by permission from Ira & Larry Goldberg Coins & Collectibles, Inc.*

"When was the New Testament written? This is a question that the outsider might be forgiven for thinking that the experts must by now have settled. Yet, as in archaeology, datings that seem agreed in textbooks can suddenly appear much less secure than the consensus would suggest."

—John Robinson, *Redating the New Testament*

I accept the scholarly consensus on the composition ranges for many of the remaining sources in the ECW list, but not all. Recent work into the dates of the NT texts and other sources argue for more precise dates. It is essential to examine the approximate composition dates of some of the texts, since any redating may change the status of a text; it may become too late to qualify according to the Date Rule, that is, after the 100 CE cut-off (and be dropped from consideration), or become earlier than expected, thereby requiring review. There have been compelling arguments put forward by scholars to revise some traditional dates, sometimes with dramatic changes. Four works in ECW should be assigned a post-100 CE date. This will eliminate them from consideration:

## THE EGERTON GOSPEL

This gospel is found on four papyrus fragments discovered in 1934. It includes four fragmentary stories about Jesus, but scientific analysis has revealed that the papyri were created around 150 CE. Its dating, therefore, can be adjusted to 150–200 CE versus the 70–120 CE date suggested in the ECW.[1]

## THE GOSPEL OF PETER

This is not a gospel per se but rather a Passion narrative—a text relating to the death and burial of Jesus. It is comprised of fourteen paragraphs, supposedly composed by Peter. Scholars have argued for either an early date, around the time of the composition of the Passion narrative(s) in the four Gospels, therefore either pre-dating the Gospels or being created at the same time or after the four Gospels were in circulation. There is, indeed, a lot of overlap between the *Gospel of Peter* and the Passion narratives as found in the four Gospels. However, there is enough evidence to attribute a late date to the *Gospel of Peter*, which is after the date of composition of the four Gospels.

Firstly, within the *Gospel of Peter*, we can observe what I would call "two-stage embellishment." As we shall see when discussing the Synoptic Problem, Mark's Passion narrative was written first. Matthew and Luke later drew on it to compose their narratives,[2] each embellishing Mark's rather spare account in the process and adding new elements to the story. For example, in Matthew, we first hear that Jesus was offered wine with gall, that there was an earthquake, and that the guards sealed the tomb with a single seal. Luke includes, for the first time in the story, Herod's presence at Jesus' trial, the repentant criminal being crucified next to Christ, and the two angels present at the tomb. But while none of these details are found in Mark's early version of the Passion, they are included in the *Gospel of Peter*, where they are further embellished. There is indeed wine vinegar *and* gall; a more significant earthquake; high priests and crowds present with the guards, who sealed the tomb with seven seals; the repentant criminal punished by not having his legs broken; and two glowing angels descending spectacularly from the sky. All the details embellished by Matthew and Luke have been further embellished in the *Gospel of Peter*, which shows that this gospel was written later, using Luke and Matthew as sources.

Secondly, some historical errors in the gospel are telling. The gospel first includes Luke's story of Jesus being presented to Herod Antipas during his trial. It then further embellishes it by having Herod condemn Jesus despite not having the authority to do so in Roman Judea, a power only Pilate had. The expression "Lord's Day" is used twice in the gospel,[3] but it is a later theological concept, dating to the 100s CE.

Thirdly, there are in Peter's text unlikely and even fantastical elements. The gospel relates how the Jewish leaders "camped out" for three nights near Jesus' tomb over Passover in violation of the festival customs and purity laws regarding proximity to corpses. And the sudden remorse displayed immediately upon Jesus' burial by those who had demanded his death earlier in the day:

"the Jews and the elders and the priests, perceiving what evil they had done to themselves, began to lament and to say, Woe for our sins: the judgement hath drawn nigh, and the end of Jerusalem." (*Gospel of Peter* 7)

---

1    "Ever since their initial publication, most scholars have concluded that the *Egerton Gospel* is later than the New Testament Gospels, and dependent on them …" (Stanton 1997, 83).

2    The order of composition of Mark, Luke, and Matthew is discussed in Chapter 13, The Synoptic Problem.

3    *Gospel of Peter* 9 and 12, used to signify the day of the resurrection.

The text also says that at noon, darkness covered all of Judea while Jesus was on the cross and caused people to trip and fall. Similarly, the resurrection occurred with truly fantastical elements, including a voice from Heaven, two giant flying men, and a walking, talking cross:

"And in the night in which the Lord's day was drawing on, as the soldiers kept guard two by two in a watch, there was a great voice in the heaven; and they saw the heavens opened, and two men descend from thence with great light and approach the tomb. And that stone which was put at the door rolled of itself and made way in part, and the tomb was opened, and both the young men entered in. When therefore those soldiers saw it, they awakened the centurion and the elders; for they too were hard by keeping guard. And, as they declared what things they had seen, again they see three men come forth from the tomb, and two of them supporting one, and a cross following them: and of the two the head reached unto the heaven, but the head of him that was led by them overpassed the heavens. And they heard a voice from the heavens, saying, Thou hast preached to them that sleep. And a response was heard from the cross, Yea." (*Gospel of Peter* 9–10)

Fourthly, the *Gospel of Peter* bears some of the hallmarks of a Docetic interpretation. Docetism was a version of Christianity that denied that Jesus had a real body; thus, he could neither be hurt nor killed. This doctrine developed over time and became prominent in the 100s CE, indicating a post 100 CE date for composition. In the *Gospel of Peter*, when Jesus is crucified, "he held his peace, as though having no pain," (*Gospel of Peter* 4), and the author does not say Jesus died; instead, he says that Jesus was "taken up" (*Gospel of Peter* 5). Later, Church Fathers, such as Serapion,[4] condemned this gospel for its Docetism.

Finally, as we will see, we already have an earlier *Gospel of Peter*: the Gospel of Mark. Obviously, the author did not realize this.

It thus seems the *Gospel of Peter* was composed quite late after all. According to the scholars who argue for a late date, an untrustworthy author claiming to be Peter wrote the text, perhaps in the mid or late 100s CE. This individual would have been out of touch with the historical reality that was contemporary to Jesus' death, embellishing Luke's and Matthew's accounts and creating a semi-farcical Passion story in lieu of a reliable narrative. The *Gospel of Peter*'s date range should thus be adjusted to 150–200 CE.

## THE GOSPEL OF THE EGYPTIANS

There are only two remaining fragments from this work, cited by Clement of Alexandria[5] around 200 CE. As a result, it is hard to know exactly the intent, origin, and form of this "gospel." The fragments deal with how to break the birth-death cycle and a return to androgyny. The scholarly consensus places composition between 120 and 150 CE.

## THE GOSPEL OF THE HEBREWS

This is a tricky text. There are only seven surviving fragments, which appear to present a syncretic Jewish-Christian work of Gnostic origins. This gospel may have been initially written in Hebrew, Aramaic, or Greek. It is referred to by the title "Gospel of the Hebrews" by Early Church Fathers. However, it is not clear whether the original consisted of one work or a collection of works. It may also have existed in different versions through time, with additions and cuts regularly made to the text. Scholars are still debating the issue. There is, however, a scholarly consensus, which places the initial composition between 120 and 150 CE.

## ROBINSON'S RE-DATING

John A. T. Robinson, in his famous investigation into the dates of the NT texts,[6] successfully questions the surprisingly almost non-existent evidence for the "orthodox" scholarly opinion that the Gospels and much of the NT were written quite "late," that is, after 70 CE.[7] For instance, he explains that Mark was written no later than 70 CE and provides a critical examination of both

---

4       (The Editors of Encyclopaedia Britannica, Saint Sarapion 2020).

5       (The Editors of Encyclopaedia Britannica, Saint Clement I 2013).

6       (Robinson 2000).

7       ECW has the latest dates for Mark, Matthew, Luke, John at 85, 100, 130, and 120 CE respectfully.

internal and external evidence to offer a better-established set of dates than those presented in the ECW list. I find his reasoning for re-dating specific works convincing, and he provides a good jumping-off point for me to sharpen some dates further so that I will be following in large part his argument for better dating. His central finding is that many texts, including the four Gospels and Acts, are earlier works than commonly accepted. Here are the composition dates (all CE) that he argues for:

- 40–60: *The Didache*
- 40–60: Gospel of Matthew
- 40–65: Gospel of John
- 45–60: Gospel of Mark
- 47–48: James
- Early 50: 1 Thessalonians
- Early 50 or 51: 2 Thessalonians
- Spring 55: 1 Corinthians
- Autumn 55: 1 Timothy
- Early 56: 2 Corinthians
- Late 56: Galatians
- Early 57: Romans
- Late Spring 57: Titus
- 57–60: Gospel of Luke
- 57–62: Acts
- Spring 58: Philippians
- Summer 58: Philemon
- Summer 58: Colossians
- Late Summer 58: Ephesians
- Autumn 58: 2 Timothy
- 60–65: 1, 2, 3 John
- 61–62: 2 Peter
- 61–62: Jude
- Spring 65: 1 Peter
- 67: Hebrews[8]
- Late 68–70: Revelation
- Early 70: *1 Clement*
- 75: *Epistle of Barnabas*
- 85: *The Shepherd of Hermas*

I have replaced the ECW data ranges with these specific dates in Appendix 7.

So what is the impact of this redating on the remaining 42 Christian sources in ECW? The four re-dated sources gospels of Egerton, Peter, Egyptians, and Hebrews are eliminated by the Date Rule, leaving 38 sources. However, Robinson's re-dated Pauline Epistles of 1 Timothy, 2 Timothy, Titus, and 2 Peter and the *Shepherd of Hermas* have moved back into the set, since the new dates are pre-100 CE, bringing the count to 43. You can see the effect on the list set in the "before and after" comparison presented in Appendix 7. As sources are excluded, I will cross them off, and as better dating is uncovered, I will alter the existing dates with bold-faced, new dates.

---

8    Book of Hebrews is sometimes also called the Letter to the Hebrews, distinct from the *Gospel of the Hebrews.*

# CHAPTER 12

# APPLYING THE CREDIBLE FACTS RULE

In this chapter, I shall apply the Credible Facts Rule to the remaining 45 sources. Although pre-100 CE and Christian in theme, the nine sources below have no useful facts about Jesus that help answer the Three Questions. They can all be excluded: 4 Maccabees, *the Wisdom of Solomon*, the Epistle of Jude, *the Christian Sibyllines, Apocalypse of Adam, Eugnostos the Blessed, The Sophia of Jesus Christ, The Shepherd of Hermas, The Testaments of the Twelve Patriarchs,* The Epistle of James, 2 John, and 3 John. This leaves 33 sources.

# CHAPTER 13

# ASSESSING THE FOUR GOSPELS (PLUS ACTS)

*Figure 8* ***The Oldest Surviving Latin Bible***

*This is the first page of the New Testament showing the four gospel writers in the Codex Amiatinus. The Codex is the oldest surviving Latin Bible (the Vulgate, as translated from Greek by Saint Jerome) and was created in the late 600s or early 700s CE in the Anglo-Saxon Kingdom Northumbria, near the time of Cuthbert. It is a huge book; it is almost two feet thick and weighs 75 pounds. It was sent as a gift to the pope in 716, but the pope died before it could be delivered, and it wound up in Florence, where it is kept. The Codex was loaned to the British Library in 2018, returning to England after 1,302 years. The dedication page has been altered mysteriously, naming the giver as "Peter of the Lombards" rather than the original "Ceolfrith of the English."*

"Long before there was ever a King James Version of our Bible, there was a gospel truth … and long before doctrines and denominations, the pre-eminence of the gospel was already ripe to harvest. Before man had ever thought about creating symbols to represent spiritual things … there was a gospel."

—Chandel L. White, *Romans to Jude — Precise Christian Scripture Revealed*

The next step in sifting the sources is to consider the four Gospels, for they are, by far, the richest sources about Jesus. Each is a lengthy work claiming to detail who Jesus was, what he taught, and what he did, as they each share the story of the earthly career of Jesus, which ends in his death and supposed resurrection. However, inconsistencies exist between them, they are different in terms of content and style, and each seems to draw a different portrayal of Jesus.

## THE NAMES

None of the Gospels explicitly say who their author was.[1] Traditional scholarship suggests the names associated with each Gospel is false, given the traditional "late dating" of their compositions. This implies that the Gospels were attributed to a false author to lend them authority. But the argument is unlikely for the following reasons:

- I will argue the Gospels are quite early, created during the lifetime of eyewitnesses who could guarantee authorship.

- Early Christians (like anyone) would not have accepted bogus authorship claims, especially on documents that promised them eternal salvation.

- Why assign names of relatively obscure personages, such as non-eyewitnesses of Jesus like Luke and Mark, who were said not to be involved in the events they relate? If you are fabricating authorship, why not assign a much more authoritative choice, such as disciples Peter or Andrew?[2]

- There is not one instance of the Early Church or its opponents ever questioning the authorship of the four Gospels.

- The Gospels were never known by titles other than the ones we have.

When the gospels were first written, they were not anonymous, and making copies was expensive and slow. The first copies would have circulated amongst friends, acquaintances, and local groups, with an oral description accompanying them: "this was written by so and so." When ancient scrolls were stored, the author's name would be written either on the outside or on a tag attached. Many ancient works were thus formally anonymous. When copies spread further afield and became collected together with other gospels, this then necessitated an identification to differentiate each Gospel.

## THE CORE MESSAGE+

After Jesus died, his followers spread the story of Jesus through preaching and teaching.[3] A consistent "script," which I call the "Core Message," would have been needed almost from the very start. It would have been quickly formalized and agreed on by those followers who were the "insiders" and who had been present in whole or part for Jesus' mission, for they each knew the essence and specifics of Jesus' message. The core Jesus material arose quickly in the days, weeks and months immediately

---

1    Not strictly true for the Gospel of John, which I shall discuss in my chapter on the Gospel of John.

2    Again, not strictly true, in this case for the Gospel of Matthew.

3    Acts describes this activity in detail.

following Jesus' death.[4] As the followers dispersed geographically and started preaching and teaching, the Core Message's retelling over and over to diverse audiences would have formed the basis for the disciples' speeches and answers to questions from listeners.

As the Core Message spread, new information would accrete to the Core Message. A disciple teaching in a village that Jesus had visited earlier would be informed by villagers what Jesus had done and said there. Also, individuals who had interacted directly with Jesus would be circulating their own stories, such as the man in the tombs and his fantastic story of Jesus healing him (Mark 5:2–20). We are told explicitly that the man spread his story all over a region called the Decapolis. Eventually, this additional information, here the man's story, would have been added to the general core message material. Some of these stories and their authors wound up in the written Gospels as discrete sources, creating an augmented core story that I call the "Core Message+." No doubt, many other stories did not make it into written form and have been lost.

As speculated by some academic models of gospel formation, there would be no anonymous malleable oral tradition, since all the facts on Jesus' mission would have been immediately available and guaranteed by eyewitnesses for decades after. Also, written materials during Jesus' mission and soon after were no doubt in use. It would seem incredible that through the whole of Jesus' ministry, no written records were kept, especially as Jesus interacted with many people, including the educated elites, and we know that some of Jesus' followers were well educated and literate.[5] It is only natural that lists of short sayings, preacher's notes, a collection of discourses and parables, and a factual record of people and places visited would have been created. Early Christian writer Papias mentions disciple Matthew creating a written set of sayings in Aramaic, and Lost Sayings Gospel Q (40–80 CE)[6] is a written recollection of Jesus' sayings. Although all now lost, these notes and logs would have helped to underpin the Core Message+.

## CAN WE IDENTIFY THE SOURCES USED BY THE AUTHORS?

The Gospels of Mark, Luke, and Matthew relate the highly colourful story of the beheading of John the Baptist by King Herod Antipas due to his stepdaughter's dancing (Matthew 14:1–12; Mark 6:14–29; Luke 9:7–9). We can be confident the author(s) were not at the private court function for Herod's birthday (only his high officials and military commanders and the leading men of Galilee were invited, according to Mark 6:21). So where did this story come from? Who was the source?

So far, I have been examining the sources from an external point of view to arrive at my Source List, but with each Gospel, I want to move inside and take a hard look to see what can be said for the sources used by the author and the implications this has for the contents. For instance, this Herod story is most certainly not an eyewitness report. We can then be wary of accepting the story at face value. This is a helpful method when discussing some of the odder parts of the Gospels.

Is it possible to tease out these outside sources included in each Gospel? Richard Bauckham's work[7] suggests that yes, the authors included stories they had heard from others, and these people can be tentatively identified, such as the man in the tombs. Many people have an anonymous, episodic presence in the gospels, for example, those who are healed and then never re-appear. There is the occasional person named for no reason, namely, Jairus, Bartimaeus, Levi, Salome, Simon of Cyrene, his sons, and Joseph of Arimathea in Mark. Bauckham suggests the explanation for these exceptions might be that these named figures were eyewitnesses to *their* story. The primary tellers of the tradition associated with them; when their accounts were included in the Core Message, their names would also be added, with the eyewitness being a guarantor of the integrity of the story they told and retold during their lifetime, perhaps even becoming well known in the process. Sometimes, the story would

---

4    Robinson points out how "explosive" developments can occur over a very short period of time, all of Paul's letters were produced over perhaps eight years, Jesus' mission only occupied less then three years. (Robinson 2000, 79).

5    Such as Nicodemus, Joseph of Arimathea, tax collector Matthew, and aristocrat John.

6    As listed in ECW. It is a reconstructed source, which I will discuss in my Chapter 15 on Q.

7    (Bauckham, *Jesus and the Eyewitnesses: The Gospels as Eyewitness Testimony* 2008).

be inserted with the name of the person telling it, for instance, Jairus,[8] or someone specific but unnamed, such as "the blind man."[9] Bauckham also explains that in the cases where the stories do not include a named person, the name might have been either lost or the re-tellers were simply not the primary eyewitnesses.

For example, in Mark, the three named women who were at the cross with Jesus when he died and went to his tomb afterwards (Mark chapters 15 and 16) are Salome, Mary Magdalene, and Mary, the mother of James the Younger and Joses (assuming she is the same person). These are critical witnesses, for they saw Jesus die, where he was buried, the tomb opened, and the young man in the tomb (Mark 15:40–16:8). In the story, the disciples, including Peter, have scattered and saw none of this. Mark is very careful to mention the names of the eyewitnesses and relates *their* story, since they were the only witnesses. Linking the names to the stories allowed early followers to verify the information directly if the witnesses were alive. This shows how names can serve as a framework for detecting discrete passages in the Gospels and classifying them as "standalone stories," attributed to the people directly involved and which the author included.

I can only make the best estimate of these sources' identities based on the limited information available. Unless I identify another source, I assume, in general, that the information presented in each Gospel came directly from the author.

## THE PLAN TO ASSESS THE FOUR GOSPELS

I will assess each of the four Gospels in terms of authorship, dating, and source(s). Since Acts of the Apostles picks up where the Gospel of Luke ends and is by the same author, the two are usually referred to as Luke-Acts, so I will also consider Acts.

The traditional scholarly date ranges for composition, taken from ECW, are:

- Mark 65–80 CE
- Matthew 80–100 CE
- Luke 80–130 CE
- Acts of the Apostles 80–130 CE
- John 90–120 CE

I think these dates are too late. Why? The key is the Gospel of Mark and the date 70 CE. To explain, I will start with Mark, but first I need to examine an independent issue: the Synoptic Problem. Then I will discuss each Gospel in this order:

- Mark
- Matthew & Luke-Acts (together)
- John

---

8    The story of Jairus' daughter Mark 5:22–43.

9    The blind man who washes in the Pool of Siloam John 9:1–38.

# CHAPTER 14

# THE SYNOPTIC PROBLEM

*Figure 9 **James, son of Joseph, brother of Jesus.***

*A close up of an inscription on an ossuary, a limestone box used to bury bones commonly used by Jews from about 20 BCE to 70 CE. The inscription reads: "James, son of Joseph, brother of Jesus." Although each name was quite common, this combination would have been almost unique. Also fascinating is the inclusion of a brother, a unique element among the thousands of ossuaries discovered; this indicates that the Jesus in question must have been famous and important. If the inscription is authentic, then this is probably the ossuary of James, brother (or some relation) of Jesus, said to be, along with Peter, one of the Early Church leaders. He was killed in 62 CE, according to Josephus. Scholars are divided over the authenticity of the inscription. However, the ossuary itself is not doubted. Recent work, though, has tipped toward authenticity. See (Shanks, "Brother of Jesus" Inscription Is Authentic! 2012). The James Ossuary was on display at the Royal Ontario Museum from November 15, 2002 to January 5, 2003. Image courtesy of Paradiso via Wikimedia Commons.*

Comparing the four Gospels reveals strong parallelism between three of them, namely Mark, Matthew, and Luke. These indeed include many of the same stories, often in a similar order, with very similar or identical wording. These three gospels are called the "Synoptic Gospels," synoptic meaning "seen together;" we call the puzzle of how this came about the "Synoptic Problem."

## WHO COPIED WHOM?

According to John S. Kloppenborg,[1] when reading the three Synoptic Gospels, we see a very high degree of verbatim agreement between the texts, not only in terms of essential details but also in the factual order of the narratives, as well as the presence of superfluous details. For example, we can compare the story of Jesus calling the two fishermen to discipleship in Matthew and Mark:

---

1    (Kloppenborg 2008, 1–41).

As Jesus walked beside the Sea of Galilee, he saw Simon and his brother Andrew casting a net into the lake, for they were fishermen. "Come, follow me," Jesus said, "and I will make you fishers of men." At once they left their nets and followed him. (Matthew 4:18–20)

As Jesus was walking beside the Sea of Galilee, he saw two brothers, Simon called Peter and his brother Andrew. They were casting a net into the lake, for they were fishermen. "Come, follow me," Jesus said, "and I will make you fishers of men." At once they left their nets and followed him. (Mark 1:16–18)

Another example is the story of Jesus calling the tax collector Levi/Matthew to be one of his followers. It is found in Luke, Matthew, and Mark:

As he walked along, he saw Levi son of Alphaeus sitting at the tax collector's booth. "Follow me," Jesus told him, and Levi got up and followed him. While Jesus was having dinner at Levi's house, many tax collectors and "sinners" were eating with him and his disciples, for there were many who followed him. (Mark 2:14–15)

After this, Jesus went out and saw a tax collector by the name of Levi sitting at his tax booth. "Follow me," Jesus said to him, and Levi got up, left everything and followed him. Then Levi held a great banquet for Jesus at his house, and a large crowd of tax collectors and others were eating with them. (Luke 5:27–29)

As Jesus went on from there, he saw a man named Matthew sitting at the tax collector's booth. "Follow me," he told him, and Matthew got up and followed him. While Jesus was having dinner at Matthew's house, many tax collectors and "sinners" came and ate with him and his disciples. (Matthew 9:9–10)

Kloppenborg also points out some interesting facts about the three Synoptic Gospels. They often agree when it comes to relating the same stories in the same relative order. Matthew and Luke tend to give a more detailed account of the stories than Mark does, while Mark tends to be laconic compared to Matthew and Luke. However, Matthew and Luke do not contradict Mark—that is, they do not agree together against Mark. But the passages that make Matthew and Luke's accounts more complete rarely agree. This would indicate that Matthew and Luke were not directly connected but were somehow connected through Mark. Matthew and Luke do relocate stories out of sequence with Mark, but there is no instance of them relocating the same story to the same position. Finally, Kloppenborg notes that no unnamed person in Mark is ever named in Matthew or Luke. Mark, then, is the common link, without Matthew and Luke being directly connected.

During the creation of one or more of these three Gospels, copying from a physical text must have occurred, since the similarities are too close (so close that they cannot be explained as mere memories of texts or a recording of an oral tradition). That gives us four possibilities: Matthew was copied by Mark, who Luke then copied; Luke was copied by Mark, who Matthew then copied; Mark copied from both Matthew and Luke; or Matthew and Luke both copied Mark.

The first three options, in which Mark is copying from a source, are not likely scenarios. Indeed, Mark tends to be much briefer than Matthew and Luke, reports fewer stories, and has less overall content. If Mark copied from either Matthew and/or Luke, he discarded essential elements of the narratives, such as entire parables, Jesus' infancy, essential teachings (e.g., the famous Sermon on the Mount), and, most awkwardly, the resurrection appearances of Jesus. This possibility does not seem reasonable.

Another aspect points to the fourth option. Mark reports this interesting event:

"…Jesus entered a house, and again a crowd gathered so that he and his disciples were not even able to eat. When his family heard about this, they went to take charge of him, for they said, 'He is out of his mind.'" (Mark 3:20–21)

But this contradicts both Luke and Matthew's stories on Jesus' youth, for they both clearly say that his parents (Joseph in Matthew and Mary in Luke) knew who Jesus really was, a divinely ordained man, and would not have thought his activities surprising. Therefore, in our first three scenarios above, Mark would have actively dropped the positive birth stories about Jesus and inserted the negative scene. His family is actively against him and thinks he is insane, a scene that Matthew and Luke do not mention. It is difficult to see why Mark would have done this.

Finally, it is widely acknowledged that Luke and Matthew used better grammar than Mark did—including conjunctions and connectives—as well as better ancient Greek overall. We find in their Gospels some wonderfully composed speeches, such as the Sermon on the Mount, in addition to improved versions of the stories present in Mark. For example, Mark briefly relates a two-verse tale of Jesus appearing after death to two followers while they were walking in the country (Mark 16:12–13). Luke relates the same story in 22 verses, including dialogue, the walker's destination of Emmaus, the name of one, Cleopas, a meal, Jesus "explaining" aspects of the JS (which are not related), and then Jesus disappearing and the disciples returning to Jerusalem (Luke 24:13–35). In another instance, Mark describes Jesus' time of solitude in the desert in two verses (Mark 1:12–13). In comparison, Matthew recounts it in 11 verses, with details of Satan's three attempts to have Jesus show his authority and Jesus giving pithy rebukes each time. To have Mark "dumb-down" better versions and cut elegant details makes no sense.

In any case, Matthew's and Luke's handling of Mark is within well-established conventions in Antiquity,[2] while the other alternatives are less so.

## MARK WAS FIRST

It thus seems reasonable to assume (as does almost all the scholarship on the Synoptic Problem) that the fourth model is the most reasonable, that Mark is the common source for Luke and Matthew. They copied from Mark independently of each other. It is easy to see Luke and Matthew filling out, clarifying, and improving Mark's more primitive stories while retaining the story order, disagreeing only when they deviate from that order. Luke and Matthew also added new content, including the birth narratives (which they disagree on), and dropped all embarrassing and contradictory information, such as Jesus's family reaction. Matthew and Luke also upgraded Mark's style with better Greek grammar and more sophisticated literary structures.

Therefore, Mark's Gospel was produced first, early enough for it to be circulated and generally known so that Luke and Matthew could use separate copies. Matthew and Luke, working independently, incorporated edited parts from a written copy of Mark into their material. As we can see from Figure 10, Matthew included 94% of Mark; Luke included 79% of Mark; only about 3% of Mark was left out between the two. It follows that both Luke and Matthew introduced their unique material. This earlier date for Mark's Gospel has important implications, as we shall see.

---

2    (Stanton 1997, 69).

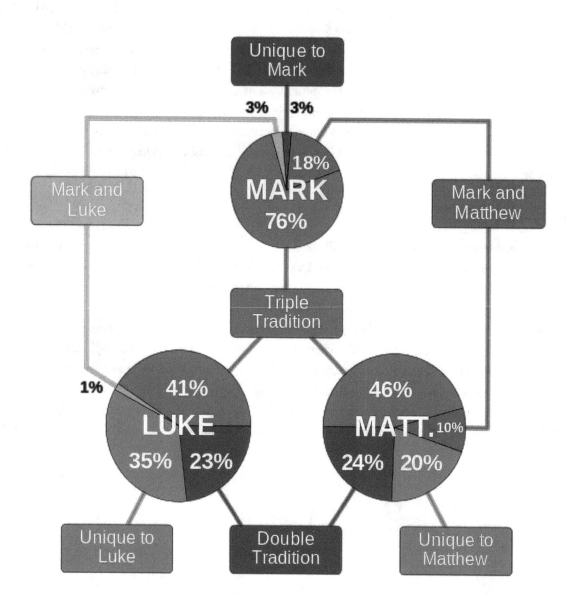

*Figure 10 **The Relationships Between the Three Synoptic Gospels.***

*Image courtesy of Alecmconroy derived from Popadius via CC BY-SA 3.0.*

## THE DOUBLE TRADITION

I have established that both Matthew and Luke had a copy of Mark in front of them when they were independently composing their respective Gospels and thus sharing portions of Mark. However, there is another puzzle: Matthew and Luke also share some material that they did not get from Mark, about 4,500 words in total (or about 230 verses), marked as The Double Tradition in Figure 10, representing nearly a quarter of each Gospel.

We can note three things about the overlaps found in Matthew and Luke. In general, there is a remarkably close agreement. For example, here is a speech from Jesus, not found in Mark, as he admonishes villages that have not believed in him:

"Woe to you, Korazin! Woe to you, Bethsaida! If the miracles that were performed in you had been performed in Tyre and Sidon, they would have repented long ago in sackcloth and ashes. But I tell you, it will be more bearable for Tyre and Sidon on the day of judgment than for you. And you, Capernaum, will you be lifted up to the skies? No, you will go down to the depths. If the miracles that were performed in you had been performed in Sodom, it would have remained to this day." (Matthew, 11:21–24)

"Woe to you, Korazin! Woe to you, Bethsaida! For if the miracles that were performed in you had been performed in Tyre and Sidon, they would have repented long ago, sitting in sackcloth and ashes. But it will be more bearable for Tyre and Sidon at the judgment than for you. And you, Capernaum, will you be lifted up to the skies? No, you will go down to the depths." (Luke, 10:13–15)

In this case, Jesus' speech in Luke comprises 46 words, and 45 of them are identical in Matthew (Matthew is repeating the miracles sentence twice). Not only do the words match, but the sequence of the words is nearly identical. Unlike English, word sequences can vary significantly in ancient Greek without a difference in meaning, so this matching word sequence is highly significant. Both texts also match inflexions, verbal sequence, and use of particles, all considered the most variable aspects of ancient Greek. Furthermore, the material has the same general order in both Gospels and coheres as an entity; it is not just a random set of verses. It has an overall storyline. All of this shows that both Matthew and Luke must have used the same written text (and not oral material) to compose their respective Gospels, as they did with Mark. Even in places where the level of agreement is not high, it is still clear that a similar source was used and that the author merely adjusted the wording.

## HYPOTHESIZING Q

This is called the "Two-Document Theory." Matthew and Luke used Mark, as well as a now-lost document, which is referred to as "Q," from the German word for "source," Quelle. Other scenarios have been proposed, but this is the most widely accepted and the simplest. I will thus examine Q in the next chapter because it needs to be considered separately as a legitimate source.

# CHAPTER 15

# Q

By comparing Matthew and Luke's overlap, it is possible to extract a body of material probably contained in Q. The Q material primarily consists of sayings of Jesus, which suggests that the document was a sort of "sayings log," that is, 230 or more verses of sayings with just two short narratives: Jesus being tempted by Satan in the desert and the healing of the Centurion's son.[1]

I will use the official Q text published by the International Q Project (IQP),[2] a research cluster focused on Q. While Q makes up about a quarter of Luke and Matthew, because neither author used all of Mark, we cannot assume that all of Q is present in their Gospels; indeed, some passages must have been left out, such as an introduction, just as some of Mark was left out. It seems that this is how Matthew and Luke worked. Also, there is no reason to think that Luke and Matthew used identical material from Q. Indeed, there is no doubt that some of the material, unique to either Luke or Matthew, was derived from Q but not used by both authors. Q, therefore, could have been quite a bit more extensive. However, as Luke and Matthew were quite conservative in excluding Mark's material, our Q may preserve most of Luke and Matthew's Q.

Another aspect outlined by the IQP is that while there is close agreement within Matthew and Luke's sayings, there is no agreement on the placement of those sayings from Q relative to Mark's sequence. This fact again indicates that neither Luke nor Matthew used each other. However, there are many (about 40%) of the Q sayings and stories that are in the same order relative to each other. Therefore, Q must have been written in a specific order, which influenced Matthew and Luke.

Furthermore, the IQP speculates that there must have been some introductory section in Q and perhaps even a title that would help define Q, but these have not been preserved. The IQP team further argues that Q and Mark do overlap in some places; typically, they say the Q version is longer and includes a greater number of sayings than Mark does.

The team also explains that the Q version, which Matthew and Luke used, must have been written in ancient Greek. Indeed, the two authors' agreement is very significant, so it is doubtful that the source they used had been translated from Aramaic by both authors independently. There is also no evidence in the text that Q was initially written in Aramaic, the language in which the original sayings would have been remembered. On the contrary, in the Q text, we can find a spelling mistake, which is typical of ancient Greek, not Aramaic.[3] This further shows that the original Q was written in Greek. The Q sayings appear as standardization of scripts for oral performance, a tell-tale sign of transcription from oral Aramaic into ancient Greek. Jesus spoke in Aramaic, but Q was written in Greek by a Greek scribe because that was the scribal language.

Finally, the IQP team's work suggests that Q's "world" was rural agricultural Galilee, where Jesus taught for a time. Q is full of farming metaphors set in a rural landscape: unproductive trees, threshing, arboriculture, day labour, harvesting, and sowing. There are no urban settings. The only villages that the text mentions are those that Jesus visited, namely, Capernaum, Bethsaida, Khorazin, and Nazara—all small, insignificant locations set in rural Galilee.

---

1      Q is not our only sayings log; the Gospel of Thomas is mostly made up of sayings, suggesting that other sayings collections may have existed.

2      (The Editorial Board of the International Q Project 2001).

3      Q 12:27: should be "do not card" versus "how they grow." This example is important, so it belongs in the main text.

The simple message of Q is distinct from the more advanced theology of the other Gospels. It emphasizes the presence of the Kingdom of God, with Jesus as its messenger. The text shows no interest in Jesus' death and supposed resurrection, perhaps because it occurred away from the countryside, in Jerusalem, and accords no expiatory sacrifice or salvific significance to Jesus, in stark contrast to the Gospels, especially Luke's and Matthew's.

## AUTHORSHIP

According to John Kloppenburg, Q was a Greek document whose scripts, comprised of Jesus' sayings, were meant for oral performance, a common practice given the time's high illiteracy rates. It was composed by a scribe, or scribes, in contemporary scribal tradition, perhaps directly from Aramaic performance scripts. As such, there is no information on authorship.[4]

## DATE

Scholars agree that Q is a very early work, most probably written between 40 and 60 CE, if not earlier (i.e., not long after Jesus' stay in rural Galilee, in the early 30s).[5] It disappeared as a standalone work sometime after Luke and Matthew copied it after the early 60s CE.[6]

## SOURCES

It would be interesting to know whether an original Aramaic sayings log was preserved in a written form or was the material all memorized in oral tradition? If a written text, then what (or who) was its source? Did the disciples compile it while Jesus was alive? This seems a likely scenario; however, the ultimate origin of Q is still being debated.

Q is an early work and contains much information about Jesus, so it will be included in my Source List.

---

4    (Kloppenborg 2008, 57–60).

5    I will date Jesus' time in Galilee between mid-31 CE and September 32 CE, suggesting a possible "date" for Q.

6    Since Luke and Matthew are dated to roughly 58 to 61 CE, and both Luke and Matthew used Q, then Q most probably existed for a while after the mid-60s.

# CHAPTER 16

# THE GOSPEL OF MARK

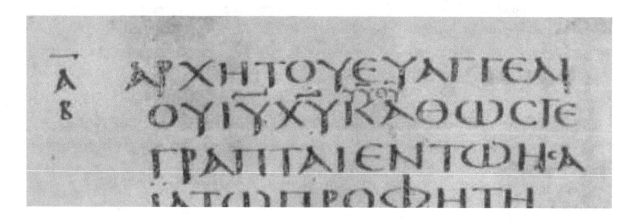

*Figure 11 **The Beginning of the Gospel of Mark***

*This image is the beginning of the Gospel of Mark in the grand Codex Sinaiticus, a complete Bible from the mid-300s CE. The first line reads αρχη του ευαγγελι ου "The beginning of the gospel (euangeliou) of," then IY and XY with lines overtop then the start of the next verse καθως "just as." IY and XY are examples of "nomina sacra," meaning sacred names; these abbreviations were a kind reverential shorthand for names considered divine. The abbreviation is a contraction of the name to the first and last letter in the name with a line on top. In this case, IY is the possessive of Ἰησοῦς or "Jesus," and XY is the possessive of Χριστός or "Christ." Hence the first verse reads, "The beginning of the gospel of Jesus Christ." Interestingly, the full name of Jesus does not occur in this Bible. Notice the later addition of two more nomina sacra after Jesus Christ, YY for Υἱός meaning "Son" and ΘY Θεός meaning "God," hence a later theological addition of "Son of God." Image reproduced by permission from the British Library. Codex Sinaiticus; Mark, 1:1-2, library: BL, folio: 217b, scribe: A.*

In this chapter, I will assess the Gospel of Mark in terms of authorship, dating, and source(s). This chapter is lengthy, as there are several additional issues specific to Mark: Mark's Chapter 13, the Longer Ending, Mark's Chapter 16, and Secret Mark, which need resolution, in that order, before this Gospel can be considered for inclusion in my Source List.

## AUTHORSHIP

Do we have any information on who created the Gospel of Mark or how it came to be? We do, from a short statement by Papias. We do not know much about Papias, apart from the odd comment from later writers who mention him. Irenaeus,[1] writing around 180 CE, described him as "an ancient man who was a hearer of John, and a companion of Polycarp …,"[2] both Early Church leaders.

---

1     Irenaeus, (130–202 CE) was Bishop of Lyons and author of *Against Heresies*. For information, please see (Hyland n.d.).

2     Irenaeus, *Against Heresies*, 5.33.4.

Papias wrote a substantial, five-volume work called the *Exposition of the Sayings of the Lord*, probably after 110 CE. It preserved a lot of oral history from the Early Church. Unfortunately, this work has been lost, but about two dozen fragments survive as citations in Eusebius's *Church History*.[3] These are the ones of interest:

"2. But Papias himself in the preface to his discourses by no means declares that he was himself a hearer and eyewitness of the holy apostles, but he shows by the words which he uses that he received the doctrines of the faith from those who were their friends.

3. He [Papias] says: 'But I shall not hesitate also to put down for you along with my interpretations whatsoever things I have at any time learned carefully from the elders and carefully remembered, guaranteeing their truth. For I did not, like the multitude, take pleasure in those that speak much, but in those that teach the truth; not in those that relate strange commandments, but in those that deliver the commandments given by the Lord to faith, and springing from the truth itself.

4. If then, anyone came, who had been a follower of the elders, I questioned him in regard to the words of the elders — what Andrew or what Peter said, or what was said by Philip, or by Thomas, or by James, or by John, or by Matthew, or by any other of the disciples of the Lord, and what things Aristion and the presbyter John, the disciples of the Lord, say. For I did not think that what was to be gotten from the books would profit me as much as what came from the living and abiding voice.'"[4]

These passages show us that Papias passed on information about Jesus that he had heard directly from his contemporaries, fulfilling the Custody Rule. Even though he was writing after 100 CE, his statement is potentially useful. Eusebius then continues to pass on Papias' information on the composition of Mark:

"14. Papias gives also in his work other accounts of the words of the Lord on the authority of Aristion who was mentioned above, and traditions as handed down by the presbyter John; to which we refer those who are fond of learning. But now we must add to the words of his which we have already quoted the tradition which he gives in regard to Mark, the author of the Gospel.

15. 'This also the presbyter said: Mark, having become the interpreter of Peter, wrote down accurately, though not in order, whatsoever he remembered of the things said or done by Christ. For he [Mark] neither heard the Lord nor followed him, but afterward, as I said, he followed Peter, who adapted his teaching to the needs of his hearers, but with no intention of giving a connected account of the Lord's discourses, so that Mark committed no error while he thus wrote some things as he remembered them. For he was careful of one thing, not to omit any of the things which he had heard, and not to state any of them falsely.' These things are related by Papias concerning Mark."[5]

We do not know when Papias wrote his work; various scholars argue that it may have been written anywhere between 110 and 140 CE. But what is more important to note is that Papias is speaking about a period in his life when, as a young man—perhaps in or around 80 CE—he was collecting information on Jesus. Hierapolis, where Papias was located, was at the nexus of two great roads that connected the region's major cities, namely, Ephesus, Antioch, Attalia, and Smyrna. Papias was thus well placed to meet various early Christian teachers as they crisscrossed the area because that region in western Turkey and Syria (Roman Asia) had become the hub of early Christianity after the destruction of Jerusalem in 70 CE.

---

3    There is also a single probable quote of Papias' work in Irenaeus.

4    Eusebius, *Church History*, 3.39.2–4

5    Ibid. 3.39.14–15.

Fragments 3 and 4 cited above read as part of a prologue, which was perhaps addressed to a particular individual (hence the use of "you"), whose name is now lost. A similar prologue starts the Gospel of Luke. Interestingly, Papias mentions that "books" were available to him, but he preferred to inquire directly. Here, he is alluding to the preferred learning technique of the scientific, historical, and technical treatises of his time; first-hand experience was considered a better learning technique than reading. He thus made careful and serious inquiries of informed sources—preferably eyewitnesses—collected their testimonies in note form, and then arranged them artistically into a piece of literature in accordance with the contemporary "best practice" of the historiography *genre*.

In his prologue, Papias mentions three groups of people:

1.  Those who "had been in attendance on the elders," that is, the people who had heard the elders teach and whom Papias had a chance to talk to. The elders were still alive and teaching when Papias spoke to these people in his youth. The elders would have been the senior Christian teachers of the time. Since they were spread through the cities of Roman Asia, Papias would not normally have had the chance to hear them unless they travelled through Hierapolis.

2.  The next group that Papias names consist of Jesus' disciples—Andrew, Peter, Philip, Thomas, James, John, Matthew—and "any other of the Lord's disciples." He was interested in what they had "said." Note the use of the past tense here. Therefore, these people must have been dead by the time Papias was inquiring, and he could only learn what they had said by asking either the elders or those who had attended on the elders. It is interesting to note that Papias expected to hear specifically what "Peter or Andrew said." He thus considered their oral history as authoritative. Papias makes it clear that he values direct information, preferably guaranteed by an eyewitness or at least coming from someone who heard directly from an eyewitness.

3.  The last group comprises "Aristion and the presbyter John, the disciples of the Lord." These are specific people, distinguishable from the previous group, for they appear to be still living and teaching: "What things they say" (present tense). Papias regards the people belonging to the last two groups, "the disciples of the Lord," as actual eyewitness disciples of Jesus.

It thus seems that there were still at least two direct disciples of Jesus alive by then and nearby geographically, namely, Aristion[6] and John. Papias calls the second John "presbyter" to distinguish him from the first John he mentioned, and one of the "elders." Note here the time Papias is referring to—the 80s CE; it nicely overlaps with my earlier analysis' timeframe, where the 90s would see any surviving companions of Jesus well into their seventies and eighties. In fact, this would be the last time in history that such an overlap would occur, and it would be reasonable to assume that this would spur authors such as Papias to write down their information. The direct link between an inquiring Papias and Jesus' companions, Aristion and presbyter John, is further reinforced by Eusebius:

"7. Papias, of whom we are now speaking, confesses that he received the words of the apostles from those that followed them, but says that he was himself a hearer of Aristion and the presbyter John. At least he mentions them frequently by name and gives their traditions in his writings. These things, we hope, have not been uselessly adduced by us."[7]

And we have already seen that Irenaeus considers it notable that Papias was "the hearer of John."[8]

Papias had direct links with information once or twice removed from Jesus, and he briefly mentions the creation of the Gospel of Mark in fragments 14 and 15; it is John the Presbyter, one of the disciples of Jesus, who told him the story.

Papias is thus very clear that Mark is indeed the formal author of his Gospel, but that Peter was the source for the material. Papias is also careful to tell us that Mark was the translator and companion of Peter but that he never saw nor met Jesus himself.

---

6    Apart from the mention here Aristion is unattested.

7    Eusebius, *Church History,* 3.39.7.

8    Irenaeus, *Against Heresies,* 5.33.4.

Moreover, Papias is not expressing his opinion or being vague on the creation of the Gospel of Mark; instead, he is reporting what John the Presbyter "used to say" as fact, and we know that he met John at least once. He is passing on information directly given to him by a companion of Jesus who would have known Peter personally, and perhaps Mark as well.

Other early traditions also have Mark writing down Peter's stories. A later writer, Justin Martyr,[9] who wrote around the 150s CE, referred to the Gospel of Mark as Peter's "memoirs": "And when it is said that He [Jesus] changed the name of one of the apostles to Peter; and when it is written in the memoirs of him [Peter] that this so happened …"[10] Justin is referring here to the incident in the Gospel of Mark where Jesus renames Simon to Peter (Mark 3:16). Eusebius, quoting Clement of Alexandria,[11] talks of a tradition with additional details coming from the primitive elders as follows:

"The Gospel according to Mark had this occasion. As Peter had preached the Word publicly at Rome, and declared the Gospel by the Spirit, many who were present requested that Mark, who had followed him for a long time and remembered his sayings, should write them out. And having composed the Gospel he gave it to those who had requested it. When Peter learned of this, he neither directly forbade nor encouraged it."[12]

An additional story comes to us directly from Clement:

"Mark, the follower of Peter, while Peter publicly preached the Gospel at Rome before some of Caesar's *equites* [wealthy aristocrats], and adduced many testimonies to Christ, in order that thereby they might be able to commit to memory what was spoken, of what was spoken by Peter, wrote entirely what is called the Gospel according to Mark."[13]

The source of the Gospel of Mark is thus very well attested in the early literature as being Peter.

There is also a frequently used ancient (and modern) rhetorical technique called the *inclusio* ("inclusion") that can be used as evidence for identifying Peter as the source of Mark. An *inclusio* serves to link a theme appearing at the close of a work back to the beginning of the narrative; in other words, it is a literary bracketing technique. Its use signalled to the reader that the story was soon to end, highlighted a theme that the author wanted to emphasize, and lent a sense of elegance and symmetry to the whole. Examples are common in both the OT and the NT. In Mark's Gospel, the first disciple of Jesus named is Simon (later renamed by Jesus to Peter): "As Jesus walked beside the Sea of Galilee, he saw Simon and his brother Andrew casting a net into the lake, for they were fishermen" (Mark 1:16). Peter is also the last disciple named in Mark: "But go, tell his disciples and Peter, 'He is going ahead of you into Galilee. There you will see him, just as he told you'" (Mark 16:7). Mark uses this *inclusio* to point to Peter and indicate that the enclosed material is the testimony of Peter, not Mark's.

Furthermore, the Gospel of Mark reads like a dictated oral history. Each story is easily visualized with short narratives, including a teaching point. The Gospel of Mark reads much like an assembly of detachable stories strung together because they are seldom linked logically; instead, they follow one another with a series of vague expressions, such as "On another occasion," "He left that place," "On leaving those parts," or "Once." Also, the structure consists of repetitive patterns that would aid an oral performer. This structure, of course, is the direct result of Mark attempting to string the discreet oral units together to create a unified written narrative.

It seems both Luke and Matthew, who were not eyewitnesses of the events they relate, knew that Peter was behind the Gospel of Mark, given how carefully they used its material. Between the two of them, they practically used all of Mark; only 3% was discarded. They both, in general, followed Mark's sequence of events and embellished the stories without ever contradicting Mark on the main facts. They obviously held Mark in very high regard, and he was their primary source. In his prologue,

---

9    An early Christian philosopher and writer (c. 100–165 CE). For more information (The Editors of the New World Encyclopedia, Justin Martyr 2018).

10    Justin Martyr, *Dialogue with Trypho*, 106.

11    A Christian apologist and writer (c. 150–c. 215) distinct from Clement I of Rome. See (Fredericksen 2020).

12    Eusebius, *Church History*, 6.14.6-7.

13    Clement of Alexandria, *Fragments* 1.

Luke even mentions the information "handed down to us" (Luke 1:1–2) from eyewitnesses; presumably he means Peter, whose testimony he is using.

Luke also seems to use the *inclusio* technique. However, he does not copy Mark's *inclusio*, but he creates his own. In his Gospel, Simon/Peter is the first (Luke 4:38) and last disciple (Luke 24:34) named. Again, the author, Luke, is pointing to Peter as the most important source of information.

Peter figures prominently in Mark's Gospel, which frequently adopts Peter's perspective on events. For instance, the Transfiguration event (Mark 9:2–8) is reported from Peter's point of view, and Mark's Gospel is the one that mentions Simon/Peter the most frequently amongst all the Gospels, despite all the other Gospels being longer works. Both would be expected if Peter was the source.[14]

Additional sources have Rome as the setting for the initial "publication" of the Gospel of Mark. This makes sense, as Mark seems to have only a vague knowledge of the geography of Galilee (so he cannot have spent much time there and, therefore, probably lived chiefly in Rome). Several words from his Gospel were borrowed from Latin, such as "Praetorium" (Mark 15:16) and "denarius" (Mark 12:16), the language of Rome. Mark also finds himself explaining Hebrew and Aramaic terms, such as "Talitha koum!" (Mark 5:41) and "Corban" (Mark 7:11). His Gospel was thus probably intended for a Roman audience. Moreover, a "Mark" is mentioned in the letter 1 Peter, which further points to the place of composition: "She [a sister church] who is in Babylon, chosen together with you, sends you her greetings, and so does my son Mark" (1 Peter 5:13). Assuming that Peter did indeed write this letter, there is no doubt that the Babylon in question here refers to Rome (a common metaphor at the time); therefore, Peter was writing from Rome, and a Mark was closely associated with him there.

Papias states that Mark was the "interpreter" of Peter. This could mean he was either a translator or someone who explained things. Papias is very clear that Mark altered nothing of Peter's testimony; he must, therefore, mean "translator." Peter himself was probably raised bilingual, in Aramaic and koine Greek. He came from Galilee, a Jewish region within the more prominent Greek culture of the Eastern Roman Empire. He would have improved his Greek as he pursued his ministry, although we do not know if he could write in Greek. Richard Bauckham suggests that while Peter could speak well in rough Greek, he may have preferred to preach in his native Aramaic (also making it easier to report Jesus' original Aramaic teachings).

Based on the information we have, it is possible to recreate the sequence of events that led to the composition of the Gospel of Mark. Peter was teaching and preaching the Core Message+ in Rome. Some wealthy persons approached Mark, Peter's assistant, and asked for a written Greek record of Peter's teachings, which is understandable if Peter was teaching in Aramaic (or poor Greek). These people no doubt offered to pay for the copies, as scribes were not cheap. So Mark started to copy down Peter's preaching—the stories, parables, short sayings, and so on that we can find in his Gospel. Peter told whatever was needed in whatever order that suited the occasion. Interestingly, Clement of Alexandria seems to indicate that Peter only found out about the Gospel of Mark after it had been disseminated and did not seem to be interested in it. Mark took the project on himself. Papias asserts that Mark neither omitted nor added anything to Peter's testimony. Thus, the result was not a connective, "regular" narrative but a collection of disorderly discrete stories—memories and anecdotes from Peter, which makes sense if Peter was indeed unaware of Mark's Gospel project. And no doubt not all of Peter's information was heard by Mark. There would be gaps in the overall story as well as certain scenes that would be told over and over. Any information Peter presented in Aramaic, Mark would have translated into Greek. Mark's notes then consisted of discrete pieces of accurately recorded information, in Greek, of varying length, from a pithy saying of a few words to lengthy sequences, such as Peter's version of the Passion Story. But other than a general story arc encompassing Jesus' appearance, mission, and then last week and death, there was no order to the events. Mark was left with the task of ordering his notes to create a readable version of Peter's account of Jesus.[15]

It is interesting to note how different Mark's Passion Narrative (the story of Jesus' arrest, trial, and death) is in comparison to the rest of his Gospel. While most of Mark is made up of discrete units, the Passion Narrative has an integrated story arc, from

---

14    For a complete discussion on the literary features of Mark see (Lunn 2014, 209–240).

15    I picture Mark starting out in front of a large table covered in pieces of papyri, large and small, in no order.

Jesus arriving in Jerusalem through to his arrest, trial, and death, that spans four chapters (11, 14, 15, and 16) out of the total 16 chapters—a quarter of the Gospel. This suggests Peter recounted this story as a whole unit embedded in the Core Message+.

Without a lot of time and place markers, Mark would at times have had to guess the actual order of events. This is implied when he uses his frustrating expression "sometime later." He simply does not know when. Other times the gaps in the narrative forced Mark to make sequencing errors. For example, I will show that he placed the cleansing of the Temple during the third Jerusalem visit (Mark 11:15–17), conflicting with the author of the Gospel of John,[16] who says it occurred two years earlier (John 2:15–16). Mark wanted to include the story but only had material from the last Jerusalem visit, so he had to place it there. Also, some sections are not very informed, like chapter 16, and there are significant gaps in Jesus' story, such as his activities in Jerusalem before his final visit. Mark's notes probably also included lots of random miscellanea about which he needed to make decisions on whether to include them or not. I will argue that some of these "leftovers" make up his odd Chapter 13. No doubt Mark possessed extra material that he chose to leave aside.[17] Mark's guesswork over sequencing is the reason for Papias' fussing over "ordered form" and Luke boasting of his "orderly account" (Luke 1:3).

Mark Gospel contains numerous problems—factual errors, a sketchy trial sequence, a sparse, post-burial sequence, and an odd Chapter 13. It certainly seems as if Mark had "released" the document to his patrons before Peter knew of its existence, as Peter did not "proof" the final document to fill in gaps, correct sequence issues, and fix errors. After release, perhaps Peter considered the Gospel too imperfect and beyond retraction, so he had no interest in it. Maybe Peter was planning to write his own complete account at some point.

In any case, Mark's errors are pretty numerous. If not all, I attribute most of those to Mark, for Peter, being a Galilean Jew, would most certainly not have made such mistakes. Indeed, they all pertain to Mark's lack of knowledge of Galilee. First, the evangelist knew very little about the geography of that region. For instance, he indicates that Sidon is south of Tyre, when it is actually to the north. He also suggests that the Sea of Galilee is in the Decapolis area, when it borders it to the northeast (Mark 7:31). Later on, Mark places Judea to the west across the Jordan from Capernaum, when it is due south (Mark 10:1). In another instance, Mark says that when coming from Jericho, one goes through Bethphage first and then Bethany, but, in fact, Bethphage is reached after Bethany (Mark 11:1).

Other errors show that Mark did not know Galilee very well. For instance, Mark says that ceremonial washing applies to all the Jews, when it only applies to priests (Mark 7:3–4). In another example of factual error, Herodias was previously married to Herod II, not Phillip (Mark 6:17).

As for his chronology, it is often incorrect or non-existent. As already pointed out, Mark's timing of the cleansing of the Temple is off by two years, and he gets the Last Supper[18] timing wrong; it was a day earlier. For Mark, Jesus' mission lasts about a year, whereas in John, it lasts two and a half years. In places, Mark's narrative runs "thin," with little detail and even gaps, and it shows some odd features. This is especially true of Chapters 13 and 16, which I shall treat separately.

But Mark alone cannot be held responsible for all the problems encountered in his Gospel. Peter's narrative has odd content issues. These include his superstitious healing interpretations; all of Jesus' demon healings are indeed reported only by Peter (Mark 1:23–26, 1:34, 1:39, 3:11, 5:8–10, 7:29, 9:25–26).[19] They also have odd, superstitious, and fantastical stories, such as Jesus' forty days in the desert, complete with Satan and angels (Mark 1:12–13); the folk tale of the Baptist's beheading (Mark 6:17–28); the rumour of the two travellers seeing Jesus after the Crucifixion (Mark 16:12); the dream-like transfiguration (Mark 9:2–8); the centurion spontaneously and confusingly declaring Jesus the Son of God upon his death (Mark 15:39); the

---

16    For the rest of this chapter, when comparing content of Mark to content in the other Gospels, I will only refer to the Gospel of John, as Matthew and Luke simply reproduce Mark's content. There is also an additional reason for ignoring Matthew and Luke, which I will discuss in Chapter 17.

17    This is shown to be true in my discussion of Secret Mark below.

18    The Last Supper was the final evening meal Jesus had with his followers just before he was arrested.

19    Q also has one demon story (11:14).

weird story of the pigs (Mark 5:1–20); the "darkness" appearing just before Jesus' death (Mark 15:33); and the curtain protecting the inner sanctum inside the Temple spontaneously tearing in two upon Jesus' death (Mark 15:38).

In Antiquity, the Gospel of Mark was held in lower esteem than the other three Gospels, for it was deemed rougher and simpler. This is certainly true when compared to John's complex and more detailed Gospel. As he explains in his prologue, Papias was concerned about truth and orderly composition, which were, at the time, the main features of good history. He thus praises Mark's fidelity to Peter's account. He argues that it is not Mark's fault if the account reads as a haphazard collection of anecdotes, perhaps in response to implied criticism of that gospel.

*Figure 12* **Peter**

*A very early representation of Peter (Petrus) from a Roman catacomb dated to the 300s. Above the name is the Chi-Rho symbol which is the overlap of the first two capital letters in ΧΡΙΣΤΟΣ, Greek for Christos, first used as an abbreviation for Jesus Christ during Emperor Constantine I's reign (306–337 CE).*

So what can we say about Peter? Peter, via Mark, tells us nothing about himself before the advent of Jesus. However, we can gather some information about his life from John's Gospel, which explains that Peter was originally from Bethsaida, a village at the top of the Sea of Galilee (John 1:44). Peter tells us that he was living in nearby Capernaum with his brother Andrew, where they worked as uneducated fishermen at the time of Jesus. Peter was married and probably had children, and they all lived in a house in Capernaum (Mark 1:29–30). His father was called John (John 21:15). There is no reason to suppose that Peter was an older man, as frequently shown in later works of art. He was to live another three decades, so he was probably around the same age as Jesus while he was a disciple. Initially, he seems to have followed the Baptist, as he was near the Baptist's camp when he first encountered Jesus. As told by John (John 1:42), Peter later followed Jesus but only when the latter was in Galilee. Later, though, as Jesus goes further afield, Peter states, "We have left everything to follow you!" (Mark 10:28), which presumably means that he has left family and friends to follow him. Peter had a superstitious nature; he believed in demons, had visions he thought were real, and told fantastic tales. Tradition has him being killed around 64 CE, under Emperor Nero. He was killed in the Roman Hippodrome on Vatican Hill just outside Rome, and buried in a primitive cemetery nearby.[20] St. Peter's Church was built over what are thought to be Peter's bones.[21]

For my Source List, I will include an edited version of Mark, which I shall call the Gospel of Peter-Mark—Peter-Mark for short—to distinguish it from the original and to emphasize that Peter is the source. I will still refer to Mark when discussing the original. For my Peter-Mark, I will leave Mark's errors in the text and just note them.

## DATE

We have established that of the three Synoptic Gospels, Mark's was written first and then used by Matthew and Luke. But when did Mark "publish" his Gospel? We know that Mark probably arranged and published his Gospel while in Rome. As I explained earlier, we do indeed have an indication in 1 Peter of Mark being in Rome with Peter, which is dated to the spring of 55 CE. The rest of the external evidence is unclear and contradictory. There is, however, one internal clue.

According to the scholarly opinion, if Mark is "late"—between 65 and 80 CE—then Luke and Matthew must be even later. Many scholars assume that Mark is "late" because of one passage in the Gospel, contained in the famous and odd Chapter 13, which mentions the destruction of the Temple and a "desolation."[22] The traditional interpretation is that it describes the events of the First Jewish-Roman War that went on from 66 to 70 CE, when the Jews revolted. Rome put down the revolt, destroying both Jerusalem and the Temple in 70 CE. According to that interpretation, Mark must have been composed after 70 and put the description of the event on the lips of Jesus to make it appear a successful prediction of the future. But does Chapter 13 refer to the year 70?

According to Robinson, there is nothing to support such an assumption.[23] He indeed points out several problems that dispel the notion that this passage has anything to do with 70 CE. Firstly, in Mark's Chapter 13, the disciples ask Jesus when the Temple will be destroyed, but he never answers them; in fact, he never mentions the Temple's destruction again. There is a parallel Temple-destruction verse in the Gospel of John, which the author explains is metaphorical (John 2:19–21), not a reference to an actual event. So it seems reasonable to assume the "destruction" in Mark is also metaphorical.

Secondly, Robinson explains that this famous verse—"When you see 'the abomination that causes desolation' standing where it [or he] does not belong—let the reader understand—then let those who are in Judea flee to the mountains" (Mark

---

20    A fascinating speculation places Peter's death on October 13, 64 CE. The Great Fire of Rome burned down much of the city from July 19 to 28 of that year. According to Tacitus the Christians in the city were made the scapegoats by Nero, probably to deflect suspicion away from Nero's administration or other groups, initiating the first official persecution of the Christians. Tacitus specifically mentions "a show in the circus" where many were killed (Tacitus, The Annals, 15.44). Since the Circus Maximus in the city had been destroyed in the fire the games would have been staged at the Hippodrome, located outside the city on Vatican Hill. The persecutions would have started after the end of the fire in August-September 64 and no doubt Peter, being the Christian leader in Rome would have been arrested then. In the Roman calendar there were two very important public celebrations related to the emperor, his ascension day and birthday. These days would be celebrated with sacrifices, public ceremonies, and games. Nero became emperor on October 13 54, so October 13 64 would have been his tenth anniversary, a very important date. No doubt it would have been the high point of the celebrations and important criminals such as Peter would have been executed as part of the games.

21    See this fascinating video series that details the evolution of Peter's burial place (The Editors of Cultural Travel Guide 2012). See also (Guarducci, The Tomb of St. Peter: The New Discoveries in the Sacred Grottoes of the Vatican 1960) and (Walsh 1982).

22    I have provided a copy of Chapter 13 in Appendix 2.

23    (Robinson 2000, 13–31).

13:14)—has traditionally been interpreted as a reference to Roman General Titus' soldiers sacrificing to their standards on the Temple Mount after winning the siege of 70. However, Robinson believes that there is a much better solution to this reference. Indeed, he writes, after the events described in this verse, where Jesus urges his listeners to flee to the mountains after the "desolation," it would have been too late for anyone to flee, since Jerusalem was surrounded and the Romans had seized most of Judea three years before. The predicted events simply do not fit history.[24] Also, Robinson remarks that the details of the conflict given by Jesus are generic and could refer to any period. According to him, anyone could have predicted that any type of revolt against the Romans could lead to nothing but complete destruction. Therefore, if we are to trust Robinson's argument, then the events related by Mark do not pertain to the year 70 CE. As a result, Mark has become unmoored in time, and his Gospel could be either later or earlier. But since the dates of Luke and Matthew are dependent on Mark's date, they too have become unmoored in time. There is no reason to accept the traditional dating of these three Gospels. So let us try and pin the correct dates down.

By reading Chapter 13 carefully and digging further into its historical background, we can find a clue to Mark's date. Verse 14, cited above, is the key. Verse 14 contains the only instance where Mark addresses the reader directly: "let the reader understand." It also includes the expression "the abomination that causes desolation," sometimes termed the "Awful Horror"—a JS expression. It occurs only three times, all three in the book of Daniel (Daniel 9:27, 11:31, 12:11). But what does it mean?

In 168 BCE, the Hellenistic Seleucid Empire ruled over Judea. The reigning emperor, Antiochus IV Epiphanes, decided to outlaw Judaism and ordered that the Temple in Jerusalem be turned over to pagan worship. The JS book 1 Maccabees describes this event in the following words: "Now on the fifteenth day of Kislev [November to December], in the year 145 [168 BCE], they set up a disgusting and destructive thing on the altar for entirely burned offerings in the sanctuary" (1 Maccabees, 1:54). The "disgusting and destructive thing" was probably a statue of Zeus, since 2 Maccabees mentions the temple being dedicated to the "Olympian god Zeus" (2 Maccabees 6:2), the new object of prayers and offerings. This action kicked off a Jewish revolt, which eventually freed Judea from the Seleucid Empire. The book of Daniel[25] was written in the immediate aftermath of the rebellion, and it addresses the defilement of the altar in these terms: "And at the temple he [Antiochus] will set up an abomination that causes desolation" (Daniel 9:27). But why is Mark using this expression found in the JS? Was there a similar event taking place during his time?

Early in 40 CE, the unstable Roman Emperor, Gaius Caligula, ordered that the Temple of Jerusalem be modestly renamed "The Temple of Illustrious Gaius the New Jupiter". He thus ordered a massive gilt statue of himself to be placed in the Temple for prayers and offerings. He meant to convert the Jewish Temple into a place of pagan worship, again, where he would be worshipped as a divine being; in other words, he deified himself. The Jews rioted at the news. In response, the Emperor ordered half of the Eastern legions to accompany the statue into Jerusalem to ensure its installation; this amounted to invading Judea, marching into Jerusalem, and setting up his statue. Publius Petronius, the Syrian governor put in charge of the whole operation, expected war to break out as a result.

Philo of Alexandria[26] described officially meeting with Caligula[27] while these events unfolded. For the occasion, Philo was carrying a petition to secure the rights of the Jews:

> "What sayest thou, O master? Are you making war upon us, because you anticipate that we will not endure such indignity, but that we will fight on behalf of our laws, and die in defence of our national customs? For you cannot possibly have been ignorant of what was likely to result from your attempt to introduce these

---

24    Josephus, who was present at the siege and acting as a translator, describes the siege in detail.

25    The book of Daniel is an odd book. It was written contemporary to the rebellion but claims to have been written centuries before, so when it describes current events, it couches them as successful predictions of the future. Hence, the "desolation" is described here as a future event.

26    A Hellenistic Jewish philosopher and writer, (c. 20 BCE– c. 50 CE). For more information see (The Editors of Encyclopaedia Britannica, Philo Judaeus 2020).

27    The only surviving transcript of an interview with a Roman emperor.

innovations respecting our temple; but having previously learnt with perfect accuracy what was likely to happen as well as if it had already taken place, and knowing the future as thoroughly as if it were actually present, you commanded your general to bring up an army in order that the statue when erected might be consecrated by the first sacrifice offered to it, being of a most polluted kind, stained with the blood of miserable men and women."[28]

A massive Jewish revolt thus seemed imminent in 40 CE! If the statue went up, it would indeed lead to yet another "abomination that causes desolation," as foretold in Daniel. This explains the advice as found in Mark 13:14: "let those who are in Judea flee to the mountains," just as the rebels were reported to have done in the revolt. Therefore, the year 40 CE matches Mark's warning about "the abomination that causes desolation standing where it [Or he] does not belong." In his Greek writings, Mark usually prefers the gender-neutral "it," but here he uses the masculine version to refer to the desolation. Notice how Mark is cautious not to mention the ruling emperor directly; it would undoubtedly get him into trouble, especially as he was in Rome at the time. Because of the risk, he subtly encodes his warning with an obscure reference from a book only Jews would know and finishes with the admonition: "let the reader understand." Mark also indicates that the event is still to come—"When you see"—so it has not happened yet. Mark can thus not be referring to events that occurred before 40 CE. The crisis in question was only averted by Caligula's assassination on January 22, 41; therefore, Mark also cannot be referring to events that happened after 40.

Other verses in Chapter 13 are an excellent fit for events occurring between the late 30s and 40 CE. In the first place, it was a time of tension; serious rioting broke out in Alexandria and Jamnia in 40 CE. More rioting broke out when the plans for a statue in the Temple were announced: "Brother will betray brother to death …" (Mark 13:12). Secondly, earthquakes were an issue at the time: "There will be earthquakes in various places, and famines" (Mark 13:8). There had notably been a large earthquake in Antioch and parts of Syria in 37 CE. There was also a famine in the late 30s. We suspect this because, during that period, the Jewish aristocracy asked for taxes to be lifted on agricultural products, something they typically did during times of food anxiety or famine.

Moreover, messianic pretenders were a common feature when Mark writes: "For false messiahs and false prophets will appear and perform signs and wonders to deceive …" (Mark 13:8). For example, Simon Magus, a Samaritan prophet who led a group up Mount Gerizim— possibly in 36 CE—preached and performed magic (hence his name) in Samaria and Rome. "Wars and rumours of wars" also fit that time period. A few years before, from 36 to 37 CE, Herod Antipas, the ruler of Galilee, fought a short war with the neighbouring Nabatean Kingdom, the Nabateans invading Herod's domain until Rome restored order. There were also military tensions between the nearby Parthian Empire and Rome, which led to a brief border war in 36 CE. Finally, the first period of crisis for Christianity occurred in the mid to late 30s with persecutions, hence "You will be handed over to the local councils and flogged in the synagogues." Persecutions had already started even before Jesus' death when he was arrested (Mark 14:46), and his followers were prosecuted (John 9:22) and scattered. Soon after Jesus' death, both Peter and John were imprisoned by the Jewish authorities (Acts 4:3, 5:19), flogged (Acts 5:40), and threatened with death (Acts 5:33). A Jewish mob had killed Christian Stephen in 34 CE (Acts 8:1–2), and Saul/Paul was imprisoning Christians and preparing to travel to Damascus to persecute more of them there (Acts 8:1–3, 9:1–2). No other time period fits Chapter 13 as well as this period. Mark 13, and presumably all of Mark, was thus most certainly "published" (that is, released for scribal copying) during the year 40, before Caligula was assassinated at the beginning of 41, and before the threat of revolt had passed.

Can we refine the date even more? Yes, the following verse indicates that winter had not yet arrived: "Pray that this will not take place in winter" (Mark 13:8). We can assume that this passage can be dated to the spring, summer, or fall of 40 CE. But spring is too early, as the order for the statue was issued early in 40 CE, and time was needed for the crisis to build. By winter 40, Mark could have retrieved and altered the passage if only a single or a few copies were published. But by winter 40/41, multiple copies must have been already circulating, and it was too late to change the text. As I pointed out earlier, Clement of Alexandria, via Eusebius, records a tradition saying that "many" people asked Mark for a written Gospel. He obliged; therefore, many copies may have been created initially, making later alterations impossible. This oversight also gives Mark an incentive to

---

28    Philo, *On the Embassy to Gaius,* 31.208.

create an updated gospel later in life; he would undoubtedly have heavily edited Chapter 13.[29] Given all the available evidence, Mark must have published many copies of his Gospel in Rome during the summer or fall of 40 CE.

## MARK'S ODD CHAPTER 13

Chapter 13 has always been the focus of much debate. It is a discourse by Jesus covering the destruction of the Temple and deceptive teachers, along with all sorts of topics, such as warnings, stars falling from the skies, people fleeing, the "Elect," abominations, and fig trees in a disordered sequence. It is 37 verses long, making it the most extended sustained teaching in Mark. The next longest sequence of teaching in Mark is 29 verses, with the Parable of the Sower (Mark 4:3–31), which is actually half this length, for Jesus repeats it twice. The Sower is cohesive and sensible, unlike the odd chapter 13. I review this chapter in Appendix 2 and conclude it consists of short, independent, authentic sayings of Jesus (verses 2, 5–6, 9–13, 28, and 31–37) that Mark thought necessary to record but had no other place for, so he created a discourse structure, added his own material (the rest of the chapter), and fitted them together as best he could, along with his "public service announcement" on the imminent disaster that Caligula's statue would cause.

As a result, I will exclude Mark's verses from Peter-Mark and my Source List.

## THE LONGER ENDING OF THE GOSPEL OF MARK

*Figure 13 **Shorter Mark***

*The ending of the Gospel of Mark in the Codex Vaticanus with the words kata Markon meaning "according to Mark". Vaticanus is the oldest existing complete Bible, created 300–325 CE during the reign of the Roman emperor Constantine. It has been held in the Vatican Library since the 1400s, perhaps brought there after the fall of Constantinople in 1453. The format of the codex is three columns per page. This figure shows the end of the last column of the Gospel of Mark, which ends at verse 8 of chapter 16, the Short Ending of Mark. Notable is an additional blank column left after this section. Throughout the rest of the manuscript, each new book was started in the next column. Only at the end of Mark is there an extra blank column, suggesting the scribe was aware that 12 verses of the Longer Ending would not fit at the bottom of this column, so a blank column was left, allowing for later inclusion.*

The earliest intact bibles, the Codex Vaticanus and the Codex Sinaiticus,[30] dating from the early 300s CE, terminate Mark's Gospel at an odd verse in the last chapter, called the Abrupt or Short Ending (Mark 16:8). Both bibles have heavily influenced modern translations, which usually end at verse 8, but frequently a 12-verse Longer Ending is provisionally included in brackets or with notes.[31] Interestingly, Roman Catholics are not required to believe that Mark added anything after verse 8. However, a more extended and more complete ending was heavily attested by Church Fathers and manuscript tradition before and after these codices were created. My Source List currently has Mark ending at chapter 16, verse 8. The question is: Should I include the Longer Ending of Mark? If so, should I include it completely, in part or with a *proviso*? Given that the Longer Ending

---

29    I will cover this issue when discussing Secret Mark.

30    A codex, plural codices, is a handwritten book typically made from vellum or papyrus. It is the ancestor of the modern book.

31    My copy of the NIV does include the additional verses without notes nor brackets. If you have a Bible handy, flip to Mark chapter 16 and see how your publisher handles the ending.

mentions post-resurrection appearances, and that Mark is a source of primary importance, the issue deserves a complete discussion, given in Appendix 3.

Based on the arguments put forth, I can thus conclude that the Longer Ending is indeed the original ending to the Gospel of Mark, published in 40 CE. The Abrupt Ending was a brief and localized manuscript tradition, probably springing from the Gnostic denial of bodily resurrection, which made its way into the two Codices before the original, Longer Ending form was re-established in all traditions. I shall, therefore, include the Longer Ending in Peter-Mark.

## MARK'S PROBLEMATIC CHAPTER 16

Mark's last chapter, including the Longer Ending containing Peter's resurrection stories, has its own problematic features. Peter's account is odd; it is a relatively short and disordered resurrection sequence of just ten verses, while John has 56 verses to describe the resurrection. Just as with chapter 13, Mark's ending seems to be the work of an author who did not have a lot of material to finish his Gospel satisfactorily. Peter must thus not have spoken much about the resurrection in Mark's presence. Besides, the latter has included two different versions of the first sighting; the first is found in verses 1 to 8, where a group of women find the empty tomb and are told by a mysterious young man that Jesus is not there anymore. The second version is found in verses 9 to 11 and essentially matches the Gospel of John (John 20:1–8), with Mary Magdalen telling her story of seeing Jesus at the tomb and relating the information to the rest of the group, who do not understand (notice in superstitious Peter's version that demon-healing has reappeared). Mark says that Jesus says he will see them in Galilee, but no Galilee meeting is ever described; this must be another story Mark simply never heard. In Mark's verses 12 and 13, we find the nascent "Road to Emmaus" story, later embellished by Luke. It consists of a rumour saying that two people walking in the countryside saw Jesus in a "different form." Peter again has passed on a superstitious rumour that Mark then included. As for Mark's verses 15 and 16, they certainly conform to the kind of things that Jesus says elsewhere, so they are probably accurate (John 20:21–23). At this point, Mark does not seem to have any other information to share, which might explain why he quickly wraps things up. And this is where Mark inserted some obvious editorial material, as he did in chapter 13, as well as some odd verses that seem to be related to the rumours circulating about the activities of certain early Christians, such as speaking in tongues (Acts 2:4; 1 Corinthians 14:4–5), the laying of hands, driving out demons, poison resistance, and snake handling. I am unsure where Mark got these from (perhaps superstitious Peter),[32] but it is the first and only time Jesus is associated with tongues, snakes, or poison. Jesus otherwise never taught or practised these activities.[33] Mark's second last verse (19) recounts an event that neither Peter nor Mark could know, and a generic, final verse attests to the success of the disciples spreading Jesus' message. I will thus set aside this dubious material from Mark for my Peter-Mark and retain only verses 9–11 and 14–16.

## SOURCES

Now I want to go through Peter-Mark's verses and identify the most probable eyewitness sources to blocks of material from the beginning through to the Last Supper.[34]

Peter seems to have accompanied Jesus through most of the mission Mark relates. Peter's eyewitness information provides the text with detailed, vivid, and, at times, extraneous details. For instance, in Capernaum, when Jesus was besieged in Peter's house by the crowds, the people bearing the paralytic man to be healed mounted the house and unexpectedly dug through the mud and thatch roof to lower the man to Jesus' level (Mark 2:2–12). Suppose the story recounted consists of something that either Peter witnessed directly or was in the immediate vicinity of the event being recalled. In that case, Peter can be identified

---

32    Both Acts and Paul's Epistles mention at least some of these activities occurring, involving both Paul and Peter sometimes, in the chaotic first few decades of the after Jesus' death. So it is possible this was, in fact, passed on by Peter.

33    Perhaps this is an example of what Papias called "strange commandments" in Mark.

34    For the material after the Last Supper, which is the Passion Narrative, I will treat it in more detail when answering the question: What Did Jesus Do?

as the source of information. For example, when Jesus approaches Jerusalem, he sends two disciples to get him a colt to ride on (Mark 11:1–2). If Peter were not one of the two, he would have gotten the details afterwards from them. But Peter was not always present, so he used stories from other people to augment his account. For the rest of the Gospel, we can make reasonable identifications for the sources used in Peter-Mark from this point on until the Last Supper:

**1:1–9.** After an opening verse probably written by Mark, Peter introduces the Baptist and Jesus. According to the Gospel of John (John 1:40–42), when Andrew (Peter's brother) and another person, who both appear to have been close followers of the Baptist, first encountered Jesus, Andrew fetched and introduced Peter (then called Simon) immediately to Jesus. Peter, who lived in Capernaum (Mark 1:21, 29), must have travelled south to the Baptist's camp at Bethany-Beyond-Jordan. Peter would have been familiar with the Baptist's appearance and his core message, which he describes.

**1:10–1:13.** Peter was probably not on hand for Jesus' baptism, as Peter relates the episode from Jesus' point of view; the information is terse, seems second hand, and differs from John's account. The latter purports that the Baptist saw "the Spirit" descend on Jesus at some point. Peter, in turn, describes Jesus' experience with "the Spirit," and Peter says it descended while he, Jesus, was being baptized.[35] Interestingly, Peter's is the only account of Jesus being baptized. Peter's account could only have come from Jesus. Did Peter later embellish a solitary spiritual time in the desert with angels and Satan? Or perhaps it was meant to be a metaphor for an inner struggle described by Jesus.

**1:14–7:24.** Peter probably returned with the group to Galilee for the wedding in Cana (John 2:1–12) and then went on to Capernaum, where he was living. Peter had nothing to relate until later encountering Jesus in Capernaum at the beginning of Jesus' extended Galilean mission. Sometime later,[36] Jesus reconnected with Peter and Andrew in Galilee. Peter and the disciples accompanied him around Galilee. Peter has included three narratives with details outside the disciples' knowledge: the man in the tombs, the bleeding woman, and the fanciful story of Herod beheading the Baptist.[37] First, the story of the man in the tombs was told by the man himself because the disciples do not appear in it; there is only the man and Jesus. It contains vivid and extraneous details, and the man told the story over and over (Mark 5:20). He most certainly added the bizarre demon and pig incident to embellish his account (he did seem disturbed). Peter must have heard the story later and incorporated it. Secondly, the bleeding woman recounted her story with her inner thoughts, condition, and odd interpretation of "power" flowing out of Jesus. Finally, the death of John the Baptist is clearly a folk tale inserted awkwardly into the action, for it is full of drama. Herod was the evil king, and John the hero, and there were illicit yearnings and a gruesome, bloody death. No one from Jesus' or the Baptist's party would have been there, since the event occurred in the royal court closed to outsiders.[38] The story must have been circulating, and Peter believed it was true and retold it. Mark has awkwardly inserted the tale into the story of the disciples being sent out to preach by Jesus.[39]

**7:24–7:30.** This terse account of Jesus secretly travelling north seems to imply that he was alone, with only one short story: the reluctant healing of the child of the Syrophoenician woman, who must have been the source of this story. Peter must, therefore, have heard her story later.

---

35    Neither Peter nor the Baptist (related in John) describe this mysterious "Spirit" further, although both authors seem to indicate its descent was a visible phenomenon.

36    According to the sequence in the Gospel of John, I estimate it was between six months and a year before Jesus came back to Galilee.

37    Josephus contradicts the story by saying the Baptist was killed due to fear of an uprising. He also points out that Herodias was not previously married to Antipas' brother but his half-brother, Herod II.

38    The invitees were "… his high officials and military commanders and the leading men of Galilee" (Mark 6:21).

39    Perhaps Mark is trying to line up the timing of the Baptist's death, the date of which is obscure as we will see, with this phase of Jesus' mission in Galilee.

*Figure 14* **Caesar's Denarius**

*This is a denarius minted during Emperor Tiberius's reign (14-37 CE). The denarius was the standard silver coin of the Roman Empire, and at the time, a legionnaire was paid about 225 denarii a year. This coin is one possible candidate for the "denarius" ("denarion" in Greek) in the famous teaching: "Give to Caesar what is Caesar's and to God what is God's," (Mark 12:17) that Jesus was reported as saying when asked if people should pay taxes. The observe bears a portrait of the emperor. The inscription reads: "Ti[berivs] Caesar Divi Avg[vsti] F[ilivs] Avgvstvs" (Caesar Augustus Tiberius, son of the Divine Augustus), essentially proclaiming Augustus (the previous emperor) a god and Tiberius, his son. The reverse shows the emperor as Pontifex Maximus (or "high priest"). Image reproduced by permission from Classical Numismatic Group, Inc. www.cngcoins.com via CC BY-SA 3.0.*

**7:31–14:17.** Jesus returns south to Galilee and then the Decapolis. Peter and the disciples and detail re-appear. Peter and the disciples thus seem to have remained in Galilee until Jesus returned. They go over to the far side of the River Jordan, then approach Jerusalem via Jericho. Peter includes three independent healing stories from that journey, as told by a deaf-mute man, a blind man in Bethsaida, and Bartimaeus of Jericho. Here, Peter's external source is thus a deaf-mute man who provides vivid detail—the brief interaction between himself and Jesus that occurred away from the crowd—which he must have repeated on many occasions. The blind man in Bethsaida also knows inside information about his healing, which happened away from the village. It includes an odd observation on the first attempt at healing, which was, we are told, only partially successful. Again, he must be the source of Peter's story. Finally, Bartimaeus must be the one who told others, for Jesus' actions were, again, unseen by the crowd. After this, Peter and the disciples accompany Jesus to Jerusalem and the Last Supper.

## SECRET MARK OR MARK V. 2.0

Of all the sources I am examining, this source is by far the most mysterious. It all started in 1958 when scholar Morton Smith visited the ancient Mar Saba monastery near Jerusalem. While cataloguing its library, he came across an unknown letter by Clement of Alexandria responding to a Theodore. The latter seemed to have questions regarding a variant Gospel of Mark that he had encountered. This letter is interesting because it includes quotes from a previously unknown, updated version of the Gospel of Mark, claimed to have been completed by Mark himself later in life. This gospel is called Secret Mark, or Hidden Mark. Here is an excerpt from the letter:

> "As for Mark, then, during Peter's stay in Rome, he wrote an account of the Lord's doings, not, however, declaring all of them, nor yet hinting at the secret ones, but selecting what he thought most useful for increasing the faith of those who were being instructed. But when Peter died a martyr, Mark came over to

Alexandria, bringing both his own notes and those of Peter, from which he transferred to his former book the things suitable to whatever makes for progress toward knowledge. Thus, he composed a more spiritual Gospel for the use of those who were being perfected. Nevertheless, he yet did not divulge the things not to be uttered, nor did he write down the hierophantic teaching of the Lord, but to the stories already written he added yet others and, moreover, brought in certain sayings of which he knew the interpretation would, as a mystagogue, lead the hearers into the innermost sanctuary of that truth hidden by seven veils. Thus, in sum, he prepared matters, neither grudgingly nor incautiously, in my opinion, and, dying, he left his composition to the church in Alexandria, where it even yet is most carefully guarded, being read only to those who are being initiated into the great mysteries."[40]

The letter then quotes two until then unknown verses from this updated Mark, which I will call Mark 2.0. Here are the two new verses that Clement quotes from Mark 2.0, with instructions where they should be inserted:

"To you [Theodore], therefore, I shall not hesitate to answer the questions you have asked, refuting the falsifications by the very words of the Gospel. For example, after 'And they were in the road going up to Jerusalem' and what follows, until 'After three days he shall arise,'[Mark 10:34] the secret Gospel brings the following material word for word:

'And they come into Bethany. And a certain woman whose brother had died was there. And, coming, she prostrated herself before Jesus and says to him, "Son of David, have mercy on me." But the disciples rebuked her. And Jesus, being angered, went off with her into the garden where the tomb was, and straightway a great cry was heard from the tomb. And going near Jesus rolled away the stone from the door of the tomb. And straightway, going in where the youth was, he stretched forth his hand and raised him, seizing his hand. But the youth, looking upon him, loved him and began to beseech him that he might be with him. And going out of the tomb they came into the house of the youth, for he was rich. And after six days Jesus told him what to do and in the evening the youth comes to him, wearing a linen cloth over his naked body. And he remained with him that night, for Jesus taught him the mystery of the kingdom of God. And thence, arising, he returned to the other side of the Jordan.'"[41]

And

"And after the words, 'And he comes into Jericho,'[Mark 10:46] the secret Gospel adds only, '… the sister of the youth whom Jesus loved and his mother and Salome were there, and Jesus did not receive them.'"[42]

Further on, the letter mentions a third version of Mark, stolen and edited by a heretical Gnostic sect led by Carpocrates of Alexandria (died 138 CE) that added in elements of Gnostic theology:[43]

"But since the foul demons are always devising destruction for the race of men, Carpocrates, instructed by them and using deceitful arts, so enslaved a certain presbyter of the church in Alexandria that he got from him a copy of the secret Gospel, which he both interpreted according to his blasphemous and carnal doctrine and, moreover, polluted, mixing with the spotless and holy words utterly shameless lies."[44]

---

40    (Clement of Alexandria, *Letter of Clement of Alexandria on Secret Mark* n.d.). It is interesting that mention is made of Peter having notes, perhaps to aid in preaching and teaching or the beginnings of his own gospel, as I speculated earlier.

41    Ibid. To be added between Mark 10:34 and 35. Interestingly, the first fragment seems to be the story of the raising of Lazarus as told in the Gospel of John.

42    Ibid. To be added after Mark 10:46.

43    As happened in the composition of the Gospel of Thomas, to be discussed in Chapter 23.

44    (Clement of Alexandria, *Letter of Clement of Alexandria on Secret Mark* n.d.).

This explains Clement's odd mention of "the secret ones," "things not to be uttered," and "hierophantic teaching," which are all Gnostic ideas; he is mentioning them to indicate they are not original to Mark to distinguish the Christian version from the Gnostic version.

So it seems Mark, in later life, moved (or fled) from Rome to Alexandria after Peter was killed (64 CE) in the Neronian persecution.[45] He created a more "spiritual" gospel for the benefit of local Christian believers, using the notes of his and Peter's stories to expand his original Gospel, which was kept carefully in Alexandria.[46]

The original letter, now called the Mar Saba Letter, was transferred after discovery to the Greek Orthodox Church in Jerusalem. It then disappeared sometime after 1990; all that remains are photos made by Smith and a later custodian. Therefore, ink and paper cannot be tested for dating purposes, but based on visual examination, if authentic, it was probably written around 200 CE.

There has been a lot of debate over this letter. Some claim authenticity, while others, such as Smith, argue that it is a forgery, either ancient or modern. Others yet argue that Clement is correct or mistaken on different points. Some believe Smith forged it to advance his theory that Christianity was a mystery religion with erotic initiations, implied in the meeting of Jesus and the young man. Finally, a 1940 novel called *The Mystery of Mar Saba* recounts a mysterious and embarrassing Christian letter discovered at the Mar Saba Monastery (!), which critics of Smith argue is the source for the idea of the forgery.

As for me, I find it rather odd that this secret gospel is never mentioned anywhere else in the literature. Of course, it seems this version of Mark was not widely distributed. Just as Clement is about to explain the passages quoted above, the letter breaks off inconveniently. Because most scholars—and Clementine scholars in particular—argue that the letter is indeed genuine, I will include these quotes in my Peter-Mark. I have four additional reasons for thinking the letter is genuine. First, it makes sense that Mark would flee Rome at the time indicated (i.e., Nero's widespread persecution). It is only natural he would bring any source material with him to save it from certain destruction. Second, as I have argued, he undoubtedly wanted to fix chapter 13, and probably other features as well, due to criticism of the incompleteness and disorder of his gospel. It had circulated for over 20 years by then. And since Peter was dead, there was no possibility for Peter to complete a revised Peter-Mark or create a new work on his own. Third, the second fragment fixes an odd gap in Mark. In 10:46, Jesus and his followers come to Jericho, and then in the following sentence, they are leaving. The new insertion has them doing something before leaving and reads more naturally.

The final argument in favour of authenticity has to do with an odd remark in Mark's original version. When Jesus is arrested in Jerusalem by an armed group in the Garden of Gethsemane, they also seize an unnamed young man with an outer linen garment who escapes "naked," leaving his garment behind (Mark 14:46–52). Linen tended to be worn by the wealthier class. So who was this person, and why mention him? Until we uncovered the first new verse proposed by Clement, it was a total mystery. Clement introduces a wealthy young man who wore an outer linen garment over his "naked body" and must be the escapee in question, because it fits his description.[47] But Clement adds an additional detail that points to his identity: Jesus raised him from the dead. This is obviously Lazarus, as described in John (John 11:17–44). So the first new verse links to the later story in this respect, making it more likely to be authentic.[48] Therefore, I will insert these two fragments into Peter-Mark.

Peter-Mark's Gospel is acceptable under the Date Rule and contains direct eyewitness factual testimony. Therefore, I will include it, with all my edits, into my Source List.

---

45    Eusebius links Mark with Alexandria in 62/63 CE in *Church History* 2.24.1, also see (Lunn 2014, 240).

46    No doubt he would have "fixed" his faulty chapter 13 and other errors. It is unclear exactly what Clement means by "spiritual" in this context; perhaps he means more compelling, given the additional information added to Mark 2.0.

47    I will have more to say about this figure when I discuss the Gospel of John.

48    As to why Mark chose not to include it in his original Gospel, I shall discuss in Chapter 18.

CHAPTER 17

# THE GOSPEL OF MATTHEW, THE GOSPEL OF LUKE, AND ACTS OF THE APOSTLES

"There will always be a war between light and darkness, between Science and superstition, between education and ignorance. Ignorance is easier; it requires no study."

—Nicholas Meyer, *The Adventure of the Peculiar Protocols.*

We have examined the first of the three Synoptic Gospels and concluded that Mark was written before Matthew and Luke, around 40 CE, and was used, along with a now-lost document called Q, by Matthew and Luke for their Gospels. Both the Gospels of Matthew and Luke are like Mark's in that they tell the story of Jesus up to his death. Acts picks up where Luke left off and tells the story over the next thirty years of the Early Church in Jerusalem following Jesus' resurrection and Paul's subsequent missionary trips. It then ends with Paul being under house arrest in Rome. There is little doubt that the author of Luke also wrote Acts, for not only does it read like a sequel to Luke, but it has the same style, is addressed to the same patron, Theophilus, and refers to the Gospel of Luke as "in my former book" (Acts 1:1). So I will include Acts in my discussion of Luke.

## AUTHORSHIP

We have established that Peter-Mark is based on eyewitness testimony. But is this true for Luke and Matthew? If so, then it increases the reliability of their accounts. However, the short answer is no. How do I know this? The great bulk of their works was simply copied from other sources, namely Q, the Gospel of Mark, and other unknown sources.[1] An actual eyewitness would relate their own stories rather than repeat someone else's account. As already discussed, their unwillingness to deviate from Mark's Gospel, despite its deficiencies, bellies eyewitness status. Luke himself indicates that he has no first-hand information in his prologue:

> "Many have undertaken to draw up an account of the things that have been fulfilled among us, just as they were handed down to us by those who from the first were eyewitnesses and servants of the word. Therefore, since I myself have carefully investigated everything from the beginning, it seemed good also to me to write an orderly account for you, most excellent Theophilus, so that you may know the certainty of the things you have been taught." (Luke 1:1–4)

Luke thus says to Theophilus, who was probably the patron who funded him to do this "research project," that he must carefully investigate the life of Jesus himself, since he has no direct knowledge. He indeed says that the information "was handed down to us." The Early Church Father Irenaeus also states that Luke only appears many years later, after Jesus' death, when Paul

---

1   This is especially true for the source(s) for the birth narrative found in Luke and Matthew, since neither author would just have happened to be present at Jesus' birth.

was travelling: "Luke also, the companion of Paul, recorded in a book the Gospel preached by him."[2] It is thus clear that Luke never met Jesus and relied on at least second-hand testimonies to write his Gospel.[3]

We have no information on the author of the Gospel of Matthew. Disciple Matthew is mentioned in some surviving fragments from Papias, again preserved by Eusebius: "But concerning Matthew he [Papias] writes as follows: 'So then Matthew wrote the oracles [*logia*] in the Hebrew language, and everyone interpreted [translated to Greek] them as he was able.'" [4] There has been much debate on what these "oracles" could be, but they are not the Gospel of Matthew for several reasons. First, the Gospel of Matthew incorporates Mark, which was initially written in Greek, not Hebrew. Second, Papias seems to think that there were multiple Greek translations of the *logia*, but these are otherwise unattested. Third, scholars agree that the Gospel of Matthew was originally composed in Greek and is not a translation. While it cannot be the "oracles" mentioned, it establishes that there was a tradition that a Matthew, disciple or not, wrote something. In any case, the author of Matthew was not an eyewitness and relied on other sources.

## SOURCES

We know that both authors used Q and Mark.[5] When you strip out the Mark and Q material, you are left with 35% and 20% of new, outside material present in Luke and Matthew, respectively, about 402 verses for Luke and 214 verses for Matthew. Since neither author was an eyewitness, they must have gotten this unique material from other unknown sources, meaning we have no way of assessing accuracy.

## PROBLEMS WITH THE AUTHORS OF MATTHEW AND LUKE

Both Luke and Matthew show troubling tendencies, which do not make them credible as independent authors writing original material. This is clear from a few examples:

Of the four Gospels, only Luke and Matthew have anything to say about Jesus before his baptism by John the Baptist. Both include odd and conflicting birth and youth narratives that have Jesus being born of a virgin in Bethlehem and include wonderous events. These are great stories, including the original Christmas story: the Star of Bethlehem, no room at the inn, the manger, and singing angels. However, these narratives cannot be accurate. Both Peter and John say that Jesus was from Nazareth, they never mention Bethlehem,[6] and neither mentions or even alludes to anything unusual about Jesus' youth, yet they[7] spent a fair amount of personal time with Jesus, while Luke and the author of Matthew never knew Jesus. If you are trying to convince your audience that Jesus is unique, then why would Peter and John not include a fabulous youth narrative? Or his virgin birth? The fact that they did not make it reasonable to infer that, in fact, Jesus was a rather unremarkable person with mundane origins, as opposed to Luke's and Matthew's second or third-hand information. As for the place of birth, there was an incentive for Luke and Matthew to move Jesus to Bethlehem because they wanted to portray Jesus as the Christ/Jewish

---

2     Irenaeus, *Against Heresies* 3.1.1.

3     Another argument for Matthew not being an eyewitness is that he adopted the same approach to Gospel creation as non-eyewitness Luke—copying from other sources.

4     Eusebius, *Church History* 3.39.16.

5     Much speculation has occurred pertaining to what written records about Jesus were circulating soon after his death. Here, Luke and Matthew independently used only two substantive sources, Q and Mark. Therefore, we can reasonably conclude these two were the only major written sources about Jesus existing at the time. If others existed no doubt Matthew and Luke would have used them. It also seems likely that Matthew's "oracles", as mentioned by Papias, had been subsumed into Mark or Q by this time and were no longer circulating as an independent text.

6     Matthew simply states that Jesus is originally from Bethlehem, even though Matthew copies Peter's title thereafter, "Jesus of Nazareth," in his Gospel. See also Mark 1:9 and John 7:41–42.

7     I will establish that the Gospel of John, like Peter-Mark, is also based on eyewitness evidence.

Messiah who must be of the linage of King David and from Bethlehem. However, in their eagerness to redefine who Jesus was, such as connecting Jesus with Bethlehem, they committed numerous errors and included stories disturbingly wrong on many counts.[8]

Peter-Mark tells us that initially, Jesus' family thought Jesus was insane and tried to seize him upon realizing that he was preaching. Again, this is a mundane and ordinary reaction: "When his family heard about this, they went to take charge of him, for they said, 'He is out of his mind'" (Mark 3:21). John adds: "For even his [Jesus'] own brothers did not believe in him" (John 7:5). These otherwise perfectly reasonable reactions would be doubtful if even some of the fantastic birth events were true, again undermining Luke and Matthew's veracity.

Besides, Matthew's and Luke's birth/youth narratives conflict. They are quite separate stories. Matthew has Mary and Joseph living in Bethlehem when Jesus was born via virgin birth, then fleeing Herod the Great to Egypt, returning and settling in Nazareth. Luke has Mary and Joseph living in Nazareth and travelling to Bethlehem for a census, where Jesus was born at an inn. Forty days later, Luke explains, they left to visit Jerusalem and then returned to Nazareth. While Matthew affirms a virgin birth, Luke never explicitly indicates one. He states, instead, that, "He [Jesus] was the son, so it was thought, of Joseph" (Luke 3:23). Both Matthew and Luke, though, seem desperate to have Jesus associated with Bethlehem in some fashion to fulfil a Messianic verse from Scripture: "But you, Bethlehem Ephrathah, though you are small among the clans of Judah, out of you will come for me one who will be ruler over Israel, whose origins are from of old, from ancient times" (Micah 5:2). Therefore, while Matthew and Luke agree on this goal, their narratives are not in accordance, which suggests that they are not reliable.

The birth narratives themselves stand out as obvious literary constructs that read more like JS stories, with a typical cast of characters, including angels, virgin births, Magi, evil kings, elaborate speeches, old-fashioned language, and heavenly hosts. Virgin or otherwise, fabulous birth stories were a common feature of famous people's biographies in Antiquity. For instance, Alexander the Great, Plato, Emperor Augustus, Buddha, and Lao Tzu, to name a few, all have stories of wondrous births attached to their persona. It is easy to see how these folk tales about Jesus came about, given the tension between his perceived status and humble origins. Luke's and Matthew's birth narratives are entirely out of character with the simple narratives provided by Peter-Mark. They obviously constitute two false but interestingly independent stories, invented to raise Jesus' status by embellishing his birth, then distant in time from the time of composition, with miraculous events. Again, Matthew and Luke have included these false tales to re-define Jesus into something they desired and perhaps to appeal to potential Graeco-Roman converts by adopting a literary genre that would sound familiar to them.

The Gospel of Luke reports Jesus' conception as occurring during the reign of King Herod the Great, and his birth during the empire-wide census of Roman governor Quirinius, which required Jesus' family to travel to King David's hometown, Bethlehem. There are many problems with this account. King Herod died in 4 BC, but Quirinius carried out a census in Judea, Samaria, and Idumaea only when it came under Roman rule in 6 CE (ten years later). Also, there were no "empire-wide" censuses during the reign of Emperor Augustus (27 BCE–14 CE). Furthermore, no Roman census ever required people to travel to their hometowns. Any census requiring such travel is non-sensible, as it would cause massive economic disruption and population displacement (i.e., millions of people spending months travelling all over the empire simply to be counted). And still, according to Luke, King David had lived 42 generations before Joseph, so unless Joseph grew up in Bethlehem, it would not be his hometown. Also, we know that Jesus' family lived in Galilee under the rule of Herod Antipas, outside of Judea, and that they would be unaffected by any Roman census occurring in Judea. Luke apparently did not fact-check his material before inclusion in his Gospel.

Matthew is very keen to show many aspects of Jesus' life as the fulfilment of JS prophecies. However, his scriptural references are frequently inaccurate, his interpretation does not square with the reference itself, and he makes clumsy mistakes. Indeed, he cited the story of 30 silver pieces[9] as being from the book of Jeremiah, but it is actually from Zechariah (Matthew 27:9; Zechariah 11:12–13). His use of Malachi 3:1 is incorrect, as he alters the pronoun from "me" to "you" (Matthew 11:10).

---

8    I do not doubt that they both believed the stories true and they were doing the right thing.

9    About a legionnaires' wage for a month.

Matthew quotes Isaiah concerning the virgin birth: "'The virgin will be with child and will give birth to a son, and they will call him Immanuel' (which means 'God with us')" (Matthew 1:23). However, Matthew is using the Greek translation of the JS (called the Septuagint). His Greek quote is not precisely what Isaiah says in the Hebrew original, which reads: "Look, this young woman is about to conceive and will give birth to a son. You, young woman, will name him Immanuel" (Isaiah 7:14). There is no mention of her being a virgin. Isaiah, in chapter 7, is discussing the Syro-Israelite crisis of 734 BCE, not announcing the future. The scriptural text is thus referring to an event that has already happened. And Jesus was named Jesus, not Immanuel.

Matthew also alters Peter-Mark's account of Jesus entering Jerusalem (Mark 11:4–9). Peter said that Jesus rode in on a colt, but Matthew claims that Jesus was riding both a colt and a donkey (Matthew 21:1–7), to better fit another saying from Zechariah (Zechariah 9:9) inferring that Jesus is a king entering Jerusalem. Matthew wants to show that Jesus was the son of David, and thus lists a genealogy (Matthew 1:1–16) that starts with Abraham and goes all the way to David and then to Joseph, Jesus' father. Ignoring for the moment the issue of using JS as historical fact, as I have discussed, Matthew then goes on to say that Jesus is not a blood relation of Joseph anyway, since Mary conceived via the Holy Spirit, making the whole issue pointless, as genealogy is transmitted through one's biological father (Numbers 1:18; Jeremiah 33:17). But Matthew is also careless; he draws on the second and third chapters of 1 Chronicles, which lists 18 generations from David to Jeconiah but leaves four names out, probably to match the fourteen that came before David and the fourteen that came after Jeconiah. He aims to make the following claim: "Thus there were fourteen generations in all from Abraham to David, fourteen from David to the exile to Babylon, and fourteen from the exile to the Christ" (Matthew 1:17). Clearly, Matthew is fixated on the number 14. But again, he is mistaken; there are only thirteen names in the last sequence! Luke also gives a genealogy for Joseph (Luke 3:23–38), but it diverges quite radically from Matthew's after David. Indeed, Luke has 41 generations, while Matthew only has 27. It is troubling to see Luke and Matthew attempting to redefine Peter's Jesus.

Matthew also alters the sayings of Jesus. Rather than "blessed are the poor" (Q 6:20), which, given Q's simple, rural context, meant lacking money, Matthew has changed it to a more theological and confusing "poor in spirit."[10] Also, Jesus does not teach that divorce was acceptable in cases of marital unfaithfulness in Peter-Mark, but he does in Matthew.[11] Finally, Peter-Mark reports Jesus as frequently speaking about the "kingdom of God." However, Matthew alters almost all instances to "the kingdom of the heavens."

As I discussed earlier, Peter-Mark has some significant problems that Luke and Matthew just reiterate rather than correct. Mark makes a mistake about the date of the Last Supper by indicating it was a Passover meal but then says Jesus was killed the day before.[12] The Gospel of John states correctly that the crucifixion occurred on the day before Passover. A simple mistake easily corrected; however, Matthew and Luke simply copied the blatant error into their accounts with no hesitation. Several unconvincing proposals have been made to sort this out; for instance, it was a Passover-like meal, or a different, sectarian calendar. The best solution is that, again, Luke and Matthew were simply careless and uninformed and did not fact-check their stories.

Both Luke and Matthew added freely to Peter's resurrection sequence to pursue their agenda of making Jesus the fulfilment of JS prophecies. Again, both showing poor editorial control in the process. Luke added the story of two gleaming men in the empty tomb that eyewitnesses Peter and John do not mention, and Matthew added an earthquake and an angel who descended to roll away the stone conveniently. Jesus was entombed for two nights and one day, but Matthew claims that Jesus was in the bowels of the Earth for "three days and three nights" (Matthew 12:40) to conform to the story of Jonah. On the death of Jesus, Matthew has "many holy men" rise from their tombs and walk around Jerusalem (Matthew 27:52–53). Again Peter-Mark (and other contemporaries, such as Philo and John) do not mention such a fantastic event.

Finally, both Matthew and Luke eliminated details they consider embarrassing about Jesus. The story found in Peter-Mark regarding Jesus' family, who thought he was insane (Mark 3:21), has been dropped in both their accounts. Both also dropped two episodes: one where Jesus must re-heal a blind man (Mark 8:22–26), and a second where he uses a magic word to heal a

---

10    Matthew 5:3. The author of Matthew may simply have misunderstood the saying.

11    Matthew 5:32 versus Mark 10:11–12.

12    Mark 15:42 versus Mark 14:16–17.

mute (Mark 7:31–37). Both Luke and Matthew also left out the episode in the synagogue where Jesus gets angry (Mark 3:5). Furthermore, Luke simply ignores the passages where Jesus says that he does not know when the end of all things will come (Mark 13:32). All these problems add to the unreliability of Matthew's and Luke's Gospels.

## DATES

Mark was published in 40 CE, so Luke and Matthew would have been composed sometime after 40. Scholars, according to ECW, date Luke-Acts to 80–130 CE and Matthew to 80–100 CE. But more can be said about their dating.

As mentioned, Luke and Matthew did not know each other's work, since nothing linking them can be found in their texts. They both composed their Gospels by using written sources, and, undoubtedly, if the other's Gospel had been available, they would have used it somehow, for example, to harmonize their conflicting birth narratives. Also, both Luke and Matthew, to a large extent, duplicated each other's project, combined Mark and Q, and added some extra material. It thus seems reasonable to think that they were both writing around the same time, unbeknownst to each other. Still, both Gospels offer no internal evidence that could allow us to date them; however, Acts does.

Luke wrote Acts after he had written his Gospel. If I can date Acts, I should work back from its date and get a better range for Luke's and Matthew's Gospels. There are, in my opinion, two main reasons that explain why the date ascribed to Acts by scholars (between 80 and 130 CE) is too late.

Firstly, Acts, Luke, and Matthew do not mention or even foreshadow the tumultuous events of the 60s CE.[13] Indeed, the Great Fire of Rome, which destroyed two-thirds of the city over ten days in July 64 CE, is absent from their accounts. The ensuing persecution of Christians, ordered by Nero probably between 64 and 65 CE, is also conspicuously absent. The three "pillars" of the Early Church were killed in the early 60s: Paul and Peter in Rome by Nero around 64 CE, and James in Jerusalem a few years earlier, in 62 CE. But none of these events are mentioned in Acts, yet the execution of the relatively minor figure of Deacon Stephen thirty years earlier is depicted in detail in Acts.

Another disastrous event of the 60s was the First Jewish-Roman War (starting in 66 CE), when the Jews revolted against Roman rule. In retaliation, Roman armies marched through Judaea, destroying all opposition, scattering the population—including the Jerusalem Church—and besieging, taking, and destroying Jerusalem and its Temple in 70 CE. They thus effectively terminated Jewish Temple worship, which changed the nature of Judaism forever. Furthermore, during this war, a bloody civil war broke out between the newly formed Judean provisional government and Zealot factions in and around Jerusalem. At roughly the same time, there was also a rebellion against Emperor Nero, causing his sudden suicide. As the resulting civil war and chaos descended onto Rome and the Empire, three would-be emperors rapidly came and went in the Year of the Four Emperors[14] (69 CE) before Vespasian re-established order. No reference or allusion to any of these events is ever made in Acts, which ends with Paul in Rome freely preaching at the very epicentre of most of the action. Finally, the events leading up to Paul's arrival in Rome are reported in detail, without any hint of trouble. Certainly, Acts must be from a period preceding the chaos and persecutions that erupted after July 64 CE.

Secondly, Acts ends rather abruptly with Paul's stay in Rome. Here are the last verses: "For two whole years Paul stayed there [Rome] in his own rented house and welcomed all who came to see him. He proclaimed the kingdom of God and taught about the Lord Jesus Christ—with all boldness and without hindrance!" (Acts 28:30–31). And then the text simply breaks off. However, the last six chapters of Acts are a build-up to Paul's trial in Rome. His initial arrest in Jerusalem, his imprisonment, further adventures, and journey to Rome are all recounted in great detail. But the outcome of the trial is never revealed. It is clear then that Acts must have been completed and "published" around that time (i.e., before or shortly after Paul was presumably taken into custody for trial). Paul had been in Rome for two years, so if we can determine the date of his arrival and add two years, that will give us the date of Acts.

---

13    Especially odd since Acts is a historical work.

14    For more information see (Vermeulen 2020).

## WHEN DID PAUL ARRIVE IN ROME?

Acts chapters 24 to 28 tell of Paul's arrest and journey to Rome for trial. Paul was arrested and then incarcerated in Caesarea, Judea, for two years by the Roman procurator of Judea, Marcus Antonius Felix. We know he served from 52 to 59 CE because archaeologists have noted a change in Judean coinage, indicating a turnover in procurators around those dates. Felix was replaced by Porcius Festus, who then went on to serve from 59 and 62 CE. Within a few weeks of Festus taking office, Paul was brought before him and took that opportunity to request a hearing from Emperor Nero, arguing that it was his right as a Roman citizen. Festus agreed to send him to Rome via ship under guard in 59. Remarkably, this section of Acts, which is usually written in the third person, uses the first-person plural—"we"—indicating that Luke (the author and narrator) was with Paul. The two men wintered in Malta and arrived in Rome early in 60. If we add two "whole" years, we have early in 62 CE as the publication date of Acts. We know Luke did not wait longer, otherwise he would have added the details and outcome of the trial. Now that Acts has been dated, we can turn to the date of Luke.

## THE DATE OF LUKE

What about the dating of Luke? At the beginning of Acts, Luke says: "In my former book, Theophilus, I wrote about all that Jesus began to do and to teach …" (Acts 1:1). Again we note an ascription to Theophilus who, presumably, was his patron and was paying for this two-book research project. Luke states that his Gospel was a "former book," a standalone work; that sounds as if it was already published when he wrote Acts, again with Theophilus as his patron. We have established that the Gospel of Mark was written in 40 CE and that Luke copied from Mark. The Gospel of Luke might thus have been composed between 40 and 62. But 62 is probably too late because Acts was being published at the time, and the Gospel of Luke was already out. So how long did the two-book project take? Surely Theophilus would not want a 20 or even 10-year gap between the works, at the extreme. It seems more reasonable that the works were published not too far apart in time, probably less than five years, and maybe even just two or three years. That would place Luke reasonably between c. 58 and 61.

# WHO WAS LUKE?

In his letters, Paul refers to a certain Luke as a "co-worker" (three times), a "fellow-worker" (Philemon 1:24), "Our dear friend Luke, the doctor" (Colossians 4:14), and a "companion" (2 Timothy 4:11). But is the author of the Gospel of Luke also the companion of Paul? I think so. Luke is mentioned in neither Acts nor the Gospel of Luke, but Early Church tradition is nearly unanimous that the author of Luke was also the colleague that Paul mentions. No other alternative is proposed. As I mentioned earlier, I see no reason to doubt the Early Church's ascription of Gospels to specific people, including Paul's Luke here. And until positive proof can be brought to bear, I am inclined to accept at face value that an individual named Luke was a physician and an occasional companion of Paul. His literary style and vocabulary indicate that he was indeed an educated man, as is generally expected from a physician, even in ancient times.

## THE "WE" PASSAGES IN ACTS

The author of Acts describes most events in the third-person singular or plural ("he" and "they") until chapter 16, where he relates Paul's travels. There are then discrete sections where "we" is used. These transitions between first person and third person coincide with arrivals or departures from specific locations. The "we" portions are internally consistent and more detailed than the surrounding third-person sections, suggesting that the author is joining Paul's group for particular legs of their journeys. For instance, in the following passage from Acts 16:8–10, the narrator speaks of a time when he started accompanying Paul and his companions:

"So they passed by Mysia and went down to Troas. During the night Paul had a vision of a man of Macedonia standing and begging him, 'Come over to Macedonia and help us.' After Paul had seen the vision, we got ready at once to leave for Macedonia, concluding that God had called us to preach the gospel to them."

It thus seems that the author joined the group at Troas. Later verses indicate that he then travelled with the group to Philippi, after which point "they" left, presumably leaving him behind in Philippi. Another extended, third-person segment then starts. Here are the three "we" sections and their corresponding travels and dates:

1.  Troas to Philippi, probably 50 CE;[15]

2.  Philippi to Jerusalem, probably 57 to 58 (Acts 20:4–21:19);[16]

3.  Caesarea to Rome, 60 to early 62 (Acts 27:1–28:30).

Therefore, it seems clear that Luke stayed in Philippi—and perhaps even lived there or nearby— before he re-joined the group there five years later to go to Jerusalem. Upon arrival, Paul was almost immediately imprisoned for two years in Caesarea under Roman Procurator Felix, at which point the "we" segment ends.

The three letters by Paul, which mention Luke, were written during the summer and autumn of 58 CE,[17] when Paul was in prison in Caesarea. Presumably, Luke was tending the imprisoned Paul, as the latter was given "some freedom and permit [for] his friends to take care of his needs" (Acts 24:23). As he awaited Paul's trial during this period, Luke was in an excellent position to start composing his two works, because he was in an ideal location to conduct inquiries. Jerusalem with the early church was indeed just a couple of days away. Luke then travelled with Paul to Rome, where he published Acts while waiting (again) for Paul's subsequent trial.

## WHO WAS THE AUTHOR OF MATTHEW?

The traditional view is that the disciple and companion of Jesus, Matthew, wrote the Gospel of Matthew. But as I have explained, this is not the case, since the author was not an eyewitness. So who was the author? Only one small piece of information can serve as a clue, but it is unclear; Papias' reference to disciple Matthew writing "oracles," with subsequent translations that I have shown, cannot be the Gospel of Matthew. But does Papias think these "oracles" were the Gospel of Matthew? To answer that question, we must look at the context of the fragment in Eusebius' work. Richard Bauckham hypothesizes that Papias is here explaining why both the Gospel of Mark and (incorrectly) the Gospel of Matthew lack "good rhetorical order," a concern of Papias'.[18] In Mark's case, this is because his Gospel was based on oral history—that is, the way Peter dictated his stories—and in Matthew's because translators changed his order around and added new material, as was common translation practice. Papias thought these two gospels contrasted with the "proper" literary ordering of the Gospel of John. Papias was thus addressing the apparent differences in the order of these three works. Eusebius appears to have disagreed with him on this, so he probably dropped Papias' statements on the matter.[19] Therefore, Papias thought Matthew's "oracles" were the original Gospel of Matthew. Papias' linking of these very early "oracles" by Disciple Matthew to the Gospel of Matthew probably led to the traditions within the Early Church that Matthew wrote his Gospel before the other Gospel authors did. This is indeed what Origen[20] says:

> "Concerning the four Gospels which alone are uncontroverted in the Church of God under heaven, I have learned by tradition that the Gospel according to Matthew, who was at one time a publican and afterwards an Apostle of Jesus Christ, was written first; and that he composed it in the Hebrew tongue and published it

---

15    See (Kostenberger, Kellum and Quarles 2009, 400).

16    See also (Brown 1997, 428).

17    (Robinson 2000, 84).

18    Papias stresses in the preface to his now lost work, quoted by Eusebius, that he put his information "into ordered form." Eusebius *Church History* 3.39 3-4.

19    Eusebius even states Papias "appears to have been of very limited understanding" (*Church History* 3.39.13).

20    An early Christian theologian (c. 184–c. 253). See (Edwards 2018).

for the converts from Judaism. The second written was that according to Mark, who wrote it according to the instruction of Peter…"[21]

Eusebius mentions a similar comment made by Clement of Alexandria:

"Again, in the same books, Clement gives the tradition of the earliest presbyters, as to the order of the Gospels, in the following manner: The Gospels containing the genealogies, [Luke and Matthew] he says, were written first."[22]

However, I have explained earlier that the Gospel of Mark came before the Gospel of Matthew. Therefore, the disciple Matthew wrote something in Hebrew or Aramaic before Mark wrote his Gospel (i.e., a proto-Matthew). Richard Bauckham is careful to assert that Papias uses the word *logia*, which means "short accounts" of Jesus' sayings and deeds. The exact content of this collection of *logia* remains unknown. However, Early Church Fathers came to associate this collection with the Gospel of Matthew mistakenly. Perhaps this proto-Matthew was even eventually subsumed into the teaching and preaching of the Early Church, the Core Message+. It could also be that these short accounts were pulled out and somehow influenced Q, even though scholars affirm that Q was composed in Greek and is not a translation from an Aramaic or Hebrew text. Perhaps even the inclusion of Q or the original short accounts associated somehow with Matthew into the Gospel of Matthew was enough to name the Gospel after him. But these are all speculations, and, therefore, this is where I must leave it.

## THE DATE OF MATTHEW

Several arguments can help in dating the Gospel of Matthew. Robinson remarks that Matthew seems to be directed at the needs of a community suffering an "identity crisis" regarding their traditional Jewish customs. He makes several points that indicate a time when traditional Judaism and the new Christianity were still in an uneasy co-existence. According to Robinson, just like in Luke and Acts, Matthew does not mention anything that could refer to, or even foreshadow, the tumultuous years that followed 64 CE. Also, Matthew discusses Jewish temple practices in a way that indicates they were still in place; this again points to a pre-70 CE composition date. Similarly, the Christian community's concerns about the temple tax seemed current, again suggesting a pre-70 CE date. Robinson thus concluded that the Gospel of Matthew appears to correspond to the situation in the 50s and early 60s in Palestine. I noted earlier that according to the synoptic problem, we could tell that Luke and Matthew were composed independently; this would suggest a roughly parallel composition time. As a result, I believe we can use the same timeframe for both Matthew and Luke, c. 58 to 61 CE.

---

21    (Origen, *Commentary on the Gospel of Matthew* (Book I) n.d.).

22    Eusebius, *Church History*, 6.14.5-6.

# WHO WAS MATTHEW?

*Figure 15* **The Calling of Saint Matthew by Caravaggio (1599–1600)**

*This scene captures the moment when Jesus, on the extreme right in the background sporting a slight halo, points to Matthew, in a manner reminiscent of Michelangelo's Adam from the Sistine Chapel, the hunched figure on the left. Astral light streams from right to left, while another standing figure with Jesus, probably intended to be Peter, is conversing with seated figures. Literally in the dark and oblivious to the action, Matthew is absorbed in counting money while the other seated figures seem dubious by Jesus' selection.*

Of the four Gospel authors, the author of Matthew is the least known. His Gospel provides no clues as to its author. Tradition holds that the author does signal his identity; Peter's story of the calling of Levi, son of Alphaeus, the tax collector (Mark 2:14–15), is also present in Matthew, but with the name "Matthew" inexplicably swapped in for "Levi" (Matthew 9:9–10). So what does this imply? Was this Matthew's way of signalling himself in the narrative? Probably not, as according to Bauckham, Peter never identified Levi with Matthew. When listing the disciples, Peter mentions Matthew but no Levi. Also, it would be very unusual for a Palestinian Jew to have two different, Semitic first names: Levi and Matthew. So it is not clear why the name change has occurred.

As I have pointed out earlier, the Gospel of Matthew is not the product of an eyewitness account, so the disciple Matthew, being an eyewitness, could not have composed it. I think it is most likely that the unknown author linked the disciple Matthew to the Gospel through the Levi renaming device for some reason, perhaps to elevate the authority of the Gospel,[23] or the author may have been a certain Matthew—a common name—who later became confabulated with the disciple Matthew (the same thing happened to John, after all) and is otherwise unknown. More obscurely, the author may have acknowledged Matthew as the source of some unique material in the Gospel, correctly or not, by reaching back to the "oracles" of Matthew. Scholars argue that whoever the author was, he was probably Jewish and writing for a Jewish-Christian audience. Indeed, he does not bother to explain Jewish customs to the reader, and he portrays Jesus from a Jewish perspective. He may also have been based in Antioch. All in all, the author is unknown but was undoubtedly not the disciple Matthew.

In summary, we can safely say that Luke wrote both his gospel and Acts. He was an educated man and a physician and perhaps came from Philippi. But he never met nor saw Jesus. He accompanied Paul briefly in 49 CE and remained with him from 54 to at least early 62. He probably started his two-volume research commission in 57 while sojourning in Palestine and waiting for Paul's release. His Gospel was probably published between 58 and 61 CE, and Acts was published in early 62.

As for the Gospel of Matthew, the disciple Matthew probably wrote a very early collection of some of the sayings and deeds of Jesus in Aramaic or Hebrew, but it is now lost as an independent text. On the other hand, an anonymous author wrote the Gospel of Matthew, which came to be ascribed to the disciple Matthew. That author was not an eyewitness of Jesus, and his Gospel was probably published roughly between 58 and 61 CE.

So all three works, the Gospels of Luke and Matthew and Luke-Acts, are early and contain much information about Jesus. However, I will *not* include Luke-Acts and Matthew in my Source List. Both Luke and Matthew distort the information provided by Peter in significant ways, freely embellishing with, at times, unbelievable claims, and they appear not to have performed even minimal fact-checking. And, more troubling, they are not above suppressing or altering aspects of Jesus to re-define him, doing so even clumsily at times, for their dubious theological purposes. They present Jesus as a figure rooted in the JS by portraying him as fulfilling messianic prophecies. Because neither Matthew nor Luke were eyewitnesses to Jesus, and both used anonymous sources for the new material they provide, we cannot assess their sources. In any case, these sources are quite dubious in places, and both authors exercised poor editorial control over the information they introduced into their narratives. To conclude, according to the Credible Facts Rule, I find neither author credible, and I will thus exclude Luke's and Matthew's Gospels from my Source List. Since Luke also authored Acts, I deem the very minimal information on Jesus present in Acts also unreliable, and I shall also drop the book from my list.[24]

I think it is possible that Matthew and Luke included some accurate and unique material about Jesus, such as the wonderful parable of the Good Samaritan found in Luke, which seems in keeping with things that Jesus might have taught. However, I just cannot tell if it is authentic, given Luke and Matthew's poor reputation, so I would rather lose a bit of authentic material than introduce a lot of false information. How much unique material could I be excluding by doing so? I calculate that once I drop the birth and youth narratives and the genealogies, we arrive at about 20% and 14% that is unique to Luke and Matthew, respectively. That is the worst-case scenario, assuming that everything in the unique material is authentic, but given Matthew's and Luke's reputations, this is highly unlikely. Therefore, the loss of authentic material, while unfortunate, is probably minimal. We have Q and Peter-Mark, so we do not need Luke and Matthew's distorted repetition of that same material.

---

23    Since the author of Matthew was clearly attempting to redefine Jesus and his legacy it would not be too much of a stretch to falsely assign his Gospel to a disciple such as Matthew and insert the Levi name switch to support the façade.

24    I do consider the later "we" sections accurate eyewitness accounts.

# CHAPTER 18

# THE GOSPEL OF JOHN

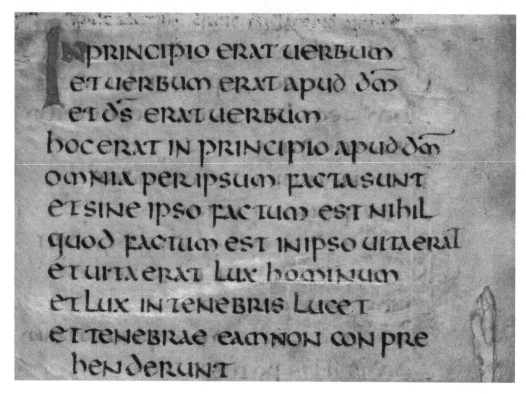

*Figure 16 **First Paragraph of the First Page of St. Cuthbert's Gospel of John.***

*A Gospel of John thought to have been owned by St. Cuthbert or associated with him. He was a famous Northumbrian bishop who died in 687 CE. It is the oldest bound book surviving in Western Europe and a rare Anglo-Saxon book. It is un-illuminated and written in simple Latin. The text above reads: "In the beginning was the Word [Verbum], and the Word was with God [Deum abbreviated as a sacred name], and the Word was God. He was with God in the beginning. Through him all things were made; without him nothing was made that has been made. In him was life[vita], and that life was the light [lux] of all mankind. The light shines in the darkness, and the darkness has not overcome it (John 1:1–4)."*

The Gospel of John is entirely independent of the other three Synoptic Gospels. There is no apparent overlapping material or sources with any other NT text. Its literary style is distinctive compared to the other Gospels; it is highly structured with a detailed timeline.

## AUTHORSHIP

This gospel is also unique in that the author identifies himself to the reader and establishes himself in the narrative. At the very end of the Gospel, the author tells us the following:

"Peter turned and saw that the disciple whom Jesus loved was following them. (This was the one who had leaned back against Jesus at the supper and had said, 'Lord, who is going to betray you?') When Peter saw him, he asked, 'Lord, what about him?' Jesus answered, 'If I want him to remain alive until I return, what is that to you? You must follow me.' Because of this, the rumour spread among the brothers that this disciple would not die. But Jesus did not say that he would not die; he only said, 'If I want him to remain alive until I return, what is that to you?' This is the disciple who testifies to these things and who wrote them down. We know that his testimony is true." (John 21:20–24)

According to Bauckham, in keeping with the practice of ancient writers when referring to themselves using the first-person plural "we," the author is referring to himself. So the final sentence should be read as an authoritative affirmation: "I know that my testimony is true." The author is, therefore, solemnly claiming eyewitness status "to these things." This solemn first plural "we" is used only in one other place, near the end of the Word Prologue of John (John 1:1–18), where the author states, "We have seen his [Jesus'] glory …" (John 1:14). Again, he is claiming eyewitness testimony by forming a standard "we" *inclusio* which brackets the author's testimony.

Otherwise, the author uses the third-person singular "he" or "his" most of the time, to keep himself hidden and not to intrude on the narrative. This is also a standard ancient biographical practice. Thus, the author is playing the role of the witness and actor in the story but modestly staying out of view.

In the last verse, the author talks directly to the reader and identifies himself as the disciple who wrote "these things" (i.e., the preceding Gospel of John). He is also quite emphatic regarding the reliability of the information he presents. In an earlier verse, he refers to his own testimony of a momentous event: "He who saw this has testified so that you also may believe. His testimony is true, and he knows he tells the truth."[1] All this indicates an eyewitness account written by the witness himself.

Another interesting feature of John is the use of the phrase "the disciple whom Jesus loved" to refer to a mysterious unnamed follower of Jesus, whom scholars refer to as the Beloved Disciple. In a Gospel that uses names heavily, the presence of an unnamed central character calls for scrutiny. The phrase is used six times, starting at the Last Supper through to the last occurrence in the opening sentence quoted above (John 13:23, 19:26, 20:2, 21:7, 21:20). This places the Beloved Disciple explicitly at the Last Supper, at the crucifixion, at the empty tomb, and at the third resurrection appearance in Galilee.[2] In the scene above, Peter and Jesus are discussing the Beloved Disciple. Immediately after, the author states, "This is the disciple who" wrote the Gospel, and then he affirms its reliability. The author claims to be the Beloved Disciple, a follower of Jesus, an eyewitness who relates information truthfully.

This quote also identifies the Beloved Disciple/author as the figure who, at the Last Supper reclining next to Jesus, leans over on him momentarily to ask him who would betray him (John 13:23–25).

There are also two other instances in the Gospel of John where an unnamed disciple (John 1:37, 18:15) is mentioned close to the action, Bauckham argues.[3] In each case, the unnamed disciple is the author and hence the Beloved Disciple.

In the first instance, two disciples, an unnamed disciple and Andrew, are "following" Jesus; the latter looks back and sees them. They are the first of his followers, even before Peter. At the end of the Gospel, the Beloved Disciple/author is "following" Jesus, who is with Peter. Both men are looking back at him. Together with the final reference to "him" (John 21:23), the Beloved Disciple is the last disciple mentioned in John. Thus, the author created an oblique *inclusio* that signals his identity; he and

---

1    John 19:35. The occasion for emphatic testimony is the piercing of the dead Jesus' side while on the cross and witnessing blood and water come out of the wound. The author saw this as a momentous event, as he identified Jesus as the Paschal, or sacrificial, lamb because Jesus did not have any broken bones, as was explicitly commanded of the Paschal Lamb in Numbers 9:12, the blood identified with the purifying blood of the Passover lambs being shed at the same time in the Temple, and the water being symbolic of life in Judaism. Also, John the Baptist called Jesus the Lamb of God. For the author, this all comes together in this event to show Jesus is the true Passover Lamb.

2    One of the "two other disciples" in 21:2.

3    (Bauckham, *Jesus and the Eyewitnesses; The Gospels as Eyewitness Testimony* 2008, 388–393).

Andrew are the first followers, and he is also the last one.[4] Clearly, the author uses this "disciple-following *inclusio*" to signal the Beloved Disciple as one of the first two followers of Jesus. He thus emphasizes the author's eyewitness reports as the essential source for the Gospel.

The second instance of an unnamed disciple is the following: "The other disciple, who was known to the high priest" (John 18:16). This figure is also the Beloved Disciple/author. In this case, his authority as witness is established by the relationship with the high priest and not as the disciple that Jesus loved, hence the absence of the term Beloved Disciple. The courtyard scene is also rich in vivid detail: the fire, the time of day, the cold, and Peter's interactions with the courtyard's residents. This level of rich eyewitness detail and dialogue is like all the sequences which include the Beloved Disciple,[5] the Baptist's conversation with the Pharisees, the intimate actions at the Last Supper, the activities of the soldiers at the cross, the position of the grave clothes in the empty tomb, and the setting of the breakfast with Jesus in Galilee at the end—all recounted with great precision. The author was thus present at these events.

But who exactly was this author and eyewitness? We know nothing of his life before he met Jesus, except that he was a disciple of John the Baptist. We know he was long-lived and a well-known figure later in life, since he goes out of his way to scotch a rumour circulating "among the brothers" that he would not die.

There is universal agreement amongst Early Church writers that a certain John wrote the Gospel of the same name. Polycrates[6] wrote the following line at the end of the 100s CE, where he identifies the Beloved Disciple as being named John: "John, moreover, who reclined on the Lord's bosom [at the Last Supper], and who became a priest wearing the mitre, and a witness and a teacher - he rests at Ephesus."[7] Eusebius cites a far more telling passage from Clement of Rome concerning the identity of the author of John:

> "They say that John, who had employed all his time in proclaiming the Gospel orally, finally proceeded to write for the following reason. The three Gospels already mentioned having come into the hands of all and into his own too, they say that he accepted them and bore witness to their truthfulness; but that there was lacking in them an account of the deeds done by Christ at the beginning of his ministry."[8]

Irenaeus, just after he mentioned the Gospels of Matthew, Mark and Luke, says that "... John, the disciple of the Lord, who also had leaned upon His breast, did himself publish a Gospel during his residence at Ephesus in Asia."[9] Still, according to Irenaeus, this author, John, lived until the time of Emperor Trajan (98–117 CE) and was thus quite elderly. Clement of Alexandria too links the author of the Gospel of John to the Apostle John,[10] who, he says, lived until after Emperor Domitian's death in 96 CE. He also refers to John as "the old man."[11] In the Early Church literature, we cannot find an alternative identity for the author of the Gospel of John.

There is one last, small indicator that the author was a John. The author of the Gospel of John liked to encode numbers into his text. One example is the numerical value of the Hebrew version of the name "John," which is 129. Interestingly, the 129th word into the epilogue of John marks the beginning of the use of the phrase: "that disciple whom Jesus loved" (John 21:7). So it seems John encoded his name into the text.

---

4     It may also be meant as a tribute to Mark's own *inclusio* indeed in John, Peter is the second named follower and the last-named follower.

5     (Bauckham, Jesus and the Eyewitnesses; The Gospels as Eyewitness Testimony 2008, 398).

6     Bishop of Ephesus, which is on the coast of the Aegean Sea in present-day Turkey (c. 130–196 CE). For more information, please see (Polycrates of Ephesus n.d.).

7     Polycrates, *Epistle to Victor and the Roman Church Concerning the Day of Keeping the Passover*.

8     Eusebius, *Church History*, 3.24.7.

9     Irenaeus, *Against Heresies*, 3.1.1.

10     We shall see the ascription of this John to the disciple John, son of Zebedee, by Irenaeus is incorrect.

11     Clement of Alexandria, *Who Is the Rich Man That Shall Be Saved?* 42.

Most, but not all, of the Early Church fathers assumed, incorrectly, that this "John" was the disciple John the Apostle, the brother of James the Apostle; both men were sons of Zebedee, and both were members of the Twelve called by Jesus and mentioned in Peter-Mark (Mark 1:19, 3:17). However, another influential and contemporary John was confused with John the Apostle, John being a common name. Therefore, Papias mentions two distinct Johns when he describes his methodology of collecting information "… what was said … or by John … and what things… the presbyter John … say."[12] He is very careful to distinguish between John, son of Zebedee, who had died by then, was a disciple, and travelled along with other members of the Twelve Disciples in Galilee, from Presbyter John, who was also a disciple and who was still teaching when Papias was a young man in the 80s CE. After quoting Papias, Eusebius continues:

"It is worthwhile observing here that the name John is twice enumerated by him. The first one he mentions in connection with Peter and James and Matthew and the rest of the apostles, clearly meaning the evangelist [John son of Zebedee]; but the other John he mentions after an interval, and places him amongst others outside of the number of the apostles, putting Aristion before him, and he distinctly calls him a presbyter. This shows that the statement of those is true, who say that two persons in Asia bore the same name and that there were two tombs in Ephesus, each of which, even to the present day, is called John's. It is important to notice this. For it is probable that it was the second if one is not willing to admit that it was the first that saw the Revelation, which is ascribed by name to John."[13]

Papias, therefore, called the latter "John the Presbyter" to distinguish him from John the Apostle. The word "presbyter" also translates as "elder." Both Papias and Polycarp[14] heard John the Presbyter speak while young men,[15] which implies that he was quite elderly by then. If John knew Jesus in his twenties and was still teaching Papias and Polycarp, who were both born in the 60s, in the 80s, he would be well into his seventies or eighties by then. Later in life, John the Presbyter was based in Ephesus, which was only 200 kilometres away from Papias in Hierapolis, and only 8 kilometres away from Polycarp in Smyrna. John the Presbyter, therefore, could have easily met both men. He was thus quite elderly but still teaching, in line with Clement of Rome's description of the author John as a prodigious teacher.

So was the Gospel author John the son of Zebedee, or the Presbyter? The author of the Gospel of John cannot be the son of Zebedee, a rural fisherman based in Galilee, due to specific facts about the author found in the text.

First, the author is very familiar with the environs of Jerusalem. Much of the detailed action takes place in and around Jerusalem. He describes extraneous details about pre-70 CE structures, such as the Bethesda Pool, the Pool of Siloam, and the portico of Solomon's Colonnade, suggesting that he lived there. He also details Jesus' trips to Jerusalem but does not seem to have travelled much with Jesus in Galilee; he provides very little information about Jesus' activities there. Still, these activities were quite extensive, according to Peter. Again, it seems the author was Jerusalem based and not Galilee based. He also possesses "behind-the-scenes" information on the activities of the Jewish leaders. He was "known to the high priest" and perhaps was a family relation and had privileged access to elite circles, which would be impossible for a humble fisherman (John 18:16). He was wealthy too; he had a home in Jerusalem because he mentions "homes" when referring to himself and Peter, indicating that John had a house in Jerusalem (John 20:10). We know that he hosted Jesus at the Last Supper,[16] since Jesus was seated to John's left in the place of honour, while Peter was seated to John's right (John 13:23–25). The meal was held at the top of a two-storey building, with a large upper room waited on by servants, suggesting John was very wealthy (Mark 14:13–15).

Second, his Gospel is very well written, and he uses sophisticated, literary constructs, which suggests that the author was well educated. For example, the Gospel has a parallel two-stage prologue and two-stage epilogue. The book opens with the famous "Word became flesh" prologue, which stretches from verses 1 to 18 and speaks of the beginning of time (the first

---

12    Eusebius, *Church History*, 3.39.4

13    Eusebius, *Church History*, 3.39.5–6. Here Eusebius is referring to the author "John" in the Book of Revelation, which I will examine in Chapter 22.

14    Bishop of Smyrna (c. 65–155 CE). See also (The Editors of Encyclopaedia Britannica, Saint Polycarp 2020).

15    Eusebius, *Church History*, 5.20.6. Irenaeus confirms John as an eyewitness of Jesus.

16    (Whiteley 1985).

beginning). The actual story then starts with John the Baptist's testimony (the second beginning) (John 1:19). The Gospel then ends with a two-stage conclusion, starting with the first ending at the end of chapter 20, followed by the narrative epilogue and a second ending (John 21:24–25). The second beginning and the first ending are the start and end of the story of Jesus and his disciples, while the first beginning and the second final ending bookend the story of the Beloved Disciple, making the story of Jesus and his disciples wrapped in the interpretations and testimony of the Beloved Disciple.

As mentioned earlier, the text features two distinct *inclusios*: the we-*inclusio* and the "following anonymous disciple" *inclusio*. Also, the structure of John is filled with subtle, numerical metaphors that further point to his background. Jesus' last saying in the Gospel includes the three words "until I come" (John 21:22). These match the first three words of the gospel: "In the beginning …" Both the beginning and the end are thus reaching backwards and forward in time. This symmetry extends to the number of syllables in the prologue, which matches the words in the epilogue: 496. The number 496 is also a perfect number,[17] and its numerical value in Greek equals "only son." Also, both endings—20:30–31 and 21:24–25— consist of 43 words. This number play was typical in ancient literature; here, they indicate the careful structure and unity of the Gospel and dispel the scholarly speculation that the second epilogue is a later addition. The numerical value of "Jesus" and the expression "the lamb of God," used twice in John, are both 391. In the last scene of the gospel, 153 fish are caught, and 153 is a triangle number with linkages to the JS.[18] John loves the number 7. There are 7 witnesses in the epilogue, 7 miraculous signs performed by Jesus, 7 "I am" sayings by Jesus, and 7 discourses. The use of these sophisticated literary devices points to a very educated and creative mind. This suggests John was a well-educated young religious man from the priestly or aristocratic class based in Jerusalem, not a rural fisherman.

There is also an interesting but debated tradition passed on by Polycrates claiming that John was a priest who had worn the "mitre" or, in other translations, "the sacerdotal plate" (i.e., part of the head regalia worn only by the High Priest). It means that at some point, author John served as High Priest. Acts does mention a John, distinct from John, the son of Zebedee, who appears in a passage as part of the high priest's family.[19] But John was a popular name. Either Polycrates knew this information independently, or he picked it up from Acts. Whatever its source, this tradition reinforces the notion that John the Presbyter had links to, or was part of, the High Priest's family and was based in Jerusalem.[20]

John the Presbyter is not named as a member of the Twelve Disciples in Galilee, but he was part of the wider group who followed Jesus. Interestingly, Peter never mentions him, nor does he single him out; perhaps they were not well acquainted.[21] Indeed, both John and Peter seem to accompany Jesus at alternating periods, with little overlap until at the end of Jesus' life.

There is one more interesting link—the three epistles of John in the NT. Most scholars agree that all were written by the same person who wrote the Gospel of John. However, they reject the idea that John, son of Zebedee, could have written these works. Now we know why: John the Presbyter wrote them. The second and third epistles, generally attributed to the same author as the Gospel, are short letters written by someone who refers to himself as "the Elder" (John 2 and John 3). Remember that "presbyter" also means "elder." So John the Presbyter/Elder composed the Gospel of John and the epistles at Ephesus (according to Irenaeus), where he was buried. Coincidently, Ephesus is also the burial place of John, son of Zebedee. This must have led to the conflation mentioned above and created confusion about how a Galilean fisherman could have composed a complex gospel, as well as the epistles.

To summarize, the Gospel of John was written by eyewitness John the Presbyter/Elder, who was not one of the Twelve Disciples but a companion of Jesus nonetheless. He was a wealthy young man of the aristocratic or priestly class living in

---

17    A perfect number is a positive integer equal to the sum of its proper divisors: 496 = 1+2+4+8+16+31+62+124+248, for instance 6, 28 496 and 8,128, and so on.

18    A triangle number is a number which is the sum of the simple sequence of numbers; 1+2+3+4 … Also see (Bauckham, *The Testimony of the Beloved Disciple* 2007, 271–284) for a full discussion of John's use of numbers.

19    Acts 4:6.

20    See (Bauckham, *The Testimony of the Beloved Disciple* 2007, 41–50).

21    There is a more compelling argument why Peter does not mention John, which I will cover in the next chapter.

Jerusalem.[22] At the outset, he was a disciple of John the Baptist and then became one of the first followers of Jesus. He was present at many of the significant events in Jesus' mission. He was long-lived; he moved to Ephesus and composed his Gospel later in life, while he continued to teach about Jesus and have contacts with Papias and Polycrates.

# DATE

*Figure 17 **P52—The Earliest Surviving Gospel Fragment.***

*The Rylands Library Papyrus P52 is a fragment from a papyrus book or codex. It is dated from 100 to perhaps 200 CE, making it probably the earliest fragment of the New Testament in existence. It contains part of the trial of Jesus before Pilate from the Gospel of John.*

When did John write his Gospel? Unfortunately, there is not much to go on.

The latest estimated date for John comes from physical evidence. The earliest existing NT fragment is part of the Rylands Papyrus Library and is designated as P52. It stands for the 52nd catalogued papyrus. Discovered in Egypt, it is about the size of a credit card and comes from a codex. We know this because there are writings on both sides of the piece of papyrus. The text contains parts of seven lines from John, chapter 18 (the investigation by Pilate into Jesus as related in the Gospel of John). Overall, scholars estimate that dating is roughly between 100 and 200 CE, although the majority leans toward the years 100 to 150 CE. If we allow some time for transmission and then copying, we can reasonably place the earliest composition date of John to, say, 90–140 CE.

## COMPARED TO THE SYNOPTIC GOSPELS

As I have already stated, Matthew and Luke had a copy of Mark before them when writing, which heavily influenced their Gospels. However, they did not seem to know John. Indeed, they rigorously follow Mark but completely ignore the substantial additions made by John to Jesus' story. For instance, John describes the many festival visits by Jesus to Jerusalem and adds two whole years to Jesus' mission, but Matthew and Luke show no interest! Matthew and Luke also repeat Mark's mistakes and ignore the correct information available in John. For instance, as I explained earlier, both authors repeat Mark's error regarding the Last Supper being a Passover meal, while John places it correctly on the previous day. Elsewhere, Mark mistakenly places the incident of Jesus chasing out the money changers at the final Passover visit, when John correctly places it at the first of three Passover visits.[23] Here again, both Luke and Matthew copied Mark's error. When John offers additional information in overlapping accounts, neither Luke nor Matthew uses it. For instance, Luke and Matthew tell the story of the anonymous women who anointed Jesus with perfume (Luke 7:37–38; Matthew 26:7). John names the woman as Mary and indicates the amount and name of the perfume and describes how the aroma filled the house. But Luke and Matthew do not use any of those details despite their inclination to embellish Mark's stories. Further on, John tells the story of how Jesus washed the disciples' feet at the Last Supper and, by doing so, taught an important message on followership. Yet again, Luke and Matthew only seem to know Mark's version, and they do not mention that event. Neither author appears to know the Gospel of John.

Early Church Fathers say that John's Gospel was published last after the other three. Indeed, both Clement of Rome and Irenaeus state this.[24] Luke and Matthew would undoubtedly have consulted John, as they did with Q and Mark, if they had known John, as neither were eyewitnesses. Therefore, John must have been composed either at the same time or after Luke and

---

22    This would explain John's "behind-the-scenes" information on the activities of the priestly class and for his apparent immunity from arrest despite his affiliation with Jesus.

23    I discuss this point in Chapter 26.

24    See Eusebius, *Church History*, 3.24.7, & Irenaeus, *Against Heresies*, 3.1.1.

Matthew. I have concluded earlier that both Luke and Matthew were written roughly between 58 and 61 CE; it follows that John must be from that date range or later.

## THE 60S CE

We can deduce John's date by looking into some details from the text. John describes a pre-70 CE Jerusalem, with its Pools of Bethsaida, Siloam, and Solomon's court; these were all destroyed during the war with the Romans. John also speaks as if Jerusalem was still standing: "Now there is in Jerusalem near the Sheep Gate a pool, which in Aramaic is called Bethesda and which is surrounded by five covered colonnades" (John 5:2). Therefore, John must be pre-70. Like Luke-Acts and Matthew, the Gospel of John never mentions or even foreshadows the tumultuous years of the mid-60s and early 70s CE, including the start of the First Jewish-Roman War in 66 CE. So if John's Gospel was published last and John had access to the three other Gospels, as Clement indicates, he probably wrote his Gospel in the early to mid-60s (in line with Robinson's assessment),[25] after Luke and Matthew had become available and before Jerusalem was destroyed.

I believe John was prompted to leave his testimony and fill in the blanks left by Peter, as suggested by Clement, upon hearing the news of Peter's death in Rome (c. 64 CE) and realizing no new information would be forthcoming from Peter.[26] It is no coincidence then that John discusses events from Jesus' mission not covered in Peter-Mark; there is minimal overlap between the two except for the Passion Story, where John wanted to fill in the gaps to provide a complete account (and his interpretations) of Jesus' death. This casts new light on the final sequence of the Gospel; both Peter and Jesus are followed by John, with Peter and Jesus "gone" at this point, while John is still alive and still following. There is no reason to doubt Irenaeus when he says that John composed his gospel in Ephesus, the same location where he lived in later life and where he was a bishop and died. Thus, we can assume that the Gospel of John was written last, probably in the mid-60s, perhaps between 64 and 65 CE, in the city of Ephesus.

## SOURCES

Now I want to outline the most probable eyewitness sources for blocks of material present in John until the Last Supper, when John and Peter come together formally.

**1:1–14 and 16–18**. This sequence is the famous Prologue of John, where Jesus is said to be the "Word." This Prologue has variously been called a poem, or an adapted early hymn. It serves as a summary of John's theological themes in the Gospel: Jesus as the light, his pre-existence, him becoming flesh, and his unity with God. It also introduces themes that John repeatedly uses: "light," "flesh," and "truth." So even if the Prologue was adapted from a pre-existing hymn, we can say John is responsible for its final form.

**1:15 and 1:19–3:21**. In this sequence, we learn that John was a disciple of the Baptist and was with him when he gave his "testimony" on Jesus. There is no mention of Jesus being baptized, so if Jesus was, then John must not have been present. Over a four to seven-day span, John met Jesus and Peter, joined their small group, followed them to Galilee, and then attended a wedding in Cana. John accompanied Jesus during his subsequent Passover visit and probably attended the Nicodemus meeting. So John himself is the source of these events.

**3:22–4:54**. Here a lack of detail suggests that John did not accompany Jesus when he was baptizing in Judea and then travelling north. Three independent and detailed sequences include personal knowledge that must have been gained despite John being away from the group that was accompanying Jesus. In the first sequence, a follower of the Baptist familiar with the evangelist John relates a discussion he had with the Baptist. In the second instance, a Samaritan woman's detailed account of her one-on-one discussion with Jesus, with apparently no one else around, is recounted, as well as the events that occurred

---

25    (Robinson 2000, 254–311).

26    I have argued for a similar scenario in the creation of Mark 2.0.

later in the village. In the final instance, only the royal official would have known the hour of healing, and, as a result, he is acknowledged as the source of that information.

**5:1–47.** John relates the stories as he accompanies Jesus while in Jerusalem.

**6:1—7:1** This sequence seems lacking in detail at places, so it is not clear whether John was with Jesus or not. However, I believe John was with the group for the feeding of the 5,000 people, walking on water, and teaching the next day in Capernaum. Why? This section is the only retelling of a Peter account by John outside the Passion Story. He must be retelling the story because the earlier account lacked something or was in error, and he would only do so if he knew the correct version, so he must have been present. [27]

**7:2–10.** An odd little story perhaps related by Jesus' brothers.

**7:11–10:39.** Here John accompanies Jesus while in Jerusalem. It seems that John was present during the interrogation of the blind man and his parents, or got the details from a source who was in attendance. John indeed mentions that other disciples were present, but he does not name them.

**10:40–42.** Lack of detail of Jesus' activities across the Jordan River indicates John was not present.

**11:1–17.** Detail returns, so John must have travelled to Jesus' location and then travelled back with him to Bethany and Lazarus, or the disciples related the story to John.

**11:18–11:53.** John vividly recounts the raising of Lazarus and its consequences, indicating he was present.

**11:54.** John probably did not withdraw to the wilderness with Jesus, as there is no detail, so he must have gotten the information from people who accompanied Jesus.

**11:55–13:1.** John accompanies Jesus upon his return to Bethany up to and including the Last Supper.

## PROBLEMATIC FEATURES IN JOHN

After waiting twenty years, John produced a more cohesive, elegant, and carefully detailed narrative than Mark. And this is to be expected, for Mark is relating scattered oral stories that he has arranged. John provides more detail and is to be preferred when both are reporting the same information. As I have shown, Peter also has a more fantastical turn of mind than John.

In general, there is little to find fault with within John. His most glaring insertion is the very long speech that Jesus gave after the Last Supper, as it is four chapters long (John 14–17). Jesus undoubtedly did pass on his final teachings for the group then, but Jesus' long, rambling, and repetitive teaching seems to be made up of distinct shorter teachings. John was trying to insert several lengthy teachings and sayings of Jesus into one long, artificial discourse. As with Mark's chapter 13, this was a convenient placement before the start of the cohesive Passion Story.

I only have minor complaints about the rest of his Gospel. First, John (or an early copyist) makes spelling mistakes. When Jesus was on the cross, a sponge with wine was offered to Jesus on the tip of a spear (ὑσσῷ), not a small, bushy plant like lavender called hyssop (ὑσσώπῳ).[28] Since hyssop or similar plants were used in Jewish rituals to sprinkle the blood, later editors probably did not correct the mistake, as they would have understood the meaning metaphorically.

Also, John reports that Nicodemus brought a hundred *litrai* (the ancient Greek plural for *litra*—about 0.72 pounds,[29] roughly 75 pounds in total) of a mixture of myrrh and aloes, which is a wildly extravagant amount (John 19:39). It is undoubtedly an odd statement coming from the usually sober John. The amount may be accurate, as Nicodemus was a very wealthy man, and tremendous amounts of spices for burial were not unheard of, especially for kings.[30] Perhaps Nicodemus, as a well-off follower of Jesus, had arranged for a "kingly" burial. However, I think the answer may be more prosaic: another spelling mistake.[31]

---

27    I will discuss the changes in the retold account in the next chapter.

28    John 19:29 and sometimes Mark 15:36, although my NIV uses "stick."

29    (The Editors of Sizes.com n.d.).

30    Josephus, *Antiquities of the Jews* 17, 199.

31    (Brug 2012).

Rather than λίτραν ἑκατόν, or "100 litrai," adding back one letter yields λίτραν ἕκαστόν, rendering a "litra each," a standard measure of myrrh and aloes—still an expensive amount, though. It is also reasonable to suppose that the marketplace would not have 75 pounds of these spices on hand; it is an amount that would have taken some time to stockpile. Therefore, I am sure that we are merely facing a spelling error here, made either by John or a copyist. Again, it was never corrected, for it read metaphorically that Jesus was buried like a king, an adequate metaphor given his importance.

Lastly, John seems to think that Jesus withdrew to the village of Ephraim (John 11:54), but it is more likely that he simply passed through the region of Ephraim on his way beyond the Jordan, as described by Peter-Mark. John was not with Jesus on that trip. And lastly, John's use of number-play distorts the actual amount in places; for instance, was numerically interesting 153 fish caught in the last scene? Probably not. Other than these issues, we have no reason to doubt John's reliability.

John is an early work written by a companion of Jesus. It is full of information about Jesus and, according to the Rules, will be included in my Source List.

# CHAPTER 19

# JOHN AND PETER

*Figure 18 **The Burial Places of Peter and John***

*A study in contrasts. Peter is buried directly under the Dome of Saint Peter's Basilica in Vatican City (top). The view is almost straight up from the High Altar, centred under Bernini's pavilion directly under the highest dome in the world part of the largest church in the world. The current altar sits over at least four other shrines and altars going back 2000 years which are all centred directly over Peter's simple burial plot. Image courtesy of MatthiasKabel via CC BY-SA 3.0. The simpler tomb (bottom) is believed to be that of John the Elder in Ephesus set amongst the ruins of an ancient Byzantine church.*

"No story can be devised by the wit of man which cannot be interpreted allegorically by the wit of some other man."

—C.S. Lewis, *On Stories: And Other Essays on Literature*

Two of the four Gospels, John and Peter-Mark, come from eyewitness testimony. By comparing the two, can we gain insights into each account? Yes, we can.

John and Peter are contrasting individuals: John was a Jerusalem based, urban, educated Jew who was a member of the elite, while Peter was an uneducated and superstitious rural Galilean. However, both give complementary information on different aspects of Jesus' mission. John primarily reports Jesus' Jerusalem activities, and Peter reports Jesus' time in Galilee. John provides a more coherent, time-defined, and hard-headed account, while Peter's account is uneven and episodic, consisting of Mark's stitched together notes.

## CREDIBILITY

Peter's Gospel includes fantastical and "dodgy" elements, some of which I enumerated in chapter 15; it is hard to know how many elements Peter believed to be accurate, how many were meant as metaphors or were due to Mark or were entertaining embellishments as part of the stock and trade of getting and keeping an audience's attention, since Peter was performing for an audience.

### DEMONS

The stories of Jesus include descriptions of demon possession and Jesus casting out said demons to heal people. Surprisingly, only Peter reports demons.[1] John never mentions demons, even though he describes Jesus performing healings.[2] No doubt John would have heard these stories of demons, but clearly he did not believe in them and considered reports of them to be incorrect. So what is going on?

The rural peasants in and around Galilee, like most ancient communities, believed in demon possession. For instance, the Syrophoenician woman diagnosed her daughter's sickness due to a demon and specifically asked Jesus to drive it out (Mark 7:24–30). Peter, the rest of the disciples, the spectators, and the healed people probably all believed in demon possession and interpreted specific healings in that light. Interestingly, Peter is careful to delineate healing of the sick versus demon possession, so two different types of disorders are indicated (Mark 1:32, 34, 6:19). Do we have any indication as to the nature of the condition taken for demon possession? We do, but in a negative way. The story of the boy with the evil spirit is telling (Mark 9:17–29). Jesus is approached by a man who claims an evil spirit possesses his son. He describes past symptoms, and then the boy has a seizure; both descriptions conform to a grand mal epileptic seizure;[3] however, this is ascribed to an evil spirit. The disciples have failed to throw out this demon; only Jesus could cure with "prayer" to God. Earlier, the disciples had been given "authority over evil spirits," and they had been successful in healing, but not when it came to this case, an actual condition. So this "authority" must be limited to faith healing, where the afflicted believes demon possession is the explanation for imagined or psychosomatic illnesses (the result of, for instance, stress, anxiety, developmental, eating, or sleeping disorders). Using the power of suggestion, spreading the news of Jesus' mission, or performing a placebo treatment (for example, anointing with oil),

---

1     There is a single demon healing in Q set in rural Galilee.

2     John only mentions demons when others are discussing them or in the context of an accusation against Jesus.

3     Generalized Tonic-Clonic Seizures, a brief episode of stiffening limbs, thrashing on the ground, loss of bladder and bowl control, and foaming and biting of tongue and cheek tissue. Afterwards, the person is weak and confused (Davis 2020).

they "healed" people. Certainly given their association with Jesus, they would have been a potent force in faith healing.[4] We also hear of an unassociated healer performing the same types of healings in Jesus' name (Mark 9:38).

In this milieu that accepted demon possession as a matter of course, Jesus seems to have "played along" with his expected role of demon thrower on several occasions, for example, in the case of the epileptic boy, presumably since acknowledging the demon aided in the recovery. But even this is hard to say for sure, since this is refracted through Peter's acceptance of demons, and almost all the accounts of Jesus interacting with a demon come from embellished secondary sources.[5]

John, the better witness, indicates there is no such thing as demon possession. He also never once suggests that someone is healed because of their faith; healings occur solely due to the authority of Jesus. So I will set these embellished elements in Peter's narrative aside.

## FANTASTIC EVENTS

The other stories from Peter probably started as metaphors, such as Jesus' solitary time in the desert (Mark 1:12–13) (Jesus communing with the divine), the darkness (Mark 15:33) (condemning the world for Jesus' death), the centurion (Mark 15:39) (perhaps appealing to the Roman audience to accept Jesus), and the ripping curtain (Mark 15:38) (eliminating the barrier between God and man). Mark, perhaps not understanding the symbolic element of the stories or because Peter "performed" these segments as real, reported these as facts. As I will argue, apart from most of the healings, Peter was not present at any of these events. The only story Peter is a part of is the Transfiguration (Mark 9:2–8). However, this event cannot be true, since Moses, who appears in the scene, is a mythical figure. The rest of the story reads more like a hallucination or a dream: a high mountain, dazzling whiteness, a voice from Heaven, and everything suddenly disappearing. Peter took all of this as real, so he included it in his preaching.[6] Peter also included the folk tale of the Baptist's beheading (Mark 6:17–29) and the rumour of the travellers in the country (Mark 16:12–13).

John reports none of these other stories.[7] John would have undoubtedly heard some of them, but obviously he did not believe them, or he would have included or alluded to some of these events. As a result, as with the demon stories, I do not think these elements in Peter's narratives are true.

John had a much higher standard for inclusion than Peter; Peter included some fantastic material that I have attempted to excise from my Peter-Mark. Mark also included non-original and conflicting material in several chapters to "fill out" chapters 13 and 16. Again, I have attempted to excise these from my Source List.[8] I am thus sceptical of Peter's editorial judgement (and Mark also has his issues). So if Peter and John are conflicted on a point, I would take John's version over Peter's, for it sounds more credible, being devoid of extraordinary additions.

# TWO ROLES

Bauckham notes how John is very careful to hold himself forth as the ideal witness by contrasting himself with Peter. This takes the form of a rivalry between the two men in John's Gospel: John follows Jesus first before Peter, John helps Peter into the courtyard, John beats Peter to the tomb when they run to it, John serves as the intermediary between Peter and Jesus when Peter wants to know who the betrayer is at the Last Supper, John witnesses Peter's denial of Jesus, and John was present at Jesus' trials and death, while Peter was not, being in hiding.

---

4    Only Peter links healing with "having faith." Certainly, believing in the healer and his power would be a pre-requisite for these types of healings.

5    The man in the tombs, the Syrophoenician woman, and the man with the epileptic son.

6    There is also a story in Acts of Peter having another vision of a sheet with animals being lowered from the sky with a voice from heaven that he took as being significant (Acts 10:9–16).

7    Luke and Matthew, since they copied from Mark, include most of these fantastical elements and even embellish them further.

8    *Salt & Light II* will include my annotated version of Peter-Mark.

Peter is depicted as the man of action, the leader; he's investigating, hauling in the net, and building the Church. John's role, in turn, is as ideal witness. While affirming Peter's centrality, he modestly displaces Peter to establish his role as unobtrusive witness who had, however, a deeper understanding of Jesus. For example, when they both go to the empty tomb, Peter enters and investigates, while John peers in and suddenly "believes" (John 20:8). And in the epilogue, the Beloved Disciple is the first to perceive "the Lord." Peter acts from then on. As Bauckham put it, "the Fourth Gospel implies [that] Peter has not said the last word about Jesus or the most perceptive word."[9] Thus John, in his way, although he acknowledged the importance of Peter's testimony, was reacting to Peter-Mark's perceived deficiencies, probably the ad-hoc nature of Peter-Mark, which left out important information by setting the record straight. Indeed, John does fill in around Peter's narrative with Jesus' Jerusalem activities to create one complete record; Peter-Mark and John need to be read together. I believe John wrote after hearing of Peter's death and realizing Peter would never update his gospel. There was indeed no one left with sufficient authority to bear witness to the rest of Jesus' story.[10]

In sum, Peter died pursuing his active role in building the Church, while the Beloved Disciple did, through this "book," continue to testify, a role assigned to him by Jesus himself (John 1:39). Therefore, the Beloved Disciple started witnessing before Peter and continued to do so after his death, until the end of time, through a Gospel. Both roles represent different types of activity—namely, active service and anonymous witnessing.

## A QUESTION OF NAMES IN JOHN AND MARK

John's and Peter-Mark's Gospels point to an early date for Mark and a late date for John. Bauckham raises the fascinating issue: Why are some people named and others unnamed in the two Gospels?[11]

There is, remarkably, a pronounced reluctance in Peter-Mark to name the people who attended the events that occurred during Jesus' last week, while John has no problem naming many of these people.

For instance, in Peter-Mark, the mysterious woman who anoints Jesus (Mark 14:3–9) with an expensive perfume just before the Last Supper is not named, which is very odd, as Jesus insists her story be retold "in memory of her." At least to some observers, this woman appears to designate Jesus as anointed in the messianic sense,[12] whether that was her intention or not. This would have placed her in a dangerous position, as the elites were on guard for messianic pretenders. She could be seen as complicit in a conspiracy to challenge the existing political order. However, John has no problem naming her; she is Mary, sister of Lazarus.

Peter-Mark relates the story of raising "the young man" and the "certain woman" who was his sister.[13] From John, we learn they are called Lazarus and Martha. According to Peter-Mark, when Jesus was arrested in the Garden of Gethsemane, an unnamed man "standing near" drew a sword and injured a servant of the High Priest by cutting off his ear (Mark 14:47). Peter-Mark not only does not name the attacker, but it also obscures the relationship with Jesus; he was just standing around. John, in turn, informs us that Peter wielded the sword and was part of Jesus' group, and Malchus was the name of the injured servant. Peter-Mark does not give the name of the High Priest who condemned Jesus, while John does. He was Caiaphas.

Elsewhere, Peter-Mark tells us Jesus instructed two unnamed disciples to borrow a colt (Mark 11:1–7). They do so from "some people standing there." Obviously, this was a pre-arranged action, and Peter is very vague about who the disciples and the

---

9    (Bauckham, Jesus and the Eyewitnesses; The Gospels as Eyewitness Testimony 2008, 128). This also fits with the idea that John wrote to "fill out" Peter's account.

10    Hence John's concern to establish his authority as ideal witness.

11    (Bauckham, *Jesus and the Eyewitnesses; The Gospels as Eyewitness Testimony*, 2008, chapter 3).

12    Kings and great leaders were traditionally anointed with oil or other perfume at their investiture.

13    Mark 10:34b, re-inserted from Mark 2.0.

people were. When Jesus rides the colt into Jerusalem, the religious elite would have seen this as another threatening messianic declaration,[14] and anyone complicit, including the owner of the colt, would be seen as politically subversive.

In another passage from Peter-Mark, Jesus sent two unnamed disciples into Jerusalem, where they contacted an unidentified "man carrying a jar of water," who leads them to the pre-arranged secret location for the Last Supper, a place owned by another unidentified man (Mark 14:12–16). The secrecy of the operation is evident because men typically did not carry jars with water (women did), and Jesus has already pre-arranged everything. As I have argued, the location is John's home, and the servant was John's also, but he remains anonymous in Peter-Mark.[15]

So what is going on here? The Gospel of John was written more than two decades after Mark's, yet John, when recounting the last week of Jesus' life, can name quite a few people whom Peter could not. Gerd Theissen[16] argues that after the anointing of Jesus and the report of the raising of Lazarus, the Sanhedrin would have gone on high alert, since the events described occurred just before Passover, and they sound like Jesus was planning to lead a messianic uprising. The Sanhedrin's response was to order the arrest and death of both Jesus and Lazarus (John 11:53 & 12:10). Therefore, this would have been a time of danger for Jesus and anyone associated with him. Thiessen further argues that Peter provided protective anonymity for all of those involved by leaving people's names silent, being vague about their association and being generally evasive in places. This was necessary, as Peter's account (and the Core Message+) came from a time when people were still in danger, which supports the case for the very early date for Peter-Mark, 40 CE. Thus, the people involved were still "wanted" by the authorities in the few years since the crucifixion. Jesus was dead, but one of his followers (Peter) had attacked a person during a lawful arrest, the young man of Peter-Mark (Lazarus) had resisted arrest and was probably still sought on a death warrant, and the young woman (Mary) who had anointed Jesus was a ringleader in the messianic plot, which included all of Jesus' followers. Decades later, when John was writing in 64–65 CE, it was finally safe to name people.

This also answers two odd facts about Peter's account. First, we know John accompanied Jesus almost constantly after the Last Supper, but Peter never mentions him. Why? John was from the priestly or aristocratic class, so he was also at risk. Being from Jerusalem and no doubt well known, he could easily be identified, so Peter simply did not mention him at all. The second odd fact consists of Lazarus's encoding as "the young man with the linen cloak." Peter-Mark introduces this figure in the passage reintroduced from Mark 2.0 (Peter-Mark 10:34b), which I have added to Peter-Mark as reliable. He then mentions "the young man" again at the arrest of Jesus (Mark 14:51–52). Remember, there was a warrant out for both Jesus and Lazarus. Hence, they seized him as well. But "the young man" fled, leaving his linen cloak behind. Peter felt it important to signal to readers that Lazarus had faithfully been with Jesus when he was arrested. This may also explain why the initial passage from Mark 2.0 was not originally published; it was too revealing and could have got Lazarus in trouble.

So the people who were named in Peter-Mark were either no longer in power (Pilate, in particular), of no consequence (Barabbas), or no longer "wanted" persons (for instance, Bartimaeus, Salome, Simon of Cyrene, and Mary of Madelene) who may have died and no longer needed anonymity by 40 CE. The rest of the unnamed needed protective anonymity. Later, by the time of John's Gospel, many of the unnamed could safely be named.

---

14      Zechariah 9:9 indicates a king would come seated on a colt and the attendant crowd hail him as a king.

15      I speculate that the mysterious owner of the colt is John, as Jesus was already in confidential communication with him; several people (John's servants?) had the colt ready. But there are no facts other than this to support this surmise.

16      (Theissen, *The Gospels in Context* 1991).

# OVERLAP

*Figure 19* **Detail of the Tabgha Bread and Fishes Mosaic**

*Detail from a mosaic in the Church of the Multiplication of the Loaves and the Fishes at Tabgha near the Sea of Galilee, the traditional location of the Feeding of the Five Thousand. Dated to the 400s CE.*

Peter-Mark and John do not often overlap, which makes sense, for John wrote last and would have had Mark's Gospel in front of him upon writing. Therefore, he did not see the need to rehash Peter's existing information. He wanted to contribute the sequences that Peter could no longer detail after his death. There are only two areas of overlap: the Feeding of the Five Thousand/Walking on the Water sequence (John 6:5-13; Mark 6:34–44) and the Passion story (John 13:1–20:31; Mark 14:1–16:20). John needed to reiterate the Passion story since he was an eyewitness to almost all of it and deemed the final day of Jesus was not being interpreted correctly. Peter's account was not complete and was in part second hand, since he was in hiding after almost being recognized in the courtyard.[17]

But why did John repeat the dual miracle story? His chapter 6 has the feeding and walking on water followed by the Bread of Life teaching. In Peter-Mark, the feeding and walking are followed by a teaching on the evils coming from the inside of a person. So what is going on?

As discussed, John saw himself as the ideal witness to Jesus. By reiterating the events he had seen, he could give it an essential meaning that Peter had missed. When we put the two sequences side by side, we can see they both occupy about twenty verses. However, John provides quite a bit more detail than Peter does; the men were on a mountain, Passover was near, Jesus was testing his followers, Phillip and Andrew are quoted,[18] there is an un-named boy present, Jesus said not to waste the leftovers, and the people thought he was a prophet and wanted to make him king forcefully.

---

17   Peter-Mark's and John's Lazarus stories are not overlaps since Mark did not include the Lazarus incident in the original version of Mark. John obviously considered it crucial, as he includes much detail of the incident.

18   Depending on the version, Phillip estimates it would cost eight months' salary, half a year's salary, or 200 denarii = 1,600 dupondius = 3200 loaves of bread, a large and accurate amount.

In contrast, John omits two pieces of information that Mark included. First, that the followers thought Jesus was a ghost walking on water, and second, the followers "did not understand about the loaves; their hearts were hardened" (Mark 6:49). We have already seen how John dismisses Peter's supernatural interpretations. As a result, he must want to make it clear that at least he did not think Jesus was a ghost walking on water, so he claims that he believed. Second, John seems to take exception to the suggestion that he did not understand and his heart was hard … again. He insists that he understood and believed.[19] John emphasizes Jesus' momentous actions at the previous and the next Passover in his Gospel. Since this overlapping material occurs around Passover, momentous events such as the feeding, walking on water, and the Bread of Life teaching, must be happening that needed full "witnessing."[20]

---

19    We see this again in the story of the reaction to Mary Magdalene telling the disciples she had seen Jesus alive in Peter-Mark: "they did not believe." However, in John, he insisted he "believed."

20    John may have travelled to Jesus in Galilee on this Passover for precisely this reason.

# CHAPTER 20

# PAUL OF TARSUS

*Figure 20 **A Roman Road in Syria***

*It was along a road such as this that Saul, a member of the Pharisee sect, later called Apostle Paul, had his conversion experience. Saul had been persecuting Christians in Jerusalem and was on his way to Damascus in Syria to arrest Christians among the Jewish community there. According to Paul, a bright light knocked him to the ground about noon near Damascus, and he heard a voice that identified itself as Jesus, and he became temporarily blind. From that point on, he joined the Christian mission. The details of the conversion experience are given in three places in Acts of the Apostles: first in 9:1–9, then in 22:6–21, and a third time in Acts 26:12–18. Three times Paul alludes to the conversion experience in his letters: 1 Corinthians 15:3–8, 2 Corinthians 12:1–7, and Galatians 1:11–16, in which he variously describes the experience as "seeing Christ," "heard things" in Paradise, and receiving a "revelation from Jesus Christ." Image courtesy of Bernard Gagnon via CC BY-SA 3.0.*

The Dunning-Kruger effect: The less you know, the more confident you are.

"All my means are sane, my motive and my object mad."

—Herman Melville, *Moby Dick*

Of the 27 books in the NT, thirteen were written by or attributed to the Apostle Paul. His epistles are early texts considered foundational to orthodox Christianity. Robinson's dating puts them all within eight years, stretching from early 50 to Autumn 58 CE, well within the Date Rule.[1] All of Paul's writings are in the form of letters addressed to various communities or peoples from which the titles are drawn. After initial receipt, the letters undoubtedly started to be circulated amongst Christian audiences, and eventually quite a few were added to the NT. Others are known to have been lost. The contents consist, in general, of Pauline Christian doctrine, counsel, argumentation, encouragement, instruction, and conflict resolution.

Paul did not know Jesus, but according to him and Acts, he interacted with many Early Church members, including the senior leadership of Peter, John, and James. His activities and extensive missionary journeys are covered in detail in the Acts of the Apostles. In Acts, we thus learn that Paul was born a Jew—his Jewish name was Saul—of the tribe of Benjamin and that he joined the Pharisaic Jewish faction.[2] In his letter to the Galatians, he describes himself as "extremely zealous for the traditions of my fathers" (Galatians 1:14). He indeed started by persecuting the Early Church members in Jerusalem, and Acts has him guarding the cloaks of those who stoned an early Christian. He was travelling to Damascus when, according to him, he had a transformative, hallucinatory experience, which caused him to spend the rest of his life preaching an odd form of Christianity (called Pauline Christianity) throughout Asia Minor, Greece, and Italy. He founded several churches and, during a stormy career that included various life-threatening adventures, he conflicted with the Jewish establishment, Jesus' disciples, and Roman authorities. Eventually, he was arrested and sent to Rome for trial, where the last we hear of him is in 62 CE.[3] We do not know the outcome of that specific trial, but it is generally accepted that he perished along with Peter during Emperor Nero's persecutions of Christians around 64 CE in Rome.

Paul's letters have been of great importance, for they are traditionally considered the earliest, discrete Christian writings—with, perhaps, the exception of the Epistle of James. As such, they are invaluable to scholars attempting to understand the Early Church and its activities. Paul's letters are also the only known texts from a member of the Jewish sect of the Pharisees, of which Paul claimed he belonged to in his early years. Therefore, they are also crucial to our understanding of first-century Judaism during the period preceding the Temple's destruction in 70 CE. Apart from their scholarly value, they also espouse beautiful sentiments in places, making them popular down to the present day. However, in my quest for the historical figure of Jesus, Paul's letters are (almost) completely useless.

Scholars have come to view only 7 of the 13 letters as actually written by Paul;[4] two others have evenly divided opinions on authorship, and the remaining five are rejected as not being directly from Paul. They were either written pseudonymously by someone else or were composed by a scribe based on notes that Paul may have given him. We know of a few other letters that did not survive because they are mentioned in extant epistles. I will not treat the authenticity of the Pauline Epistles, except for two cases.

According to the Credible Facts Rule, four of Paul's letters contain no facts about Jesus: Philemon, 2 Thessalonians, Ephesians and Titus, so they can be excluded immediately.[5] The remaining ten (including Hebrews) contain only a handful of

---

1        (Robinson 2000, 84).

2        Acts 22:3 has Paul a student of the great teacher Gamaliel, who was based in Jerusalem. If true, Paul would probably have been "around" during Jesus' mission, and he may have seen or spoken with Jesus.

3        I discussed the justification for this date in Chapter 17.

4        However, Robinson argues convincingly they all originate from Paul in one form or other, as originals, drafts, or re-copies.

5        I have adopted the shortened title for Paul's letters. So Philemon refers to the Letter to Philemon, and 2 Thessalonians to the Second Letter to the Thessalonians.

facts scattered amongst them, so they need to be considered. Also, 1 Corinthians has embedded a tantalizing early statement of belief passed on to Paul and which I call the Corinthian Creed.[6]

## THE CORINTHIAN CREED

Corinthians is considered an authentic letter of Paul's, in which he makes an interesting statement about some information he "received" and is passing on to his readers:

> "For I delivered to you as of first importance what I also received, that Christ died for our sins according to the scriptures; and that he was buried; and that he hath been raised on the third day according to the scriptures; and that he appeared to Cephas [Peter]; then to the twelve; then he appeared to above five hundred brethren at once, of whom the greater part remain until now, but some are fallen asleep; then he appeared to James; then to all the apostles, and last of all he appeared to me also …" ( Corinthians 15:3–7)

This text appears to be a formal creedal statement (i.e., a core statement of belief) that Paul was told and is now repeating. This text block is linguistically and textually distinct from the text surrounding it, indicating it is from a different source. This letter was written in the Spring of 55 CE.[7] Paul was thus passing along a tradition that must pre-date 55 CE. He refers to having related this creed in the past and reminds his readers, the members of his group in Corinth, of it. Paul had previously visited Corinth in 49 or 50 CE (Acts 18:1–17), so the Creed must pre-date 50 CE. Most scholars acknowledge that it is a very early tradition that goes back to the first Jerusalem Church. However, we should note that Paul got the "Twelve" wrong; indeed, at that point there were only eleven disciples, since Judas had left the group. Unless Paul uses the "Twelve" to mean "disciples" in general, there may have been more than just eleven witnesses. Also of note, Paul slips himself into the Creed at the end; this will help with my interpretation later

## DATE AND SOURCE

The Creed pre-dates 50. But when and where did Paul get it?

Two imperfect sources recount the events preceding this date: the early chapters of Acts, which cover the activities of the followers of Jesus in and around Jerusalem starting immediately after the crucifixion, and another authentic letter from Paul, titled Galatians, written in late 56,[8] where he recorded his version of interactions with the church leaders in Jerusalem. If we can construct a timeline for Paul, we can conjecture the timing for his reception of the Creed and establish at least a date when the Creed was in use. Acts introduces Paul (also called Saul) at the stoning of Stephen.[9] What is the timing of the latter's death? Unfortunately, Acts is the only source available, and it is vague regarding the timelines of that period. The crucifixion occurred on the day before Passover, April 1, 33; Acts relates that forty days then passed, and Pentecost was celebrated 50 days after Passover, so in May or June 33. Days passed, "day after day" (Acts 4:42), which is somewhat imprecise; finally, Stephen was then stoned to death. The text thus allows us to place Paul in Jerusalem during the summer of 33.

As I discussed earlier, Luke wrote Acts 30 years later (around 62 CE) and related a collection of second-and third-hand stories from the Early Church that he had assembled into a narrative. He obviously had no precise timeframe for the events between the death of Jesus and the stoning of Stephen, since he simply did not know. He undoubtedly was unsure of the order of events and what had happened (surely Stephen did not deliver his famous set-piece "death speech" [Acts 7:2–53]. Luke

---

6     First Corinthians 15:3–7.

7     (Robinson 2000, 84).

8     Ibid.

9     Stephen was a Christian deacon appointed by the disciples who is traditionally held to be the first Christian killed for his beliefs.

would have invented it, as was the practice of the day). The events Luke does describe in this section of Acts, chapters 1 to 7, would take no more than a month or two to complete. The Church, however, even if it expanded rapidly, obviously needed far more time to do so. The period from Pentecost to the death of Stephen could thus be months or even years.

What happened next, as well as our dating math, depends on which source is used. According to Acts, Saul/Paul was prosecuting the Church in Jerusalem and had received permission to travel to Damascus, which is about 200 kilometres away at a slow horse gait of 40 kilometres per day. So with stopovers, it was probably a 10-day trip. There he would have arrested any Christians. Enough time must have elapsed for Christianity to spread to Damascus. As he neared Damascus, Paul had his famous conversion experience, and after "many" days spent in Damascus, he returned to Jerusalem, where he joined the Apostles. This is what is recounted in Acts:

> "When he came to Jerusalem, he tried to join the disciples, but they were all afraid of him, not believing that he really was a disciple. But Barnabas took him and brought him to the apostles. He told them how Saul on his journey had seen the Lord and that the Lord had spoken to him, and how in Damascus he had preached fearlessly in the name of Jesus. So, Saul stayed with them and moved about freely in Jerusalem, speaking boldly in the name of the Lord." (Acts 9:26–28)

However, Paul has a contradictory version of events following his conversion. In Galatians, considered an authentic letter of Paul's, written over a year after 1 Corinthians, he has this to say of his post-conversion:

> "But when God, who set me apart from my mother's womb and called me by his grace, was pleased to reveal his Son in me so that I might preach him among the Gentiles, my immediate response was not to consult any human being. I did not go up to Jerusalem to see those who were apostles before I was, but I went into Arabia. Later I returned to Damascus. Then after three years, I went up to Jerusalem to get acquainted with Cephas [Peter] and stayed with him fifteen days. I saw none of the other apostles—only James, the Lord's brother. I assure you before God that what I am writing you is no lie." (Galatians 1:15–20)

The "reveal" he mentions must be his conversion to Christianity. He is emphatic—and swears an oath—that he did not go to Jerusalem to see Jesus' companions there; instead, he writes, he consulted no one and left Damascus for Arabia (i.e., the eastern lands of the Nabateans, or the region around Babylon). Only then, after three years, he says, did he go to Jerusalem and meet the two people he mentions in the Creed with authority to teach the Creed. Presumably, it is then that he learnt the Creed that he passed on to the Corinthians in his letter, 20 years or so later.

There are thus two mysteries that remain to be solved. First, the timeline between the deaths of Jesus and Stephen could be months—say six months. This places the death of Stephen toward the end of 33. It could also be years, say three years, thus setting the death in 36 (the scholarly consensus).

The second mystery involves Paul's first visit to the Apostles in Jerusalem and his picking up the Creed. Was it a month or a few months after his conversion according to Acts, or was it three years according to Paul in Galatians? Coupled with our admittedly conjectured dates, casting the broadest possible net, the Creed was then passed on to Paul between 33 and 39. While Acts relies on old stories that Luke has no way of dating precisely, Paul may be fibbing or exaggerating about the three years. As his other letters show, he was at pains to make himself out as an Apostle, for he never met Jesus, and to let his followers know that his doctrine came directly from Jesus, not the Jerusalem Church. Therefore, he had something to gain from denying early contact with the leaders in Jerusalem and appearing as any other convert.

I am inclined to think that Acts is nearer the truth. Indeed, after a dramatic conversion experience, why not go to Jerusalem first to learn what you can rather than go off to a remote region for three years? However, I think I may have reached the limits of what I may reasonably assume and so am left with a date range of 33 to 39 for the transmission of the Creed to Paul. The Creed itself is not only very early but also very simple; it could have been composed in a short amount of time, probably almost immediately after the death of Jesus, as part of the creation of the Core Message+. The source would then be the Jerusalem

Church—the initial group who followed Jesus—with Peter and James as leaders. So given its source and date, I will include it in my Source List.

## PAUL'S LETTERS

Setting aside the Corinthian Creed, Paul surprisingly relates a very short list of facts about Jesus. Why so short? It seems certain that Paul did not know Jesus during his lifetime; he never mentions the stories found in the Gospels, nor the sayings and teachings of Jesus, even in instances where a quote from Jesus would have clinched an argument. According to Graham Stanton, this is baffling.[10] If he knew more, would he not have mentioned some information? Paul's long letters—very long, by ancient standards—are so oddly bereft of details about Jesus' life and death that Richard Carrier touts the letters as primary evidence that Jesus, in fact, never existed. Paul's primary purpose is to resolve countless moral and doctrinal disputes, which Carrier finds "bizarre" if Jesus did indeed exist. He says:

> "Paul's Jesus is only ever in the heavens. Never once is his baptism mentioned, or his ministry, or his trial, or any of his miracles, or any historical details about what he was like, what he did, or suffered, or where he was from, or where he had been, or what people he knew. No memories from those who knew him are ever reported. Paul never mentions Galilee or Nazareth, or Pilate [sic incorrect—Paul does mention Pilate] or Mary or Joseph, or any miracles Jesus did or any miraculous powers he is supposed to have displayed ... or anything about the life of Jesus not in the Gospels. Paul never references any event in Jesus' life as an example to follow (beyond the abstractions of love, endurance and submissiveness), and never places anything Jesus said in any earthly historical context whatever."[11]

However, stories about Jesus and his sayings were available in various texts when Paul was writing. Mark's Gospel had been circulating for a decade at least; Q was probably also in circulation by then. Paul even says that he met Peter for fifteen days (Galatians 1:18–20), while Luke assures us that Paul was interacting with the Jerusalem group almost from the beginning (Acts 7–9). Also, many eyewitnesses to Jesus still lived.

In short, there is no way he could not have known at least some facts about Jesus. I must conclude, then, that Paul simply did not see Jesus' teachings and actions as relevant in the context of his letters. Perhaps they were even contrary to Paul's teachings. I say "contrary," as he seems to go out of his way to avoid factual information and insists that *his* gospel, "the gospel of Christ," which came to him directly from a celestial Christ by revelations, should take precedence over any other gospels.

"I am astonished that you are so quickly deserting the one [Paul] who called you to live in the grace of Christ and are turning to a different gospel—which is really no gospel at all. Evidently some people are throwing you into confusion and are trying to pervert the gospel of Christ." (Galatians 1:6–7)

This is made explicit in the following astonishing remark:

"For I make known to you, brethren, as touching the gospel which was preached by me, that it is not after man. For neither did I receive it from man, nor was I taught it, but it came to me through revelation of Jesus Christ." (Galatians 1:12–13)

Paul is also quite insistent he did not interact with the followers of Jesus in Jerusalem for at least three years after his conversion, presumably strengthening the "originality" of *his* gospel. He says he only spent time with Peter and James for a couple of weeks, which is flatly contradicted in Acts.[12] He returned to meet them a second time only fourteen years later (Galatians 1:16–22), and when he did so, he was almost contemptuous of the "reputed" leaders— Peter, James, and John—and insisted they had nothing to teach him. Indeed, he writes:

---

10    (Stanton 1997, 131).

11    (Carrier 2014, 34742).

12    In Acts 9:26–28, Paul returns to Jerusalem soon after his conversion and spends time with the apostles.

"As for those who seemed to be important--whatever they were makes no difference to me; God does not judge by external appearance--those men added nothing to my message." (Galatians 2:6)

According to Carrier, "… the only sources Paul ever refers to for anything he claims to know about Jesus are private revelations and hidden messages in scripture …"[13] So Paul is adamant his "gospel" comes from "revelations" and not from the people who knew Jesus. Paul even intimates that any other stories about Jesus should be disregarded; only his revelations and the things written in the past—that is, the JS—should be considered, for his gospel reveals their hidden meaning:

"For everything that was written in the past was written to teach us, so that through the endurance taught in the Scriptures and the encouragement they provide we might have hope…" (Romans 15:4)

"Now to him who is able to establish you in accordance with *my gospel* [my emphasis], the message I proclaim about Jesus Christ, in keeping with the revelation of the mystery hidden for long ages past, but now revealed and made known through the prophetic writings by the command of the eternal God …" (Romans 16:25–26a, emphasis added)

All that Paul's Jesus does is descend from Heaven, die, and then re-ascend (Philippians 2:6–9). There is no ministry and no teaching. But why is Paul's version of Jesus' life in contradiction with the stories told by his companions, whom he dismisses? Paul describes his conversion experience by saying that Christ "appeared" to him (1 Corinthians 15:8) or was "revealed" to him (Galatians 1:16). He thus had a hallucinatory experience, upon which, he says, he acted immediately without consulting anyone (or any facts). Carrier rightly suggests that ancient converts, including Paul, exhibited schizotypal characteristics:

"They naturally and regularly hallucinated (seeing visions and hearing voices), often believed their dreams were divine communication, achieved trance states, practiced glossolalia [speaking in tongues], and were (or so we're told) highly susceptible to psychosomatic illnesses (like 'possession' and hysterical blindness, muteness and paralysis). These phenomena have been extensively documented in modern charismatic cults within numerous religious traditions, and their underlying sociology, anthropology and psychology are reasonably well understood."[14]

It seems that Paul suffered from some sort of incurable malady, probably linked to the above condition. Indeed, he speaks of "a thorn in (his) flesh" (2 Corinthians 12:7). He also says:

"I must go on boasting. Although there is nothing to be gained, I will go on to visions and revelations from the Lord. I know a man [himself] in Christ who fourteen years ago was caught up to the third heaven. Whether it was in the body or out of the body I do not know—God knows. And I know that this man—whether in the body or apart from the body I do not know, but God knows— was caught up to paradise and heard inexpressible things, things that no one is permitted to tell." (2 Corinthians 12:1–4)

We also know that Paul promulgated the notion of "Gifts of the Spirit" to his congregations; these included speaking in tongues, trances, and prophesying (1 Corinthians 12:1–11). See, for instance, the following passage: "I thank God that I speak in tongues more than all of you" (1 Corinthians 14:18).

Apparently, these practices got out of hand. We know that at least one of Paul's congregations, the Corinthians, followed his spontaneous tongues and prophesying practice and that it became so disruptive that Paul had to issue guidelines (1 Corinthians 14:26–40). Paul also rebukes those speakers who spout gibberish: "So it is with you. Unless you speak intelligible words with your tongue, how will anyone know what you are saying? You will just be speaking into the air" (1 Corinthians 14:9).

---

13    (Carrier 2014, 34753).

14    (Carrier 2014, 4403).

Moreover, Paul had odd theological ideas not attested by John or Peter, including a "third heaven," worshipping Jesus as God, Jesus' death having cosmic consequences, Gifts of the Spirit, Paradise with "unspeakable words," and baptism and communion that were spiritual events (2 Corinthians). As James D. Tabor put it:

> "The fundamental doctrinal tenets of Christianity, namely that Christ is God 'born in the flesh,' that his sacrificial death atones for the sins of humankind, and that his resurrection from the dead guarantees eternal life to all who believe, can be traced back to Paul—not to Jesus. Indeed, the spiritual union with Christ through baptism, as well as the 'communion' with his body and blood through the sacred meal of bread and wine, also trace back to Paul. This is the Christianity most familiar to us, with the creeds and confessions that separated it from Judaism and put it on the road to becoming a new religion."[15]

Paul was a vigorous organizer, an elegant letter writer, and very good at spreading the name of Jesus. Still, his theology was his own, which brought him into conflict with the followers of Jesus in Jerusalem, as described by Paul and in Acts. He was a loose cannon with no interest in the actual Jesus, and he was primarily out of control—from the perspective of Jesus' companions, at least. According to the famous Jesus scholar, Albert Schweitzer: "the Gospel of Paul is different from the Gospel of Jesus ... the Greek, the Catholic and Protestant theologies all contain the Gospel of Paul in a form which does not continue the Gospel of Jesus but displaces it."[16] And Thomas Jefferson called Paul: "the great Coryphaeus[17] and first corrupter of the doctrines of Jesus. These palpable interpolations and falsifications of his doctrines led me to try to sift them apart."[18] Well known biblical scholar Geza Vermes says this about Paul's status as an authority on Jesus: "Paul, who never set eyes on Jesus or John the Baptist, would have failed the qualifying examination."[19] Reza Aslan comments that Paul's teachings about Jesus would have been viewed as "shocking and plainly heretical"[20] by the followers of Jesus, and they took action to send representatives to Paul's congregations to "correct"[21] the damage of Paul's message.[22]

In conclusion, Paul was not an eyewitness of Jesus. His letters provide little factual information about Jesus, as he actively ignored existing information. His letters served to assert his reputation as an authority on Jesus, proclaim Paul's theological doctrines, and formulate community rules. Paul suffered from schizotypal tendencies that caused him to hallucinate "revelations" from a celestial Jesus and find meanings in reading between the lines of JS. He thus created a new mystical religion, Pauline Christianity, which displaced Jesus' teachings and was based on the worship of Christ and ecstatic revelations derived solely from his hallucinations.

Paul's letters contain a few facts about Jesus, including The Corinthian Creed, unattested elsewhere and the fact that Jesus suffered outside the city gate (Hebrews 13:12). So, for the moment, the letters containing any facts will be added to my Source List.

---

15     (J. D. Tabor 2013).

16     (Schweitzer, *The Mysticism of Paul the Apostle* 1998).

17     The leader of a group or sect.

18     (Jefferson 1820).

19     (Vermes, *The Changing Faces of Jesus* 2001, 64)

20     (Aslan 2013, 139).

21     Ibid. 140

22     In Galatians 1, Paul responds by reproving his congregation for "turning to a different gospel" preached by "some people." Aslan ably describes the conflict between Paul and Jerusalem (Aslan 2013, 139–141).

# CHAPTER 21

# APPLYING THE CUSTODY RULE

Before proceeding, I will review the progress in reviewing sources. At the end of Chapter 11, there were 33 sources still to review, and my Source List contained three entries. Since then, I have added five new sources: Q, Secret Mark, Peter-Mark, Gospel of John, and the Corinthian Creed to my Source List, bringing the total number to eight sources of information on Jesus. Seven sources have been surveyed and excluded: Matthew, Luke, Acts, Philemon, 2 Thessalonians, Ephesians, and Titus. So 33 less 4 accepted, less 7 rejected leaves 22 sources still to be reviewed.[1]

As the title suggests, in this chapter I will review those authors who produced written works after 100 CE (so outside our remaining 22 sources, except for 1 Clement) who may have had a documented, direct connection with one or more people who knew Jesus; these authors did not, however, know Jesus directly. If true, then according to the Custody Rule, the source should be added considered.

To be considered in the ECW list:

Ignatius of Antioch (105–155 CE), *Polycarp to the Philippians* (110–140 CE), Papias (110–140 CE), *1 Clement* (80–120 CE), and Quadratus of Athens (120–130). Tacitus, Josephus, and Mara Bar Serapion have been included, and Suetonius (115 CE) and Pliny the Younger (111–112 CE) were dropped, as per Chapter 9. Quadratus was discussed in Chapter 8 and is included for discussion.

## IGNATIUS

Ignatius of Antioch (c. 35 to c. 107) was the Bishop of Antioch for many years.[2] When he was an old man, he was arrested, taken to Rome, and executed. On his trip to Rome, he wrote a series of seven letters to various congregations along the way and to his friend Polycarp that have come down to us. Although tradition holds, he knew John the Presbyter, and Ignatius was undoubtedly in the right place and time to have met John and other people who knew Jesus; I can find no source that confirms this, so I must set aside Ignatius' letters.

## POLYCARP

He was the Bishop of Smyrna in the early to mid-100s CE.[3] Irenaeus has this to say about him:

> "… Polycarp also was not only instructed by apostles, and conversed with many who had seen Christ, but was also, by apostles in Asia, appointed bishop of the Church in Smyrna, whom I also saw in my early youth, for he tarried [on earth] a very long time, and, when a very old man, gloriously and most nobly suffering

---

1    Five were added, not 4, to the Source List, since the Corinthian Creed was not in the original ECW list.

2    For more information, please see (O'Connor 1910).

3    (The Editors of Encyclopaedia Britannica, Saint Polycarp 2020).

martyrdom, departed this life, having always taught the things which he had learned from the apostles, and which the Church has handed down, and which alone are true."[4]

Eusebius also preserves a fragment of a letter by Irenaeus:

"... so that I am able to describe the very place in which the blessed Polycarp sat as he discoursed, and his goings out and his comings in, and the manner of his life, and his physical appearance, and his discourses to the people, and the accounts which he gave of his intercourse with John [the Presbyter] and with the others who had seen the Lord."[5]

So we have documentary evidence that Polycarp was in touch with early witnesses, and John the Presbyter in particular. Only one piece of his writings survives, the Letter to the Philippians, which he wrote to the Christian congregation at Phillipa around the 130s or 140s CE, so we will consider this letter.

## PAPIAS

In the discussion of the Gospel of Mark, we saw that Papias was in direct touch with John the Presbyter, an eyewitness to Jesus. Both Eusebius and Irenaeus quote fragments of his lost *Exposition of the Sayings of the Lord*, and one from Irenaeus appears to offer previously un-attested teaching of Jesus[6] handed down by Papias. This fragment will be included.

## CLEMENT OF ROME

Clement of Rome's only surviving work is his *Letter to the Christian Church in Corinth*, called *Clement 1*, dated 96 CE. Since his work is under my cut-off of 100 CE, I will include this letter.

---

4    Irenaeus, *Against Heresies*, 3.3.4.

5    Eusebius, *Church History*, 5.20.6.

6    Irenaeus, *Against Heresies*, 5.33.3–4.

# CHAPTER 22

# APPLYING THE REPETITION RULE

I have shown that Peter-Mark, John, and Q are, by far, the richest and earliest sources for facts about Jesus. Luke and Matthew are early sources as well, although unreliable. It is now profitable to apply the Repetition Rule to see if the information in any potential source, or a source already in my Source List, is simply a repetition of information we already have in earlier sources. If so, the source is redundant and can be discarded. For instance, if a source's only fact about Jesus is that he was crucified, and Peter-Mark, being an earlier source, states that he was also crucified, then according to the Repetition Rule, the source is redundant and can be excluded from my Source List.

I apply the Repetition Rule to all 25[1] sources yet to be reviewed and the sources in my Source List in Appendix 6. The result: 17 sources can be eliminated[2] as redundant, plus 3 from my Source List are also redundant[3] and can all be excluded in their entirety.[4] Five remaining sources need to be discussed in the next chapter.

Three scraps of information unattested in the earlier sources have moved into my Source List:

- 1 John has a short quote from Jesus: "God is light and in him is no darkness at all."[5]

- A surviving teaching from Papias.[6]

- The Letters of Paul yield the single fact: "He suffered outside the city gate."[7]

In the next chapter, I will review the last five sources and then finalize my Source List.

---

1 The last chapter added three sources for consideration.

2 *1 Clement, Polycarp to the Philippians, Quadratus of Athens,* 1 Corinthians, 1 Thessalonians, Philippians, Galatians, 2 Corinthians, Romans, Colossians, 1 Timothy, 2 Timothy, 2 Peter, *Fayyum Fragment,* 1 Peter, *Epistle of Barnabas,* and *Oxyrhynchus 1224 Gospel.*

3 Tacitus, Mara Bar Serapion, Corinthian Creed.

4 Josephus' *Testimonium Flavianum* is eliminated, but the second statement about James remains.

5 1 John 1:5, most certainly authored by John the Elder/Presbyter.

6 Irenaeus, *Against Heresies,* 5.33.3–4.

7 Hebrews 13:12.

# CHAPTER 23

# THE LAST SOURCES

*Figure 21 **Emperor Nero.***

*Nero Claudius Caesar Augustus Germanicus, also known as Nero, was Roman emperor from 54 to 68 CE. Later commentators have contributed to a very negative assessment of his rule: he is alleged to have had his mother killed, kicked his pregnant wife to death, and started or abated the Great Fire of Rome in 64 CE. It is hard to say if this is accurate, since there are no historical sources from his reign, only secondary sources written 50 years after his death that were derogatory in order to tarnish his legacy. He was also the first persecutor of Christians. In 68 CE a military rebellion caused his supporters to abandon him. Nero panicked and killed himself on June 9, 68 CE, leaving no heirs and ending the Julio-Claudian dynasty started by Julius Caesar and Augustus. The resulting power vacuum sparked a brief civil war in the Year of the Four Emperors (69 CE).*

*Image courtesy of the American Numismatic Society via CC BY-SA 0.0.*

"I cordially dislike allegory in all its manifestations …"

—J.R.R Tolkien.

# THE BOOK OF REVELATION

The Book of Revelation—not Revelations, as it is commonly referred to in error—is probably the oddest book in the NT. The author, who calls himself John, reports that he is on Patmos, a small Greek island in the Aegean Sea off the coast of Turkey. He had a vision in which an angel sent by Jesus dictated seven letters addressed to seven congregations in Asia Minor. After this, he was whisked away to see fantastic things, including vivid apocalyptic and prophetic imagery, as well as various weird visions, such as seven-headed dragons, the four horsemen of the Apocalypse, lakes of fire, the Serpent, the famous 666 numbered Beast, the Second Coming of Christ, the 144,000 saints, and New Babylon being destroyed—that is, all things to come. It ends with the angel commanding John to communicate what he has seen. Since the contents are extravagant and obscure, Revelation is open to and has been given an extensive range of interpretations in the past and at present (for instance, Hollywood loves this book!).

While odd in the context of the NT and literature in general, Revelation is a typical example of the Apocalyptic literature genre developed in Jewish and early Christian culture. The word "Apocalypse" means "the revealing of divine mysteries." Typically, Apocalyptic literature details the authors' visions of future events, such as the "end of time" or other divine information as revealed by an angel or other heavenly messenger. The Apocalyptic literature genre is characterized by heavy use of symbolism, references to time periods, the use of numbers and additional numerical information, and cryptic or hidden ideas and themes. It is seldom written by the person claiming authorship.

Apocalypses were a popular medium for authors who desired to spread their ideas, especially if the ideas might be regarded as unacceptable. For instance, Revelation criticizes the Roman Imperial power structure by couching criticism in obscure symbolism. Also, apocalypses would have been popular; they could be regarded as an early form of science fiction. They could be read for entertainment, as a puzzle to be decoded, for political and theological analysis, or as a study into esoteric information. And they need not be stand-alone works; the JS, for instance, has apocalyptic sections scattered throughout.

There are plenty of Jewish and Christian apocalypses surviving, and they are very similar to Revelation.[1] So Revelation is by no means unique. It is distinctive only for being included in the NT and being a relatively early Christian work.

## DATE

Robinson provides an interesting analysis of the book.[2] According to him, Revelation was probably written at a time when Jews and Christians had not yet formally parted ways, which they only did after 70 CE when the Temple was destroyed. Revelation indeed seems to present a time when the Temple was still standing and functioning, again pre-70:

"I was given a reed like a measuring rod and was told, "Go and measure the temple of God and the altar, with its worshipers. But exclude the outer court; do not measure it, because it has been given to the Gentiles." (Revelation 11:1–2)

Still, according to Robinson, Revelation seems to document intense persecution of Christians in Rome:

"Then the angel carried me away in the Spirit into a wilderness. There I saw a woman sitting on a scarlet beast that was covered with blasphemous names and had seven heads and ten horns. The woman was dressed in purple and scarlet and was glittering with gold, precious stones and pearls. She held a golden cup in her hand, filled with abominable things and the filth of her adulteries. The name written on her forehead was a mystery:

---

1    For instance, we have the Book of Daniel, *the Apocalypse of Adam, the Apocalypse of Peter, the Apocryphon of John, the Apocalypse of Paul, the Apocalypse of Thomas, the First Apocalypse of James, the Second Apocalypse of James, the Coptic Apocalypse of Paul,* and *the Coptic Apocalypse of Elijah.*

2    (Robinson 2000, 221–254).

BABYLON THE GREAT

THE MOTHER OF PROSTITUTES

AND OF THE ABOMINATIONS OF THE EARTH.

I saw that the woman was drunk with the blood of God's holy people, the blood of those who bore testimony to Jesus." (Revelation 17:3–6)

These few verses of dramatic imagery are easily decoded.

"This calls for a mind with wisdom. The seven heads are seven hills on which the woman sits. They are also seven kings. Five have fallen, one is, the other has not yet come; but when he does come, he must remain for only a little while. The beast who once was, and now is not, is an eighth king. He belongs to the seven and is going to his destruction. The ten horns you saw are ten kings who have not yet received a kingdom, but who for one hour will receive authority as kings along with the beast." (Revelation 17:9–12)

The woman who sits on "seven hills" and is named Babylon is Rome because the ancient city was famous for its seven hills, and the word "Roma" in Latin is feminine.[3] The woman is wearing purple and scarlet, the imperial dye worn by Roman elites. So Rome, the capital of the Roman Empire, is "… the great city that rules over the kings of the earth" (Revelation 17.18). Apparently, "those who bore testimony to Jesus" must refer to Peter and Paul, who had recently been killed in Rome. Robinson argues that Revelation is most probably referring here to the savage persecution under Nero, which started in 64 CE.

*Figure 22 The Earliest Existing Number of the Beast*

*A fragment, called P. Oxy. 4499, of Revelation from c. 225–275 CE only recently deciphered and published.*
*The number of the beast is on the third line, XIϚ, reading 616 versus the more common 666.*

---

3    In 1 Peter 5:13, Peter states that he is writing from "Babylon," a code name for Rome used by those who wished to avoid trouble with the Roman authorities.

The "Beast" refers to a Roman emperor. The text thus speaks of the "kings" (or emperors) of Rome. The numbers appearing in the text offer clues as to the Beast's identity, who, presumably, had mistreated Christians. The number of the Beast, 666 (or 616 in some early manuscripts), is the sum of the Hebrew letters for "Nero Caesar." In the Hebrew alphabet, letters also had numerical values. If you spell the Greek version of "Nero Caesar" in Hebrew, you get נרון קסר. Substituting the number value for each letter, the following series is created: 50, 200, 6, 50, 100, 60, 200; when the numbers are added up, the total is 666. The Latin version of the name in Hebrew drops the second נ, which is valued at 50. This yields the other value attested in early manuscripts: 616. Clearly, the 666 Beast mentioned in Revelation refers to the emperor Nero, the instigator of the first Imperial persecution against Christians (sorry, Hollywood!).[4]

Furthermore, we learn that the sixth king is currently reigning: "five have fallen, one is, the other has not yet come." Nero was the fifth Roman emperor ("the first beast"), and the first upstart emperor after Nero's suicide was Galba, who marched on Rome with his army and then ruled from June 68 to January 69 CE; he is thus the one who "is." It was a period of civil war and upset in Rome, referred to as the Year of the Four Emperors. We can read in Revelation that "they will bring her [Rome] to ruin and leave her naked; they will eat her flesh and burn her with fire," which seems to match Galba's actions (Revelation 17:16). Perhaps, therefore, "the other (who) has not yet come" may refer to the next upstart emperor, Otho, who rebelled at the beginning of 69 CE.

Nero committed suicide in June 68, six months earlier. But a false rumour, called Nero Recidivist, circulated that he still lived and, with the aid of the Parthian Empire in the East, would return. "Who once was" might refer to Nero returning to claim the throne and become the eighth "king" of Rome. Therefore, Revelation must have been written after Otho rebelled in early 69 CE but before the third upstart, Vitellius, defeats Otho in April 69 CE.

It is probable that the author, a certain John, a common name at the time, was in Rome during those events and witnessed the chaos and the "impending" implosion of Rome and its empire. He then fled for Asia Minor, perhaps to Patmos, where he may have been from, to write letters to the seven churches to prepare them for a time of unrest. Regardless of the exact circumstances of the authorship, we can reasonably date the composition of either Revelation or the background events to early 69 CE.

Revelation, therefore, passes the Date Rule. Also, it mentions Jesus 16 times; in fact, the very opening phrase of the book reads as follows: "The revelation from Jesus Christ." However, Revelation contains no information to help us with the Three Questions. Jesus is the focus of faith and the source of testimony, but there is no factual information about Jesus or his deeds. So, according to the Credible Facts Rule, I will not include Revelation in my Source List.

## THE GOSPEL OF THOMAS

The Gospel of Thomas is an early collection of 114 sayings attributed to Jesus, more akin to the Q sayings document than to an actual gospel describing the life and death of Jesus. The Gospel of Thomas claims that the sayings of Jesus it reproduces are "secret" and were recorded by a certain Didymos Judas Thomas, hence the name.

Scholars have long known about the existence of a Gospel of Thomas through scattered comments made by Early Church Fathers, but no copy was believed to be extant. In 1945, however, some Egyptian farmers uncovered a clay pot with 13 books containing 52 mostly Gnostic works (the Nag Hammadi collection), all written in Coptic (late Egyptian); one of those was the Gospel of Thomas. It is speculated that monks from a nearby monastery may have buried the books when Athanasius, Bishop of Alexandria, in his annual letter of 367 CE (the same letter that lists the canonical books of the NT for the first time), condemned the use of non-canonical works.

Before going further, it is important to take a quick look at the Gnostics.

---

4    And the famous "mark of the beast" needed to buy or sell would be Roman coinage that showed the portrait of the emperor with inscriptions claiming they were divine, a lot of the coinage at that time would show Nero, since the new emperors had not reigned long enough for wide circulation of their coinage. Other speculation states the mark was a brand using hot coinage.

## THE GNOSTICS

Gnosticism is a label for various odd religious ideas that arose in and around Alexandria in the late first and early second century CE. It encompasses multiple esoteric teachings drawn from different aspects of Judaism, Christianity, and Greek philosophy. The Gnostics saw the material world as corrupt; they thus rejected the idea of bodily resurrection as presented by Christianity. They only accepted the concept of "resurrection" if redefined as an "ascent of the soul," for, to them, the soul is immaterial and, therefore, incorruptible (unlike the body).

Early Church Fathers wrote extensively against Gnosticism because the Gnostics, they argue, would take both Christian themes and entire gospels and re-write them with their ideas interwoven into Jesus' teachings. Moreover, the Gnostics claimed that Jesus had passed down "secret" teachings that had only been revealed to the Gnostics. This is what Irenaeus has to say about the activities of the Gnostics:

"By transferring passages, and dressing them up anew, and making one thing out of another, they succeed in deluding many through their wicked art in adapting the oracles of the Lord to their opinions."[5]

Tertullian[6] states that the Gnostics' doings "… pervert by means of additions and diminutions, for the accomplishment of its own purpose …"[7]

With this in mind, let us turn back to the Gospel of Thomas.

The Gospel of Thomas records sayings of Jesus that are like those found in the four Gospels. These sayings are interleaved with other sayings that are unattested elsewhere and have Jesus (confusingly) espousing Gnostic ideas. It appears that the author of Thomas is using the four Gospels and then placing a layer of Gnostic teachings over them.

From the discussion on the Gospel of Mark, we know of another Gnostic "gospel" written by a teacher called Carpocrates. The latter produced a Gnosticized version of the Gospel of Mark, that is, with Gnostic teachings inserted. It would appear that Thomas is another example of this.

The author (or editor) of Thomas is unknown. Most scholars believe that Thomas depends on the four Gospels and place the date of composition to the early to mid-100s CE. Therefore, using the Date Rule, Thomas can be excluded from my source list.

# THE SIGNS GOSPEL

This is a hypothetical text, just like Q, initially suggested by Rudolf Bultmann as an older text that John may have relied on when writing his Gospel. There is the vestige of a numbering system of the miraculous actions or signs by Jesus; the first (John 2:11) and second signs (John 4:54) are numbered in John, but not the later ones. It has been suggested that John had a list of "signs" in written form in front of him as he taught and composed, but what it contained is widely debated. Various reconstructions of the list have been proposed based on extracting a text from the Gospel of John. Stylistic arguments have been put forward, suggesting that the author of the Signs Gospel was also the author of John's Gospel. As regards dating, obviously the list would have to pre-date the Gospel of John. Interesting as this is, there is no existing Signs Gospel, only an extracted text from John, so the Gospel of John subsumes any information on Jesus, and we can set the Signs Gospel theory aside.

# THE PASSION NARRATIVE

Scholars have debated whether there was a stand-alone Passion story that Peter and John later used in their Gospels. I think it likely existed, although there is no direct evidence. As I mentioned previously, right after Jesus' death, his followers would have quickly assembled a standardized version of events for Jesus' last week as part of the Core Message+. The stories would have been solidified by repeated retelling over the years. Peter told a version of this Passion Narrative, and parts of it were captured

---

5    Irenaeus, *Against Heresies*, 1.8.1.

6    Tertullian was an early Christian author (c. 155–220). For more information on Tertullian see (Wilken 2020).

7    Tertullian, *The Prescription Against Heretics*, 17.

by Mark, making his Passion Narrative a very early "work." It would have been distinctive from the other teachings and stories in terms of the drama and length—it is easily the most extended narrative we have on Jesus. We see that John also follows the Passion Narrative story arc found in Pater-Mark but has his version of it based on his personal experiences of that week. However, both versions of the narrative already exist in Peter-Mark and John; I need not speculate further on the issue.

## THE DIDACHE

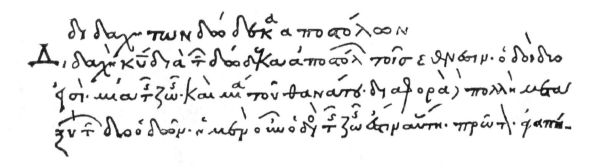

*Figure 23 **The Didache***

*The title of the complete copy of the Didache, unexpectedly rediscovered in 1887 by Philotheos Bryennios after it was lost for 1,500 years. He was browsing in a small library in Constantinople when he came across the manuscript, bundled and unrecorded, with a group of six other manuscripts. This text was copied by a scribe who signed it himself as "Leon, notary, and sinner" and says he completed the copy on June 11, 1056.*

The *Didache* (pronounced Did-ah-Kay), also called the *Lord's Teaching Through the Twelve Apostles to the Nations*, has been of intense interest since the chance rediscovery in 1887 of a complete text in Istanbul.

Until its rediscovery, the *Didache* was known only through fragments and second-hand commentary from Early Church Fathers. Compared to the fragments of another copy of the *Didache*, grouped under the title *Papyrus Oxyrhynchus*—discovered a century earlier and dated from the 300s CE—it appears minimal alteration had occurred when compared to the later 1056 copy.

The *Didache* is an anonymous, short, 16-paragraph work, about a third the length of Peter-Mark and written in very simplistic Greek. It consists of a "Two Ways" section (chapters 1–6), a liturgical manual (7–10), instructions on the reception of travelling prophets (11–15), and a short apocalypse (16). Scholars agree that the *Didache* is a very early work, no later than the early 100s AD. Its primitive nature and markings of oral transmission indicate it probably goes back to the very Early Church of the 40s and 50s. It was included in some early versions of the NT but later dropped since it dealt with practical matters.

Jesus is mentioned three times but not with any usable information. So using the Credible Facts Rule, I shall set the *Didache* aside.[8]

---

8    However, in another aspect the *Didache* is very important, and I will explore in *Salt & Light II*.

# PERICOPE ADULTERAE

*Figure 24 **John 7:53–8:12***

*A sketch by Rembrandt portraying the famous scene of Jesus and the adulteress. Jesus is drawing on the ground after telling the mob (all garbed as 1650s Dutch people in this sketch) "Let any one of you who is without sin be the first to throw a stone at her" (John 8:7). Rembrandt completed many sketches and is known for his images from the Gospels.*

The last source[9] to be assessed is the beautiful story (*pericope*) of the woman caught in adultery and brought before Jesus, or the "cast-the-first-stone" story. Here it is, as found in modern copies of the Gospel of John:

"Then they all went home, but Jesus went to the Mount of Olives.

At dawn he appeared again in the temple courts, where all the people gathered around him, and he sat down to teach them. The teachers of the law and the Pharisees brought in a woman caught in adultery. They made her stand before the group and said to Jesus, 'Teacher, this woman was caught in the act of adultery. In the Law Moses commanded us to stone such women. Now what do you say?' They were using this question as a trap, in order to have a basis for accusing him.

---

9    The *Pericope* is not found in the ECW list as a stand-alone work.

But Jesus bent down and started to write on the ground with his finger. When they kept on questioning him, he straightened up and said to them, 'Let any one of you who is without sin be the first to throw a stone at her.' Again, he stooped down and wrote on the ground.

At this, those who heard began to go away one at a time, the older ones first, until only Jesus was left, with the woman still standing there. Jesus straightened up and asked her, 'Woman, where are they? Has no one condemned you?'

'No one, sir,' she said.

'Then neither do I condemn you,' Jesus declared. 'Go now and leave your life of sin.'" (John 7:53–8:11)

According to the JS, the penalty for adultery is death,[10] but Jesus does not condemn her. Most scholars believe the story was not original to the Gospel of John because it is absent from the earliest manuscripts (from the 300s and 400s CE), although many more later adopted it; however, even today the story may be absent or footnoted in various versions of the NT.[11] But Early Church Fathers seem to attest to it, notably Papias, according to Eusebius:

"And he [Papias] relates another story of a woman, who was accused of many sins before the Lord, which is contained in the Gospel according to the Hebrews."[12]

Scholars are not sure what this *Gospel of the Hebrews* was. Still, it seems likely that Papias was reporting the *Pericope Adulterae* as a traditional story, which was either written somewhere or told orally from before the year 100 CE.[13] Therefore, I will insert it into the appropriate place in John in my Source List.

---

10    *Leviticus* 20:10 & *Deuteronomy* 22:22. In *Exodus* 20:14, the ban on adultery is one of the Ten Commandments.

11    This passage is excluded in my copy of the NIV New Testament.

12    Eusebius, *Church History*, 3.39.16.

13    Interestingly, Papias was taught directly by John the Presbyter, author of John, so he could have picked this story up directly from John, which would not be surprising, as the incident takes place in Jerusalem where much of John's information is situated. It was then later, naturally, associated with John's account. If true, why John did not include it originally in his Gospel is a mystery.

# CHAPTER 24

# MY SOURCE LIST

"OK, so ten out of ten for style, but minus several million for good thinking, yeah?"

—Douglas Adams, *The Hitchhiker's Guide to the Galaxy*

Finally! From all the starting sources, I have established the only sources that have useful information on Jesus that can be used to answer my Three Questions. Here is My Source List:

There are three primary sources:

- The Gospel of Peter-Mark, dated 40 CE, was dictated by eyewitness Peter.

- The Gospel of John, written in the mid-60s CE by eyewitness John the Presbyter.

- The Q source, dated to the early to mid-30s CE, a sayings collection.

And five fragments from different sources:

- The *Pericope Adulterae*, an early story connected with John the Presbyter, as alluded to by Papias, was inserted into John at 7:52.

- Hebrews 13:12, probably repeated by Apostle Paul.

- Josephus' *Antiquities*, which tells us that Jesus had a brother, James, who was murdered in 62 CE.

- A teaching passed on by Papias, as quoted by Irenaeus in his *Against Heresies* 5.33.3–4.

- According to John the Presbyter in 1 John, Jesus said, "God is light and in him is no darkness at all."

I am now ready to move on to Part 2 and answer the Three Questions:

1. What did Jesus do?

2. What did Jesus say?

3. Who was Jesus?

I will answer the first question over the following five chapters by first providing some background on Palestine during Jesus' time and then see what we can say about his early life. I then establish some dates and build a detailed itinerary of Jesus activities through to his death, burial, and events after. I will then discuss the miracles he is alleged to have performed. Finally, I will answer the last two questions in Chapters 30 and 31 respectively.

# CHAPTER 25

# THE EARLY LIFE OF JESUS

## PALESTINE DURING JESUS' TIME

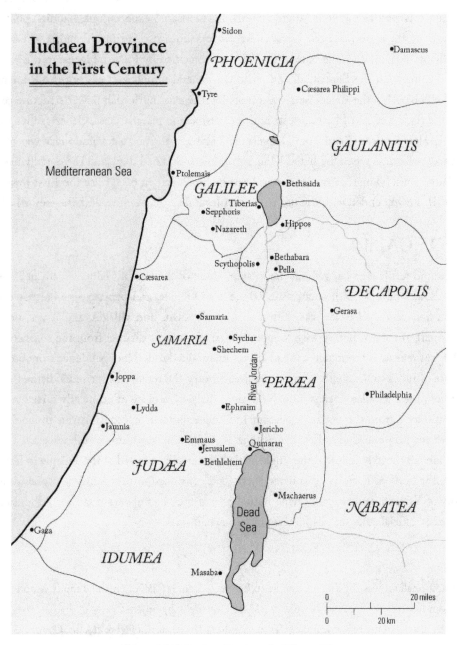

*Figure 25* **Palestine During the Time of Jesus.**

*Image courtesy of Andrew c via CC BY 3.0.*

Rome conquered Palestine in 63 BCE, ending Jewish independence. In 34 BCE, the Roman Senate appointed Herod the Great as "King of Judea," making him a vassal of Rome. He famously expanded the Second Temple[1] from 19 BCE onwards in a massive building program that finished—quite ironically—just before its destruction in 70 CE. Herod died in 4 BCE, and his kingdom was then split into Judea, Galilee, Peraea and Gaulanitis by the Romans between his three sons, as shown above. At the time of Jesus' youth, the Romans had dismissed one of the three sons, Archelaus, for incompetence and taken direct control of Judea (including Idumea and Samaria), making it a province of the empire.

Herod Antipas ruled Galilee and Peraea, and Herod Philip II ruled the area northeast of the Sea of Galilee, Batanea Auranitis or Gaulanitis. The major Roman province of Syria bordered the region at the top, and the Decapolis—an independent group of ten Greek cities—sat to the east. The Roman power centre was in Syria, where some legions were stationed. Syria's governor was also the regional military commander, outranking the Judean governor, since Judea was a relatively minor Roman holding.

First-century Palestine was very tumultuous. There were rising messianic expectations, bandits, political revolutionaries, and constant conflict ravaging the region. Various Jewish rebel leaders arose at this time: Theudas, "the Egyptian," Athronges (who declared himself "King of the Jews"), the Samaritan (who was crucified by Pilate), Hezekiah the bandit chief, Judas the Galilean, and others, including John the Baptist, all adding to the general tumult and placing the Romans and Jewish elites en-garde for possible rebellions. Also, the Essene sect was criticizing the existing Jewish power structure centred in Jerusalem, which was made up of the Sadducee and Pharisee sects and the aristocratic priestly class. Other groups were causing trouble for the authorities: the Zealots and the Sicarii (or "Daggermen") agitated to start a revolutionary war to expel the Romans. The first century encompassed a time when the hated King Herod the Great had died, and the equally hated Romans handed kingship to his much-hated sons. Numerous small riots and revolts finally led, in 66 CE, to the First Jewish-Roman War and a simultaneous civil war. This revolt ended with the destruction of Jerusalem, its Temple, and, thenceforth, Temple Judaism.[2]

## THE PEOPLE OF GALILEE

Galilee is a mountainous and fertile area lying along the western shore of the Sea of Galilee, north of Jerusalem. Small farms produced grapes, almonds, and olive oil; fisherman fished the Sea of Galilee; and papyrus was harvested along the banks of the Jordan River. In the first century, Galilee was dotted with small towns and villages, and it was not heavily populated. Historically, Galilee was part of the northern Jewish kingdom of Israel and was distinct from the southern Jewish kingdom of Judea. Although Galilee was repeatedly conquered, it had always maintained rough independence from both the conqueror and the surviving Jewish state of Judea to the south. During the first century, the region comprised a distinct cultural and religious mix, as it had been for centuries. "Galilee" means literally "nations district," a place of ethnically mixed semi-nomadic peoples with Hittite and Mitanni blood from the north. A peasant in Galilee under Emperor Tiberius probably would have shared relations, rituals, and customs from the Canaanites, Samaritans, Phoenicians, Assyrians, and Aramaeans.

While the Jewish urban elite strictly followed the single-male Yahweh cult, centred at the Temple in Jerusalem, the Galilean "people of the land,"[3] as the book of Ezra had dismissed them, had continued until recently to worship fertility deities, such as Asherah, the consort of Yahweh, and revered divine nature just as they had always done for a thousand years. Also, they followed, in varying degrees, official cults such as Judaism or Samaritanism.

---

1    So called since traditionally it was the second temple to be erected, in 516 BCE, on the Temple Mount in Jerusalem after the destruction of Solomon's Temple, the First Temple, in 587 BCE by the Babylonians.

2    For a more in-depth history of the region, please refer to (Sanders, *The Historical Figure of Jesus,* Chapter 3) and (Sanders, *Jewish Palestine at the Time of Jesus* 2021).

3    Ezra 10:10–11. In the 400s BCE, Ezra led a group of Jewish elites out of Babylon exile to Jerusalem and oversaw the enforcement of the Yahweh cult in part by calling on the Jews who had remained and intermarried, "the people of the land," to forsake their diverse religious practices and follow Yahweh.

The Galileans had a reputation; quite a few rebels came from Galilee, so they were seen as either admirable rebels or hotheads that needed to be put down. The Jerusalemites considered them as unsophisticated and coarse, and they apparently spoke with a distinct accent.[4]

As far as we know, Jesus probably spent most of his life in and around Galilee, including his ministry, apart from occasional festival trips to Jerusalem and several trips outside Palestine. Other than Jerusalem, we have no record of him teaching in any other urban setting, such as Sepphoris or Tiberius, the two leading Galilean cities, or Damascus, Caesarea, or Tyre. Jesus was a rural Galilean who grew up amongst the derogated "people of the land."[5]

## NAZARETH

Our evidence suggests that Jesus was born and raised in Nazareth. John states that he was known as Jesus of Nazareth to distinguish him from other people named Jesus (John 1:44, 18:5–7). Peter, however, specifies that Jesus came from Nazareth in Galilee, a helpful precision, for Nazareth was a very obscure place. John mentions that the disciple Nathanael derided Nazareth (John 1:46) and that people were generally confused by the suggestion that the Christ, or any prophet, could come from Galilee (John 7:41, 52). The titulus, or sign, on Jesus' cross also stated that he was from Nazareth (John 19:19).

Nazareth sits on the jagged brow of a windy hilltop at the end of a valley in lower Galilee. To the south, a high rocky ridge cuts off movement, while a gentle slope leads to the Sepphoris Valley to the north. It counted a few hundred relatively poor people with no roads in the early Roman period; it was just a huddle of houses. Everyone lived in simple dwellings with courtyards, some partially cut into the hillside. They raised a few crops and kept some animals. Recent excavations indicate that Nazareth was well served by at least three wells. There is no evidence of Hellenistic or Roman culture in Nazareth. The town appears to have been destroyed during the First Jewish-Roman War, for archaeologists have found that at that time, the stones of houses were quarried and then reused as tombs, which usually indicates a phase of depopulation. Mark says that Nazareth had a synagogue (Mark 6:1–2), like any other Jewish small town or large village. It is quite remarkable, though, that no ancient historian or geographer ever mentions Nazareth until the 200s or 300s CE. Josephus, the military governor of Galilee during the First Jewish-Roman War, mentions 45 cities and villages in Galilee, but not Nazareth. Neither the Mishnah nor the Talmud ever refers to it. Nazareth must have indeed been an obscure place.[6]

None of the sources in my Source List mentions the events in Jesus' life before his appearance at the Baptist's camp. As John and Peter would undoubtedly have had many opportunities to inquire into these, and since they were writing works meant to exalt Jesus' status, it is safe to assume that Jesus was not extraordinary—that he led an unremarkable early life. However, he seems to have undergone a radical change at some point in his life, as evidenced by the reactions of those who knew him. In one instance, as I mentioned earlier, his family showed up while he was teaching and tried to seize him because, they said, "he [was] out of his mind" (Mark 3:21). Later, his mother and brothers again attempted to contact him, but he rebuffed them (Mark 3:31–35). When Jesus taught in Nazareth, the people—most certainly including his friends and family —were "amazed," offended, and confused in equal measure; it seems that Jesus' behaviour had become totally out of character, and no one could recognize the man who had grown up around them (Mark 6:1–3; John 6:42, 7:5). In return, Jesus complained about his relatives (Mark 6:4, 6).

---

4    Interestingly "Galilean" was also a term for a cursed lawless person (G. Vermes, *Jesus the Jew: A Historian's Reading of the Gospels* 1981, 55).

5    For more detail see (G. Vermes, *Jesus the Jew: A Historian's Reading of the Gospels* 1981, 42–57).

6    For more information see (Aslan 2013, 25–33).

# FAMILY

*Figure 26 **A Typical House***

*A reconstruction of a typical house common to first-century Galilee, they typically had an interior courtyard, living quarters, storage areas, and a place for animals. This would have been the Galilean village environment familiar to Jesus and his followers.*

Jesus, as mentioned earlier, had a family. His mother was Mary, and he had brothers— James[7], Joses, Judas[8], and Simon—and at least two sisters (Mark 6:3, 15:40). Mary had a sister-in-law, also called Mary, who was married to Jesus' uncle Clopas (John 19:25). According to John, Jesus' father was Joseph (John 6:42, 1:45), although it seems that he was not around, for Jesus is consistently referred to as "Mary's son" (Mark 6:3). Perhaps Joseph had passed away before Jesus became a young man. It is also possible that he was born out-of-wedlock, since he is referred to as Mary's son in his hometown, which is very unusual.[9] In any case, Jesus undoubtedly had an extended family of grandparents, uncles, aunts, and cousins, like most people of the time.

---

7    Killed in 62 CE, according to Josephus.

8    Traditionally thought to be the author of Epistle of Jude.

9    There is an interesting speculation pursued by some scholars that Jesus was fathered by a Roman soldier named Panthera. Origen, in his work *Contra Celsum*, in which he refutes various attacks on Christianity made by Greek philosopher Celsus, mentions a rumour about Mary "when she was pregnant she was turned out of doors by the carpenter to whom she had been betrothed, as having been guilty of adultery, and that she bore a child to a certain soldier named Panthera," which he calls a fable. This rumour also seems to have circulated in Jewish rabbinic circles, which refer to a "Yeshu ben Pantera," or Jesus son of Pantera, Chullin 2:22–24. Interestingly, a tombstone for a Tiberius Julius Abdes Pantera (c. 22 BCE–40 CE) has been discovered, whose career it has been hypothesized by James Tabor in (J. D. Tabor 2006) would have placed him in Galilee around the time of Jesus' conception. However, this is all interesting speculation.

*Figure 27* ***The Father of Jesus?***

*After Jesus' death, there circulated a rumour among the opponents of Christianity that Jesus' mother had committed adultery with a Roman soldier named Panthera, or Pantera, and Jesus was his child. This tombstone, discovered in 1859 in Germany, is for a Tiberius Julius Abdes Pantera (c. 22 BCE–40 CE), an archer who came from Sidon, a city north of Galilee, so he probably spoke Aramaic. After Herod the Great's death in 4 BCE, rebellions broke out, serious enough for the Syrian military governor to bring three legions to Palestine. During that action, Sepphoris, which is just a few miles from Nazareth, was destroyed by the Romans. It could be that a young 18-year-old Pantera was serving in those legions that were in and around Galilee in 4 BC, which is close to the estimated time of Jesus' birth. It is also interesting to speculate that if he was born via adultery, did this contribute to the idea that he was born of a virgin? Is this also behind Luke's statement, "He was the son, so it was thought, of Joseph" Luke (3:24)? However, there is no way to know if this is true or not. Most scholars do not believe it to be true, since Pantera was a common name. Also, this whole story seems to be a polemic, plus the dating is off for this Pantera; according to his inscription, he did not join the Legions until age 22.[10] Image courtesy of JordiCuber via CC BY-SA 4.0.*

---

10    (Casey 2010, 153–154).

There is no evidence, even from polemicists, that Jesus ever married and had a family. However, it would have been relatively uncommon for a 30-year-old, first-century man to be single (and celibate?). Most men were expected to wed, perhaps as early as 18. Maybe an unknown wife of his had died at a young age, for death in childbirth was not unusual at the time. But we have absolutely no information on his marital status. Despite other family members, such as his brother James, being prominent within Early Church literature, there is no mention of a wife or offspring of Jesus; they would have been of interest to others. We can thus suppose that he was either never married or was a young widower with no children.

## PROFESSION

Peter-Mark calls him a *tekton* by profession,[11] which is commonly translated as "carpenter," but could also mean builder, mason, artisan, contractor, or handyman. This type of occupation would have required him to travel to seek work, for poor Nazareth would not have offered enough opportunities.

Sepphoris, the administrative city for Galilee, was only a 45-minute walk away from Nazareth and would have provided him with such opportunities. Affluent and cosmopolitan, it was heavily influenced by Greek culture and had a population of over 40,000. During Jesus' time, Sepphoris was undergoing a significant building program, since Herod Antipas, the ruler of Galilee, was transforming it into his royal capital city to become the "ornament of all of Galilee."[12] Along with his father and brothers, Jesus would have undoubtedly visited and worked there over the years witnessing urban Greco-Roman life, probably on public buildings and ornate houses for wealthy elite members. There is also no reason to doubt that Jesus might have travelled to other nearby settlements, such as Capernaum, Magadan, or Gennesaret, for all were within walking distance.

## EDUCATION

Jesus probably had no formal education. He belonged to the lowest class of society, namely peasants, just above beggars and slaves. Although nearly 97% of the Palestinian peasantry could neither read nor write, Mark alludes to the fact that Jesus could at least perform the former, for he regularly quoted scripture and taught in synagogues, which always involved reading. Craig E. Evans argues, "there is considerable contextual and circumstantial evidence that suggests that in all probability he was literate."[13] To what degree is unknown. Perhaps he had rudimentary religious training, enough to be familiar with the JS. He may have even picked up some writing ability from work; how this influenced his lack of written output, if at all, is unknown. He would have spoken Aramaic and probably some Greek too, for business. Hebrew was the language of the elite and scribes, and he would not have had much interaction with either.

---

11     Mark 6:3. Geza Vermes states the term for carpenter in Talmudic sayings stands for "scholar" or "learned man," perhaps linking to Jesus' suggested celibacy. (G. Vermes, *Jesus the Jew: A Historian's Reading of the Gospels* 1981, 21).

12     (Josephus, *The Antiquities of the Jews,* 2017, 18.27).

13     (Bockmuehl 2003, 17).

# CHAPTER 26

# THE DATES OF JESUS

Wat can be said about dating Jesus and his activities? No source gives a precise, dated chronology of his life, so we must rely on indirect evidence from a few sources that sometimes appear to conflict. However, we can reconstruct the chronology of his whereabouts with surprising precision. At the outset, in my opinion, we have only one firm date—the day of his death. Once I establish this date, I will work backwards and make some reasonable estimates to detail a chronology for Jesus.

## THE JEWISH CALENDAR AND FESTIVALS

The Jewish calendar is lunar; accordingly, the times of festivals shift each year. The Jewish day starts at sunset and ends with the next sunset. As for the weekly Sabbath, it lasted from Friday at dusk until Saturday—also at dusk—while the first day of the week was Sunday. At the time of Jesus, several festivals were held throughout the year, including the three pilgrimage festivals—Passover, Pentecost, and Tabernacles—in which all males had to visit the Temple in Jerusalem.

The annual Passover festival, also called the Feast of Unleavened Bread, commemorates the departure from Egypt of the ancient Israelites as told in the book of Exodus. The festival occurred on the fifteenth day of the month of Nisan (beginning at dusk), which typically falls in March or April. Occasionally, Passover would fall on the same day as a Sabbath; it would then be called "Special Sabbath" or "High Day." The typical Jewish family would offer a lamb or goat for sacrifice to the Temple priests on the afternoon of the fourteenth—the Preparation Day—and eat it with unleavened bread that evening after dusk as the Passover Meal, which would mark the beginning of the fifteenth and the Passover.

## A FRIDAY OR SATURDAY?

Now we need to establish the date of Jesus' death. John provides a clear and straightforward timeline. He states that Jesus died on the Preparation Day, and the next day was a "special Sabbath," that is, Passover was falling the next day on a Sabbath day, a Saturday. So Jesus died the day before, on a Friday. The Day of Preparation had started at dusk the previous evening (Thursday). Jesus attended the Last Supper, was arrested, brought before Pilate in the morning (John 19:42), then crucified, died, and was buried,[1] all on the Preparation Day.

Mark agrees with John that Jesus was killed and buried on the Preparation Day before the Sabbath (Mark 15:42). However, Mark is confused about the timing of the Last Supper; he says that "on the first day of the Feast of Unleavened Bread" they got ready to eat the Passover meal (Mark 14:12). The first day of Unleavened Bread is Passover, which conflicts with his later statement that Jesus died the day before Passover.

I take it as a given that John's chronology in this regard is the correct one. So Mark has the trial, death, and burial timing correct but was mistaken and placed the Last Supper—a day too late.

---

1  Jesus had to be buried before dusk, the start of the next day. "… the Jews did not want the bodies left on the crosses during the Sabbath," since Deuteronomy 21:22–23 commanded that dead bodies were not to be exposed overnight.

# DATE OF DEATH

According to my sources, Jesus was crucified when Pontius Pilate was procurator of Judea; he served from 26 to 36 CE. Jesus died on a Friday before a Saturday Passover. Colin J. Humphreys and W. G. Waddington[2] count only three dates during Pilate's rule that has a Friday falling on the day before Passover: April 9, 27 CE, April 5, 30 CE, and April 1, 33 CE.[3] We can eliminate two of these dates since they do not fit with other timelines based on two indirect dates: the start of Jesus' mission and the year of Jesus' first Passover, according to John (John 2:13).

## THE START OF JESUS' MISSION

Both Mark and John are clear that Jesus started his mission after encountering the Baptist. But when did this happen? In Luke's unique material, he carefully states that the Baptist began his mission in "the fifteenth year of the reign of Tiberius Caesar" (Luke 3:1–2). Tiberius became Roman emperor in September 14 CE; if Luke was using the Julian calendar (which is most likely, as it was the method used by Roman historians) and thereby followed the standard accession-year system,[4] the fifteenth year would have been the calendar year 29 CE (14+15). But if Luke was using the regal-year system,[5] the fifteenth year would be situated between September 28 to August 29 (14+15). Taking the outer dates of the two ranges means that the Baptist's mission must have started sometime between September 28 and the end of 29 CE, and Jesus' mission thus started no earlier than September 28. The first option, April 9, 27, therefore, for Jesus' death can be excluded as being far too early. Also, Pilate seems to have been prefect for some time before Jesus' death (Luke 13:1, 23:12), and he started his rule in 26; so again, April 9, 27 is too early for the crucifixion.

---

2    (Waddington and Humphreys 1992).

3    Humphreys and Waddington do their analysis using the old Julian Calendar and not the current Gregorian Calendar, introduced in 1582. In the first century, deducting two days converts from Julian to Gregorian, which I have done. Going forward, I will use Gregorian dates.

4    The first partial year that the emperor ruled would be called the Accession Year, and Year 1 would start at the New Year; in this case, year 15 CE would be Year 1.

5    Year 1 starts from the date of the first day of the reign, so in this case September 14 CE to August 15 CE would be Year 1.

*Figure 28* **The Jerusalem Temple Warning Inscription**

*It warns pagan visitors, in Latin and Greek, to go no further into the temple grounds on pain of death. Several of these warnings were placed around the temple to protect the temple precincts from defilement by non-Jews. This one was discovered in 1871 and reads, "No stranger is to enter within the balustrade round the temple and enclosure. Whoever is caught will be himself responsible for his ensuing death."[6] Image courtesy of Istanbul Archaeology Museums via CC BY-SA 3.0.*

## THE DATE OF JESUS' FIRST PASSOVER VISIT

John relates the first Passover visit in Jesus' mission in which he indicates that the Temple proper had taken 46 years to build (John 2:20). Josephus tells us about the start of the construction work in some (but not all) detail.[7] In 20 or 19 BCE, King Herod the Great made a speech stating his intention to refurbish and expand the Temple. The Jewish elite insisted he stockpile the necessary supplies (a thousand wagon loads) and train all the required workmen (a thousand) before starting any demolition work, which he did. Assuming that some time elapsed to do the preparation work—say a year or two—and remembering there is no year 0, 46 years later means that the construction referred to was finished at the earliest by 26 CE, and at the latest in 30 CE, according to scholarly estimates.[8] If he started his mission at the earliest in September 28, the earliest possible Passover visit for Jesus would be the Passover of spring 29 CE.

John also reports that Jesus attended at least three Passover festivals during his mission (John 2:13, 6:4, 11:55) and was crucified at the last one. Mark, however, only reports Jesus' last Passover visit to Jerusalem. John mentions other visits by Jesus to Jerusalem for feasts, and he names them all except one (John 5:1), which may have been another Passover or another festival. Assuming these are consecutive Passover festivals, it seems that Jesus attended either three (or four) Passover festivals in total, which would indicate a mission time of two-plus (or three-plus) years. Jesus thus attended at least two more Passovers after his first, the earliest being spring 29 CE; if I add two more years, the absolute earliest the crucifixion could have occurred would be at the Passover of 31. Therefore, I can exclude the second date, April 5, 30, for Jesus' death, as it is too early.

---

6    (Palestine Exploration Fund 1872, 132).

7    Josephus, *Antiquities of the Jews*, 15.11.

8    If 20 BCE, the year of Herod's speech, is Year 1 and very little time was taken to ready the work, then the 46th year is 26 CE. At the other extreme, if Year 1 is the construction start, the speech was in 19 BCE, and it took two years to start, Year 1 is 17 BCE, and the 46th is 29 CE. We should add an extra year to account for the possibility that the person speaking of 46 years to build is speaking of whole years in the past, and completion was not until the 47th year of construction. Adding this last addition makes 30 CE the absolute latest date.

## THE MYSTERY FESTIVAL OF 5.1

In John 5:1, John is uncharacteristically vague: "Sometime later, Jesus went up to Jerusalem for a feast of the Jews." Was this mystery festival a Passover festival? Did Jesus visit three or four Passovers in John? I believe the number is 3; that is, the mystery festival was not a Passover festival. Indeed, John is generally meticulous about chronology; he would not have left out a Passover festival, as he was careful to mention all the others, even the one that Jesus did not attend (the second one). Besides, not enough events seem to have passed between the 2:13 Passover festival and the 5:1 festival for it to be a whole year. John says that Jesus spent "some time" in the countryside, travelled to Galilee with a brief stop in Samaria, and then "sometime later" went back to Jerusalem for the mystery festival. No other festivals are mentioned, which is odd if there was a year interval. There were also five festivals per year, so the mystery festival was most probably a non-Passover festival.

So what festival was it? It was probably one of the other two pilgrimage festivals (Pentecost or Tabernacles). I think it is the Tabernacles Festival that John is mentioning. Why? There are four reasons. First, Pentecost is a one-day festival, while Tabernacles is a seven-day festival, so it seems more likely that the multiday travel from Galilee to Jerusalem would be expended for a more extended festival rather than a single day festival. Second, the crowds would be bigger for Tabernacles, making it easier for Jesus to reach out to more people than during Pentecost. Peter has Jesus in Galilee that summer when the wheat was mature, which in Galilee precisely occurs around Pentecost.[9] And finally, John does not mention Jesus ever attending a Pentecost but specifically mentions Jesus going to Tabernacles and Hannukah in 32 CE, so Pentecost does not seem to have been a preferred festival for Jesus. So I conclude John 5:1 is referring to the Tabernacle Festival of 31 CE, held September 17 to 24.

## APRIL 1, 33 CE

This leaves us with the remaining date of April 1, 33 CE, for Jesus' death. However, given the constraints I mentioned above, does this date fit?

If there were indeed only three Passover visits and we work backwards to date all the Passovers found in John, then Jesus was crucified at the 33 CE Passover. His previous (second) Passover day (John 6:4) must be in the year 32, and the first Passover visit (John 2:13) must refer to the year 31 CE. A 31 CE visit fits with the completion year of the sanctuary, since 30 is the absolute latest estimate for that completion.

This dating also fits with the start of the Baptist's mission. Jesus could have met the Baptist anywhere from September 28 to just before Passover 31 CE at the latest. It seems most likely that Jesus started his mission in early 31, since John chronicles a short time, or "days," (John 2:1) between the Baptist pointing out Jesus and Jesus getting his first followers, going to the wedding in Cana, and spending "a few days" (John 2:12) in Capernaum before going to the first Passover festival in 31. This also makes sense since it would take time for the Baptist's message and fame to spread and attract the crowds that had gathered; a movement like this could easily have taken months to get started before Jesus arrived on the scene.

Therefore, Jesus most likely started his mission in early 31 CE and died on April 1, 33.

# DATE OF BIRTH

None of my sources provides any direct indication of the year in which Jesus was born. All that is available is John's comment that Jesus was "not even fifty years old" during his mission (John 8:57). Casting further afield to imperfect Matthew and Luke, we can make some estimates based on their indirect information. Matthew, in turn, states that Jesus was born during Herod's reign (Matthew 2:1). The latter reigned from 37 BCE to March 4 BCE, while Jesus was still a "child" in Egypt, writes Matthew (Matthew 2:14–15). As for Luke, he places Jesus' birth during the Census of Quirinius (6 to 7 CE) (Luke 1:5, 2:1–2). Luke also says that "Jesus himself was about 30 years old when he began his ministry" (Luke 3:23).

---

9    (Morrison n.d.).

We have no other information about Jesus' age. Unfortunately, Matthew and Luke contradict one another by about 15 years, making their chronology unreliable. Luke also seems to contradict himself: if Jesus was born in 6 or 7 CE (Luke 2:1–2), then he would have been in his early twenties when he began his ministry in 31, not a vague "about thirty." There must have been separate age traditions, which Luke put in his Gospel without reconciling. I am inclined to set aside Matthew and Luke's comments on birth date, as both their birth narratives are quite fantastic. As for the "about thirty" remark in Luke, it must have come from a separate and unique tradition. In any case, it points to the fact that Jesus was still young enough to start his ministry but seasoned enough to have some measure of authority. If we allow "about thirty" to correspond to, say, between 28 and 32 years of age, and assume he started his ministry in 31 CE, this places his birth between 1 BCE and 3 CE (again, there is no year 0).[10] However, we only have a passing comment from unreliable Luke as evidence. Therefore, at his death in 33 CE, Jesus would have been aged between 30 and 34 years old.

Given the dates I have established along with dates of the festivals he visited,[11] it is possible to flesh out the timeline of Jesus' life and mission:

- He was born between 1 BCE to 3 CE.

- John the Baptist's mission started sometime in late 28 or 29 and continued until his arrest.

- Jesus met and might have been baptized by the Baptist in late 30 or early 31 CE, and after some short interval, during which Jesus spent some time on his own ("in the desert for forty days") (Mark 1:13), he started his mission in early 31.

- He visited Jerusalem for the first Passover starting on March 24, 31 (John 2:13).

- Jesus went to Jerusalem for the pilgrimage Festival of Tabernacles, September 17 to 24, 31 CE (John 5:1).

- Jesus was away from Jerusalem in Galilee for the second Passover 32 CE starting on April 12 (John 6:4).

- He attended the Feast of Tabernacles between October 6 and 13, 32 CE and the Eighth Day of Assembly on the fourteenth (John 7:2, 37).

- He was in Jerusalem for the Feast of Dedication between December 14 and 22, 32 CE (John 10:22).

- Jesus came to Jerusalem for the third and last Passover, which started on April 2, 33 CE (John 11:55).

- Jesus died around 3:00 p.m. (Mark 15:34) on Friday, April 1, 33 and would have been placed in the tomb around 6:00 p.m. at the latest, since Passover started at dusk.

- Reportedly, Mary Magdalene (with others she mentions) found the tomb empty on the "first day of the week" (Mark 16:9; John 20:1) early in the morning, before or at sunrise, at about 6:30 a.m. on Sunday, April 3, 33.

## THE DATES OF JOHN THE BAPTIST

The mission of the Baptist starts before Jesus' and parallels it until the Baptist is arrested. If I can establish some timeline for the Baptist, it will help me in dating the points of contact between the two missions and fill in Jesus' timeline. I have already established two dates associated with the Baptist: the start of his mission, which occurred sometime in late 28 or 29 CE and continued until he was arrested, and the date when Jesus met him, that is, late 30 or early 31 CE.

According to John, Jesus left Jerusalem after the Passover of 31 and spent "some time" in the Judean countryside with his followers. John is careful to state that this was before the Baptist was arrested, suggesting the arrest was soon after this

---

10   The Sources give no date for Jesus' birth; it is almost certainly not December 25, which was the Roman Solstice and which several cults considered as a sacred day, including the Sol Invictus, the victorious sun cult. Christians may have re-interpreted the victorious sun as the victorious son, Jesus, and kept the festival date. (Sheldon 2018).

11   I use hecal.com for the Gregorian calendar dates of ancient Jewish festivals.

time (John 3:22–24). The Baptist was located across the River Jordan in the region of Peraea, ruled by Herod Antipas.[12] John then states something odd:

"The Pharisees heard that Jesus was gaining and baptizing more disciples than John [the Baptist], although in fact it was not Jesus who baptized, but his disciples. When the Lord learned of this, he left Judea and went back once more to Galilee. Now he had to go through Samaria." (John 4: 1–4)

It is not clear what "this" refers to. Attention from the Pharisees? Or is something else not mentioned? Whatever it was caused Jesus to leave Judea immediately for Galilee, and he "had" to go through Samaria, the implication being that this was not the preferred route.[13] It must be that Herod Antipas had arrested the Baptist, and Jesus heard that his activities had come to the notice of the authorities in Judea, so he feared arrest also because he too was attracting crowds.[14]

Jesus then decided that it was time to go to the relative safety of Galilee via the less popular route, through Samaria. So the arrest of the Baptist most probably happened in April 31, at the tail end of the rainy season, "there was plenty of water" (John 3:23), and while the arrestee was still in Herod's territory (John 3:22–26). This sequence squares with Peter's account that after the Baptist was arrested by Herod and held in prison,[15] Jesus went to Galilee and started his Galilean mission (Mark 1:14–6:15). The next we hear, after Jesus spends some time in Galilee and just before the Feeding of the Five Thousand, Peter states Herod has beheaded the Baptist (Mark 6:16). John has a parallel account of the Feeding of the Five Thousand, which he says happened when (the next) Passover of 32 CE "was near" (John 6:4). That year, Passover occurred between April 12 and 20, 32. Consequently, according to my best estimate, the Baptist was imprisoned in April 31 and was dead by Spring 32.

## JOHN THE BAPTIST AND JESUS

I find the relationship between Jesus and the Baptist confusing. Both Peter and John say that the Baptist preached about the coming of one greater than him. According to John, the Baptist subsequently declared Jesus the Son of God and the Lamb of God from afar, but the two men do not seem to have ever met—indeed, the Baptist "did not know him" but for a supernatural descend of the Spirit in the form of a dove (John 6:4). John, whose Gospel I prefer to follow, does not say that Jesus was baptized. Peter-Mark says the Baptist baptized Jesus, but I showed earlier that Peter was not present for this event, so baptism remains unclear. Jesus did not follow the Baptist and maintained a separate ministry. So why was Jesus in the vicinity of the Baptist, and what was their relationship?[16] Despite his initial identification of Jesus, the Baptist seems to be confused by his actions; he dispatches some disciples to question Jesus about his status, asking him: "Are you the one to come, or are we to expect someone else?" (Q 7:18–19) I am thus inclined to think that Jesus was not the leader that the Baptist was expecting.[17]

Now that I have established an overall sequence anchored with the dates I have supplied, I will work through Jesus' mission itinerary in detail up to the Last Supper.

---

12    John says the Baptist was at Aenon near Salim. There is debate whether this was on the Judean (west) or Peraean (east) side of the river; however, as the Baptist was arrested by Herod, it must have been on the east side where he had jurisdiction. In support, the Madaba Map places Aenon near Salim on the east side near Jericho, where the road from Jerusalem crosses the Jordan.

13    There were two major routes from Jerusalem to Galilee: the main north-south Roman road on the further side of the River Jordan, or the local north road that ran through Samaria. As there was long standing enmity between the Samaritans and Jews, the latter route was the least favoured route to Galilee. See also (Capper, The New Covenant Network in Southern Palestine at the Arrest of Jesus 2003, 17).

14    John 4:3–4 and Josephus *Antiquities* 18:118–119.

15    Josephus' account also corroborates this by mentioning the Baptist was imprisoned and killed at Herod's nearby castle of Machaerus, which was just 25 kilometres south from Aenon near Salim. Josephus, *Antiquities of the Jews*, 18.5.2.

16    Perhaps Jesus was present for the same reason he seems to have attended the Jerusalem festivals, the presence of crowds of receptive people.

17    To add to the confusion, Josephus does speak of the Baptist's teaching in *Antiquities* 18:117 but does not mention the Baptist signalling a future leader.

# CHAPTER 27

# JESUS' ITINERARY

*Figure 29 **Ancient Road Atlas***

*A close up of the Tabula Peutingeriana, a 1200s CE copy of an original Roman road atlas showing all the roads in the Roman Empire. It is thought to be based on a map created during the reign of Emperor Augustus (Pompeii is still shown although destroyed in 79 CE), with later additions. This section shows Palestine, with the North to the right and the West at the top, where the island of Rhodes can be seen. Jerusalem can be seen above the orange blob, centre left (Mont Oliveti, or "Mount of Olives"). The city is also labelled as Aelia Capitolina, as Emperor Hadrian had renamed it. The Dead Sea is below, and the River Jordan runs from the Sea of Galilee right to left, with Tiberius (Tyberus) on its shore. The major north-south Roman road can be seen below and parallel to the River Jordan. Image courtesy of the Austrian National Library.*

In this section, I want to see how far I can go in creating an integrated timeline for Jesus' actions and movements by dating events and naming places to answer: What did Jesus do? My sources provide me with some time and place markers, so I will thus weave these together to create a detailed narrative of Jesus' actions.

Apart from John and Peter-Mark, the other sources in my Source List yield almost no markers. Therefore, I will rely on John and Peter-Mark to obtain the correct overall sequence of events. If Peter-Mark states that Jesus stayed x days in some place, then I will rely on this information. It is to be remembered that Jesus' operational area was small and easily accessible on foot over a few days. For instance, the distance between the tip of the Sea of Galilee and Jerusalem is around 200 kilometres and can be walked by a healthy person within four to six days. Most other trips could be made in much less time; for instance, Jerusalem is about 45 kilometres away from Bethany-Beyond-Jordan, which could be walked in a day or two, so little time is to be assumed for travel.

## MARKERS FROM THE SOURCES

A marker is any information that establishes the time or location for Jesus. For instance, if Jesus went to Jerusalem for Passover and we know the year, we have the location and dates of his presence. I have assembled all the markers in my Source List. As I noted earlier, John did not see the need to rehash Peter's information, so there is not much in the way of overlap between their stories. The two narratives start together with the Baptist in early 31 CE, diverge, and then come together at the Last Supper in late March 33 CE, where I will stop this section and pick up the Passion Narrative in the next chapter.

## O. JOHN THE BAPTIST

Late 28 or 29 CE onwards (Mark 1:1–8; John 1:6-28; Q 3:02–3:17).

John the Baptist started his mission in late 28 or 29 CE. Both John and Peter-Mark start their Gospels with the Baptist baptizing people in the Jordan River (or the springs and brooks near it, as the main river could be treacherous) at a place called Bethany-Beyond-Jordan, probably at the current site of Al-Maghtas on the eastern bank of the Jordan. The old road from Jerusalem via Jericho crosses the Jordan nearby, making it accessible to the people in Judea and Jerusalem who came to him (about one- or two-days travel). The Baptist attracted crowds, followers, and the interest of the Jewish religious leaders.

## 1. JESUS APPEARS, THEN TO GOES GALILEE.

Early 31 CE (Mark 1:9–13; John 1:28–2:1; Q 3:21–4:13).

Jesus appears at the Baptist's mission at the opening in Peter's and John's narratives. He must have heard of John in Galilee and was attracted to his mission for the crowds. Peter says that he was baptized, but John does not mention this; instead, he says that the Baptist saw the "Spirit" descend on and remain on Jesus. Also, the Baptist states that he did not know who Jesus was until he saw that sign. Jesus then immediately collected some followers and started his mission, so he was not a follower of John. Peter implies that something transformative occurred around this time; he went to a remote area by himself for a while (or a long time, i.e., "forty days"), but we have no eyewitness details.[1]

At the time, John and Andrew were disciples of the Baptist. They were both present when the Jewish authorities interrogated the Baptist over a few days and directly heard his testimony on Jesus. John, the evangelist, carefully related this testimony, saying that "John gave [it]," as well as where and when the event occurred. Afterwards, he and Andrew met Jesus and decided to follow him (at about 10:00 a.m., "the tenth hour"). Jesus later met Andrew's brother—Peter, Phillip, and Nathanael—who all seemed to be associated with the Baptist because they were nearby. They started following him as well; the exact timing is not precise, however. Jesus, and presumably this group, then went to Galilee—a journey of two or three days—to the village of Cana, the hometown of Nathanael, where they were all invited to a wedding, witnessed by John. It is on that occasion that Jesus turned a large amount of water into wine. They then stayed in Capernaum, the hometown of Phillip, Andrew, and Peter, for a few days. I assume that John was not present since we have no details; he must have returned to Jerusalem.

---

1        I am inclined to think Jesus had his transformative experience first and then mingled in the Baptist's crowd seeking followers, since it included many young people seeking spiritual guidance. I do not think Jesus was baptized, as he was intent on starting his own independent mission, and John is explicit that Jesus did not himself baptize during his mission. As soon as he collected some followers, he straight away left the Baptist's camp, never to return. It is not clear what the Baptist means by the "Spirit."

## 2. JERUSALEM PASSOVER 31 CE

Late March 31 CE (John 2:13–3:21; Mark 11:15–16).

*Figure 30* ***The Southern Temple Steps***

*These steps were built by Herod the Great as part of his expansion of the Temple Mount in Jerusalem. They lead to a double gate and a triple gate in the south retaining wall, now bricked up, which would be used by pilgrims to access the Temple above. They were buried in 70 CE after the destruction of the Temple and excavated in 1967. These original steps were undoubtedly used by Jesus in his visits to Jerusalem.*

Jesus then travelled to Jerusalem for the 31 CE Passover Festival, occurring March 25 to the 31 of that year. John was present when Jesus drove out the animal sellers and money changers from the Temple's courts and attempted to stop the flow of merchandise. While in Jerusalem, Jesus performed unspecified, miraculous signs, which gathered a following. But due to the upset in the Temple, he probably needed to keep out of sight, so he had a nocturnal meeting with a member of the Sanhedrin, Nicodemus, at which John was also present.

## 3. JUDEA AND GALILEE

April 31 to April 32 CE (John 3:22–4:54; Mark 1:14–6:31; Q 4:16, 7:01–7:24; 10:13–15).

Jesus and his followers left Jerusalem and were in the Judea countryside, somewhere west of the Jordan, baptizing. Jesus spent some of his time there, as the Jewish authorities were still undoubtedly looking for him. John was not present, however, since there are no details in his Gospel about that period. The Baptist was also baptizing, at Aenon, a spring near Salim, probably east of the Jordan. But Jesus' group appeared to be drawing more adherents than the Baptist.

Suddenly, Jesus went back to Galilee because Herod Antipas arrested the Baptist across the river, and the Judean authorities were turning their unwelcome attention to Jesus' movement.[2] He and his disciples decided to go through Samaria, the less popular route north, versus crossing the Jordan and going up east of the Jordan in Peraea, where Herod Antipas had jurisdiction. After a day or two, they arrived at Jacob's Well near the Samarian town of Sychar, at dawn "the sixth hour" (John 4:6), or 6:00 a.m., indicating a stealthy night journey. As related by an eyewitness referred to as the "Samaritan woman," Jesus interacted with her at the well while the disciples were in town. After two days,[3] they continued toward Galilee, which is a day's travel.

Jesus was then welcomed by many Galileans who had heard and seen him during the recent Jerusalem festival. He then returned to Cana and met a royal official (the eyewitness) from Capernaum, who had an ill son. Jesus healed him around 7:00 a.m. (the seventh hour), but the official only found out on the road going home the next day.

This is the start of the bulk of Jesus' time in Galilee, as narrated by Peter, who accompanied Jesus for this part of the mission. John does not appear to have gone to Galilee; he probably accompanied Jesus as far as Samaria and then soon turned back to Jerusalem, since he has nothing to say about this Galilean mission except for the Five Thousand Feeding event, which he repeats. Peter must have stayed in Galilee when Jesus departed back in March to go to the Passover. Peter returned to fishing; after all, he did have a family to support in Capernaum, a fishing village on the Sea of Galilee. Jesus then went to Capernaum and reconnected with the fishermen Peter, Andrew, John, and James by the seaside, who followed him. Mark's timeline is a little murky here; there is no precise start time, aside from a reference to the Baptist, who had just been imprisoned. We mostly have a sequence of events with some place markers but no absolute time markers. However, a reference to Jesus and his disciples eating raw grain (Mark 2:23) indicates an early summer 31 CE time, and again springtime, since the grass is green (Mark 6:39), which corresponds to the April 32 Passover timing that John provides in his overlapping material at that point. John's time markers allow me to place bookend dates around Peter's Galilean account, that is, April 31 CE to October 32 CE.[4]

Jesus taught and healed in the Capernaum synagogue on the Sabbath. People were amazed, and the news spread. The crowds went to Andrew and Peter's house, where Peter lived with his wife and family in Capernaum and where Jesus healed Peter's mother-in-law. That same evening, large crowds gathered around him, and he healed many people brought to him.

2    This suggests a conspiracy between Judean and Herodian authorities regarding the Baptist and Jesus. Mark 3:6 relates how soon after this, while Jesus was in Galilee, the Pharisees, the Judean authorities, and the Herodians, Herod Antipas' people, were still conspiring to kill Jesus.

3    Samaria was a good resting place, as it was probably out of reach of the Jewish authorities in Jerusalem.

4    If this Galilee mission sequence seems vague it is because Mark provides no overall structure for the narrative— as explained, the latter consists of a collection of discrete stories strung together into a stream.

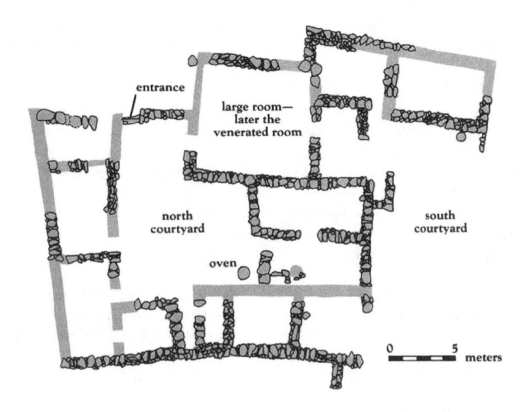

*Figure 31* **Peter's House.**

*The layout for a house found under a 400s CE ruined basilica in Capernaum. The lowest layer indicates an average house from the mid-100s BCE to the mid-100s CE, with a large room (about 20 feet by 20 feet) plastered and given a permanent roof (unusual in Capernaum for houses of the time) and turned into a public space, probably as it was the room Jesus taught and healed in. In the 300s CE, walls were built around the house, turning it into a public compound. A pilgrim visiting sometime between 381 to 395 CE said this was Peter's house and that although it was now used as a church, the original house walls had been left unchanged. In the second half of the 400s, the house church was covered over, and a new octagonal church was built on top, centred on the main room below. A pilgrim visiting in the 560s remarked on Peter's House now being a basilica. The basilica was destroyed in the 600s. It has been excavated and can be seen today. Image reproduced by permission from Studium Biblicum Franciscanum Photographic Archive .*

## CAPERNAUM

Capernaum was a prosperous Jewish fishing village on the upper north shore of the Sea of Galilee, close to where the River Jordan entered the sea. As a first point of entry from Jordan, it had a custom toll house (Mark 2:14) and probably a small garrison of Herod's troops—Q mentions a centurion or a military officer in Capernaum (Q 7:1,3). It seems that Peter and Andrew's house in Capernaum was Jesus' main base in Galilee. It was situated just a couple of doors away from the synagogue. This part of Capernaum has been excavated. Archaeologists notably uncovered the layout of a house under a 400s ruined basilica in Capernaum that corresponds to Peter's house.

Mark's chronology is not entirely clear after this. The next day, Jesus and his disciples travelled throughout Galilee, teaching and healing. Jesus healed a man with some skin disease. Despite trying to keep his healings secret, the news spread to the point that he could no longer enter towns. He thus returned to Capernaum after a few days, and another crowd developed around Peter's house. There he taught, and he healed a person with paralysis lowered through the straw roof because too many people blocked the entrance to the house. He called Levi, the tax (or toll) collector, and ate at his home. He further taught and healed and then started to have run-ins with the Pharisees, especially over his Sabbath activities. The latter eventually approached Herod Antipas' people to have Jesus killed, since Herod had the authority to do so in Galilee. Meanwhile, Jesus healed a man with a shrivelled hand on a Sabbath in front of a crowd in the synagogue. He then selected the Twelve Apostles.[5]

## WHO WERE THE TWELVE?

Typically, this would be a contentious question, for Mark, Matthew, and Luke have different sets of names for the Twelve. But since I have decided to discard Matthew and Luke's information, and John does not enumerate the Twelve Apostles, we can rely on Peter-Mark's list to inform us. It reads as follows:

"These are the twelve he appointed: Simon (to whom he gave the name Peter); James son of Zebedee and his brother John (to them he gave the name Boanerges, which means Sons of Thunder); Andrew, Philip, Bartholomew, Matthew, Thomas, James son of Alphaeus, Thaddaeus, Simon the Zealot and Judas Iscariot, who betrayed him." (Mark 3:16–19)

Jesus thus gave nicknames to Peter (Rock) and brothers James and John (Sons of Thunder). Jesus further gave them the authority to represent him in preaching and healing.

After Jesus had performed miracles, healings, and selected the Twelve, even more people were drawn from the whole region, and crowds accompanied him everywhere he went, many seeking healing for themselves and relatives.[6] Jesus took to teaching from a boat near the shore to address the many people. He also visited the Galilean villages of Chorazin and Bethsaida.

# 4. TABERNACLES FESTIVAL 31 CE, BACK TO GALILEE

Mid-September 31 CE (John 5:1–5:47).

*Figure 32* **Codex Vaticanus 354.**

*This codex is a Greek copy of the four Gospels and the earliest cursive version precisely dated. The scribe's name was Michael, a monk who finished his work as follows: "In the month of March, the fifth day, the sixth hour, the year 6457, the seventh indication." That is, about noon, March 5, 949 CE. This section is from John 5:4, about an angel stirring up the waters in the Pool of Bethesda. Michael marked the story of the angel with asterisks as being dubious.*

---

5     Also called The Twelve Disciples, however Peter uses the term "apostles."

6     Jesus healed for free contrary to the other healers and priests at that time, increasing his appeal.

Jesus returned to Jerusalem for the Feast of Tabernacles starting on September 17 that year. There is no break in Peter-Mark to indicate when this occurred in Peter's account. Jesus healed a lame man (either he or John were the eyewitness) at the colonnaded Sheep Gate Pool (Bethesda) on a Sabbath day, perhaps on September 20, the only Sabbath during the festival. Jesus told him to walk and carry his mat and then slipped away. Unfortunately, carrying a mat violated Sabbath rules and led to a confrontation between the man, Jesus, and certain Jews. Jesus' actions on the Sabbath launched a persecution against him. He responded with a lengthy discourse, mentioning the embassy sent to the Baptist earlier in the year. John says that Jesus went back to Galilee "sometime after" the festival (John 6:1). He then breaks off his story and jumps ahead to April 32 CE.

## THE POOL OF BETHESDA

*Figure 33 **A Portion of the Pool of Bethesda***

*This is the only part of the pools still visible today. This view shows a portion of the original steps down into the eastern edge of the southern and lower pool, the wall on the upper left is where the colonnade separating the north and southern pool would have stood. This could be the site of the healing; as those seeking healing would gather on the edges of the south pool when water was released into it from the northern pool. These steps along with those on the western side would have been the closest they could gather to the released water (the water "troubled" by the angel).*

The Pool has been partially excavated.[7] It was laid out with two pools, north and south, side by side, one slightly higher than the other. Four colonnaded arcades ran around the outside, and a fifth ran across the middle, separating the two pools. The complex in Jesus' day was probably an Asclepion, a pagan healing centre dedicated to the God of healing and well-being, Asclepius. Such centres were numerous across the empire, and this one probably served the Roman garrison stationed in the nearby Antonia Fortress. As a result of its pagan association, the complex and pools were located outside the city walls, away from the Jewish part of town. The water was "stirred" whenever freshwater was released from the upper reservoir into the lower one. People seeking treatment from the god apparently entertained the superstitious belief that this stirring effect was an opportune time for immersion. Later, scribes Christianized the phenomenon by linking it to the action of an angel. When Jesus told the healed man to sin no more, he assuredly meant "do not appeal to a false pagan god for help." Jesus must have then returned to Galilee after the festival.

Q has two free-floating reports that are probably from Jesus' period in Galilee since they do not fit anywhere else in our timeline. The first claims that Jesus healed a centurion's son (or serving boy) in Capernaum, and the second has to do with the Baptist who, while in prison, inquired of Jesus, asking if he was the one expected. Since the Baptist would appear to still be alive at this time, this would have to be before April 32 CE and thus occurred during this interval. As mentioned earlier, the Q sayings log springs from Jesus' time in Galilee, so the sayings it contains must date from April 31 to October 32 CE.

---

7    Please also see (Lizorkin-Eyzenberg 2014) & (Biblical Archaeology Society Staff, The Bethesda Pool, Site of One of Jesus' Miracles 2018).

His family thought he was crazy, Mary and his brothers came to take him away, and the teachers of the laws accused him of demon possession. He taught the crowds with many parables and explained them to his disciples and the others "around him" (Mark 4:10).

One evening, after teaching the crowd from the boat, Jesus and his group crossed over the Sea of Galilee. A storm arose, and Jesus "calm(ed) it," which terrified his disciples (Mark 4:38–40). Later, they arrived in the "region of the Gerasenes," which probably refers to the fertile Valley of Kursi, which is midway on the eastern shore of the sea. That region was part of a non-Jewish Hellenized area called the Decapolis (the "Ten Cities"), with several urban centres nearby, including Hippos, Gedara, and Gerasa. This would explain the presence of pigs, unclean animals in Judaism, in the story from the man of the tombs. There Jesus healed the man, but the locals asked Jesus to leave. The man then spread an embellished version of his story around the Decapolis (Mark 5:20).

Jesus later returned to the other side of the sea (probably to Capernaum), where crowds gathered. He healed the daughter of a man called Jairus, the "ruler" of the synagogue (Mark 5:35), and a bleeding woman, our eyewitnesses.

Jesus and his disciples then went to Nazareth, where he taught in the synagogue and performed healings. Some people who knew him and his family took offence at his teaching. He toured around Galilee again and sent his disciples out in pairs to teach and heal.

When Herod Antipas heard about Jesus, John the Baptist was already dead, beheaded sometime before.

The disciples then returned to Capernaum.

## 5. GALILEE

April 32 CE (Mark 6:32–7:23; John 6:1–71).

Apart from the Passion Narrative, this sequence is uniquely told by both John and Peter. John came up from Jerusalem to visit, perhaps when he found out Jesus did not plan to go to Jerusalem for Passover, and as discussed in Chapter 18, felt the need to re-tell his version.

Close to the Passover Festival of 32 CE (April 13 to 20), Jesus and his disciples went by boat to "a solitary place" to rest on the far side of the Sea of Galilee. Still, crowds of people followed on foot, indicating the group was probably in the region beyond Bethsaida.[8] Jesus went to a mountainside from where he taught the people, and then Jesus' followers fed about 5,000 men.[9] In response to this miracle, Jesus was concerned that the crowd might act on messianic expectations and declare him the Messiah. Therefore, he told his disciples to get in the boat and head west to Capernaum while he went off by himself. Between 3:00 and 6:00 a.m. (the fourth watch in the Roman time system), the disciples, including John, rowing against a contrary wind, saw Jesus walking on water about five or six kilometres out from shore, come near, and embark on the boat. They were amazed and confused.

They all landed across the Sea at Gennesaret (Kinessaert) to the south of Capernaum. Again, crowds gathered, and people arrived in boats from the other side, confused as to how Jesus had crossed over unseen. Both Peter and John relate that Jesus gave two important speeches related to consumption. At the synagogue in Capernaum, his teaching caused many followers to drop away, but the Twelve remained (John 6:66–68).

Jesus later clashed with the Pharisees about purity laws and taught further. He then arrived at "the house," in Capernaum, Peter's presumably, where he explained some of his teachings. He also healed people in the marketplace by touch and by them touching his cloak.

---

8    According to John 1:44, Bethsaida was the hometown of Phillip, Andrew, and Peter. The exact location of Bethsaida is still being debated. According to Josephus, *Antiquities* 18.2.1 and *Wars* 2.9.1, it lay in Herod Phillip's domain at the northern tip of the Sea of Galilee just east of where the Jordan flows into the sea. Apparently, there must have been a river crossing there, given the odd fact although Jesus and his followers sailed across the sea, the crowds followed on foot to their location.

9    Both John and Peter accurately relate the fact that it would have cost eight months' salary, or 200 denarii, to feed all those people.

## 6. GALILEE

May 32 to September 32 CE (Mark 7:24–9:50; John 7:1).

John left Jesus at this point, as John had no details to relate until Jesus arrived in Jerusalem in October 32 CE for the Tabernacles Feast.

Avoiding Judea due to the threat from the religious officials, Jesus headed anonymously north to the region around Tyre. Along the way, he "healed" a Syrophoenician woman's daughter, her mother being our eyewitness. Jesus then travelled south into the Decapolis, where he healed a deaf man (the witness). Jesus was probably on his own for this trip, as neither John nor Peter provide any detail.

Jesus then fed 4,000 men, with the disciples present, and then headed by boat to the region of Dalmanutha, an unknown location, perhaps on the northwest coast of the Sea of Galilee. There he had another run-in with Pharisees, taught, and sailed back over to Bethsaida, where he healed a blind man whom he swore to secrecy (and who is our witness). Jesus and his disciples then went to the villages around Caesarea Philippi, which is north of Bethsaida. He told his disciples not to say that he was the Messiah and taught some more. After six days—and it is unclear whether this was after arriving near Caesarea Philippi—Peter had a hallucination or a vivid dream: the Transfiguration (Mark 9:2–8).

Crowds gathered, and Jesus healed a man's son after the disciples had failed to cure him. They then returned to Peter and Andrew's house in Capernaum, where Jesus continued teaching.

## 7. FEAST OF DEDICATION AND TABERNACLES IN JERUSALEM 32 CE

October 32 to year-end 32 CE (John 7:2–10:40; Mark 10:1).

Soon after, Jesus left Galilee for the last time. At this stage, the sequence of events is confusing, as Peter-Mark seems to have a three-month gap before he and John are in unison again, with Jesus placed beyond the Jordan. John saw Jesus twice in October and December 32 CE in Jerusalem for festivals, but there is no detail indicating that he remained there between the festivals. Mark has him leave Galilee to go into Judea—and more precisely to Jerusalem, according to John—and then he is placed across the Jordan. Therefore, Jesus probably stayed in Jerusalem with John from October to the New Year, while Peter and the other disciples remained across the Jordan "in the house" (Mark 10:10) until then, perhaps for security reasons. Also, John mentions no disciples being with Jesus during that visit, including Peter, hence the gap in Peter-Mark (i.e., Peter had no information for Mark).

Jesus started in Galilee and went to the feast of Tabernacles, which lasted from 7 to 13 October, 32 CE. Interestingly, John mentions at this point that Jesus' brothers did not believe in him. Jesus then went to the festival late and in secret.

Both the people and authorities wondered if Jesus would appear at the festival. Halfway through the festivities, he started teaching in the Temple, accompanied by John, and the Jewish leaders ordered his arrest. However, Jesus avoids arrest, thanks to the crowds.

It was perhaps around this time that Jesus saved the adulteress in the *Pericope Adulterae* story. As I mentioned earlier, this free-floating story has traditionally been inserted at this point in John, but other than the fact that it occurred in Jerusalem on a day after which Jesus had been teaching in the Temple courts, it could be placed during any other Jerusalem visit and fit just as well.

*Figure 34* **Pool of Siloam.**

*One corner of the recently discovered Pool of Siloam in Jerusalem. According to the Gospel of John, Jesus directed a blind man to wash the mud Jesus had applied from his eyes on the steps of this pool, perhaps right here. The man then regained his sight. The pool was buried after the destruction of Jerusalem in 70 CE and was long thought to have been a literary invention. It was only re-discovered in 2004 by accident.*

The crowds who heard Jesus while he was teaching in the Temple were divided on who he was. Despite this, he continued his contentious discourse. He even narrowly escaped a stoning upon leaving the temple. On a Sabbath, on the steps of the Pool of Siloam, Jesus applied mud to the eyes of a blind man and then directed him to wash it off. The man thus regained his sight. The man and his parents were then interrogated by the Pharisees, who disbelieved the story.[10] But Jesus continued to teach and cause controversy.

---

10    Given the extraneous detail of the interrogation, either John was present or got the details later from one of his contacts in the priestly class.

Jesus was in the Temple during the Feast of Dedication in Jerusalem between December 14 and 22, 32 CE. Again, John accompanied him, given the level of detail in the account. On that occasion, while Jesus was walking in the Temple area of Solomon's Colonnade, the crowd pressed Jesus to declare himself the Messiah, but both his refusal to comply and his inflammatory response angered people to the degree that they attempted to grab him and stone him. He managed to escape, though. Jesus then crossed the Jordan, leaving the jurisdiction of the Jerusalem elites, to where the Baptist used to operate, Bethany-Beyond-Jordan.[11]

## 8. BEYOND JORDAN, THEN TO BETHANY.

January 33 CE to March 33 CE (John 10:40–11:57; Mark 10:1–45).

At this point, it is year-end 32 CE. The timeline from here until Jesus arrives in Bethany in late March 33 CE has traditionally been confused. There are contradictions between John's account of Jesus' travels and Peter-Mark's. However, with the new time-and-place marker from Mark 2.0 (Mark 10:34a), the sequences mesh almost perfectly. Here are the two complete sequences:

In John:

1.  From Jerusalem across the Jordan to Bethany-Beyond-Jordan in early 33 CE.

2.  To Bethany and the Lazarus incident.

3.  Withdrawal to the village of Ephraim near the desert.

4.  To Bethany by March 27 (six days to the Passover).

In Peter-Mark:

1.  Into Judea (Jerusalem?) and then across the Jordan.

2.  To Bethany and the Lazarus incident.

3.  To beyond the Jordan again.

4.  To Jericho and Bethany.

The only difference between the sequences is that John has Jesus leave Jerusalem and go to Ephraim—either a village a few miles to the northeast of Jerusalem close to the Jordan River or the region around the village—while Peter, who accompanied him, indicates that they went back across the Jordan. It could well be that they simply transited through the region. Because John did not accompany them, he mistook the village/region for the destination when in fact, Jesus and his group kept going over the Jordan.

Both John and Peter-Mark have Jesus beyond the Jordan River in Bethany-Beyond-Jordan in winter 33 CE. Peter says that Jesus and his group, including Peter, were staying in a house with the other disciples. John has no information about this stay, so he must have remained in Jerusalem. From there, Jesus taught many visitors. Peter mentions that they had given everything up to follow him, so Peter must have broken with his family.[12]

In response to the news that a friend called Lazarus, who lived in Bethany, was ill, Jesus and his disciples travelled there, and John met them there, as detail returns to his account. The seemingly intentional delay (he waited an additional two days after receiving word of Lazarus' illness before setting out), during which Lazarus died, could be due to the three-day rule in Jewish belief, according to which the soul stayed on Earth for three days before finally departing the body. Thereby, Lazarus would be "truly" dead after four days. Jesus thus found Lazarus dead and raised him back to life in the presence of onlookers and the

---

11    There are two Bethanys, one to the east of the Jordan River called Bethany-Beyond-Jordan, and the other called just Bethany, a few kilometres outside of Jerusalem.

12    Coming after the failure of the rich man to give everything he had, the Eye-of-the-Needle story, Peter could also be emphasizing how he and the others have indeed given up everything to follow Jesus.

disciples, including Peter and John. In the wake of this news, the Jewish leaders decided to arrest and dispose of Jesus. He and his disciples stayed a week with Lazarus and his family. They then retreated to Bethany-Beyond-Jordan,[13] probably via the wilderness of Ephraim, to keep off the main road and avoid detection.

## BETHANY

Bethany is a small village about three kilometres from Jerusalem on the road from Jericho. Bethany was out of sight from Jerusalem, since the Mount of Olives stood between it and the village. As one walked toward Jerusalem from Bethany, one went through Bethphage, up and over the Mount of Olives, down into the Kidron Valley, and through the Garden of Gethsemane. It would have been (and still is) a spectacular sight coming down, as the Temple was in full view. Bethany's name suggests "house of the poor or afflicted," probably indicating that the village had a charity alms house and was a colony of unclean required to keep a suitable distance from the Temple.[14] This may explain why Simon the Leper and Lazarus, who we know was ill, lived there (Mark 14:3–10; John 12:1). It also explains "the poor" remarks made by Jesus there, the only time he refers to them (John 12:8). At the time, many Galileans lived in Bethany, probably since it was a terminus for Galilean pilgrims coming south on the Jericho road. Jesus, therefore, may have had friends and relations there, making it a secure and natural base for him and all his followers to be billeted while near Jerusalem.[15]

Once the Jewish leaders heard of the raising of Lazarus and the people's reaction, they stepped up plans to have both Jesus and Lazarus eliminated. John was probably present during the discussion. Jesus was then a hunted man who moved about carefully. He seemed able to speak openly within the Temple premises, where there were crowds of potential supporters, so much so that the Temple police were hesitant to arrest him for fear of the crowds. But when not in the Temple, Jesus was careful to stay out of reach of the authorities. He would leave Judah to keep outside their area of jurisdiction, or he'd stay out of Jerusalem in friendly Bethany or, occasionally, be hidden by friends in remote areas. He also used the Garden of Gethsemane as a covert meeting place in the evenings. It was in this atmosphere that Judas approached the Jewish leaders about handing over Jesus to them.

# 9. THE FINAL TRIP TO BETHANY AND JERUSALEM

Up to the afternoon of March 26, 33 CE (Mark 10:46–10:52).

*Figure 35 **The Zacchaeus Tree?***

*The Gospel of Luke tells the wonderful story of a chief tax collector who was in Jericho when Jesus passed through the town on the main road. Zacchaeus, who was a short man, climbed up a sycamore-fig tree to see Jesus. The latter called him down and had dinner at his house. There are three sycamore-fig trees in Jericho believed to be that tree: two living and this stump of an ancient tree. Sycamore fig trees live no more than 1,000 years, so the original cannot*

---

13     John's assertion now confirmed by the new verse from Mark 2.0.

14     See (Capper, *The New Covenant Network in Southern Palestine at the Arrest of Jesus* 2003, 16–17) on this and his argument this alms house would have been a project of the Essenes sect.

15     (Capper, *The Church as the New Covenant of Effective Economics: The Social Origins of Mutually Supportive Christian Community* 2002).

*be still alive. However, the above stump is from a very large and old sycamore encased in plexiglass (you can see the reflections in the picture). An ancient Greek Orthodox monastery was purposely built behind it. When the author visited, he noted that the main road runs beside this stump, with a large, old living tree nearby, a cutting from the original. It is thus the most likely candidate for the actual tree from the story. Image courtesy of ProtoplasmaKid via CC BY-SA 4.*

Crossing the Jordan, Jesus and his disciples were on their way to Jerusalem for the 33 CE Passover. They passed through Jericho, as the ancient road from Bethany-Beyond-Jordan to Jerusalem passes through that city. This last trip would have taken a few days at most to complete and would have been in late March. Jesus is said to have healed Bartimaeus (our eyewitness) on that occasion, after which his group went on to Bethany.

# 10. FROM BETHANY UP TO THE LAST SUPPER

March 27 to evening March 31, 33 CE (Mark 11:1–14:17; John 12:1–13:2).

*Figure 36* **The Tiny Copper Coin**

*This is the coin (or a variant) from the Markan story of the poor widow who cast in "all she had" (i.e., two small lepta, the smallest denominated coin in Judea, the Widow's Mite, worth the least valued Roman coin, a quadrans, a sort of penny). This particular coin was minted under Judean King Alexander Jannaeus (103–76 BCE) and was still in use in the time of Jesus. However, his Hasmonean, Herodian, and Roman successors all minted many tens of thousands of these tiny bronze coins. These coins held very little value and were very crudely made (this is an exceptionally well-made specimen). Even today, they are very inexpensive—you can buy a worn one for about $5. A lepton could perhaps buy one loaf of low-grade barley bread—barely enough food for a day. Image courtesy of Classical Numismatic Group, LLC, www.cngcoins.com.*

To help navigate the Last Week, please use Figure 37. I have listed events as described by John and Mark side-by-side. I have bracketed several problematic events reported by Mark with asterisks.

| Jewish day starting at dusk. Days before Passover. | Gregorian day starting at midnight | Phase of the day (6 hour blocks) | John | Mark (Items bracketed with *s have incorrect timing.) |
|---|---|---|---|---|
| 7 Sabbath | March 25 Friday | evening | | |
| | March 26 Saturday | night | | |
| | | morning | | |
| | | afternoon | | |
| 6 | | evening | | |
| | March 27 Sunday | night | | |
| | | morning | | |
| | | afternoon | Jesus arrives in Bethany | Jesus arrives in Bethany and *rides triumphantly into Jerusalem.* |
| 5 | | evening | Dinner with Lazarus. Jesus anointed. | Return to Bethany. |
| | March 28 Monday | night | | |
| | | morning | Jesus rides triumphantly into Jerusalem. | Fig tree is cursed. Jesus goes to Jerusalem *and cleanses the Temple.* |
| | | afternoon | | |
| 4 | | evening | Jesus teaches. | Return to Bethany. |
| | March 29 Tuesday | night | | |
| | | morning | | Fig tree dead. Jesus goes to Jerusalem and teaches. |
| | | afternoon | | *Chapter 13 Discourse* then return to Bethany |
| | | evening | | |

| | | | John | Mark |
|---|---|---|---|---|
| 3 | March 30 Wednesday | night | | |
| | | morning | | |
| | | afternoon | | |
| | | evening | | Dinner with Simon the Leper. *Jesus annointed.* Judas meets with priests. |
| 2 | March 31 Thursday | night | | |
| | | morning | | |
| | | afternoon | | |
| | | evening | 1. The Last Supper. | |
| 1 Preparation Day | April 1 Friday | night | 2. Arrest & Trials | |
| | | morning | 3. Crucifixion and Death. | |
| | | afternoon | 4. Burial | Death & Burial. |
| | | evening | Start of Passover & Passover Feast | Start of Passover & Passover Feast |
| 0 Passover & Sabbath | April 2 Saturday | night | | |
| | | morning | | |
| | | afternoon | | *Preparation at the Upper Room.* |
| | | evening | | *Last Supper.* |
| Passover & First Day of the Week | April 3 Sunday | night | | *Arrest.* |
| | | morning | 5. Empty Tomb. Mary Magdalene "sees" Jesus. | *Trials & Crucifiction.* |
| | | afternoon | | |
| | | night | 5. Jesus first "appearance" before his followers. | |

*Figure 37 The Last Week 33 CE*

*Image by the author.*

The first three columns show the timing of the days leading up to the death of Jesus within context of the start of the Passover festival that year. Two columns show events according to John and Mark side-by-side. Asterisks denote events, as discussed, whose timing or content are incorrect. As mentioned, when Mark and John disagree, John is to be preferred. Mark's confusion over the timing of the Last Supper and the "cleansing" and the problems with the chapter 13 discourse has already been discussed. Mark has Jesus perform his triumphant ride into Jerusalem a day too early and has the anointing by Mary three days too late. Otherwise, the sequences mesh nicely.

Working back from the first day of Passover, both John and Peter have Jesus arriving in Bethany on March 27, six days before the Passover Festival, which started on April 2. With John and Peter present at a dinner in Lazarus' house that night, Mary anointed Jesus. According to John, the next day, Jesus rode into Jerusalem and taught. No doubt the next three days fell into the same pattern. Jesus leaves Bethany for Jerusalem in the morning, he then teaches in and around the Temple precincts, returning in the evening for rest and a meal.

After the preparations for the Last Supper in John's Upper Room described by Peter on the afternoon of March 31, both John and Peter, literally and figuratively, come together at the Last Supper, held after dusk. These last few events lead us to the Passion Story.

# CHAPTER 28

# THE PASSION STORY

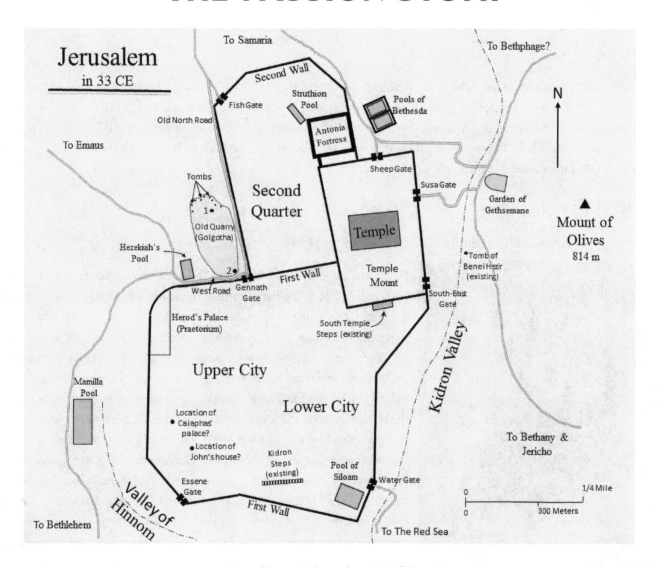

*Figure 38 **Jerusalem in 33 CE***

*Very little of Jerusalem from 33 CE is existing today, the city having been destroyed and rebuilt many times since. Some locations are only conjectural, such as the extent of the Praetorium or the locations of John's house (the location of the so-called Upper Room, the site of the Last Supper) and Caiaphas' mansion. The location labelled 1 in the Old Quarry is the traditional site of Jesus' crucifixion, today inside the Church of the Holy Sepulchre. As outlined in Appendix 4 location 2 is the more likely site of the crucifixion. Image by the author.*

So far, I have reconstructed Jesus' itinerary up to just before the Last Supper. In this chapter, I want to reconstruct the story of Jesus from that meal through to his burial, as well as the events that occurred right after. The Last Supper is where our two eyewitnesses, John and Peter, literally come together and tell the same story. Traditionally, this sequence has been called the

Passion Story, taken from the Latin *passio*, which means "suffering" or "enduring." Both John and Peter witnessed much of the events depicted. To aid the discussion, I have broken the Passion Story into five sections:

1.  The Last Supper

2.  Arrest and Trials

3.  Crucifixion and Death

4.  Burial

5.  After the Burial

In Appendix 5, I examine several alleged physical items associated with the Passion Story, namely the Chalice of Valencia, thought to be the cup Jesus drank from at the Last Supper; his alleged burial cloth, the Shroud of Turin; and the Sudarium of Oviedo, claimed to be the headcloth used to wrap Jesus' head after death. I conclude the Chalice might be the cup used but cannot say so definitively. However, I conclude that both the Shroud and the Sudarium are authentic, and they provide additional detailed information on the sequence of events.

# 1. THE LAST SUPPER

The evening of March 31, 33 CE (John 13:1–17:26; Mark 14:12–14:42).

Peter details the events leading up to the meal, while John starts as the meal is served. While in Bethany, during the day of March 31, Jesus sent two disciples into Jerusalem to prepare the meal. Jesus had already arranged a room. The operation was done in some secrecy, as the disciples met a man carrying a water jug, usually something a woman would be doing, and were led to a large furnished upper room. As pointed out by Denys Edward Hugh Whitely,[1] John was the host of the Last Supper, as Jesus is seated on his left in the place of honour, and Peter, the leader of the disciples, was to John's right, making intimate conversation possible. This would imply that the house was John's home, and he was wealthy; it had a large upper room, and servants were tending to the guests, including the man with the jug encountered earlier in the story. Probably John also supplied the colt that Jesus rode into town a few days before. In the evening, Jesus and the Twelve arrived, most certainly accompanied by others. According to Peter, Lazarus was in attendance also, since he was with the group at the arrest following the meal.

*Figure 39* **Jesus Washing the feet of his Followers at the Last Supper.**

*As reported in the Gospel of John (13:4–10). In this image, Jesus is cleaning Peter's feet, again depicted as an older man, although he was around Jesus' age or younger. Peter appears hesitant, while Jesus is insistent. Judas, no doubt, is the scowling man on the right, the only one without a halo. Jesus appears to have cleansed Judas' feet as well, despite knowing that he would betray him. Created by an unknown artist called the Master of the Housebook between 1475 to 1500.*

---

1    (Whiteley 1985).

As the food was being served, Jesus washed his disciples' feet. Since people reclined at a low table to eat with feet near, walking in sandals through dust and dirt made it essential that feet be washed before a communal meal, and this was performed by the lowliest of servants. Jesus, therefore, took a most humble position amongst his followers.

While eating, Jesus announced that he was about to be betrayed by one of the Twelve.[2] At Peter's suggestion, John leaned on Jesus and asked who the betrayer was. Jesus then indicated Judas surreptitiously, after which point Judas left. Having missed that exchange, the others carried on eating, thinking Judas was simply on an errand.

Jesus then engaged in a lengthy discourse—covering three and a half chapters in John— answered questions, and imparted final commands, since he anticipated that arrest was imminent, given the departure of Judas. During the meal, Jesus passed the bread and wine and instituted the covenant between himself and his followers.[3] He then famously predicates that they would all desert and disown him.[4] Afterwards, they sang a hymn. Finally, Jesus prayed for his followers.

*Figure 40* **Existing Steps to the Kidron Valley**

*Probably used Jesus and his followers the night of his arrest. They left John's house in the upper-class region of the Upper City after the Last Supper. They probably descended to the Kidron Valley and walked along it to the Garden of Gethsemane, staying outside the city where possible.*

---

2    Perhaps John was the source this "inside information" he had gotten from his contacts in the priestly class.

3    A covenant is a solemn promise. Note Peter does not use the more theologically advanced term terms "New Covenant" or "Covenant" but the more prosaic "covenant".

4    Interestingly, just as with John's other refusals to agree with Peter's statements that Jesus followers did not understand, in this case the statement of Jesus' followers deserting him is not repeated by John, only Peter's famous thrice disownment—presumably John did not consider it true that he too deserted Jesus.

After the supper, Jesus and his followers departed for Gethsemane,[5] an olive grove (John 18:1) in the Kidron Valley at the base of the Mount of Olives. Gethsemane was where he often met with his followers (John 18:2); it provided some security, and the location was conveniently located just outside Jerusalem and close to the road to Bethany. Since the place where the Last Supper took place, John's mansion, is unknown (it was probably situated in the swanky Upper City part), all we can say for sure about the route taken is that the group had to pass through one of the gates of Jerusalem's eastern wall. In the grove, Peter relates that while the main body of followers sat and waited, Jesus prayed off by himself, and Peter, James, and John, son of Zebedee, fell asleep repeatedly, despite being told to keep watch.

## 2. ARREST AND TRIALS

Night and morning of April 1, 32 CE to 6:00 a.m. (John 18:1–18:12; Mark 14:43–14:52).

*Figure 41* **The Garden of Gethsemane in Jerusalem**

*Some of the older olive trees in the garden have been dated back over 1,000 years. However, as olive trees grow, the older interior hollows out, so the oldest samples are gone, suggesting they are even older than the living portion of the tree. Another fact that makes them interesting is that olive trees can regrow from the roots, even if they are cut down. So perhaps the root systems are older than 2,000 years and would be living witnesses to Jesus, the night of his arrest and frequent meetings with followers. Image courtesy of Stacey Franco.*

From the Sanhedrin's point of view, it made perfect sense to eliminate Jesus. To allow seditious groups to arise, especially if led by a charismatic leader, risked a reaction from the invincible Roman government, which was contrary to the national interest and put not only the main actors in jeopardy but also, potentially, thousands of innocent people and the existing Jewish government structure. Much blood had been spilt already, and more would undoubtedly be spilt if rebel groups challenged Roman dominance. The Sanhedrin were right to fear reprisals: the revolts of 66 and 132 CE would completely destroy Jewish Palestine. Like the Baptist's, these upstart movements needed to be silenced one way or another before they went too far.

---

5    Gethsemane is derived from the Aramaic word for "oil press." John called it simply "a garden" while Mark calls it a "place" or "estate" named Gethsemane.

But why pick this particular Passover to arrest Jesus? Jesus had been leading a group of followers and attracting large crowds for several years already. His teaching was something new and counter to Judaism; he frequently clashed with traditional teachers of the Law and criticized the existing power structure, but he did have supporters in the Jewish leadership. Jesus was from Galilee and spent most of his time in rural areas, away from the reach of the urban elites. He moved about secretly, knowing the elites were after him, especially after the Baptist was killed. There were already rumours that Jesus was considered, at least by some, as the Messiah.[6] So why now? When he approached Jerusalem that Passover, alarming reports were reaching the leadership. They heard the story of Jesus raising Lazarus, and the crowds this attracted; Mary had publicly anointed him,[7] and he had made a kingly triumphant entry into Jerusalem (John 12:12–16)—all portentous events signalling Jesus' imminent declaration of kingship or Messiahship. So when Judas offered to betray Jesus, the time was ripe to forestall what the leadership feared would be yet another messianic uprising.

I will be following R.P. Booth's legal analysis[8] of the details of Jesus' arrest and trials. At the time in Judea, Booth notes there were two different legal systems: the Jewish Religious Law system administered by the Sanhedrin, and the Roman Imperial Law system. As the Jewish system did not have a capital execution option, something lost when Judea became a Roman province, the trick for the Sanhedrin was to have Jesus condemned under Jewish Law and then appeal to the Roman Law system to put Jesus to death under its standards.

Judea being a province of the Roman Empire, the Romans could arrest anyone they liked, but direct Roman involvement was usually reserved for instances where Roman dominance was threatened. Rome's main concerns were public order and tax flow. Thus, the Romans were content to leave civil and other criminal matters to local authorities, which in this case included the religiously based Sanhedrin, the chief priests, scribes, and elders. However, the Romans did so with the understanding that they could intervene at any time if they so desired. The Sanhedrin, therefore, had powers to arrest people by using the Temple police and trying the accused under Jewish Law. The Temple police were later used to arrest some of the disciples and Paul (Acts 21, 32). According to John, they had attempted to arrest Jesus earlier, but he had slipped away (John 7:32).

On the fateful night of April 1, Judas guided an armed group of Temple police and some Jewish officials to Gethsemane. He, as a member of Jesus' inner circle, was naturally familiar with the meeting place where they encountered Jesus and his followers. Jesus was arrested after Judas had identified him, or Jesus had self-identified. Jesus offered no resistance, but there was a scuffle, with Peter striking a man, who John tells us was a servant of the High Priest, with a sword before Jesus' supporters fled. The Temple police also attempted to arrest another unnamed man who evaded capture—Lazarus, anonymously identified in Peter-Mark with the code words "a naked young man with a linen cloak" who lost his outer garment and who was also sought by the authorities (John 12:10). To say that the young man fled fully naked is incorrect. Men usually wore an outer cloak, usually a large, undyed fringed shawl called a "tallith" (or "sleeved cloak"). Under the outer garment, men wore an under-tunic that came to the knees. At Jesus' crucifixion, the soldiers split up his outer garment but played dice for Jesus' under-tunic rather than tear it apart, as it was all in one piece. To be seen in just your under-tunic was termed "naked," hence when the arresting officers grabbed Lazarus, they came away with his outer garment while Lazarus fled "naked" in his under-tunic. Also, when Lazarus came to Jesus "naked" (Peter-Mark 10:34b), this meant that he was not wearing his outer cloak.[9]

---

6      In John 10:24, a few months earlier at the last festival, crowds in the Temple demanded Jesus declare himself the Messiah.

7      John 12:3 Anointing was reserved for Israelite kings and prophets.

8      (Booth 2012).

9      (Pope 2017).

## JUDAS

*Figure 42* **The Taking of Christ by Caravaggio (1602)**

*It shows Judas kissing (or attempting to in this version) Jesus to indicate who is to be arrested, as told in the Gospel of Mark 14:43–45. Notice Jesus demurring contact with Judas as an armoured soldier seizes him. In contrast, the others grasp the outer cloak of Lazarus, who is fleeing on the left and resisting arrest.*

We do not have a lot of information about the disciple Judas. John tells us that he was the son of Simon Iscariot, with Iscariot probably meaning "the man from Kerioth,"[10] a town in the south of Judea. Judas was a very popular name, so adding "the Iscariot" would have been needed to distinguish him. Jesus recruited him as one of the Twelve Disciples. John mentions that Judas oversaw the money bag and helped himself from time to time (John 12:6). After a rebuke from Jesus in Bethany over wasting expensive perfume, Judas approached the Jewish leaders and agreed for some amount of money to deliver Jesus to them, thus betraying Jesus. Jesus was aware of this arrangement,[11] so at the Last Supper, he urged Judas to be quick about it. The disciple later led officials to Gethsemane, where he identified Jesus so he could be arrested. At this point, Judas disappeared from history.[12]

But what was Judas' motivation? We can never know. Perhaps he was angry at Jesus for the very public rebuke in Bethany, or he had been caught stealing, or he may have simply been annoyed that Jesus was not going to assume the Messiahship and betrayed him either as a parting gesture or as a way of forcing him to "show himself" more forcefully. Or maybe he just wanted the cash.

## JEWISH TRIAL

Night of April 1, 33 CE (John 18:13–18:28; Mark 14:53–15:1).

---

10    (Bauckham, *Jesus and the Eyewitnesses: The Gospels as Eyewitness Testimony* 2008, 105–106).

11    Perhaps warned by Joseph of Arimathea, Nicodemus, or one of John's contacts in the aristocracy.

12    Matthew reports Judas attempted to return the money then hanged himself. Other early traditions state he was run over by a wagon, or he simply burst.

*Figure 43 **The Ossuary of Caiaphas, the High Priest, in the time of Jesus of Nazareth***

*The ossuary, or bone box, of Caiaphas, the High Priest who questioned Jesus during the Jewish trial. In 1990, a family tomb was uncovered just south of Jerusalem, with two ossuaries inscribed with the Caiaphas family name and a coin minted between 37 and 44 CE, also found in the tomb. The crude inscriptions are just a few characters long but are sufficient to indicate "Joseph, son of Caiaphas." The "son of" probably means "of the Caiaphas family." Josephus explains that Joseph, nicknamed Caiaphas, was High Priest from 18 to 36 CE, so this is the Caiaphas who confronted Jesus. The inscriptions themselves are very crude, done with the cursive Jewish script of the time in the manner of graffiti. This is due to the inscriptions being added after the ossuaries were placed in their niches in an awkward position to help differentiate them from later ossuaries.*

Jesus was bound and taken. Both Peter and John followed the arresting party to Annas'[13] house, where John, due to his relationship with the High Priest, was admitted to the interrogation. Notably, Annas asked Jesus about his followers who had scattered, and Jesus was beaten about the face with fists when his response was not what was expected.

This unofficial stop at Annas' makes sense because it was night time, and any formal proceedings had to take place at the High Priest's house, since the regular meeting place was locked behind the Temple's gates. The arresting party thus had to wait for the council to gather at Caiaphas' mansion.

John got Peter admitted to the courtyard so that he could keep warm. There, Peter mingled with some of those who had arrested Jesus. They suspected him of being a member of Jesus' following, perhaps because of his accent. They suggested he was Galilean, which led Peter to eventually deny Jesus three times before the cock-crow—a pre-dawn crow—just as Jesus had predicted. Meanwhile, the latter, still bound, was taken to the High Priest Caiaphas' house (John 18:24), where the whole

---

13    John 18:14 indicates that Annas was the father-in-law of the High Priest Caiaphas. Josephus in *Antiquities* 20.9.1 indicates Ananus/ Annas had been High Priest and had five sons, who all performed the role of High Priest as well; therefore, he would have been a person of importance.

Sanhedrin gathered and decreed that Jesus had committed blasphemy.[14] John, however, gives no details of these proceedings, so it seems that he remained at Annas' house with Peter. The exact location of these places is unknown; however, large mansions have been excavated in the wealthy Upper City of Jerusalem in the southwest part of the town, near Herod's Palace. It was undoubtedly in that area that Jesus was tried.

## JESUS AND THE JEWISH LEADERS

The Jewish leadership are shown to be suspicious of Jesus and his movement. At least early on, their suspicion was probably warranted, for the leaders were constantly being inundated with pretend Messiahs. For instance, they took an interest in the Baptist (John 1:19–25). The leadership feared that Messiah pretenders would stir up a revolt, and the Romans would have to crack down on the whole Jewish nation. They say as much in John when deliberating about arresting Jesus (John 11:47–11:48). Thus, the leaders appeared to be keeping an eye on him and his movement (John 4:1), questioning him and his actions (John 8:13, 9:13–16, 40), accusing him of demon possession (Mark 3:22), attempting to trick him on paying Roman taxes (Mark 12:13–17), and asking for a sign to demonstrate his divine authority (Mark 8:11). Ultimately, Jesus' mission progressed enough to be perceived as a direct threat, and the leaders attempted to arrest him several times (John 7:32), with the last time being successful (John 8:3–12). The insistence of the Jewish leaders would eventually lead Pilate to order his execution.[15]

The Jewish leaders were diverse if we take into account the number of terms used to refer to them: Pharisees, priests, chief priests, Levites, Experts and teachers of the Law, the Jewish Ruling Council, Rulers, the Sanhedrin, and the Elders. But not all members were hostile to Jesus and his message. We know of Nicodemus and Joseph of Arimathea, who were followers of Jesus (John 19:38–40). John also mentions "many" leaders who were supportive. Still, the zealous Pharisees kept them quiet through fear of retribution (John 12:42).

For the Sanhedrin, there was the need for haste; they feared trouble from the Passover crowds later in the day once they found out that Jesus had been arrested. They naturally wanted Jesus out of the way as fast as possible. The Day of Preparation was the last possible day for execution before the Passover started. Therefore, the Jewish leaders needed to convince Pilate that same morning to order his death.[16] They probably knew crucifixions were already scheduled for that day.[17] However, before that, the Sanhedrin needed to settle the related Jewish legal issues and decide on an argument to convince Pilate of the need for the death penalty under the Roman system— first thing in the morning, hence the nocturnal meeting.

According to Booth's analysis of these events, Jesus was not convicted by the Sanhedrin because he claimed to be the Son of God or the Messiah; this was not considered blasphemy under Jewish Law. Instead, Jesus' alluding to destroying the Temple (John 2:19) two years earlier (in 31 CE) is what got him into serious trouble.[18] According to Jewish Law, one could be accused of blasphemy for cursing or dishonouring God. The Temple had been built and was used as an honour to God, so threatening to destroy it would indeed "dishonour" God and was worthy of death. While on the cross, passers-by derided Jesus for his

---

14   Mark offers a slightly different chronology. He seems to conflate the stop at Annas, the courtyard, and the formal trial before the Sanhedrin and the High Priest Caiaphas all in one stop that night.

15   Gamaliel was a leading Jewish teacher and reputed to be one of the greatest teachers in Jewish history. He was active in the first half of the first century in Jerusalem (died c. 54 CE). He is known to have been one of the leaders of Sanhedrin at the time of Jesus, so he almost certainly was present at the trial of Jesus. What his stance was during the trial we do not know. Interestingly, Acts mentions Gamaliel as an honoured teacher of the law twice. First Acts 22:3 has Paul describing himself as a pupil of Gamaliel, and second, in Acts 5:34, Gamaliel saves the lives of the apostles by counselling the Sanhedrin to release them. For more information see (The Editors of the New World Encyclopedia, Gamaliel 2017).

16   The Roman governors of Judea normally resided up the coast in Caesarea Maritima, the provincial capital. However, the regularly travelled to Jerusalem for festivals to increase security, given the large number of attendees. So Pilate was in residence nearby.

17   John 18:40 & 19:18. Barabbas and two others were already due for execution that day, although Barabbas was later released.

18   Mark indicates this was one of the accusations made against Jesus in front to of Caiaphas.

comments on destroying the Temple (Mark 15:29). Thus, we can infer that this must have been the official public reason for his condemnation by the Sanhedrin.

The evidence seems to support the inability of the Sanhedrin to execute directly, a right probably lost when Judea became a Roman province in 6 CE. John, at least, has the Sanhedrin saying as much (John 18:31). As for Mark, he states that the Sanhedrin judged Jesus "worthy of death" (Mark 14:64), a judicial opinion rather than a sentence. The Sanhedrin needed to lay the evidence before Pilate to lead to execution under the Roman Law system. In other words, an accusation of sedition against the Emperor's authority had to be presented.

Peter's account puts himself outside during the Annas interrogation, but he omits John's presence (for anonymity); the latter was probably his source. As John offers no details for the Caiaphas' segment, we can assume that he was not present. But Peter-Mark does have inside information, so his source may have been sympathetic council members, such as Nicodemus or Joseph of Arimathea, who could attest to the Caiaphas proceedings.

## ROMAN TRIAL

*Figure 44* **Pilate's Prutah**

*A coin of Pontius Pilate called a "prutah," this one minted in Jerusalem (29 CE), so it would have been in circulation during Jesus' mission. Ten could buy you a loaf of bread, so its value was low. We can read on the obverse in Greek: TIBEPIOY KAICAPOC, that is, "Year 16 of Caesar Tiberius." In the centre, we can see a "simpulum," a ladle used in rituals of the Roman religion, a symbol of the Roman priesthood. The reverse reads IOYΛIA KAICAPOC ("Julia the Queen," the wife of Tiberius), with three bound wheat stalks. Pilate would have authorized the design. Notably, the head of the Emperor (in this case, Tiberius) is not shown, as was true of all coinage issued by the Roman authorities in Judea, so as not to offend Jewish sensibilities. However, Pilate had a reputation for alienating his subjects, so the unusual inclusion of an instrument used in Roman religious rituals may very well have been intentional.*

Dawn April 1, 33 CE (Peter-Mark 15:1–15:15; John 18:28–19:16).

Jesus was led from Caiaphas' house to Pilates' palace, called the Praetorium (Mark 15:16), "Very early in the morning." (Mark 15:1) The Jewish leadership[19] presented him to Pilate outside the palace. According to Booth, Pilate, as governor, had under Roman court practice complete freedom in the cases he accepted to look into and the penalties he imposed, apart from specific, mandatory death sentences in cases of treason against the Emperor. Pilate was free to conduct his own investigation and was not bound by the local civil or religious law systems. When Jesus was presented to him by the insistent Jewish officials on the morning of April 1, Pilate decided to investigate the case against Jesus.

---

19    No doubt the embassy included senior Jewish leaders, perhaps even Caiaphas, to request Pilate for a favour.

Both Peter-Mark and John describe this investigation. According to Peter, "the chief priests accused him of many things" (Mark 15:3), which could have included not paying taxes, because the Sanhedrin had sent spies to trap Jesus on payment of taxes to the Romans (Mark 12:13–15). According to John, who gives a more complete and nuanced account, Pilate was understandably reluctant to get involved in a local religious spat (John 18:31). Both Peter and John say that Pilate took Jesus inside the palace and interrogated him, specifically on his claim to be the king of the Jews[20]—or the king of the Judeans, based on an alternative translation emphasizing the difference between Galileans and Judeans, an even starker accusation because the Romans ruled Judea. Pilate initially decided that Jesus was being railroaded and found nothing wrong with him. Either Jesus convinced Pilate of his innocence, or Pilate could not take the charges seriously. How could a poor, roughed-up Galilean be a threat to Roman power?

Having examined and accepted the authenticity of the Sudarium and Shroud as the linens used in the death and burial of Jesus, I will add more detail to the death and burial sequence using the empirical and forensic evidence gathered from these cloths.

Pilate then attempts to release Jesus as part of a festival amnesty custom, but the crowd demanded that another prisoner, Barabbas (or Bar-Abbas, meaning son of Abbas), be released. Pilate had Jesus flogged somewhere inside the palace. He was whipped from behind by two soldiers using Roman whips while his hands were pinned above him; whip marks show that the soldier on the right was taller. The soldiers mocked him as a false king by bowing to him and wrapping him in a purple (a colour exclusively used by Roman elites) robe; they placed a crown of thorns on his head, causing the sharp, thorn-like piercing wounds. Afterwards, he was beaten around the face.[21] The evidence from the Shroud and Sudarium confirms this. Jesus was then taken into the palace.

John saw Jesus brought out in that state and presented to the crowd, who demanded Jesus' death. On several occasions, Pilate attempted to release him. However, the Jewish leaders and crowd still demanded his death; all in all, the accusation of claimed kingship seemed to be the most convenient. Eventually, around 6:00 a.m., or "about the sixth hour" (John 19:14), the crowd convinced Pilate to have Jesus crucified, the clinching argument being that a "king," if not condemned, would make Pilate disloyal to the Emperor. So Pilate, sitting on his raised seat, sentenced Jesus to crucifixion.

## THE PRAETORIUM AND GABBATHA

The Praetorium was Herod the Great's old palace; John calls it "the palace." It was occupied by the Roman prefects when in Jerusalem—the province's capital was on the coast at Caesarea Maritima. Still, prefects would be expected to be in Jerusalem during festivals. Nominally, the Antonine Fortress was the military headquarters and barracks of the Romans in Jerusalem, but the palace was undoubtedly a much more comfortable residence for Pilate.[22] It was also situated in the northwest corner of the First Wall, adjacent to the Upper City, so the party bringing Jesus did not have far to go. The palace is described by Josephus, who explains that there was a reception room, porticos, and adjacent open spaces that allowed for public proceedings.[23] Pilate condemned Jesus while seated in his judges' seat or tribunal in a place called "the Stone Pavement" (John 19:13); the ancient Greek for this word is *Lithostrotos*, meaning "a mosaic or tessellated pavement," while the Aramaic word used to refer to that specific area near the praetorium is *Gabbatha*, which means "elevated." Pilate's seat, therefore, was a paved, raised open-air area, secured by soldiers and located in front of the palace, from which he interacted with the crowds.[24]

---

20    John 18:33 and Mark 15:2. John infers it was an accusation made against him rather than something claimed.

21    Jesus was also beaten about the head during his Jewish trials.

22    In The Wars of the Jews 2.14.8 Josephus mentions another Roman governor, Florus, who also took up quarters in the palace and Philo in Embassy to Gaius 38 relates how Pilate adorned the palace of Herod with gilt shields.

23    (Josephus, *The Wars of the Jews*, 5.4.4).

24    In *The Wars of the Jews* 2.14.8 Florus, another Roman governor, set up his tribunal just outside the palace on which he sat where he met with crowds—very likely the same space as Pilate used. Again, Josephus in 2.9.2–4 mentions Pilate setting up his tribunal to converse with crowds.

The Roman trial was carried out mainly in public, presumably with John amongst the crowd standing outside Pilate's palace and with Jesus being presented after he was flogged and abused. However, two scenes in John take place in private inside the palace between Pilate and Jesus, away from the crowd, which must have been related to John by some unknown Roman eyewitness.

As for Peter, his abridged description of the public trial and crucifixion gives the impression that he was not present. Besides adding a few odd details, Peter gives us no new information than that contained in John's more complete account. I suspect that Peter was not in the crowd for the public part of Pilate's investigation, nor did he see the crucifixion, at least up close. Moreover, John mentions that no male supporters were present besides himself. I suspect that they were all in hiding after the arrest, and Peter especially, since he had assaulted the High Priest's servant and had a near identification a few hours earlier in the courtyard of Annas' house. Therefore, Peter would have had to get the details from the crowd or perhaps from John. Peter-Mark does repeat the "inside" reports from the unknown sources in the palace that John mentions, but with differing details. Both accounts, though, have a reticent Jesus accepting some form of kingship in front of Pilate.

Who were the others condemned with Jesus? Peter-Mark states that Jesus was crucified between two "robbers."[25] Pilate had already condemned them to be crucified that day, and they are described as murderers and insurrectionists.[26] Both Peter and John also attest to an amnesty for one prisoner at the Passover, but no other sources support or contradict this custom. Historians have been puzzled by this, as it seems an outrageous action (i.e., releasing a known rebel who could resume his seditious plans). The freeing of Barabbas, a murderous revolutionary, instead of Jesus, by Pilate, is even more striking. However, I believe it is possible. Pilate had the power to release any prisoners he wanted, for he was not bound by any sort of guilty or not guilty outcome, so he had complete freedom of action. The question is: Why did he do it?

---

25    Mark 15:27. The original Greek word is ληστάς, or "lestes," meaning violent robber or brigand not the softer thieves, as is often rendered. (The Editors of Bible Hub, Thayer's Greek Lexicon, Electronic Database by Biblesoft Inc. 2011).

26    Mark 15:7 tells us Barabbas was in prison with the others who were political insurrectionists and had committed murder. In John 18:40, Peter indicates Barabbas, and presumably the others, had taken part in a rebellion. This is far more serious than thievery.

*Figure 45* **Evidence for Pontius Pilate**

*A stone dedication tablet mentioning Pontius Pilate. Discovered in 1961 at Caesarea Maritima, the Roman capital of the province of Judea. The stone bears a damaged inscription dedicating a temple to Emperor Tiberius (called a Tiberium). Pilate commissioned it while he was governor (26–36 CE). Experts read this partial inscription as follows: "To the Divine Augusti [this] Tiberieum … Pontius Pilate … prefect of Judea … has dedicated [this]."*

## PILATE

Pontius Pilate was the fifth governor of Judea (26–36 CE). His official title was Prefect. Pilate had a bad reputation. Both Philo of Alexandria and Josephus describe incidents during Pilate's prefecture that caused near-insurrections amongst the Jews. One night in 27 CE, Pilate, to subvert the Jewish laws, had ensigns with the image of Emperor Tiberius erected in Jerusalem, thereby violating the Jews' ban on the display of images. A standoff with the Jews almost resulted in slaughter before Pilate backed down.[27] Pilate installed gilt shields with the Emperor's likeness on Herod's old palace in Jerusalem in a similar incident. He only backed down when the Emperor himself intervened.[28] In 28 CE, Pilate expropriated the Temple's treasury and built an aqueduct with it. The resulting Jewish protest ended in a massacre ordered by Pilate in Jerusalem.[29] Later, in 36 CE, a large armed crowd of Samaritans following a figure known simply as "the Samaritan" tried to ascend a sacred mountain but were all massacred on the orders of Pilate. The result was a formal complaint to the Emperor that ended with Pilate's recall, ending his career.[30] Finally, I have explained earlier how he minted offensive coins. Both Philo and Josephus state that Pilate did this, in

---

27    (Josephus, *The Wars of the Jews*, 2.9.2).

28    (Philo, *On the Embassy to Gaius*, 38.29).

29    (Josephus, *The Wars of the Jews*, 2.9.4).

30    (Josephus, *Antiquities of the Jews*, 18.4.1–2).

part, to denigrate Jewish custom, in contrast to the general respect shown by the Emperors Augustus and Tiberius toward the Jews. Philo described him thus: "a man of a very inflexible disposition, and very merciless as well as very obstinate."[31]

Hence Pilate had a terrible reputation amongst the Jews, unlike the earlier prefects who were more restrained. But why would Pilate make his job more difficult by stirring up trouble? And why would Pilate, the ruler who had killed hundreds, perhaps thousands, and undoubtedly crucified many, at the 33 CE Passover suddenly be releasing prisoners, fretting over Jesus and the crowds? What changed? The answer, I believe, lies with a character called Sejanus.

*Figure 46 **Emperor Tiberius.***

*This is a bust of Tiberius Caesar Divi Augusti filius Augustus, or Tiberius for short. He is the second Roman Emperor, having succeeded Augustus in 14 CE. Augustus was the brilliant architect of the Imperial Roman system that saw the subtle transformation of the Roman Republic into the Roman Empire, making the Roman Emperor the most powerful person in the Ancient World. This system had a significant flaw, which caused the western part of the empire to collapse: how to transfer power to a new and capable emperor peacefully. Tiberius was an example of the ad-hoc-ness of this process. Tiberius was a great general but wanted to live a private life after retirement. However, after an erratic succession process that saw Tiberius married to a woman he hated, making him gloomy and unhappy, he found himself on the spot as the next emperor. He was not a bad emperor; he simply did not want the job. He delegated a lot of responsibilities and eventually left Rome entirely to live on the island of Capri. He reigned until 37 CE. It was under his rule that Pontius Pilate was sent to Jerusalem, and Jesus was crucified.*

---

31    (Philo, *On the Embassy to Gaius*, 38.301).

## THE SEJANUS BACKSTORY

Lucius Aelius Sejanus (20 BCE–October 18, 31 CE) was a soldier and an ambitious politician under Tiberius. Emperor Tiberius was a reluctant emperor, who preferred to delegate authority to trusted advisors, and who eventually withdrew to the island of Capri in 26 CE, leaving Sejanus acting as his point-man in Rome. Sejanus, who started as prefect of the Praetorian Guard, the Emperor's elite bodyguard, had risen in power over the 20s to become Tiberius' trusted chief administrator of the Empire. It is very probable that Sejanus, in his capacity as chief administrator, would have selected and appointed Pilate as prefect of Judea in 26. Eventually, Sejanus ran afoul of Tiberius, who heard of a conspiracy by Sejanus and had him and others executed in October 31 CE.[32]

Sejanus appears to have had it in for the Jews. Philo, writing a few years later in 38 CE, comments on the gentle treatment of Jews by the Romans until Sejanus came along:

> "Therefore, all people in every country, even if they were not naturally well inclined towards the Jewish nation, took great care not to violate or attack any of the Jewish customs of laws. And in the reign of Tiberius things went on in the same manner, although at that time things in Italy were thrown into a great deal of confusion when Sejanus was preparing to make his attempt against our [Jewish] nation; for he [Tiberius] knew immediately after his [Sejanus'] death that the accusations which had been brought against the Jews who were dwelling in Rome were false calumnies, inventions of Sejanus, who was desirous to destroy our [Jewish] nation, which he knew alone, or above all others, was likely to oppose his unholy counsels and actions in defiance of the emperor, who was in great danger of being attacked, in violation of all treaties and of all honesty. [After the execution of Sejanus] And he [Tiberius] sent commands to all the governors of provinces in every country to comfort those of our [Jewish] nation in their respective cities, as the punishment intended to be inflicted was not meant to be inflicted upon all, but only on the guilty; and they were but few. And he ordered them to change none of the existing customs, but to look upon them as pledges, since the men were peaceful in their dispositions and natural characters, and their laws trained them and disposed them to quiet and stability."[33]

Therefore, Pilate, because he had been appointed by Sejanus, who was anti-Jewish, was either trying to please Sejanus or was following orders in harassing the Jews. But in late 31, after Sejanus' downfall, Tiberius ordered all governors to treat the Jews fairly. This must be the reason for Pilate's uncharacteristic reluctance to condemn Jesus in early 33—that is, his appeal to the crowd and this uncharacteristic amnesty offer. He was eager to please. Pilate was also receptive to the requests of the Jewish leaders to take the bodies down from crosses, and Joseph's request for Jesus' body (John 19:38). In John, the crowds argue that releasing the "King of the Jews" would send a message that Pilate was not a friend of Caesar (the Emperor). Given Pilate's probable links to the executed Sejanus—Tiberius was purging Rome of Sejanus' co-conspirators at the time—that probably clinched his decision. Pilate thus condemned Jesus, had him flogged, and ordered his crucifixion.

Ultimately, Pilate's wish to appease the Jews and show his loyalty to the Emperor caused him to condemn Jesus with a plausible cover story of a nascent insurrection being led by a self-proclaimed "King of the Jews." The dual nature of the two condemnations, one Jewish and one Roman, is reflected in the crucifixion: passers-by commented on Jesus' blasphemous Temple destruction claim, while the Roman titulus, the sign affixed to the cross, declared Jesus as a pretend king in violation of the Emperor's authority.

# 3. CRUCIFIXION AND DEATH

April 1, 33 CE, between 9:00 a.m. and 6:00 p.m. approximately (Mark 15:16–37; John 19:17–30).

---

32    (Josephus *Antiquities* 18.6.6).

33    (Philo, *On the Embassy to Gaius*, 24.159–161).

There is no scholarly consensus on the conflict between John's and Peter-Mark's timing of events for that day. John states that Jesus was condemned "about the sixth hour" and crucified soon after. Peter says that Jesus was crucified at "the third hour;" at "the sixth hour," darkness came over the land, and at "the ninth hour," Jesus died. But are Peter-Mark and John disagreeing on what occurred at the sixth hour?

## HOW TO COUNT THE HOURS

It is important to remember that there was no way for most people to tell the hour of the day with precision at the time. Therefore, the times cited by Peter and John would have been rough estimates. There were two relevant time systems in Palestine during Jesus' time that could help us clarify the divergence between Gospel timings: Jewish and Roman.

The Jewish system used a relative hour that varied in length depending on the time of year; a day was divided into twelve "hours" regardless of the length of the day.[34] The first hour of the day would start at sunrise, the end of the sixth hour was always noon, and the end of the 12th hour was the end of the day at sunset. In Jerusalem on April 1, 33, the sunrise occurred around 5:30 a.m. and the sunset around 6:00 p.m.[35] The Jewish day of Jesus' death thus ran roughly from 5:30 a.m. to 6:00 p.m. Divided by twelve, the Jewish hour on that day would be one hour and five minutes long.

Peter, a Galilean Jewish fisherman, undoubtedly used the Jewish method. Indeed, he states that Jesus was crucified at "the third hour," that is, around 9:00 a.m. (5:30 a.m. + 3 hours and 15 minutes),[36] which fits the appearance before Pilate early on that morning. So according to Peter-Mark, Jesus was still alive around 12:00 p.m. at "the sixth hour" (8:30 a.m. to 9:00 a.m. + 3 hours and 15 minutes), and died around 3:00 p.m. at "the ninth hour," three hours or so later.

Since he claims that Pilate condemned Jesus at the sixth hour, John was not using the Jewish system, which would be around 12:00 p.m., a very long lapse in time since he had been brought to him first thing in the morning. The best explanation is that John, always careful about details, was using the Roman system. John was formally educated, so this is no surprise. This method, which we still use, marked hours forward from midnight; the "sixth hour" would mean 6:00 a.m., which is in keeping with Peter's and John's own "early morning" approach to Pilate's crucifixion proceeding soon after.

But is John's Roman method also consistent with his other time statements?[37] When John first met Jesus, he stayed the day with him starting at the "tenth hour," or at 10:00 a.m., which makes more sense to start a day's activity than the end of the afternoon, 4:00 p.m., as per the Jewish time system (John 1:39). But John also writes that as a tired Jesus arrived at Jacob's well, the disciples departed for some food to make a meal, and a Samaritan woman came to draw water at the "sixth hour," or 6:00 a.m., according to the Roman system (John 4:6). This seems like an odd time to finish a journey until we remember that this was the end of a sudden journey when Jesus needed to leave Judea quickly, so a night flight seems likely. John also relates how Jesus healed a royal official's son at the "seventh hour," or around 7:00 a.m. (John 4:52). Given that Cana is more than a day's travel by foot from Capernaum, this fits with the royal official still being on the road more than a day later when his servants met him sometime after 7:00 a.m. the next day.

Here is the timing of events on April 1, 33, remembering that times are approximate as discussed:

1. Jesus started the Last Supper with his disciples in the evening at the start of the Preparation Day after 6:00 p.m.

2. Jesus was arrested later that evening.

3. Jesus was interrogated by the Sanhedrin overnight.

---

34    (The Editors of TorahCalendar.com n.d.).

35    (Cornwall, Horiuchi and Lehman n.d.).

36    This assumes that when Peter says "the third hour" he is counting hours and not using third hour/sixth hour/nineth hour as shorthand for ways of simply saying morning, noon, and afternoon, as was used occasionally.

37    (N. Walker 1960).

4.   Jesus was sent to Pilate early in the morning before 6:00 a.m.

5.   Pilate condemned Jesus sometime after 6:00 a.m.

6.   Jesus was crucified around 9:00 a.m.

7.   Jesus was still alive on the cross around 12:00 p.m.

8.   He died around 3:00 p.m.

9.   Jesus was buried by sundown, around 6:00 p.m. at the latest.

## CRUCIFIXION AND DEATH

John accompanied the procession of the three condemned men on the short walk through the Garden Gate[38] to a place called Golgotha. In Appendix 4, I discuss Golgotha and the site of Jesus' tomb. Golgotha is an old quarry just outside the city wall where West Road and the Old North Road enter the city through the First Wall via the Gennath Gate. Tombs dotted the edges of the quarry to the north, the probable location of Jesus' tomb.

In his regular clothes, Jesus carried his cross piece to the quarry, which, according to the forensic evidence, caused abrasions to his shoulders and the back of his head. He fell at least once, face forward, injuring his knees, the back of his head, and face. At some point, Jesus must have been too weak to carry on or had passed out, which might explain why a rural bystander, Simon from Cyrene, the father of Alexander and Rufus, was pressed to carry the crosspiece to the crucifixion site.[39] Peter includes this story passed on to him either by Simon himself or his sons.

Once at the Golgotha site, the crucifixion took place. The holes and accompanying uprights were undoubtedly already in place from many previous crucifixions.[40] All that was needed was for the cross piece to be lifted into place. Jesus was crucified naked around 9:00 a.m., with a nail through each wrist at the extremities of the crosspiece, which was then hoisted onto an upright position. A single nail through both feet—left on top of the right—secured his feet. Jesus' cross stood in the middle, between those of the other two insurgents being put to death on that morning (John 19:18). The Romans put a sign on his cross, the titulus, that read: "Jesus of Nazareth, the King of the Jews" in Aramaic, Latin, and Greek. Although the chief priests objected to the declarative nature of this title, Pilate could not be bothered to change it.

Despite later artistic depictions, Jesus and his fellows would have been crucified naked to increase their shame. The Roman soldiers kept both Jesus' cloak and his under-garment.

John is explicit that he was "nearby"—within speaking distance of Jesus—while Jesus slowly died. He also saw the accompanying activity: the four soldiers separating Jesus' outer garment and dicing for the under-garment, preparing the two other victims, and installing the titulus, which many passers-by on the roads could read. Many female followers, namely the Galileans—Mary; Mary, wife of Clopas; Mary Magdalene; Salome, and others—were present. At Jesus' request, John agreed to take Jesus' mother into his home in Jerusalem. Around 3.00 p.m., Jesus drank some wine vinegar[41] offered via a sponge on a spear and then said "it is finished" and died from a great pulmonary oedema (i.e., fluid in the lungs, with death due to asphyxiation or heart failure; he could indeed no longer raise himself on his legs to get his breath).

---

38    The gate mentioned in Hebrews 13:12. Jesus died "outside the city gates."

39    This would seem to confirm that Jesus was nailed to the cross piece at Golgotha and not before at the Praetorium. Why the victims had to carry the cross piece to the site of execution is a question we can only speculate about; perhaps it was an additional public humiliation or it encumbered the victim, making escape more difficult.

40    No doubt the cross pieces were recycled also. There would be no reason to discard a perfectly usable cross after one execution. This reasoning makes the discovery of the True Cross, three hundred years later, a legend. No doubt the upright and cross piece on which Jesus died would have been used many times before and after his death, making identification impossible.

41    Called posca, the military and lower classes drank a vinegary wine mixed with various spices such as myrrh or gall to improve the taste. (Dalby 2003, 270).

The priests were slaughtering the Passover lambs in the Temple in preparation for the Passover meal at the time. This explains why John connected Jesus to the motif of the Lamb of God.

As Peter was not in attendance at the crucifixion, he may have been using John's information, that of others, or a combination of testimonies to relate what happened in Peter-Mark. However, the latter does add a few more details that are not in John: Jesus initially refusing the posca presented to him; passers-by insulting him; the time of death; Pilate's surprise at Jesus' early death; and Joseph buying a linen cloth for burial. Peter-Mark also adds superstitious details, which are probably either metaphorical embellishments or the result of confusing accounts. He talks of darkness, a tearing curtain, a centurion jarringly declaring Jesus "Son of God," as well as Jesus quoting the first line from Psalm 22. None of these events is attested to by John, who was present and would have witnessed them. Therefore, I shall set these odd elements from Peter's story aside, except for the darkness.

Peter mentions darkness covering the whole land between noon and Jesus' death in the afternoon. John mentions nothing of the sort. Luke adds to the confusion by embellishing Peter's account, saying that the darkness occurred because "the sun stopped shining" (Luke 23:45). This, in turn, spawned a host of later, esoteric Church traditions as to the astronomical phenomena associated with the crucifixion (Acts 2:20); the issue is still debated.[42] If darkness did indeed occur, it was probably due to a Khamsin sandstorm (i.e., high altitude dust blown up from the desert area to the east of Jerusalem). It typically lasts several hours, with visibility impeded but with no strong winds. Such sandstorms occur during the spring in that region. It was this phenomenon reported on that day that became linked to the death of Jesus, with ever-increasing embellishment occurring over the years.

A little later, another interesting celestial phenomenon occurred: a 60% lunar eclipse visible in Jerusalem at moonrise, about 6:20 p.m. on April 1, 33, just as Jesus was buried. It would have resulted in a blood moon, again reported and associated with the death of Jesus (Acts 2:20).

These natural phenomena spawned later astronomical legends. Just as later stories were created to obviate Jesus' humble birth, these stories were embellished to mark the significance of Jesus' death, a prevalent practice in ancient times.[43] In any case, a sort of darkness may indeed have overcome the skies on the afternoon of April 1, 33.

## THE WOMEN AT THE CROSS

Both John and Peter speak of the women at the cross, and their descriptions are confusing. John says: "Near the cross of Jesus stood his mother, his mother's sister, Mary [in Greek "of Clopas"] the wife of Clopas, and Mary Magdalene" (John 19:25). Peter, in turn, says the following: "Some women were watching from a distance. Amongst them were Mary Magdalene, Mary the mother of James the younger and of Joses, and Salome" (Mark 15:40). Later on, Mark adds: "Mary Magdalene and Mary the mother of Joses saw where he was laid. When the Sabbath was over, Mary Magdalene, Mary the mother of James, and Salome bought spices so that they might go to anoint Jesus' body" (Mark 15:47, 16:1).

Peter is clear that there was a sizable group of women present, in addition to the three he mentions. Mary Magdalene,[44] Mary, mother of Jesus (Mother Mary), and Salome are distinct people, but what of the other Marys? Amongst the ancient Jews, there were a small number of very popular names. Four out of ten men bore one of the nine most popular, and almost one of every three women were named either Mary or Salome. We are told of Mary, mother of James the younger and Joses; Mary mother of Joses; Mary, mother of James; Mary of Clopas (daughter or wife of Clopas); and Mother Mary's sister (if a distinct person and not referring to Mary of Clopas).

Peter-Mark tells us that Jesus had four brothers: James, Joseph/Joses, Judas/Jude, and Simon/Simeon. John indicates that Mother Mary was present at the crucifixion. So does Peter-Mark, but he does not mention Jesus' mother by name; instead, he confusingly refers to three different Marys—the mother of James the younger and Joses, the mother of Joses, and the mother

---

42      (Ghose 2017).

43      For a complete treatment of this topic, please follow (Waddington & Humphreys, 1992) Chapters V– XI. Note this article uses Julian calendar dates, which are two days ahead of the Gregorian dates used in this book.

44      Meaning Mary of Magdala to distinguish her from the other Marys. Magdala, now called al-Majdal, is a fishing town on the western shore of the Sea of Galilee. Peter-Mark indicates Jesus had healed her at some point.

of James. Why mention these other strange, unknown Marys while not mentioning Mother Mary, who was present? Simply because of Peter-Mark's penchant for leaving out or hiding names for protective anonymity. He is thus encoding Mother Mary with these half-titles. Early Christians would have known who he was referring to (i.e., that the mother of James and/or Joses was actually Jesus' mother). This identification eliminates three of the five Marys.

But what about Mary of Clopas? Eusebius mentions a Clopas soon after the destruction of Jerusalem in 70 CE:

"They all with one consent pronounced Symeon, the son of Clopas, of whom the Gospel also makes mention; to be worthy of the episcopal throne of that parish [Jerusalem]. He was a cousin, as they say, of the Saviour. For Hegesippus records that Clopas was a brother of Joseph."[45]

So Clopas was the brother of Jesus' father, Joseph, making him an uncle. He also married a Mary and had a son called Symeon, who became a leader of the Jerusalem Church about forty years later. Therefore, Mary, wife of Clopas, would have been a sister-in-law to Mother Mary. My conjecture about the fifth Mary thus falls away; Mary, the wife of Clopas, is the sister. Mother Mary and her sister were both present at the cross, and Mother Mary followed in the funeral procession, returning to the tomb on Sunday morning.

## JEWISH BURIAL CUSTOMS

John tells us that Jesus was buried according to the proper Jewish burial customs: "Taking Jesus' body, the two of them [Nicodemus and Joseph of Arimathea] wrapped it, with the spices, in strips of linen. This was in accordance with Jewish burial customs" (John 19:40). John uses the plural *othonia*, which is commonly (and incorrectly) translated as "strips of cloth" or "strips of linen." A more accurate phrase would be "fine linens" or "linen wrappings."[46]

Jewish burial practices dictated at death the closing of the eyes and a first anointing, which typically involved aloe and myrrh (spices), before washing the body with water or oil. A second anointing followed these steps and a final wrapping in a clean linen sheet called a *sindon*, with additional spices. Strips of linen would bind the sheet around the body, including a strip to tie up the jaw so it would not drop open. However, if the dead had lost too much blood, it was preferable not to wash the body to retain as much lifeblood as possible for burial; even if the blood had soaked into a cloth, clothes, or some dirt, these would go into the tomb with the body. In that case, the body and bloody objects would be anointed.

A procession, including family members, would then take the body on a bier or a blanket to be buried within hours of death. Between 100 BCE and the Temple's destruction in 70 CE, many people were laid to rest in rock-hewn tombs in the hill country of Galilee and Judea, while others were buried in the ground. Burial in a rock-hewn tomb was the first of two separate and distinct burials. The first burial consisted of the simple placement of the body in the tomb, either in a niche—a *loculus*, the Latin for "a little place," in Hebrew, a *kokh*—which was a shaft cut as deep as a body into the burial chamber wall, or on an *arcosolium*, a bench or shelf cut out of the wall of a tomb.

The second burial occurred about a year later, when family members re-entered the tomb, carefully gathered the bones of the deceased—once the flesh had decomposed entirely—and placed them in a specially prepared, separate container known as an ossuary, from the Latin "os," meaning "bone." These chests were then placed in small niches in the family tomb for permanent burial. Gathering the bones was considered one of the critical duties of a son and was viewed as a time of rejoicing. This practice ended by the middle or end of the 200s CE.[47]

---

45     (Eusebius, *Church History*, 3.11.2).

46     (The Editors of Bible Hub, Strong's Concordance n.d., 3608).

47     For more information see (Holzapfel, et al. 2008).

## 4. BURIAL

April 1, 33, 3:00 p.m. to 6:00+ approximately (Mark 15:38–47; John 19:31–42).

*Figure 47 **A Blood Moon***

*A blood moon due to a partial lunar eclipse like the one that occurred after sunset and at moonrise around the time of Jesus' burial in Jerusalem on April 1, 33 CE. The earth is between the sun and the moon, thus obscuring the normal bright sunshine from illuminating the moon, a lunar eclipse. This picture shows a partial eclipse as a portion of the moon appears dim in Earth's shadow. The red colour is due to Earth's atmosphere; light is bent inward and coloured red by dust and water in the atmosphere, just like at sunrise or sunset, causing a second inner shadow cone that illuminates a portion of the moon. Partial eclipses like this are relatively common. Image courtesy of Martin Adams.*

The Jews did not want dead, naked bodies on display, so sometime after 3:00 p.m., they requested the Romans to break the victims' legs to hasten death via asphyxiation, a standard procedure according to the available archaeological evidence. For instance, in 1970, the bones of a crucified man were discovered in an ossuary from first-century Jerusalem; the right heel bone still had a nail in it, the forearms showed evidence of nails, and the bones of the lower legs had been broken.[48] However, the Romans did not have to break Jesus' legs, for he was already dead by 3:00 p.m. Just to be sure, a spear was thrust into his left side, piercing his heart and causing blood and internal fluids to escape, which John witnessed.

---

48    (M. Friedman 2012).

Because Passover started after sundown around 6:00 p.m. or shortly thereafter, there were only three hours to make burial arrangements before the Sabbath and Passover started. Nicodemus[49] brought myrrh and aloes, and Joseph brought a linen cloth. Both were members of the Sanhedrin and secret supporters of Jesus. Once Jesus was dead, Joseph sought to take custody of his body. Joseph would have travelled to the Praetorium to see Pilate and waited to gain an audience. Then Pilate would have awaited confirmation of Jesus' death, and a legal document allowing the release of the body would likely have been created and signed. Around that time, the burial linens, including the face cloth, and spices would have been purchased in the marketplace. Until Joseph returned with official permission, no one would have been allowed to go near the corpse.

According to the forensic information from the Sudarium (the face cloth), the body was dead in a vertical position for about an hour before the face cloth was applied at around 4:00 p.m. Joseph's mission, therefore, took about an hour. Once rigor mortis started to set in, liquids would have started flowing again, post-mortem, from the wounds. The facecloth was most likely double folded, wrapped across the face, and pinned at the back, for it seems that the right cheek was resting on the right arm, thus preventing a full wrap-around. The cloth remained in contact with the body for about an hour until about 5:00 p.m. Then at least five persons (based on recreations), probably soldiers, lifted the body down, still attached to the crosspiece. It is probable that a preliminary shroud would have been provided at this point to keep blood from escaping the body.

The corpse was then placed in a prone horizontal position with the face partially turned to the right for about an hour until about 6:00 p.m. The cloth remained over the face. During that time, the body was moved momentarily, perhaps to remove the nails and crosspiece, while face down for about five minutes with someone—most probably a servant of Josephus or Nicodemus—attempting to staunch the flow of liquids from the nose and mouth. With the arm obstruction dealt with, the cloth was removed, unfolded, and wrapped around the entire head, and then knotted at the top, held in place to the hair by some sharp objects. The head, still face down, was held up on the cheek by a left hand, which created a clear imprint on the cloth. This all occurred over five to ten minutes. Next, the body was laid on its back around 6:00 p.m., the cloth was removed, and aloe and myrrh were applied; the cloth was then replaced. The body was not washed, since as much lifeblood as possible had to be kept with the body or soaked up.

With the face cloth and probably wrapped with the preliminary shroud, the body would have been transported by the bearers to the tomb. Those who came into contact with the body were considered unclean and needed an extended purification ritual, which meant they would miss the Passover. It is thus unlikely that Joseph or Nicodemus personally attended the body. An individual kept the cloth pressed over the face to contain blood flow while others carried the body; five bearers were probably involved, certainly servants of Joseph and Nicodemus. Following burial customs, Jesus' mother, Mary, the women, and John would have escorted the body. The procession lasted no more than five or ten minutes. There is no way of knowing if the burial was completed before 6:00 p.m. or over into Passover. Note that there is no mention of who owned the tomb, just that it was nearby, but Nicodemus or Joseph probably owned it since no permission to use it was needed.

John and Peter-Mark mention details of the burial. This is what John relates regarding the burial site:

"At the place where Jesus was crucified, there was a garden, and in the garden a new tomb, in which no one had ever been laid. Because it was the Jewish day of Preparation and since the tomb was nearby, they laid Jesus there." (John 19:41–42)

As for Peter, he says: "So Joseph bought some linen cloth, took down the body, wrapped it in the linen, and placed it in a tomb cut out of rock. Then he rolled a stone against the entrance of the tomb" (Mark 15:46).

From these statements, we can deduce that the tomb was in the same "place," Golgotha, as the crucifixion. How far away, we do not know, but it was "nearby," according to John, and the bearers needed only minutes to reach it.

We are also told that the tomb was new, with a garden or gardens next to it. Typical of tombs of the time, it almost certainly had a large, rollable "stopper" stone that would be rolled on the ground and manoeuvred into or over the ground level entrance.[50] The traditionally imagined entrance, with large, wheel-shaped stones, became common in later centuries but were extremely

---

49     Regarding Nicodemus, Richard Bauckham offers an interesting reconstruction of the Gurion family, an extremely wealthy and influential family in Jerusalem, leading up to the First Roman-Jewish War starting in 66 CE. Bauckham argues that Nicodemus was a member. (Bauckham, *The Testimony of the Beloved Disciple* 2007, 137-173)

50     (Sauter 2019).

rare at the time. The entrance was low, as one had to stoop to enter. The tomb contained a bench along the right wall (there is no mention of additional benches, although there may have been more), with the linen wrappings visible from the entrance, as John mentions later on (John 20:5). Presumably, the bench was wide and long enough for a body to rest on it, so perhaps two feet wide and seven feet long.

We are told that in the tomb, Jesus was laid on the bench made of limestone,[51] so it was a bench-type tomb or an "arcosolium." The facecloth was removed but left in the tomb due to the amount of blood it contained. The body was wrapped in the expensive, clean shroud with aloe and myrrh. Aloe and myrrh were also applied to the blood on the facecloth. If coins and flowers were present, they would have been put in place at this time. The burial was partially incomplete due to the time constraints, as Passover was only minutes away or had already started. A chin strap was applied, but the shroud mainly was draped over the body, not tightly wrapped with linen bands, nor was there a second anointing, as custom normally dictated. However, the bare minimum was completed according to Jewish burial custom, most certainly directed by Joseph and Nicodemus. John accompanied Mary Magdalene and Jesus' mother to the tomb. There, he also saw the final deposition of the linens (i.e., the linen wrapping the body and the Sudarium put off to the side). If a preliminary shroud was used, its disposition is not clear. Then the tomb was evacuated, and the rolling stone plugged the low entrance. This would have been completed at around 6:00 p.m. or a little after.

Where are the sites of the crucifixion and the tomb today? The Church of the Holy Sepulchre, *sepulchre*, meaning "stone room," claims to preserve the traditional sites. When you enter the church, the tomb is located on the left toward the back, under the central dome. Only the stone bench for the body and a portion of the wall on that side remain; the rest of the original tomb has been removed. A small structure, called the Edicule, has been built around the bench, creating a small room clad in marble. The original bench has been shown to have a slab covering it, probably from crusader times, with some fill, then the external marble slab placed on top. It was recently refurbished in 2016.[52]

The stone hill, called Golgotha or Calvary, consists of a rock column about seven metres long by three metres wide and five metres high on the right as you enter the church; ascending a set of stairs to the second level, you can see the top where a slot in the rock is claimed to be where the cross stood.

In Appendix 4, I discuss these sites and conclude the traditional tomb is probably not the one Jesus was laid in, although it is perhaps nearby. And I concur with Taylor that the crucifixion site is better identified about 200 metres south from the traditional site, in today's Old City: "a little to the southwest of where David Street meets Habad Street, but north of St. Mark Street."[53]

## 5. AFTER THE BURIAL

April 3, 33 CE 5:30 a.m. onwards (John 20:1–21:25; Mark 16:1–16:20; 1 Corinthians 15:3–8).

Mary Magdalene and Jesus' mother knew where the tomb was and could thus return to the correct site post-burial to perform the second anointing and finish any part of the burial not completed on Friday due to the hastened proceedings. Knowing the location was necessary because the tomb had been donated; they were unfamiliar with Jerusalem, and it was situated in an area where there likely were many similar tombs. They would otherwise not have known which sealed tomb to approach.

On Sunday, April 3, the first day of the week, around sunrise (about 5.30 a.m.)—John says that it was still dark, while Peter-Mark says "just after sunrise"—Mary Magdalene, Mary, and Salome went to the tomb and saw that the stone plug had been rolled away. The tomb was also empty. The burial had occurred 36 hours before.[54]

John provides a detailed account of what happened next. Apparently, he and Peter were together on that fateful morning when Mary Magdalene returned and told them of the missing body. Both men ran to the tomb and saw the burial linens, with the face cloth folded up off to the side. They both entered, and John said "He saw and believed" (John 20:8b–9) that Jesus had

---

51    As limestone dust is on the Shroud.

52    (Estrin 2017).

53    (J. E. Taylor 2009).

54    Note Jesus was entombed 36 hours, not the traditional three days.

risen, due to the flattened nature of the linen wrap. Afterwards, John and Peter each departed for their separate "homes." John relates the story told by Mary Magdalene, which includes two angels in the tomb and a conversation with Jesus, whom she mistook for the gardener—remember that the tomb was in a garden-like environment.[55] John then reveals how Jesus appeared three times to his disciples and others: once on that same evening, another a week later, and then later in Galilee. In the last instance, John was explicitly present.

As already discussed, Peter-Mark's narrative is more problematic and episodic; it is indeed chronologically incorrect. Mark first relates the story of a group of women who saw a young man in Jesus' tomb upon returning to the burial site. The man told them that Jesus had risen, after which they fled. Since John makes no mention of a group of women finding an empty tomb, this must have been a second-hand story passed on to Peter, so I am inclined to set it aside. Then Peter-Mark describes Peter's version of Mary Magdalene first seeing the risen Jesus, despite the earlier discovery by the group of women.[56] Mark does not relate Peter's viewing of the empty tomb as related by John, an important story that Mark must not have heard. Mark also includes a bizarre report (or rumour) that Jesus appeared "in a different form" to two disciples walking in the country. Again, John puts no stock in this story by not mentioning it. Peter-Mark's verse 14 matches John's version (John 20:19) of Jesus' first appearance to the group. Near the end of Peter-Mark, there is another very brief description of Jesus appearing to the eleven disciples,[57] as in John. Mark obviously had no information on the second and third resurrection visits described by John; otherwise, he would most definitely have included them. Finally, Mark has Jesus passing on some rather strange remarks, mentioning demons, glossolalia, and snake handling—things John does not mention. Afterwards, Jesus was "taken up into heaven," and Mark quickly wraps up his Gospel. As previously noted, Peter-Mark offers no reliable resurrection narrative, but rather, just like in Mark's odd chapter 13, a pastiche of overlapping and conflicting stories.

Peter-Mark's sequence only matches John's precise story in a few places. John says nothing of the other events related by Peter-Mark, thereby discounting them. John is adamant that Jesus only appeared on three occasions, and he describes each instance. Therefore, I am inclined to set aside Mark's conflicting and uncorroborated stories.

So the most likely resurrection sequence, therefore, goes as follows:

On the morning of Sunday, April 3, Jesus was seen by Mary Magdalene outside the empty tomb. That evening, Jesus was seen by his followers (including Peter and John, but Thomas was missing) inside a house where they were all in hiding. On Sunday, April 10, Jesus appeared again in the same place to his followers, with Thomas in attendance this time. Sometime afterwards— enough time for some group members (including Peter and John) to travel to Galilee—Jesus appeared for the final time while the men were fishing.

And this event marks the end of our available information on Jesus' activities.

As a concluding note on the chronology of John and Peter-Mark, I would like to stress that I was surprised by how well the accounts agree and integrate; there was little overlap, and only minor conflicts exist between these two narratives. On careful investigation, I have created a relatively complete account of Jesus' movements based on John's and Peter's distinct yet complementary eyewitness perspectives.

The resurrection, the most famous miracle associated with Jesus, is only the final in a series of similarly wonderous actions discussed in the next chapter.

---

55    The usual hard-headed John must have thought this second-hand story was true since he included it.

56    It was no wonder it was easy for some later editors to believe the truncated ending (the Shorter Ending) was a better fit.

57    The only instance Peter is an eyewitness to these events.

# CHAPTER 29

# THE MIRACLES

"The Christian religion not only was at first attended with miracles, but even at this day cannot be believed by any reasonable person without one."

—David Hume, *Of Miracles*

Both Peter and John claim that supernatural events, miracles, were associated with Jesus. It is essential to examine these miracles, so I have chosen to explore the miracles separately from my itinerary of Jesus because they are controversial and encompass many exciting features that require discussion. (Note I have already eliminated Peter and Mark's embellishments from the miracle stories.)

## NUMBER AND VARIETY

There is a strikingly large number of miracles described in Peter-Mark and John. These include the well-known miracles and healings but also Jesus' apparent precognition of future events: his betrayal, the denial by Peter, his death and resurrection, plus more minor incidental things such as his knowledge of the Samaritan woman's husbands and seeing Nathaniel under the fig tree before they meet. There are many miracles explicitly described by eyewitnesses but many more alluded to by John and Peter—so many more that the authors refer to them almost casually in a throwaway phrase like, "he did a lot more miracles, but I don't have the space to go into them."

The most numerous miracles are the healings. They indeed make up around half of the miracles reported. Healings are performed in different manners. Sometimes Jesus touches the afflicted; other times, he heals through verbal commands. Healings may also take place from a distance, as in the case of Jesus healing the royal official's son who was in Capernaum while Jesus was in Cana (John 4:46–53). Other types of healings involve some makeshift ointment, such as mud, oil, or saliva. At least some supposed healings were unintentional; the sick touched either Jesus or his garment and were healed as a result, such as the bleeding woman (Mark 5:25–29).

As for the afflictions requiring healing, they are equally varied. They range from mental illnesses to all sorts of physical ailments. We thus find instances of simple fevers, psychotic states, physical deformities, and blindness. Amongst the most severe conditions that Jesus encountered were the near-death experience of Jarius' daughter and Lazarus' four-day death.

A common characteristic of all the healings is their instantaneous effect. For instance, in Peter-Mark, a man with a deformed hand had it "completely restored" in view of a crowd at the synagogue in Capernaum (Mark 3:1–5). Jesus also ordered a paralytic man to pick up his mat and walk, as he was instantly healed (Mark 2:10–12).

But the "authority" that Jesus wields seems fallible at times. On a visit to Nazareth, Jesus could not perform any miracles apart from a few healings (Mark 6:4–6). Another example is Jesus, while in Bethsaida, being cajoled into healing a blind man. It requires several attempts, since the man reports people appear like "trees" after the first attempt.

Beyond the healings, there are also other forms of very diverse miracles. For instance, Jesus calmed the storm and walked on water; he somehow manufactured thousands of food portions and changed water into wine; he displayed unexplained knowledge, including foreknowledge; there were visible "Spirit" manifestations, disembodied voices, and a withered fig tree. Some were witnessed by a single person, others by a few people. Others yet were observed by a crowd of thousands.

Another peculiar feature is that some miracles are just odd. For instance, when Jesus changes the six vats of water into wine at the wedding in Cana. Jesus' mother initiates the miracle, not Jesus. Jesus at first refuses, then reluctantly complies with her request to sort out the shortage of wine. The miracle does nothing for Jesus' mission; it teaches no lesson but just provides more wine for a party. It happens away from the crowd, so it is unseen. The miracle is banal. There is no prayer or incantation; it just "happens." And the result is confusion; even the joking banquet master does not know what Jesus did. Another example is the healing of the blind man at the Siloam Pool in Jerusalem. Jesus applies mud to the man's eyes and departs; only later, when the man washes in the pool, did he regain his sight. Confusion ensues. His neighbours and parents do not know what to make of it; the Pharisees are divided, and the man does not understand what happened and does not know who healed him or who Jesus is. Contrast these features with contemporaneous fabricated miracles stories, in this case the nativity narratives of Matthew and Luke (Matthew 1–2; Luke 1–2). Angels frequently visit with formal pronouncements, participants deliver set-piece speeches, the heavenly host appears, an evil king is outwitted, wise men come and go, Jesus is foretold, but basic factual errors are made; each story reads as if drawn from the JS. These spectacular miracle sequences push the narrative along with no extraneous details, no vivid eyewitness colouring, confusion, or doctrinal uncertainty.

Both Peter and John include odd qualities in their miracle sequences:

- They are presented as banal, almost boring; many are only mentioned in passing.

- The miracles are reported as ultimately hindering the mission.

- They spread fear and confusion.

- They contain odd extraneous details.

- Jesus seems disinclined to perform miracles, and at times he laments the need for them, denigrates them, or refuses to perform them.

# A CONSPIRACY?

*Figure 48* **Edict of Caesar**

*The inscription, dated to around 0 to 50 CE and probably originating from the Greek island of Kos, written in Greek records an "Edict of Caesar" stating that graves and tombs, including the contents, must remain undisturbed forever. The penalty for a "tomb-breaker" is capital punishment.*

The miracles, including the various resurrection appearances, are the most controversial elements of Jesus' story. If they are not true, how did these miracles stories come about? My aim in this section is to reconstruct the most likely scenario for their fabrication.

I have established a list of all the miracles contained in my Source List. I counted any unexplained phenomenon as a "miracle," from Jesus' allusion to some three-day interval (John 2:20) to the detailed set-piece miracles, such as the Wedding in Cana (John 2:1–11). I have excluded the sections I have already deemed unreliable, such as the transfiguration dream in Peter-Mark. I also consider the demon healings as regular healings sans demons. There are 64 miracles reported: 27 in John, 35 in Mark, and 2 in Q.

If the miracles did not occur, then how did they end up in these two gospels? Both eyewitnesses, John and Peter, knowingly reported fabricated elements in their stories, so it was a conspiracy of a least these two spanning

20 plus years. But how many more were involved? Quite a few miracles occurred with the disciples in attendance, so it is hard to see how Peter (and John) could report these stories if some or all the disciples were not "in on it"—Peter and John would be called out and discredited immediately. Since John, further out from the inner disciple group, was also a co-conspirator, this would imply that the rest of the inner group and other non-disciples were also involved. For instance, Mary Magdalene reports her resurrection experience, so she would also have to be part of the conspiracy.

Mark published his gospel in 40 CE, based on the preaching and teaching of Peter, which included miracle stories. Since Peter-Mark, John, and Q have fabricated miracles, Peter cannot be the sole source (i.e., he cannot be the sole creator, so the stories must go back to the very beginning, when the Core Message+ was being fashioned in the weeks and months after Jesus' death). That way, the stories could be "kept straight" and avoid later changes and contradictions in the oral tradition.

Both Peter and John are clear about the reasons for including miracle stories as part of their narrative on the life, death, and deeds of Jesus; they wished to make the reader believe Jesus was a tremendously important person, sent from God with an important message. The conspiracy group must have thought that message so important that the movement it created could not be allowed to die after Jesus was killed. So they had to retroactively embellish their narrative, both oral and then written, with miracles to confer further legitimacy to the figure of Jesus. After all, the manner of his death, which was that of a disgraced traitor, impeded his credibility and the spreading of his message.

I sort the miracle stories into five groups, based on the risk of discovery, starting with the most straightforward to manufacture and ending with the most problematic:

1. Resurrection appearances. The conspirators move the stopper stone, take the body, dump it somewhere before Sunday morning, and then make up resurrection appearances. This would be easy and involve the least number of conspirators, although a risky approach, as a desecration of the dead was a capital offence decreed by the Emperor.[1]

2. The miracles with only the inner group present and the vague non-specific miracles. The miracles "witnessed" only by Jesus or close followers and the generic "he did many amazing things" and retro-accurate predictions (e.g., foreknowledge of Peter's denial before the cock crows) all belong in this group. This group includes walking on water, healings with just Jesus or the inner group present, calming the storm, killing the fig tree, healing the man with leprosy, claims of other unspecified miracles, and so on.

3. The soft miracles: These are all the healings that could be termed charismatic faith healings (non-physical healing witnessed by outsiders).[2]

4. The hard miracles: These miracles are ones seen or experienced by groups of outsiders. This group includes turning the water into wine, Peter-Mark's two feedings of the multitude, various physical healings performed in full view of the witnesses, such as the healing the paralytic in full view of the crowd (Mark 2:10–12).

5. The hard miracles with ramifications. These are hard miracles as in the last group but which have ramifications later in the story. These would be the most problematic for the conspirators to insert into the narrative because they necessitated fabricating the original miracle and all subsequent references and reactions to it.

The presence of witnesses complicates the creation of miracle stories. Palestine at the time was a small place with a tightly connected population, where information travelled quickly. The miracles were all claimed to have happened in the last two years or so during Jesus' mission when the powerful elites were intent on discrediting him and his movement. From the protective anonymity deployed by Peter, we can infer authorities were still on the lookout for specific followers and would have been eager to undermine any claims made by Christians for some time after Jesus' death. The most significant risk would be the group 4 or 5 miracle claims

---

1    As seen in the inscription above.

2    According to Vermes, "most of the diseases exorcised or healed in the New Testament could be recognized as hysterical." (G. Vermes, Jesus the Jew: *A Historian's Reading of the Gospels* 1981, 23)

made in the weeks or months following Jesus' death; those would immediately be at risk of de-bunking. For example, in the early part of Jesus' Galilean mission at the synagogue in Capernaum, he healed a man who had a deformed hand in front of witnesses, including hostile Pharisees (Mark 3:1–5). It was easy enough to either authenticate or disprove this story by going to Capernaum and inquiring. In fact, the authorities did precisely this after Jesus supposedly healed the blind man at the pool of Siloam (John 9:1–34). Jesus then disappears from the action, and the story follows the man interacting first with his stunned neighbours and then angry Pharisees who suggest it is all a hoax. The latter launched an investigation and subpoenaed the man's parents and the man (twice) to verify that he had been blind from birth. The Pharisees failed to detect any hoax. Again, as this fabricated event occurred just a year before, it would have been easy to disprove it, particularly as members of the elites were supposedly involved.

The Lazarus story must have been particularly risky to fabricate. It was a fantastic event: the return to life after a four-day death accomplished in front of a crowd in broad daylight, with named witnesses at that—Martha, Mary, and Lazarus himself, of course. The event occurred at a specific date in the recent past, during the day of March 27, 33 CE, and at a particular location, Bethany, which was just a few kilometres from Jerusalem (John 11:1–45). The story is most detailed in John (it takes up one entire chapter), while Peter-Mark describes the event in an extended verse, which, as I discussed earlier, Mark chose not to include in his original Gospel. In both cases, later events from the life of Jesus were greatly influenced by that alleged miracle; in John, the chief priests and Pharisees, on hearing the resurrection report, finally decided to have Jesus killed. Later, when Jesus had dinner with Lazarus, and so many people came to see the resurrected man for themselves, the chief priests decided to get rid of Lazarus too (John 12:9–10). All of this would have to be fabricated, and it all could easily be debunked. Because the miracle occurred just outside Jerusalem, at a specific time, with named participants who would still be alive, it would be straightforward for opponents to go to Bethany and inquire, even years after. If it were reported as never having happened, then Jesus' followers would be discredited. That is undoubtedly the first thing the Jewish leaders would have done. The easiest way of combating the movement would be to investigate and disprove many, or just a few, of the claimed miracles.

Would Jesus have been part of the conspiracy? This seems inevitable, as he was carrying out faith healings and would have been aware of any fabrications made while he lived. He used those stories to help proclaim his message, and he may have persuaded his disciples to continue the duplicity in the name of religious reform.

For myself, the most probable conspiracy sequence would be this. Jesus, adept in faith healings and other "tricks" akin to the widely used practice of magic, starts a religious reform movement in an environment where many people believe in demons, magic, and other supernatural events. In the weeks and months following Jesus' death, his group manufactured the resurrection narrative and the Core Message+ with miracles inserted into an otherwise realistic story of Jesus. Amazingly, the duplicity was not discovered. Eventually, two eyewitnesses writing 25 years apart created written accounts of the embellished oral traditions.

However, there are problems with this sequence of events:

- This theory easily covers groups 1, 2, and 3 miracles but not groups 4 and 5 miracles, which are more problematic. Why create the 4 and 5 category miracles at all? For instance, why create reports of massive feedings? Why not report the raising of Lazarus with just the inner group present? Why take the risk? Why fabricate outside witnesses? It risked the whole enterprise by creating the real possibility of discredit by choruses of voices shouting, "That never happened!"

- In the few cases where John and Peter tell the same miracle (e.g., the first "thousands feeding" and the raising of Lazarus), the accounts are quite varied. Although the essential story is the same, why draw attention to the fact that the versions are different?[3] Should these not have been harmonized by the conspirators?

- There is no tradition of Jesus or his followers falsifying miracles, not in the Early Church literature nor among opponents of Christianity. All through the miracle stories, Jesus' opponents have no issue with the miracles themselves; instead, they oppose them on religious grounds—they are done on the Sabbath, or the miracle's power does not come from the Jewish God. The reported debunking attempts are failures. This extends through the early history of the

---

3    Even more telling when John had a copy of Mark when composing his Gospel.

Church, as there is no evidence or even rumours of a tradition from the Church's many opponents that one or some of the miracles reported were falsified.[4] Such accusations would have been very damaging, and opponents would have repeated them. Even Jewish Josephus tells us Jesus was "a doer of wonderful works" and did not qualify it with a "claimed" or mention that these rumours were fraudulent. As I have shown, debunking would have been very easy in most cases.

- If the raising of Lazarus was a fabrication, why hide Peter's account of it?

- Why did John refuse to include demon healing miracles while mentioning other miracles?

- If the conspirators were fabricating the miracles, why document how counter-productive and confusing they were to the mission?

- Why fabricate miracle hesitancy, secrecy, and failures?

- Why fabricate the odd, eclectic mix of mostly minor miracles? Why not stick with grandiose set-piece productions with angels, speeches, and JS trappings, such as the birth narratives from Luke and Matthew, or Herod's beheading of the Baptist?

- It seems incredible that, as with any conspiracy, with so many people, so many lies over so many years, no one "told," even though Jesus' followers were excommunicated from Judaism, harassed, physically assaulted, arrested, imprisoned, tortured, and killed. Even Christianity's foes do not have any instance of someone recanting Jesus' "miracles."

It is challenging to come up with a satisfactory hoax scenario that covers all these points. If, as I have shown, the Gospel accounts were produced while eyewitnesses were still alive to contradict the miracles, it seems incredible, then, that the accounts were not immediately and easily disproved. The only other solution is that the miracles were fabricated at a much later date (40 or more years?) when there would be no danger of living eyewitnesses and the authors (not John or Peter) were free to insert whatever stories they wished. But this does not fit with the fact that John and Peter-Mark are early works written by eyewitnesses.[5]

---

4    Celsus, a second century Greek philosopher writing in the late 100s CE, did attack the stories of the Christians claiming miracles—not that they did not happen but rather that they were due to Jesus using magic or trickery versus divine power. Christian critic Porphyry also did not deny the miracles but attributed them to demonic powers.

5    Q's miracles are so slight they could be inserted from the beginning without fear of contradiction.

# CHAPTER 30

# WHAT DID JESUS SAY?

*Figure 49* **Christ Pantocrator**

*"Pantocrator" means "Almighty" and is a typical depiction of Jesus in art. This striking image is a detail from the oldest icon (a sacred image used in personal devotion) in existence, dating to the 500s CE. It survived two periods of iconoclasm, "war on icons," in the Byzantine Empire, in which religious images were deemed inappropriate and destroyed. Its survival was due to its location in a remote area under Muslim control. The image is unusual, as the face is made up of two halves that are subtly different, thought to represent the "dual nature" of Jesus.*

"… all the ideas that have the greatest results are always simple."

– Leo Tolstoy, *War and Peace*

I have established what Jesus did, as much as can be known, answering my First Question. The next question to answer is: What did Jesus say?

It is easy enough to compile a list of what he said, but behind those sayings and teachings is his central message. Using my Source List, I have compiled a list of verses that capture all of Jesus' speech, teachings, and parables and then filtered out other people's sayings, for example, John the Baptist's pronouncements on Jesus, the Gospel authors' opinions, and scriptural quotations, to obtain a complete and historical picture of what Jesus said. I am wary of ideas contained in odd "one-off" statements (e.g., Mark states that Jesus' believers can pick up snakes and not be hurt—the only time this is mentioned).

Next, based on this package of sayings, I will put together a summary that encapsulates the central teaching of Jesus, which I call the Choice.

With Jesus' actions, I have been willing to accept the level of detail as presented in the texts as accurate. Not so much with the speeches. It is unlikely that John or Peter were able to remember precisely all of what Jesus said, and over three years, he would have said a lot; he was constantly teaching, after all. Short, pithy sayings, such as "It is easier for a camel to go through the eye of a needle than for a rich man to enter the kingdom of God,"[1] and the parables, which are designed to be easily remembered, would be recalled correctly, especially if often repeated. But the long discourses, such as the post-Last Supper discourse in John 13:5–18, are partial reconstructions of ideas that Jesus would have expressed on other occasions, in this case, put together by John. So how to extract the main ideas expressed by Jesus? The following characteristics can serve as a guide:

- They would be simple, something even uneducated rural folk could absorb, remember, and practise, and not be complex doctrine.

- They would be frequently repeated using different words, imagery, and stories, but the ideas would be the same.

- Jesus' ideas would shape his actions and those of his followers.

Having read over the sayings, I have arrived at the core message that he was trying to communicate with his followers and the people around him during his mission. All his teachings can be summed up by this message. In short, Jesus was presenting his audience with a clear choice: to believe or not.

## THE CHOICE

### God, the Father, exists.[2]

"No one has seen the Father except the one who is from God; only he has seen the Father." (John 6:46)

"Why do you call me good?" Jesus answered. "No one is good--except God alone." (Mark 10:18)

"Have faith in God," Jesus answered. (Mark 11:22)

---

1    Mark 10:25. There is an old story that a small gate in the Jerusalem wall called the Eye of the Needle; its small size meant that camels and other large animals could not enter. Also, some scholars claim "camel" should be "rope" or "cable," as there is only a single letter difference between the two Greek words.

2    The male gender reference is used by Jesus in his teachings but probably does not necessarily imply divine gender identification.

Jesus looked at them and said, "With man this is impossible, but not with God; all things are possible with God." (Mark 10:27)

**God loves you, so love him in return, as best you can.**

"Love the Lord your God with all your heart and with all your soul and with all your mind and with all your strength." (Mark 12:30)

"Whoever has my commands and obeys them, he is the one who loves me. He who loves me will be loved by my Father, and I too will love him and show myself to him." (John 14:21)

**Love everyone else because God loves them too. Do as best you can.**

"The second is this: 'Love your neighbour as yourself.' There is no commandment greater than these." (Mark 12:31)

"A new command I give you: Love one another. As I have loved you, so you must love one another. By this all men will know that you are my disciples, if you love one another." (John 13:34–35)

**God's interests are more important than worldly interests.**

Jesus looked at him and loved him. "One thing you lack," he said. "Go, sell everything you have and give to the poor, and you will have treasure in heaven. Then come, follow me." (Mark 10:21)

"You have let go of the commands of God and are holding on to the traditions of men." (Mark 7:8)

"For whoever wants to save his life will lose it, but whoever loses his life for me and for the gospel will save it. What good is it for a man to gain the whole world, yet forfeit his soul?" (Mark 8:35–36)

**You are free to choose to make God's will your will or not.**

"As for the person who hears my words but does not keep them, I do not judge him. For I did not come to judge the world, but to save it." (John 12:47)

"If anyone has ears to hear, let him hear." (Mark 4:28)

Then Jesus cried out, "When a man believes in me, he does not believe in me only, but in the one who sent me." (John 12:44)

**Those who place God's interests over the world's interests will be saved, raised from death, and given eternal life someday somehow, while those who choose the world (not God) will not and die like all things in the world.**

"The man who loves his life will lose it, while the man who hates his life in this world will keep it for eternal life." (John 12:25)

"For God so loved the world that he gave his one and only Son, that whoever believes in him shall not perish but have eternal life." (John 3:16)

"When the dead rise, they will neither marry nor be given in marriage; they will be like the angels in heaven." (Mark 12:25)

"There is a judge for the one who rejects me and does not accept my words; that very word which I spoke will condemn him at the last day." (John 12:48)

"But whoever blasphemes against the Holy Spirit will never be forgiven; he is guilty of an eternal sin." (Mark 3:28–29)

"I tell you the truth, he who believes has everlasting life." (John 6:47)

**No one who chooses God will be turned away.**

"All that the Father gives me will come to me, and whoever comes to me I will never drive away." (John 6:37)

"I tell you the truth, all the sins and blasphemies of men will be forgiven them." (Mark 3:28)

**Now that you are aware of the Choice, you must decide now.**

"The time has come," he said. "The kingdom of God is near. Repent and believe the good news!" (Mark 1:15)

But another said to him: "Master, permit me first to go and bury my father." But he [Jesus] said to him: "Follow me and leave the dead to bury their own dead." (Q 9:59-60)

"Follow me!" (John 21:19b)

Having answered the Second Question, I will proceed to the Third and final Question.

# CHAPTER 31

# WHO WAS JESUS?

*Figure 50 **Salvator Mundi***

*A painting of Jesus as Salvator Mundi (Latin for 'Saviour of the World') dated to around 1500 and attributed to Leonardo da Vinci, although there is still some debate. His right hand is making the sign of the cross while the glass globe in his left hand represents the universe. When sold in 2017, it became the most expensive painting in history at $450 million.*

This is the last question that I wish to address.

I have given what I consider to be the most probable answer to what Jesus did and what Jesus said. I have discussed the miracles and proposed the most plausible scenario for their fabrication. Depending on the gentle reader's attitude toward the miracles, the question of who Jesus was has two distinct alternatives:

1.  Jesus was a regular human who, when he was about thirty, God picked as his sole spokesperson to teach humanity about the Choice. When needed, God gave Jesus powers to perform miracles to draw attention to and establish Jesus' authority to teach. Jesus assented to death and resurrection as the final "call-to-arms,"[1] for it "produces many seeds" (John 12:24) for humanity. His followers experienced Jesus' resurrection, compiled the Core Message+, and propagated his teachings.

2.  Jesus was a regular human who believed he was picked as God's spokesperson to teach humanity the Choice, which he devised. He and his followers conspired to make it appear as though Jesus had powers to perform phony miracles to draw attention to and establish Jesus' authority to teach. Jesus was unexpectedly[2] captured and killed. His followers invented Jesus' resurrection and compiled the Core Message+, including fabricated miracles, and propagated his teachings.

## WAS JESUS JEWISH?

Jesus' teaching, although set against the backdrop of Judaism, has nothing to do with Judaism. Despite what scholars argue, I think it is not clear whether Jesus was ever Jewish, strict or otherwise. First, neither Peter nor John tells us anything about his youth; to say he was assuredly Jewish is conjectural. Jesus also grew up in rural Galilee, away from the strict Yahweh cult centred in Jerusalem. As mentioned, Semitic rural peoples from that area, such as those living in Galilee, had a mishmash of different beliefs and religious traditions stretching back over a thousand years, including Samaritan, Canaanite, Phoenician, Assyrian, and Aramaean traditions, as well as Judaism and Hellenistic paganism. The Samaritans, for instance, lived just south of Galilee and practised a parallel Jewish-like cult whose worship was (and still is) centred on Mount Gerizim, and the Hellenistic pagan region of the Decapolis was just over the Sea of Galilee. While Jesus certainly knew the JS, which he used in disputations with the Jewish authorities (for example, John 7:19–23), we have no indication of what influenced his early religious background.[3]

In any case, Jesus did not follow Judaism himself. We have no explicit mention of him following Jewish customs. He did not abide by the Jewish purity laws when he ate with sinners (Mark 2:14–17), he entered tombs and touched corpses (Peter-Mark 10:34b), he did not fast (Mark 2:18), and he famously and repeatedly disregarded the Sabbath. In fact, the only time the Sabbath is mentioned in the sources is when Jesus broke and disparaged it (for example, Mark 3:1–5). Jesus did visit Jerusalem for various festivals, but he never seemed to follow any of the rituals required to be an observant Jew; instead, he used those opportunities to teach to the assembled crowds and perform miracles (John 2:23). Similarly, he taught in the Capernaum synagogue, but not in the way the regular Jewish teachers did (Mark 1:22). The only explicit instance of Jesus following a Jewish ritual is in Peter-Mark, where he instructed his followers to prepare the Passover meal (Mark 14:12–14). But, as explained earlier, this was written in error; John describes that meal simply as "the evening meal" (John 13:2).

Jesus also did not teach Judaism; he taught the Choice.[4] What he taught was vastly simpler and distinct from Judaism. He affirmed the existence of a God of love (John 13:34–35, 5:41–42) instead of the fabricated and violent tribal god of JS. He often spoke of a new understanding, pouring "new wine in new wineskins" (Mark 2:22), with a decisive break from the past. He predicted the Temple's destruction (John 2:19), and he taught positions on essential topics at variance from Judaism, such

---

1    In an act that overcomes every human's greatest fear: painful, extended public death at the hands of an enemy.

2    Or, given the way he antagonized the elites, it was expected.

3    Interestingly, Peter claims that upon his death, Jesus cried out to Eloi, "my El," the older Canaanite word for God as distinct from the name Yahweh.

4    Indeed, Vermes argues Jesus went well beyond Judaism. (G. Vermes, *Jesus the Jew: A Historian's Reading of the Gospels* 1981, 224).

as his view on adultery (John 8:3–11), divorce (Mark 10:2–9), forgiveness, and traditional family relationships (Mark 3:35, 2:21–22). Listeners were amazed at his "new teaching" (Mark 1:27), asking where it came from (Mark 6:2). And Jesus would teach everyone who would listen, whether Greeks, Romans, Samaritans, or Jews. His message was inclusive. He also instituted a covenant (Mark 14:20–24), not a "new" covenant, which would imply some previous Jewish covenant. Finally, he implemented new, simple traditions, such as baptism[5] and the bread and wine ritual (which became the Eucharist). He introduced new core values, such as love and forgiveness (Mark 11–25), that departed from Judaism.[6]

But Jesus did not stop at Judaism; he also disregarded Jewish customs. Peter tells us that Jesus declared all food as clean (Mark 7:19), in defiance of many Jewish dietary customs.[7] In Q, we are told that Jesus instructed a follower to leave his father unburied, thus contradicting one of the most fundamental requirements of Judaism—the filial duty of a son to bury his father (Q 9:59-60). In the *Pericope Adulterae* (John 7:53–8:11), Jesus did not condemn an adulteress as required by JS (Deuteronomy 22:22–25). If Jesus was a practising Jew, he was not a good one.

In addition to the above litany of open challenges to Jewish traditions, Jesus would heal people on the spot for free, thus obviating the need for a Jewish priesthood. He was even straightforward about it; in one instance, he healed a leper and then told him to present himself to the priests as already healed (Mark 1:44)! As Reza Aslan explains,[8] this let the man off the hook for the very complicated, time-consuming, and expensive procedure needed for priestly cleansing as "commanded by Moses" and described in Leviticus (Leviticus 14:1–32).

And when teaching and debating, Jesus did not systematically quote scripture, which he called "rules taught by men" (Mark 7:7) or "your own Law" (John 8:15–17), to imply that the JS were human-made and not divine. He would only do so on the rare instances when the scriptures were in harmony with the Choice.[9] And, famously, he used the Great Commandment, which is just another formulation of the Choice (Mark 12:28–34).

The Jewish authorities bitterly opposed Jesus and his teachings so much that they had him eliminated using a sham trial. They would not have done such a thing if Jesus had been strengthening and teaching Judaism. In any case, if Jesus were who he said he was, he would have known that Judaism was a fabrication by men, not divine Law. So why would he be an adherent?

Much confusion over the relationship between Jesus and Judaism comes from the evangelists and Jesus himself. Simply put, the Gospel writers attempted to make Jesus part of the Jewish narrative, albeit a new version. Both John and Peter frequently speak of JS as being fulfilled in Jesus. For instance, John interprets the soldiers not breaking Jesus' legs and wounding him in the side after death as fulfilling a specific passage from the JS: "These things happened so that the scripture would be fulfilled: 'Not one of his bones will be broken,' and, as another scripture says, 'They will look on the one they have pierced'" (John 19:36–37). As for Peter, he interprets the appearance of the Baptist as fulfilling the prophet Isaiah: "It is written in Isaiah the prophet: 'I will send my messenger ahead of you, who will prepare your way—a voice of one calling in the desert, Prepare the way for the Lord, make straight paths for him.' And so, John [the Baptist] came" (Mark 1:2–4).

This projection of Jesus back into the JS is even more prominent in Luke and Matthew, whose birth narratives were created to firmly fit Jesus into the Jewish Salvation history, making him the long-awaited Jewish Messiah. For example, what was a personal mystical experience for Jesus when he wandered the desert by himself (Mark 1:11–13), Peter casts in biblical terms; he says he was tempted by Satan (Job 2:1) 40 days and 40 nights (Exodus 24:17), and heard a voice from Heaven (Isaiah 42:1). This is understandable, as Jesus' first followers mainly were Jews whose worldview was shaped by the JS, which were viewed as

---

5    "For a number of reasons it is quite likely that Jesus' gospel also required baptism. Firstly, it seems unlikely that his disciples introduced this decisive ritual at their own initiative. Secondly, Jesus began his own career accepting the rite of repentance and forgiveness" (Bockmuehl 2003, 30).

6    Interestingly, for what it is worth, the deacon Stephen during his trial, which resulted in his stoning, was accused of preaching that Jesus will "change the customs Moses handed down to us" Acts 6:14.

7    For instance, the ban on consuming non-kosher animals in Leviticus 11:3–8 and Deuteronomy 14:3–21.

8    (Aslan 2013, 113).

9    Mark 2:25–26, 7:6–8, 13, 10:5, 19; John 8:17. This is precisely the message of the *Pericope Adulterae*.

accurate and reliable. Hence, anything as momentous as the mission of Jesus *must* somehow be linked with scripture and, by extension, Judaism. All that was needed was to search the scripture for relevant verses. Indeed, despite Jesus' teachings, the Early Church seemed just like any other Jewish sect, with followers obeying some or most Jewish customs and laws, as they always had, in addition to early Christian tenets. Early Christianity was thus a syncretic Jewish-Jesus belief system. However, Jesus' group eventually distanced itself from Judaism, for the internal conflicts became too great. We have a taste of those problems in a letter by Paul, in which he famously confronted Peter about his apparent flip-flopping on the issue of eating with non-Jews:

> "When Cephas [Peter] came to Antioch, I opposed him to his face because he stood condemned. For before certain men came from James [the brother of Jesus], he used to eat with the Gentiles. But when they arrived, he began to draw back and separate himself from the Gentiles because he was afraid of those who belonged to the circumcision group. The other Jews joined him in his hypocrisy, so that by their hypocrisy even Barnabas was led astray. When I saw that they were not acting in line with the truth of the gospel, I said to Cephas in front of them all, "You are a Jew, yet you live like a Gentile and not like a Jew. How is it, then, that you force Gentiles to follow Jewish customs?" (Galatians 11–14)

So apparently, Peter, a direct follower of Jesus who told us how Jesus did not follow Judaism, was also not following Judaism but would reverse course when James or his Jewish faction ("the circumcised group") were present.[10] Jesus' followers ultimately left Judaism, since it was incompatible with their radical new faith.[11]

## WAS JESUS THE MESSIAH?

In Jewish scripture, there are 38 references to MSYH—that is, "moshiach" or "the anointed one"[12]—referring to the Jewish practice of pouring or smearing oil on someone charged with a divine office, such as a king, a priest, or a prophet. Many of the supposed Messianic prophecies in JS are veiled references to specific people in history, like the prophet Elijah or the Persian king Cyrus. The term came to mean a future Jewish king or priest descended from King David, who would rule Israel under divine command and usher in a new era of religious purity. The few allusions to a forthcoming Messiah say nothing about there being miracles connected with him, nor is there any specific divinity attached to his figure in the JS. Since the Jews were repeatedly conquered and dominated by powerful neighbouring empires, they were naturally anxious for the Messiah to appear; they hoped that he would finally bring freedom and autonomy to their people. By the first century CE, Palestine was gripped by messianic fever, and resistance leaders frequently adopted a messianic role, as did many other individuals afterwards. However, all messianic figures were nipped in the bud by the Romans, except for Messiah-poseurs Menahem and Simon bar-Giora, who destroyed Israel in the First Jewish-Roman revolt (66–70 CE). Later on, Messiah-poseur Simon bar Kokhba would set off the Second Jewish-Roman revolt (132–135 CE), which would destroy Israel again. Overall, the Jewish messianic project was a complete failure.[13]

---

10    James appears quite conservative as regards the Jewish Law; he made Paul cleanse himself in the Temple (Acts 21:17-26) and denies rumours of a rebellion against the Torah. He probably authored the Epistle of James, a very Jewish letter. John also tells us that James was not a follower of Jesus, at least early on. Perhaps due to his family relation to Jesus and piousness, he became a Church leader despite following Jewish Law.

11    Despite this separation, it is important to note how rooted current day Pauline-Christianity is in Judaism; this can be seen in the Christian Bible, which is two-thirds Jewish writings.

12    For more information, please see (The Editors of Encyclopaedia Britannica, Messiah 2020).

13    At the end of both revolts, the Roman emperors dispersed the Jewish population across the Empire, which laid the seeds for modern-day Zionism or the idea of the Jews returning to a Palestinian homeland.

Jesus was not that long-awaited Jewish Messiah in any form. However, there are passages in both Mark and John that seem to contradict this.[14]

According to John and Peter, Jesus made a few startling claims in contradiction with his actual status. He said that he had been prophesied in scripture as the Suffering Servant:[15]

"Jesus replied, 'To be sure, Elijah does come first, and restores all things. Why then is it written that the Son of Man must suffer much and be rejected?'" (Mark 9:12)

Jesus states his coming had also been generally foretold in the JS, according to John:

"You diligently study the Scriptures because you think that by them you possess eternal life. These are the Scriptures that testify about me … If you believed Moses, you would believe me, for he wrote about me … None has been lost except the one doomed to destruction so that Scripture would be fulfilled." (John 5:39, 46, 17:12)

Jesus also said that he was the Messiah:

"The woman said, 'I know that Messiah (called Christ) is coming. When he comes, he will explain everything to us.' Then Jesus declared, 'I who speak to you am he.'" (John 4:25–26)

He even went as far as saying that he was the Messiah *and* the Son of God: "Again the high priest asked him, 'Are you the Christ, the Son of the Blessed One?' 'I am,' said Jesus."

Moreover, he claimed to be a king; indeed, he rode into Jerusalem on a colt, possibly intending to fulfil a passage from Zechariah (Zechariah 9:9). He stated he had a special relationship with the Jewish Temple's God: "To those who sold doves he said, 'Get these out of here! How dare you turn my Father's house into a market!'" (John 2:16). Finally, he said that he was that Jewish God: "'I tell you the truth,' Jesus answered, 'before Abraham was born, I am!'" (John 18:58). "I Am" is the self-referential name of Moses's God (Exodus 3:14). Therefore, as reported by the evangelists, Jesus' words are at odds with the figure of Jesus crafted by the same evangelists.

The simplest explanation for this is that these quotes were embellished by Mark and John (or their witnesses) to establish Jesus and his message as a crucial Jewish phenomenon. I am not convinced, however. Overall, Peter and John are accurate reporters; it makes more sense to suggest that Jesus was "flirting" with specific Jewish high-status identities in particular situations to gain attention for his message. Indeed, the references are few and far between. For instance, his acceptance of Messiahship occurs precisely twice, and once for his "claim" to being I Am, or God (John 8:58). Indeed, if these claims were valid, then Jesus would have repeated them often, thus making his mission more successful. Jesus also seems to be claiming various conflicting, distinct, and semi-distinct identities, which points to his seeking attention. How can you be both the Messiah and God at once? Or the Messiah and the Son of God? Or the Suffering Servant and a king? He cannot even be the traditional Jewish Messiah because he fulfilled none of the pre-conditions for the role.[16] Neither did Jesus accomplish any of the messianic prescribed goals. All these interpretations conflict with his often-repeated Choice message; indeed, Jesus publicly questions the JS doctrine of Messiahship (Mark 12:35–37). Therefore, he must have used these titles to refer to himself in a bid to attract listeners. It is also important to remember that these identities were drawn from the JS, making them fabrications; thus, they cannot be reliable representations of who Jesus was.

He later explicitly denied some of the assertions he made, which makes his message ambiguous and suggests the idea that he was struggling with defining himself. He repeatedly stated that he could do nothing "without the Father," or that one had to believe in the miracles rather than him (John 10:38). When the people attempted to force him to be a king, he went into hiding (John 6:15). When asked if he was the Messiah, and Peter asserted that he indeed was, Jesus famously reprimanded Peter for saying such a thing.[17] In fact, he immediately predicted his future suffering, directly denying his messianic role, which caused

---

14    Interestingly, the term "Messiah" occurs only twice in John and not at all in Mark.

15    For more information, please see (The Editors of Encyclopaedia Britannica, The prophecies of Deutero-Isaiah n.d.).

16    (G. Vermes, *Jesus the Jew: A Historian's Reading of the Gospels* 1981, 37).

17    Mark 8:27–30 & (Bockmuehl 2003, 29).

Peter to become angry.[18]John the Baptist himself expressed doubts that Jesus was the Messiah.[19] All in all, Jesus' lack of general self-identification is seen throughout the Gospels in the sustained confusion over his identity.

Both Peter and John are eager for the reader to believe that Jesus was the Messiah (or the Christ), and this idea accreted to the new faith. However, their formulation is a Christian Messiah/Christ, which is simply a new term for Jesus that does not fit the traditional Jewish Christ/Messiah because Jesus did not teach, definitively identify with, act as, or assume the role of the Jewish Messiah.[20]

## JESUS' FAILINGS

Jesus' flirting with Jewish identities spills over into a general discussion on the mistakes he made, which hindered his mission. Jesus made many enemies during his mission, even amongst those closest to him. His activities alienated him from his family and hometown (Mark 3:21, 6:3). Even his brothers did not believe him (John 7:5). He also alienated the non-Jewish members of his community. When he encountered the Syrio-Phoenician woman, he referred to the Gentiles as "dogs," inferring that his mission was first for the Jews (Mark 7:26). However, he did healings and travelled through non-Jewish areas such as Samaria and the Decapolis. So he was not mainly catering to the Jews; his mission was inclusive.

Some of Jesus' teachings even alienated his followers. In Capernaum, he notably taught his flock that they should, metaphorically, eat his flesh and drink his blood. John explains, "From this time many of his disciples turned back and no longer followed him" (John 6:66). Despite having performed "wonders" in the Galilean villages of Choraizon, Bethsaida, and Capernaum, Jesus did not seem to have met with success in them, as he declared "woe" to each (Q 10:13–15).

Jesus' widely known reputation for healings and miracles led to some serious issues. Indeed, huge crowds were following him, causing logistical problems; at times, he took to teaching from a boat to keep the crowds at bay (Mark 3:9), and a paralytic man had to be lowered through the roof of a house due to the dense crowds (Mark 2:4). At times, these crowds tirelessly bombarded him with healing and miracle requests, which hampered his ability to deliver his message. For example, while travelling through Galilee to preach in the villages, he healed a man with leprosy. Afterwards, he told the man not to tell anyone, but the man instead spread the news, making it impossible for him to enter villages; Jesus had to stay in "lonely places" (Mark 1:39-45). Also, his miracles fed into rising messianic expectations of Jesus, which led to him becoming increasingly secretive toward the end of his mission, both to avoid the authorities and the crowds. Eventually, the miracles were his undoing—the Jewish leaders felt increasingly threatened by the news of his accomplishments and the crowds, which led to his arrest and death.

Finally, as already mentioned, Jesus went out of his way to antagonize the powerful, thus causing his mission to be cut short. For instance, soon after starting his mission, he attacked the money lenders in the crowded Temple during Passover (John 2:14–16). He also purposely broke the Sabbath in the presence of authorities, incurring their wrath (Mark 3:2–6). As a result, he and his followers could not move about freely, especially in Judea and around Jerusalem. In the end, it was the angry authorities who finally caught Jesus and killed him, thus ending his mission after just a couple of years.

---

18    (G. Vermes, *Jesus the Jew: A Historian's Reading of the Gospels* 1981, 47).

19    Ibid. 32.

20    For more information on the distinction between Jesus and the Jewish Messiah role see (G. Vermes, *Jesus the Jew: A Historian's Reading of the Gospels* 1981, 129–156).

# CHAPTER 32

# CONCLUSION

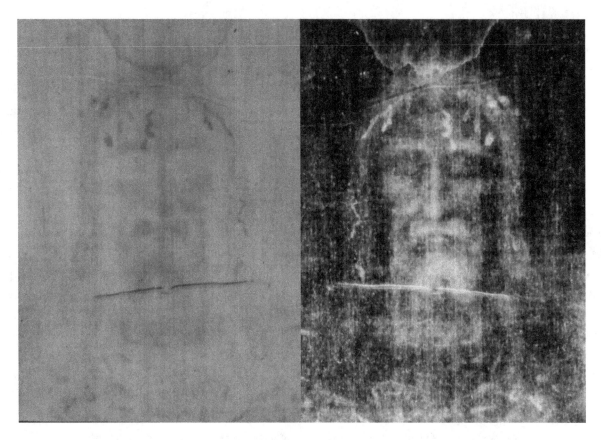

*Figure 51 **The Face of Jesus***

*This is the image of the face of Jesus from the Shroud (left) and an easier to discern negative image (right). This seems an excellent image to finish on. In contrast with the original image from Dura-Europa, where Jesus is obscured, I think we have pushed things about as far as we can go with the currently available sources and approached as close as we can to the real Jesus.*

## SUMMARY

This book started by asking three simple questions:

1. What did Jesus do?

2. What did Jesus say?

3. Who was Jesus?

To answer these questions, I completed a comprehensive survey of available ancient documents to find useful sources about Jesus. Using the resulting shortlist of eyewitness sources, I have achieved my goal of formulating comprehensive answers to each of the questions, and I have presented the most authentic and complete portrait of Jesus available, one free of later additions. Thus, for all interested in exploring and discussing Jesus, the Jesus I have described should be the starting point.

Jesus was a man intent on spreading the message of the Choice, which was new and distinct from Judaism. He flirted with various identities to spread the message. However, he was not the Jewish Messiah or God. While Jesus' mission was ultimately successful, he did make mistakes along the way, he created confusion by not definitively identifying himself, and he carelessly antagonized the powerful, who eventually killed him. But this did not stop his followers from continuing to spread his message around the world.

After his death, the simpleness of the Choice and Jesus' ambiguous identity left fertile ground for numerous theological additions. Specific people, such as Paul, and the inevitable need to increase the marketability of the Church added much to the tale of Jesus—creating the beginnings of Christianity as we know it today, with accretions not derived from Jesus.

## MY CHOICE

However, I can hear the gentle reader chiding me, "Ok, Jonathan, so far so good, but you have brought me all this way yet you maintain a neutral stance on Jesus. You have read all these sources, examined all the evidence, thought things through, and wrote this long book, but you have not indicated your assessment of Jesus. Do you believe he was who he said he was? Are the miracles real? Was he resurrected? Does God exist? What is your answer to the Ultimate Question of Life, the Universe, and Everything?"[1]

These are not independent questions. They are all asking the same thing but in different ways. If one of them is true, then all are true, I would argue; if Jesus did walk on water, then the resurrection occurred, and God exists, and so on. It is a simple binary choice: either Jesus is who he said he was and did the things attributed to him, or the miracle reports are the result of a conspiracy to hoax the reader.

Based on everything, my answer is in the affirmative. Yes, I think Jesus was who he said he was. I have accepted the Choice and follow Jesus.

Why?

## REASONS TO BELIEVE

---

""Reason is a whore, the greatest enemy that faith has;"

—Martin Luther, *Table Talk*

---

"Faith is something that you believe that nobody in his right mind would believe."

—Norman Lear, *All in the Family*

---

I'm afraid I disagree with Martin Luther; faith is useless without excellent reasons for faith. Reason and scepticism are always needed to assay one's faith continually; feelings, unexamined claims, and personal "spiritual" events are poor guides in this regard.

There are two sound reasons why Jesus was who he claimed to be.

---

1     With apologies to Douglas Adams.

## THE MIRACLES

> "'You will not apply my precept,' he said, shaking his head. 'How often have I said to you that when you have eliminated the impossible, whatever remains, however improbable, must be the truth?'"
>
> —Sir Arthur Conan Doyle, *The Sign of Four*

First, the miracles appear to have occurred, mainly as described.

The most plausible scenario of fabrication of the miracle stories, which I have outlined, seems very unlikely given all the objections.

The Shroud of Turin appears to record a real miracle associated with Jesus. The current majority scientific opinion is that the Shroud was the cloth that John the Elder saw wrapped around Jesus' body at burial and that some form of bodily dematerialization occurred, explaining the formation of the image on the cloth. This theory also explains the empty tomb and flattened state of the linens that John alludes to.

Eyewitness testimony reports many wonderous and unexplained events associated with Jesus. Both Peter and John, who were companions of Jesus, describe events they witnessed and include stories of other people who saw other events.

The miracle reporting by Peter and John are simple statements of banal facts distinct from the fabricated miracle stories typical of the time. The banality and oddness of the miracle reports make them more believable. While this is not clenching on its own, this reporting style reads as how actual unexplained events would be reported—if these events did occur, these are the kind of reports I would expect from eyewitnesses.

The miracles are a chaotic collection of events with no precedence. We hear of Jesus' reluctance to perform them, his decrying the need for them, the problems and confusion caused by them, and the times he could not perform them.

No contemporaries or near-contemporaries, including enemies of Christianity, "debunked" or even questioned the genuineness of the miracles.

All these observations lend credence to the authenticity of the miracles; while each observation on its own is not persuasive, when taken together, the matter becomes decisive.

Of course, the chief objection to the miracle reports is they cannot be true since they are unexplainable by science; for instance, if we cannot explain a person walking on water at that point in history, then the report of such an event must be false. But is that a correct interpretation? I think not.

## THE NATURE OF SCIENCE

Science is an ongoing human project that organizes our knowledge into models about what we term "reality". We engage in this activity partly because we are by nature curious and partly because our models can be very useful—consider the germ theory of disease! All scientific knowledge is empirical, meaning it is based on the best *available* data and observations. Science accepts fallibility; that is, scientists always entertain the idea that they could be wrong and that our models can constantly be improved. So science is continually evolving and updating itself with better models.

A great example of this is Einstein's Relativity Theory supplanting Newton's Three Laws of Motion, or Kepler's elliptical orbits model overcoming the simpler model of circular orbits. This is because science is contingent on our limited humanity; it is defined and limited by aspects of our human nature.[2] Thus, to claim miracles are impossible is to go too far in terms of

---

2    Consider; if humanity disappeared suddenly, our science would also disappear.

certainty, as it ignores the inherent fallibility of science;[3] the "outside-science" areas which are not describable by our current scientific models have always existed.

So as a positivist scientist, I have no rational objections to unexplained phenomena; all I can say is we cannot explain them currently. But as a supporter of vigorous scientific research, I also say that one day they may become explainable. Or perhaps the outside-science (supernatural) problem set is infinite, just as the Undecidable Problems set is in computational theory.[4]

## REACTION

The other reason to believe Jesus is who he said he was is the reaction of Jesus' followers after his death, although attested chiefly indirectly. The followers preached and taught at significant risk and cost to themselves. Many left their old lives, were arrested, persecuted, and killed like Peter, yet none recanted the miracles. Before Jesus' death, they seem cowardly and relatively slow-witted. But as biblical scholar Reginald Fuller puts it:

"Even the most sceptical historian has to postulate an X to account for the complete change in the behaviour of the disciples, who at Jesus' arrest had fled and scattered to their homes, but who in a few weeks were boldly preaching their message to the very people who had sought to crush the movement launched by Jesus."[5]

Clearly, the disciples, eyewitnesses, acted as if the miracles were real.

*Figure 52* **SDG**

*"Soli Deo Gloria," Latin for "Glory to God Alone," an initialism, either SDG or DSG, used in various works of art but most famously used by Bach at the end of most of his works, included with his signature. On the right is the end of his B Minor Mass, considered by some as the greatest music ever written, with its DSG by Bach. Image reproduced by permission from Staatsbibliothek zu Berlin - Preußischer Kulturbesitz, Musikabteilung mit Mendelssohn-Archiv, Shelfmark: Mus.ms. Bach P 180.*

# AUTHENTIC CHRISTIANITY—FOLLOWING SALT & LIGHT JESUS

Like us, Jesus was a regular human. He lived an ordinary life of pain and joy, again like us, except for those rare moments when he communed with God.[6] We cannot know his genuine relationship with God or why God "picked" him; any attempt to do so

---

3    This denial may have more to do with the critic's attitude toward a "higher" being.

4    It has been proven in computer science computational theory that the number of unsolvable problems is infinite.

5    (Fuller 1972, 2).

6    Or "was in" God or God "was in" him or was with or was working for or prayed to or became part of or joined or interfaced with or channelled and so on.

is mere speculation. He was unjustly tried, killed by the Romans on April 1, 33 CE, and buried in a tomb. About 36 hours later, the tomb was found empty, and soon after, various people saw him healthy and alive.

Directed by God, Jesus taught the Choice to all of us. We were created free so that we can be free to choose as we see fit. If you decide to try and be like God versus trying to be like the world, you choose life over death and will never be condemned. Act on the Choice!

- Be as God.
- Desire nothing in the world too much.
- Share your light.
- Love all. Condemn none.
- Have an individual and unique relationship with God.
- Keep learning as much as you can.[7]
- Become stronger in your freedom and individuality.
- Try your best.

All of Jesus' teachings are variations and restatements of the Choice.[8] Nothing in the Choice requires philosophical speculation, hidden esoteric knowledge, self-centred mysticism, or obscurantism and complex dogma. It is simple, direct, urgent, and whole. To follow Jesus is remarkably simple: choose God. That is all. QED.

Thank you, gentle reader, for coming with me on this beautiful journey! - jd

---

7    A mysterious God of Love and God of Science gave us the capacity for science and the desire to forge ahead to fulfil our potential by expanding out into the universe and expanding the inner self, to heal ourselves and perform our own miracles, and bring ourselves closer to the divine.

8    Notice with the Choice many current vexing issues fall away: gender identity, the role of science, anti-intellectualism, evolution, Christian dominations, biblical relevancy, clashing religious traditions, and so on.

# POST SCRIPTUM—COROLLARIES

*Figure 50* **Head of Christ by Rembrandt (1648)**

Following Salt & Light Jesus is not Christianity as it currently stands.

There are only three primary authentic sources about Jesus: John, Peter-Mark, and Q, with John being the preferred source over the other two since it is a cohesive whole, while Peter-Mark is refracted through a haphazard composition by Mark and Peter's superstitious nature. Everything else (including the OT, Paul, Revelation, Luke, and Matthew) are non-eyewitness material, unhelpful or irretrievably flawed. By eliminating all these conventional sources and focusing only on Jesus, many aspects of Christianity fall away[1] because there is no evidence for support anymore, some of which I shall briefly mention here.[2]

Jesus was a regular person like you and me. He was not semi-divine or divine, sinless, pre-existent, born of a virgin, predicted, the Saviour, Jewish, the Messiah, or Christ. Jesus' death (or blood) has no salvific or cosmic significance.

There is no Trinity, Hell, Rapture, Apocalypse, 666 Beast, or Spiritual Gifts such as speaking in tongues, handling snakes, and prophesying.

Other concepts need to be reviewed:

Eternal life, although real, is ill-defined according to Jesus.

The Kingdom of God is not a place or time but a personal realization.

God should be our focus, not Jesus.

Jesus is only a saviour if you accept the Choice.

There is no Second Coming, although Jesus does allude to some kind of future event.

---

1     Christianity, as are other faiths, is struggling due to the growing awareness of the public that the extensive doctrines included in the faith are insupportable. A return to Jesus would seem a helpful change.

2     For a full discussion see *Salt and Light II,* the next book in this series.

# APPENDIX 1.

# ASSESSMENT OF THE JEWISH SCRIPTURE

"It is from the Bible that man has learned cruelty, rapine, and murder; for the belief of a cruel God makes a cruel man."

—Thomas Paine, *The Age of Reason*

The JS is a collection of various texts created and edited by various people in different places and times over 500 years. Many of the original texts were redacted, edited, expanded, and then redacted again, in a process that is still hotly debated amongst scholars. The content of the JS is the story of the Israelites, one of the many indigenous Semitic people of the first millennium BCE in Palestine. It takes the form of an epic saga stretching back to the beginning of time.

Here is the JS's overall story arc, with a chronology corresponding to the Western calendar:[1]

- c. 4000–2100 BCE: the stories of Creation, Adam and Eve, the Great Flood, Noah's descendants, and the Tower of Babel.
- 2091–1700 BCE: Abraham's Wanderings, God's Covenant with him, and his descendants' adventures.
- 1700–1406 BCE: Moses and the Israelites leave Egypt; Moses delivers the Law; they wander for 40 years in the desert.
- 1406–1043 BCE: the Israelites conquer and settle in Canaan.
- 1043–931 BCE: the reigns of King Saul, King David, and King Solomon. First Temple built.
- 931–722 BCE: Israel splits into the Kingdom of Israel in the north and Kingdom of Judea in the south, a series of good and wicked kings, prophets Elijah, Elisha, and Isaiah, northern Israel conquered by Assyria.
- 722–586 BCE: King Hezekiah, prophets Jeremiah and Ezekiel, Judah is conquered by Babylon, elites exiled to Babylon.
- 586–430 BCE: the elite exiles return and, the second Temple is built, ushering the Second-Temple Judaism period, which encompasses Jesus' time and ends with the Temple's destruction in 70 CE.

But how accurate are the JS stories? I take it as a given that reality was not created around 4000 BCE. Until recently, only the JS existed for this history. However, new archaeological finds from the 1960s and later, as well as recovered reports and correspondence from the Egyptian[2] and Assyrian/Babylonian empires[3] that ruled Palestine, inscriptions, and the histories of neighbouring states such as Edom and Moab, give a very different but far more accurate history of the Israelites:

Around 1200 BCE, while Canaan was firmly under Egyptian military control, the Israelites arose peacefully as a distinct group in the highlands of western Palestine out of the existing Philistine, Phoenician, and Canaanite peoples, during the turmoil of the centuries-long Bronze Age collapse afflicting the Eastern Mediterranean world at that time. The Israelites were thus probably refugees from the collapsing Canaanite city system. They were distinct for practising circumcision and not eating pork—two practices probably borrowed from the Egyptian priesthood of the time—but in all other ways, the Israelites were just like their neighbours. And like most ancient peoples in the region, the Israelites' religious practices included purification

---

1    (Valkanet 2010).

2    c. 1550–c. 1100 BCE.

3    c. 750–539 BCE.

rituals, forbidden foods, religious calendars, and animal sacrifice. The Israelites were first mentioned as a distinct people in an inscription on the Merneptah Stele (c. 1208 BCE), stating that Egyptian Pharaoh Merneptah had conquered them. By 1000 BCE, their population was no more than 45,000 people scattered over tiny settlements. The Israelites were also relatively isolated from surrounding peoples and lived peacefully. At the time, Jerusalem was a mere small, hill-country village with a population of 2,000 people[4] and was part of the district of Judah, comprised of 20 small villages. These included farmers and pastoral groups, and all villages were isolated and rural. By 900 BCE, most Israelites had transitioned from migratory living to farming, centred around small villages.

The region of Israel, to the north, was centred at the town of Schechem, while Judah, the southern region, was centred at the town of Jerusalem. These two regions were always distinct, competing entities and societies. Judah was poorer, weaker, more rural, and less influential than Israel. It also had only one-tenth of the northern region's population. Judah had a natural development dictated by topography and climate. While Judah remained poor and backward, Israel grew and turned into an actual kingdom in the late 900s or early 800s, with a population greater than 120,000. In 722 BCE, the northern Kingdom of Israel was conquered by the Assyrian Empire. Judah then also became a vassal to the Assyrians.

The Israelites, like the other Canaanite peoples, worshipped the traditional Canaanite gods. At sites such as Tel Motza, on the outskirts of Jerusalem, the Israelites worshipped typical pagan Semitic deities.[5] "El" was the original Canaanite supreme god—the word "Israel" means "struggle with El"—along with his consort, the goddess Ashera, and their sons, including Baal, Yahweh, and a whole pantheon of minor divinities. Each son was assigned to a group of Canaanite people, and Yahweh, one of the sons of El, was given to the Israelites.

The process under which the JS was created is hotly debated; however, there is broad scholarly agreement that many authors (probably priests) created and modified material as needed by a succession of contemporary political and theological requirements, plus these materials were also edited together over centuries into larger works. Thus, two major, independently created groups of literature emerged: the Deuteronomic History and the Five Books of Moses.

## THE DEUTERONOMIC HISTORY

The Deuteronomic History refers to those texts within the JS—the books of Deuteronomy, Joshua, Judges, Samuel, and Kings—that have a theological unity that includes the covenant between Yahweh and the Israelites who, as the Chosen People, will live according to Yahweh's decrees.

The religion of the Israelites was varied and fluid, as the main deities worshipped by southern and northern kings tended to vary over time. For instance, according to 1 Kings, King Ahab, who was ruling the Kingdom of Israel in the ninth century BCE, chose to worship Baal, another of El's sons. Also, religious practice was uneven geographically. Despite the obligation to follow the official cult, as decreed in the two capitals, rural areas would continue with traditional polytheism right down to Jesus' time. This tension can be seen in specific books of the JS, notably the book of Jeremiah, which condemns the plurality of practices all over Judea,[6] and 1 Kings notes that King Solomon himself followed other deities.[7] Eventually, Yahweh and El were conflated, and Asherah becomes Yahweh's consort. Traces of this conflation can still be seen in the earliest books of the JS, which contain double stories, or the same core story told twice with variations between the two. For instance, there are two Creation stories,

---

4    (Shanks, Ancient Jerusalem: The Village, the Town, the City 2021).

5    (Kisilevitz 2016).

6    Jeremiah 11:13: "You, Judah, have as many gods as you have towns; and the altars you have set up to burn incense to that shameful god Baal are as many as the streets of Jerusalem."

7    1 Kings 11:5: "He followed Ashtoreth the goddess of the Sidonians, and Molek the detestable god of the Ammonites." Other examples exist, for instance, King Ahaz (reign 732–716 BCE) altered Temple worship to follow the Assyrians gods and may have sacrificed some of his sons to them. (2 Kings 16:2–9).

two Flood stories, and so on. In each case, one references Yahweh and the other El, or Elohim. Over time, the other gods were suppressed, at least in the urban centres.

After a reform movement, which started after 722 BCE, the monotheistic Yahweh cult was born. The urban Jews in the Kingdom of Judea then moved to strict monotheism, with their worship centred at the Temple of Jerusalem. The process was most certainly influenced by the monotheistic ideas coming from neighbouring Assyria and Egypt. [8] Between 727 and 629 BCE, pagan worship was banned and reinstated in turn, depending on the circumstances, until, under the Judean King Josiah (c. 640–609 BCE), the Yahweh cult—and, therefore, the ban on pagan worship—emerged as dominant. The first version of the Deuteronomic History was then created and, according to 2 Kings,[9] "accidentally discovered" in 622 BCE and passed off as the long-lost "true Book of the Law."

According to Deuteronomic History, Judean King Josiah, a king of the Davidic dynasty, wished to take advantage of the weakening of the Assyrian Empire by expanding the borders of Judah and re-conquering Israel. To that end, he enforced the Yahweh cult in his kingdom and backed it up with the fabricated Deuteronomic History. The worship of a single divinity, Yahweh, was centred in one temple, located in Jerusalem, the one and only capital of Judah, and national religious festivals were ordered. King Josiah, who expected to conquer the rich Northern Kingdom of Israel, thus wished to establish himself as sole ruler and impose a monotheistic cult that mirrored his centralized power. The priests of the Yahweh cult, to support Josiah's project, crafted a "national" history by using the existing folklore and recent history, enveloping them in religious propaganda, which was projected back in time. For instance, they explain in 1 Kings that the birth of the righteous Josiah was foretold 300 years before, that the kings in Jerusalem had traditionally ruled Canaan in its entity, and that Abraham had made a covenant with Yahweh a thousand years previous, which the current Israelites were breaking with their religious practices. Within that history, we find various themes, including Yahweh's covenant with Israel as "the chosen people," the Promised Land now lost, the promise of glorious conquests, of glittering cities and mighty kings, the Davidic kingship, and a repeating cycle of sin, divine retribution, and salvation by Yahweh. If Israel would only be faithful to Yahweh and follow its Davidic King, Josiah, Israel could regain her "former" wealth, glory, and territory. Unfortunately, the project failed, as Josiah was killed in a skirmish with the Egyptians in 609 BCE without achieving the conquest of the Kingdom of Israel (2 Kings 23:29). Thus, the project for which the fictional Deuteronomic History was created came to naught.

## THE FIVE BOOKS OF MOSES

The Books of Genesis, Exodus, Leviticus, Numbers, and Deuteronomy are the Five Books supposedly written by Moses. In it is the Torah, or Written Law, the laws handed down from God to Moses. The books encompass the creation of the world, the early days of the people of Israel, the exodus from Egypt, and Moses being given the Law on Mt. Sinai. They end with Moses' death just before the Israelites conquer Canaan, the "Promised Land."

Soon after King Josiah's death, the Babylonian Empire to the east had invaded Judea. It destroyed Jerusalem in 586 BCE, deporting many leading scholars, elite members, and priests to Babylon and essentially wiping the theological slate clean while leaving most rural populations to continue their pagan practices as before. Soon after that, the Babylonians were conquered by the Persians, and the elite exiles were allowed back to re-establish Jerusalem and build the Second Temple[10] in 538 BCE as the centre of Yahweh worship. These elite exiles had absorbed the Josiah-era Deuteronomic version of history and believed it to be true. To re-establish their vision of Israel, over the next 200 years, this community created the Five Books of Moses from a number of existing texts. As Israel Finkelstein and Neil Asher Silberman put it:

---

8    Egypt's brief period of monotheism under Pharaoh Akhenanten.

9    2 Kings 22:8: "Hilkiah the high priest said to Shaphan the secretary, 'I have found the Book of the Law in the temple of the Lord.' He gave it to Shaphan, who read it."

10   Ezra 1:1–11. Or perhaps it should be called the First Temple Period, since there is no archaeological evidence for a previous First Temple, also called Solomon's Temple, as described in the book 1 Kings.

"The patriarchal traditions [the Five Books of Moses], therefore, must be considered as a sort of pious 'prehistory' of Israel in which Judah played a decisive role. They describe the very early history of the nation, delineate ethnic boundaries, emphasize that the Israelites were outsiders and not part of the indigenous population of Canaan and embrace the traditions of both the north and the south while ultimately stressing the superiority of Judah."[11]

## SECOND TEMPLE JUDAISM

Over time, the Deuteronomic History, the Five Books of Moses, and other texts were edited together so that by 250 BCE, the JS had mostly reached its final form. By then, the worship of a national god, Yahweh, was firmly in place, with worship centred at the Temple in Jerusalem. Monotheism then became the rule for most Jews. The Jewish traditions that emerged during this period are called "Second Temple Judaism," which is the theological backdrop to the era of Jesus. The Second Temple existed until the Romans destroyed it in 70 CE, following Jewish revolts against Roman rule, thus ending the Second Temple era.

So the JS are a literary invention created over time (c. 650 BCE–250 BCE) to serve the Jerusalem elites' various religious and political needs. Additional books were grafted on over time, and multiple layers of redaction created the large, sprawling, and sometimes contradictory JS. As Finkelstein and Silberman put it:

"The historical saga contained in the Bible—from Abraham's encounter with God and his journey to Canaan to Moses' deliverance of the children of Israel from bondage to the rise and fall of the kingdoms of Israel and Judah—was not a miraculous revelation, but a brilliant product of human imagination."[12]

---

11    (Finkelstein and Silberman 2002, 45).

12    (Finkelstein and Silberman 2002, 1).

# APPENDIX 2.

# MARK'S CHAPTER 13

This is Mark's chapter 13:

1. As he was leaving the temple, one of his disciples said to him, "Look, Teacher! What massive stones! What magnificent buildings!"

2. **"Do you see all these great buildings?" replied Jesus. "Not one stone here will be left on another; every one will be thrown down."**

3. As Jesus was sitting on the Mount of Olives opposite the temple, Peter, James, John and Andrew asked him privately,

4. "Tell us, when will these things happen? And what will be the sign that they are all about to be fulfilled?"

5. **Jesus said to them: "Watch out that no one deceives you.**

6. **Many will come in my name, claiming, 'I am he,' and will deceive many.**

7. When you hear of wars and rumours of wars, do not be alarmed. Such things must happen, but the end is still to come.

8. Nation will rise against nation, and kingdom against kingdom. There will be earthquakes in various places, and famines. These are the beginning of birth pains.

9. **"You must be on your guard. You will be handed over to the local councils and flogged in the synagogues. On account of me you will stand before governors and kings as witnesses to them.**

10. **And the gospel must first be preached to all nations.**

11. **Whenever you are arrested and brought to trial, do not worry beforehand about what to say. Just say whatever is given you at the time, for it is not you speaking, but the Holy Spirit.**

12. **"Brother will betray brother to death, and a father his child. Children will rebel against their parents and have them put to death.**

13. **All men will hate you because of me, but he who stands firm to the end will be saved.**

14. "When you see 'the abomination that causes desolation' standing where it does not belong—let the reader understand—then let those who are in Judea flee to the mountains.

15. Let no one on the roof of his house go down or enter the house to take anything out.

16. Let no one in the field go back to get his cloak.

17. How dreadful it will be in those days for pregnant women and nursing mothers!

18. Pray that this will not take place in winter,

19. because those will be days of distress unequalled from the beginning, when God created the world, until now—and never to be equalled again.

20. If the Lord had not cut short those days, no one would survive. But for the sake of the elect, whom he has chosen, he has shortened them.

21. At that time if anyone says to you, 'Look, here is the Christ!' or, 'Look, there he is!' do not believe it.

22. For false Christs and false prophets will appear and perform signs and miracles to deceive the elect—if that were possible.

23. So be on your guard; I have told you everything ahead of time.

24. "But in those days, following that distress," 'the sun will be darkened, and the moon will not give its light.

25. the stars will fall from the sky, and the heavenly bodies will be shaken.'

26. "At that time men will see the Son of Man coming in clouds with great power and glory.

27. And he will send his angels and gather his elect from the four winds, from the ends of the earth to the ends of the heavens.

28. **"Now learn this lesson from the fig tree: As soon as its twigs get tender and its leaves come out, you know that summer is near.**

29. Even so, when you see these things happening, you know that it is near, right at the door.

30. I tell you the truth, this generation will certainly not pass away until all these things have happened.

31. **Heaven and earth will pass away, but my words will never pass away.**

32. **"No one knows about that day or hour, not even the angels in heaven, nor the Son, but only the Father.**

33. **Be on guard! Be alert! You do not know when that time will come.**

34. **It's like a man going away: He leaves his house and puts his servants in charge, each with his assigned task, and tells the one at the door to keep watch.**

35. **"Therefore keep watch because you do not know when the owner of the house will come back--whether in the evening, or at midnight, or when the rooster crows, or at dawn.**

36. **If he comes suddenly, do not let him find you sleeping.**

37. **What I say to you, I say to everyone: 'Watch!'"**

Certain aspects of this discourse stand out. It is confusing and incoherent, unlike Jesus' usually simple teachings. Most critics consider it as an artificial construct, put together from the diverse teachings of Jesus. Also, the repeated use of the undefined word "Elect" only occurs here in this chapter and nowhere else in Mark, John, or Q, but it is not clear who the Elect are. Equally confusing is that Jesus appears to repeat himself in verses 5–6.9 and 21–23. The following verses (24 and 25) were drawn from Isaiah but were misquoted. Remarkably, the end-of-time seems imminent, within the time of "this generation." Followers are thus warned to "be on guard," but then Jesus says the gospel (the good news) must first be preached to the whole world before the end of time, so it cannot be *that* imminent. And verse 30 is incorrect: that generation has passed, but "all these things" have not yet occurred, unless this is a symbolic statement. Also, verse 14 is the only time Mark talks directly to his audience, and he calls us "reader(s)," not "listener(s)," as Jesus or Peter would have said.

Scholars see this passage as an end-of-time, apocalyptic prediction, which Jesus may have uttered or which a later editor might have put into his mouth. This discourse is vivid and incoherent, allowing interpreters to draw all manner of conclusions from it. But as I have shown earlier, verse 14 was created by Mark, and we can date the Gospel of Mark's "release" to the Caligula statue incident, which occurred in the summer or fall of 40 CE. Once we accept that Mark has inserted his thoughts in the mouth of Jesus, I can take a closer look at the whole chapter and attempt to analyse it.

Chapter 13 is more sensible as a pastiche of disparate bits than as a coherent narrative. Since it was placed right before the final Passion Story, which is a well-constructed and continuous narrative, Mark probably thought this was a good point in the narrative to insert "left-over bits" (i.e., small, unused pieces of Peter's teachings Mark thought essential to report, which created a generally jumbled discourse). If we split the chapter into coherent sections, things become clearer.

Verses 1–2 were probably something that Jesus actually said. We can find a passage similar in content in John (John 2:19). John related a symbolic statement about the end of Temple worship, so the meaning here is probably the same.

Verses 3–4 have the disciples asking when "these things" will happen. What these things, plural, are is unclear, and notice Jesus never answers the question. Instead, he does a non-sequitur into avoiding deception. So Mark's initial question is a set-up for the disparate bits to come, and these verses can be set aside.

Verses 5–6 and 21, 23 are warnings about being deceived. Apropos, as in the past, there had been messianic pretenders, and no doubt would be again, who taught something different from Jesus' teachings. So Jesus probably did say something like this.

Verse 22 uses the word "Elect" and has the aside to the reader, which Mark inserted. What Mark means by the Elect and where he got the term is unclear.

Verses 7–8 are suspicious, as they are generic statements of the times and are thus far from prophetic. Wars, earthquakes, and famine were always the case, so this is not helpful. I have already discussed these verses, which fit better with recent events in 30s CE Palestine and with Mark's intent of warning—inserted by Mark.

Verses 9, 11–13 warn of conflicts with the existing order. But troubles for the disciples are, again, far from prophetic. We have already seen the blind man and Jesus cast out; these events were already occurring and are not hard to predict. John also mentions these warnings from the Last Supper (John 15:18, 16:2), so they are authentic to Jesus and remembered from here.

Verse 10 is a simple command to spread Jesus' message. Probably authentic and oft-repeated.

Verses 14–20 and 24–27, 29, 30, 32 are Mark's inserted abomination statement with accompanying fearful events of uncertain timing, some of which are taken from the JS, all of which did not transpire, as Caligula died in early 41 CE and the crisis was averted, and nothing happened. If Mark could have retrieved the manuscript from circulation later, no doubt he would have edited this section. Mark has also used "Elect" again in this section with no definition.

Verse 28 is a sudden comment on how a fig tree indicates spring, perhaps related to the earlier story of the shrivelled fig tree. Probably authentic.

Verse 31 is the enduring message of Jesus.

Verses 33–37 are a confusing short saying on being alert.

I think the only authentic sayings of Jesus are found in verses 2, 5–6, 9–13, 28, and 31–37—Temple worship, which shall pass away, a warning that followers should not be deceived and remain alert, a request that they should spread Jesus' message, and, finally, a metaphor of spring coming in the form of a fig tree. I have marked those verses in bold. In addition, each verse seems independent, with only the last seven verses, 31–37, forming a coherent short dialogue on remaining alert.

Mark created all the other verses.

# APPENDIX 3.

# MARK'S LONGER ENDING

I will be following Nicholas Lunn's recent work on this subject.[1]

Here is Mark's chapter 16, with the Abrupt Ending:

> "When the Sabbath was over, Mary Magdalene, Mary the mother of James, and Salome bought spices so that they might go to anoint Jesus' body. Very early on the first day of the week, just after sunrise, they were on their way to the tomb and they asked each other, 'Who will roll the stone away from the entrance of the tomb?' But when they looked up, they saw that the stone, which was very large, had been rolled away. As they entered the tomb, they saw a young man dressed in a white robe sitting on the right side, and they were alarmed. 'Don't be alarmed,' he said. 'You are looking for Jesus the Nazarene, who was crucified. He has risen! He is not here. See the place where they laid him. But go, tell his disciples and Peter, He is going ahead of you into Galilee. There you will see him, just as he told you.' Trembling and bewildered, the women went out and fled from the tomb. They said nothing to anyone, because they were afraid." (Mark 16:1–8)

And that is all. The narrative ends after verse 8. Many readers over the centuries have wondered at this Abrupt Ending. However, there are additional verses associated with Mark that come after verse 8. Technically, there exist three known versions of additional text, but two are attested just once or twice and are quite late, so they may be set aside from the discussion, as they could not be the original ending. The third version is overwhelmingly attested, as we shall see; it is a twelve-verse unit called the Longer Ending, which starts as verse 9:

> "When Jesus rose early on the first day of the week, he appeared first to Mary Magdalene, out of whom he had driven seven demons. She went and told those who had been with him and who were mourning and weeping. When they heard that Jesus was alive and that she had seen him, they did not believe it. Afterward Jesus appeared in a different form to two of them while they were walking in the country. These returned and reported it to the rest; but they did not believe them either. Later Jesus appeared to the Eleven as they were eating; he rebuked them for their lack of faith and their stubborn refusal to believe those who had seen him after he had risen. He said to them, 'Go into all the world and preach the good news to all creation. Whoever believes and is baptized will be saved, but whoever does not believe will be condemned. And these signs will accompany those who believe: In my name they will drive out demons; they will speak in new tongues; they will pick up snakes with their hands; and when they drink deadly poison, it will not hurt them at all; they will place their hands on sick people, and they will get well.' After the Lord Jesus had spoken to them, he was taken up into heaven and he sat at the right hand of God. Then the disciples went out and preached everywhere, and the Lord worked with them and confirmed his word by the signs that accompanied it." (Mark 16:9–20)

---

1    (Lunn 2014).

This ending seems more natural and complete, as Jesus appears, interacts with his followers, and gives them final instructions before a brief wrap up of the story.

Ancient and modern copies of Mark come in the following three versions: Case A) ending at verse 8 with nothing more (the Abrupt Ending), Case B) the Longer Ending, which proceeds naturally from verse 8, Case C) the Longer Ending, but appended with some sort of indication, separation or doubt, such as brackets, markings, or spaced apart from the Abrupt Ending. It has been suggested that the last page, or pages, were simply lost, causing this conundrum. However, there is no attestation of a lost ending in the Christian literature. Furthermore, the idea sounds purely speculative because it implies that either pages were lost early on from the original manuscript, or most or all the earliest copies, and Mark did not remedy the situation. This seems incredible. As Nunn states, serious discussion needs to be focused on Case A (Abrupt Ending) versus Case B (Longer Ending).

The current scholarly consensus supports Case A, namely, an Abrupt Ending, with some later scribe concocting the Longer Ending. It means that the Longer Ending would not be original to Mark. Interpretation of the Abrupt Ending is, in turn, widely contested. If Mark did indeed end his gospel in verse 8, it is not immediately clear his intended impact. Nunn, however, stands out by holding the opposite view; according to him, the Abrupt Ending is the anomaly, and the Longer Ending is the original ending.

In the Codex Vaticanus (created c. 300–325 CE), according to textual analysis, the same scribe copied both Mark and Luke—whose gospel immediately follows Mark's—and left an entire column blank between the two works. This is significant because in the rest of the codex, whenever a book ends before the end of a column, the remaining part of that column is left blank, and the next book starts on the next column. The Codex Vaticanus scribe was thus indicating that he was aware of the Longer Ending but did not fit in the space left; therefore, he left enough room for a potential, later inclusion. This action, leaving a gap for a disputed text, has been observed in other codices.[2]

The Codex Sinaiticus (created c. 330–360) was produced in the same *scriptorium* (or "copying house") as the Vaticanus. Again, Mark ends with the Abrupt Ending. In that case, however, decorative horizontal and vertical lines have been added to fill the empty space, which would preclude any textual addition beyond verse 8. Interestingly, all the other codices produced by this particular scriptorium, which we know of, contain the Longer Ending. The Vaticanus and the Sinaiticus codices seem to display some knowledge of an existing longer ending to Mark, but the scribes chose not to include it in Vaticanus, provisionally, and the later Sinaiticus, definitively.

There are many reasons to think the Longer Ending might be the original; most pertain to manuscript traditions. First, early Christian writings repeatedly reference Jesus as resurrected from the dead and later appearing to a select group of people. Mark, with an Abrupt Ending, is the only Gospel that does not include any post-resurrection appearances.[3] It would be odd if the original Gospel of Mark did not relate any of those appearances, since Mark's Jesus repeatedly predicts his raising. A Longer Ending is attested in manuscripts of Mark produced before the two Codices discussed above and is the only ending attested by Early Church Fathers. This means that a more extended version of Mark was circulating before the Abrupt Ending version emerged. Given that ancient writers never attempted to argue that verse 8 was the final verse, no Early Church Father ever explicitly declared that the Longer Ending should be excluded. No anti-Christian writer ever refers to, or comments on, Mark's lack of appearances; any controversy arising from the existence of two different endings is not attested. This all suggests there was no Shorter Ending version, and it was a later creation.

Moreover, the Lectionary evidence (i.e., books containing fragments of the Four Gospels, along with Christian liturgy materials) almost all contain the Longer Ending. Specific authors also appear to be using a more extended ending version of Mark; both Tatian[4] and Irenaeus quote the Longer Ending. The first doubt regarding the ending of Mark, although not a

---

2    This is also in the case of the *Pericope Adulterae,* an orphaned story sometimes inserted into the Gospel of John.

3    Most tellingly, both Luke and Matthew, who copied from Mark, include resurrection apparencies like those in the Longer Ending, suggesting their versions of Mark included it.

4    An early Christian theologian (c. 120–180 CE).

rejection, was raised by Eusebius in the early 300s CE. He was then writing from Palestine—after he had spent some time in Alexandria, the Vaticanus and Sinaiticus scriptorium location—around the same time as the two Codices were being produced. Eusebius comments that he knows of many manuscripts that have the Abrupt Ending. This is the first time the Abrupt Ending is ever mentioned, which implies existing longer ending(s) were the norm.

The other reasons that allow us to doubt that the Abrupt Ending is the original ending to Mark pertain to linguistics and literary techniques. The final word of the Abrupt Ending is "for." However, ancient Greek works never finish this way; it makes the Abrupt Ending both unique and suspicious. Additionally, according to Lunn, the Longer Ending is not linguistically distinct from the rest of the Gospel of Mark, meaning it is not a later addition but a part of the original text. Finally, we know that Matthew and Luke used Mark. Matthew does not seem to be dependent on the Longer Ending. However, analysis demonstrates that Luke used specific literary elements from the Longer Ending that can be found in his Gospel and Acts. This indicates that Luke was using a copy of Mark that contained the Longer Ending.

There are many thousands of surviving manuscripts of the Gospels, both complete and fragmentary. Since each was created by hand by copying an older text at a particular place and in a specific language, various identifiable "traditions" of manuscripts have evolved over time. The Longer Ending is found in 99% of all ancient Greek manuscripts and all major manuscript traditions. Those omitting the Longer Ending are just a handful. The Longer Ending is also heavily attested across the major traditions: Byzantine, Western, and Caesarean. It even dominates in the tradition from the region of the two Codices (the Alexandrian tradition).

It appears, then, the original Longer Ending was created by Mark, and for some reason, it was omitted from some copies made in Egypt in the late 100s or 200s CE. This allowed enough time for a body of tradition to develop copies, perpetuate the error, and Eusebius to see multiple copies of the Abrupt Ending in the adjacent region of Palestine in the early 300s. However, this omission seems to be localized geographically to Egypt. It eventually found its way into the two great Codices created in Egypt's city of Alexandria. The omission was gradually remedied by comparison to the overall manuscript tradition (we have observed the scribe of Mark in the Vaticanus some left space anticipating a correction). So the Abrupt Ending only existed in one locale for a short time.

It was either an accidental error or a deliberate act. As explained above, the original manuscript cannot have lost its ending during Mark's lifetime, since Mark would have corrected it. Under another scenario, the ending could have been lost later, in a local part of the manuscript tradition. It is hard to imagine this happening to a scroll because these were rolled up; the end of any scroll would be on the very inside. But by the 100s CE, codices were in use, and outer pages would be prone to damage, loss, or even recycled into other works. A survey of existing ancient copies indicates that 14% to 18% have a faulty final portion; damaged endings were thus not uncommon. Lunn posits that the loss of the last page of a copy of Mark could have occurred in Egypt, which started the tradition of the Abrupt Ending. However, I find the argument for deliberate tampering more compelling.

The Longer Ending, strikingly, presents a complete account of the resurrection of Jesus. But according to Philo of Alexandria, the concept of "physical resurrection" conflicted with the prevailing philosophical ideas (for instance, Gnosticism) being taught in Alexandria, so at some point, the account was dropped from the local Mark tradition by ending at verse 8. The next verse has Jesus rising and being seen. From this sprang, in Alexandria, a manuscript tradition with an Abrupt Ending, which eventually found its way into the two great Alexandrian codices discussed above. This manuscript tradition was limited to Mark, for both Sinaiticus and Vaticanus do include the resurrection appearances found in the other Gospels.[5]

---

5     This tells us the Shorter Ending of Mark was a tradition by then, not an active exclusion.

# APPENDIX 4.

# THE SITES OF THE CRUCIFIXION AND THE TOMB

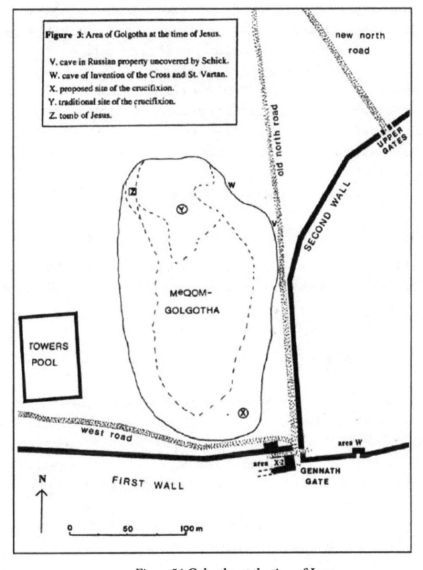

*Figure 51 **Golgotha at the time of Jesus***

*Image reproduced by permission from Taylor (J. E. Taylor 2009) Figure 3.*

The topic is confusing—at least to me—since it attempts to identify sites with no contemporary markers in a city that has been levelled and rebuilt numerous times in the last 2,000 years. The literary evidence is scant and ambiguous. I will be following Joan Taylor's analysis on this topic.[1]

---

1    (J. E. Taylor 2009) & (J. Taylor 2018).

# REPORTS ON THE CRUCIFIXION SITE

My starting point will be what Peter and eyewitness John tell me about the site of the crucifixion and the site of the burial. According to John, after being condemned, Jesus "went out to the place of the Skull (which in Aramaic is called Golgotha)" and "the place where Jesus was crucified was near the city" (John 19:17, 20). According to Peter-Mark, "They brought Jesus to the place called Golgotha (which means The Place of the Skull)," (Mark 15:22) and "(t)hose who passed by hurled insults at him …" (Mark 15:28a), "So also Jesus suffered and died outside the city gates …" (Hebrews 13:12).

According to Taylor, "Golgotha" is an Aramaic name that intimates round, skull, head, or wheel.[2] The Latin for "place of a skull" is *Calvariae Locus*, which renders "Calvary" in English; the place has traditionally been thought of as a hill or raised area, hence the Hill of Calvary. Golgotha was close to the city but beyond the walls, according to Roman and Jewish custom, which forbade burials inside city walls. It seems to have been a region—a "place," as John says— rather than a small site, large enough to encompass a cultivated area, a "garden," as John calls it, with at least one, and probably more, tombs, as well as the crucifixion site. There were passers-by to that place. The Romans would ensure crucifixion sites were situated close to busy areas to ensure public visibility as a deterrent to opposing Rome's rule. The addition of a titulus, or sign, with a description of Jesus' crime would indicate the public were close enough to read the inscription. The crucifixion site must have been large and somewhat levelled, with at least enough space for the three crucifixions, the guard contingent to secure the site, tools, and room for "operations." John indeed tells us that four soldiers were involved in Jesus' crucifixion. The site was probably larger than this estimate to accommodate more—perhaps many more—crucifixions if required, with preexisting post holes and uprights that, along with the cross pieces, were undoubtedly used repeatedly over the years. Neither John nor Peter say that this site was elevated, so it need not be thought of as a hill.

# REPORTS ON THE BURIAL SITE

Peter-Mark does not indicate the nature or location of the tomb. As for John, he reports that "At the place where Jesus was crucified, there was a garden, and in the garden a new tomb, in which no one had ever been laid. Because it was the Jewish day of Preparation and since the tomb was nearby, they laid Jesus there" (John 19:41–42).

John states the tomb was "nearby" and "at the place" of crucifixion in a garden area.

# WHERE WAS GOLGOTHA?

Based on excavations in Jerusalem, the area just north of the First or North Wall was originally a piece of ground that sloped up and away. It was used as a quarry until the 100s BCE; limestone was removed, and the quarry cut into this slope, creating a large crater with irregular rocky outcrops and caves. The area was then used for gardens or fields in the first century, since traces of ploughing have been found. Sometime later, it was filled in with debris.

Golgotha would have been a sizeable barren place. Quite a few rock-cut tombs have been discovered in the area, so it was being used as a burial site. In the first century, it lacked any sort of dwellings and was just outside the city walls. So the quarry was an identifiable "place." It also included gardens and cultivated fields. It would have been an ideal crucifixion site: it was close by and just outside the Gennath (Garden) Gate, and there were main roads nearby, providing visibility. The quarry seems to be linked to the name "Golgotha." Taylor speculates that looking out at the elongated crater from the sightline from the city, it would take on the appearance of a rounded shape, such as a head or skull, hence the name. The word "skull" may also have been associated with the region due to its use for burial sites or execution. The crucifixion, as well as Jesus' tomb, are both located within the quarry area, and the current Church of the Holy Sepulchre is situated above a portion of the quarry. All our evidence thus points toward an association between Golgotha and the quarry.

---

2    (J. E. Taylor 2009).

# TRADITIONAL SITES

Toward the end of Emperor Constantine's reign, in 326 CE, the first Christian emperor commissioned a large church complex encompassing what was claimed as both the crucifixion site and the tomb site. A few years later, in 333 CE, the Pilgrim of Bordeaux described the interior when looking in from the east through the main doors of Constantine's church:

"On the left hand is the little hill of Golgotha where the Lord was crucified. About a stone's throw from thence is a vault [crypta] wherein his body was laid and rose again on the third day. There, at present, by the command of Emperor Constantine, has been built a basilica; that is to say, a church of wondrous beauty …"[3]

Cyril of Jerusalem,[4] who was living in Jerusalem during and after the building of Constantine's church, gave a famous series of lectures—the Catechetical Lectures—in the new church (c. 348 CE). He references the sites which were in view:

"this holy Golgotha, which stands high above us, and shows itself to this day, and displays even yet how because of Christ the rocks were then riven; the sepulchre near at hand where He was laid; and the stone, which was laid on the door, which lies to this day by the tomb …"[5]

So from 326 CE onwards, the location of the two sites was fixed, as they can be seen today in the Church of the Holy Sepulchre in Jerusalem. Constantine's church survived intact, with both sites marked until it was destroyed by a local Muslim ruler in 1009 CE—an event that kicked off the Crusades. The current basilica, that is, the main building of the present Church of the Holy Sepulchre, was built by the crusaders in 1149 CE and maintained the traditional locations of the sites.

The question is, why these locations?

## THE SITES AFTER 33 CE

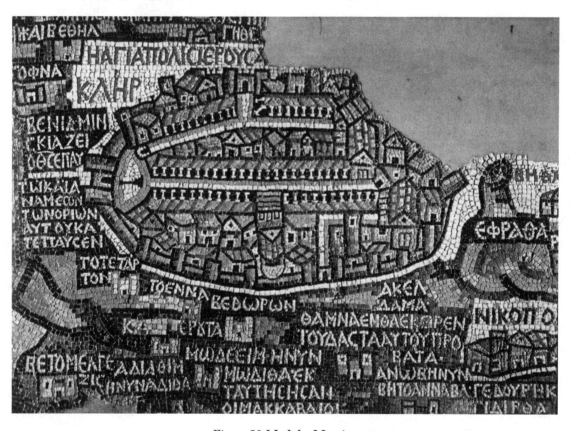

*Figure 52* **Madaba Mosaic map**

---

3     (Bordeaux Pilgrim 1885, 594).

4     A Christian theologian (c. 313–386).

5     (Cyril of Jerusalem n.d.) 13.39.

*This is from a Byzantine church in Jordan. This portion, partially damaged, shows the details of Jerusalem and is the oldest cartographic depiction of the region. The map shows the New Church of the Theotokos, which was opened in November 542 CE, but does not show any building built after 570 CE. The map, thus, was installed between 542 and 570. It depicts the north-south colonnaded main road called the Cardo, running left-right past Constantine's church (bottom centre, upside down) and ending with the second north-south road meeting at the Damascus Gate piazza, with a columnar monument on the left. The east-west road comes up the centre to the forum, next to the church on the right. The church and forum were built over Golgotha. The church has a domed structure behind it (below), which may be the structure covering Jesus' tomb site, for it lay outside the main structure.*

In 41 CE, King Herod Agrippa came to the throne and built the Third Wall north of the Old Walls and Second Wall, encompassing a large new suburb that included the Golgotha quarry. Until then, the area undoubtedly continued to be used for crucifixions and burials and was visited by people (various tombs have been found around the Holy Sepulchre Church, and some can be seen today.) With the expansion of the walls, the tombs would cease to be used, since they were now inside the city walls. However, the gardens and empty tombs would still be accessible. There is no indication of any structures being built in the quarry. During the First Jewish-Roman War, most of Jerusalem was destroyed (70 CE) and laid in ruins. After the Roman victory in the Second Jewish-Roman War, Emperor Hadrian, starting in 135 CE, built over the ruins a new Roman city called Aelia Capitolina. It used the standard Roman urban grid with a main colonnaded north-south road called the Cardo and an east-west road called the Decumanus, shown in the Madaba Map above. Typical for Roman cities, the main forum was placed where the two main roads crossed, and adjacent to it just north of the forum, a large temple to Venus was built. Both the forum and temple were built over the old quarry, much of the quarry's rock face was levelled, and other parts were filled in with dirt and debris, as discovered in the excavations mentioned above. However, a pillar of rock, currently called Calvary, was left to jut up through the temple floor for some unknown reason, perhaps as a platform for a statue.

At this point in history, I believe the precise locations of the tomb and site of the crucifixion became lost.

Until the construction of Hadrian's Temple, oral tradition, along with markers such as graffiti,[6] probably preserved both locations over the previous hundred years despite the massive upheavals of the time. It was an open-air location, never built over, with few nearby structures which were ruined. However, once the quarry was filled in and massive new pagan structures were built (the temple and the forum), the precise spots would be lost, even if the knowledge that important sites were there (somewhere) may have survived.[7]

In the Early Church literature of that period, there is no mention of the locations of the sites under the new temple or anywhere else.

The next we hear of the locations is soon after the new Constantinian church is built. Eusebius, writing in the 330s CE in *Life of Constantine*, provides some details on the preparation for building over the older temple to Venus:

"Accordingly, they brought a quantity of earth from a distance with much labour and covered the entire spot; then, having raised this to a moderate height, they paved it with stone, concealing the holy cave beneath this massive mound."[8]

While excavating in preparation for Constantine's new buildings, they accidentally found "contrary to all expectation" a tomb:

"But as soon as the original surface of the ground, beneath the covering of earth, appeared, immediately, and contrary to all expectation, the venerable and hollowed monument of our Saviour's resurrection was discovered"[9]

It seems that no one was looking for a tomb, and the find was surprising.

---

6       As can still be seen near Peter's tomb in Rome.

7       Despite later speculation, there is no evidence that Hadrian purposely co-opted the sites, thereby marking them monuments for pagan worship to spite Christian beliefs.

8       (Eusebius, *Life Of Constantine* n.d.) 3.26.

9       Ibid. 3.28.

We are given no reasons why this must be *the* tomb. Jesus was buried in a tomb like many others; over 900 pre-70 CE tombs have been discovered in and around Jerusalem, and the quarry was probably a warren of tombs. Even today, there are at least four additional tombs scattered around the outer perimeter in the Church of the Holy Sepulchre. It would be surprising if no tombs were found.

Constantine was undoubtedly pleased that a tomb was found; he was uniting the empire under the banner of Christianity. Having discovered this most sacred location could only help his program. But he never visited the site and had to rely on second-hand reports.

We are also given no reasons why the stone column coming up through the floor of the temple was identified as the crucifixion site. Indeed, it seems an awkward spot, farther from town, mainly in the centre of the quarry, too far away from the roads for passers-by to see or read the titulus. There is also no evidence from Peter-Mark or John that the crucifixion was on a high, visible point. Moreover, if we assume the Crucifixion site was quite a bit larger than seen today (both the tomb and the stone pillar have been chipped away), then the tomb would literally have to be at the very foot of the hill. This seems far too close for privacy and contradicts the information from the Gospels that the tomb was rather removed and secluded.

Can we make an educated guess as to where in the quarry the site of the crucifixion was located? I think so. I follow Taylor's research on this.

Josephus called the walls that enclosed the Upper and Lower City before Herod the Great's reign the Old Walls or First Walls. Herod the Great enlarged Jerusalem by surrounding a northern suburb with the Second Walls from a point on the Northern First Walls to the Temple Mount at the Fortress of Antonia. The point at which the First Walls and the Second Walls met was the Gennath, or Garden Gate, set in the northside of the Old Walls. The Gate may have gotten the name from the gardens in the quarry, as the latter was right outside this gate.

Taylor suggests this gate was the terminus for both the North Road and the West Road. The southern extreme of the quarry would be an ideal crucifixion site, just outside the Gennath Gate and the First Wall, close enough to both main roads for passers-by (and citizens in town) to see the crucifixions and read the titulus.

Supporting this view is Melito of Sardis,[10] writing around 160 CE after Hadrian had rebuilt Jerusalem:

"For if the murder [Jesus' death] took place at night, or if he was slaughtered in a desert place, I might have been able to keep silent. Not in the middle of the street and in the middle of the city."[11]

Melito seems to be recalling a tradition about the crucifixion site even after the area had been entirely built over. Following Taylor's reconstruction, the street Melito refers to is the new widened Decumanus road that runs parallel to the old North Wall. This probable location is about 200 metres south of the traditional site and is a much better fit for the five to ten minutes needed to carry the body to the tomb.

My conclusion is that the traditional tomb is probably not the one Jesus was laid in. No doubt a first-century tomb matching the description from John and Peter-Mark was discovered during Constantine's construction, as there were many around, and Jesus' tomb would not have been anything special. But the exact location was lost in 135 CE when the quarry was filled over. It seems certain the actual tomb was nearby, somewhere within the confines of the old quarry, as it only took five or ten minutes to carry the body to it. The site of the crucifixion is better identified about 200 meters south from the traditional site, in today's Old City: "a little to the southwest of where David Street meets Habad Street, but north of St. Mark Street."[12]

10    An Early Church Father, (died c. 180 CE).

11    (Sardis 2001).

12    (J. E. Taylor 2009).

# APPENDIX 5.

# RELICS FROM THE PASSION STORY?

*Figure 53* ***The Chalice of Valencia***

*Reputed to be the cup Jesus drank from at the Last Supper—the Holy Grail of literature.*
*Image reproduced by permission from Sta. Iglesia Catedral de Valencia.*

## THE CHALICE OF VALENCIA

In Western literature, there has been a long history of the Holy Grail, the vessel that Jesus drank from at the Last Supper. From the medieval *Perceval* by Chretien de Troyes through Dan Brown's *The Da Vinci Code*, the Grail story has inspired music, painting, and film, such as *Indiana Jones and the Last Crusade*. But did such a thing exist? For this section, I follow Janice Bennett's arguments. [1]

The short answer is, of course, yes, Jesus did drink from a cup at the Last Supper. Does that cup still exist? Perhaps. The best candidate is the Chalice of Valencia.

The Chalice of Valencia is a small ornate cup held in a chapel of the Cathedral of Valencia in Spain. It is an upper cup with elaborate gold and pearl handles and an upside-down lower cup used as the base. The lower cup and ornamentation were all added much later to the upper cup, as shown above. The (upper) cup is claimed to be the cup used during the Last Supper. Peter indeed mentions one: "Then he took the cup, gave thanks and offered it to them, and they all drank from it" (Mark 14:23).

---

1   For more information see (Bennett, *St. Laurence and The Holy Grail* 2002).

The upper cup is carved from an agate stone. It is approximately hemispherical in shape, unadorned except for a simple engraved line below the lip. It measures about 10 centimetres across and 7 centimetres high, about 4 by 2.5 inches, the size of half an orange, which is a moderate size. It has a crack after being dropped on April 3, 1744, during a religious service.

Research has confirmed that the cup dates from between 100s BCE and 100 CE and was made in Egypt, Syria, or Palestine. Expensive stone cups were considered as the "fine china" in a household that could afford them. Later, as glass became more available, glass vessels would take over. Wood drinking vessels were considered impure in Judaism, and common clay cups were not appropriate for special meals if stone cups were available. The Last Supper was held at John's wealthy home, so it is probable that the cup used by Jesus would have been a stone cup, put out for this important guest at a special meal.

Tradition states that Peter eventually brought the cup to Rome and used it for services. It was then passed down through subsequent popes. The early Roman Eucharistic prayer included the phrase: *"He took this glorious chalice,"* not found in other traditions, which indicates that a definite object was being referred to. Then under Emperor Valerian, in 258 CE, Christians were threatened with execution, and the Church saw all its wealth confiscated. According to tradition, the then Pope Sixtus II gave all the Church's relics, including that cup, to Deacon Lawrence to hide. Lawrence, who was Spanish, sent the cup to Spain for safekeeping, where, after further adventures, it found its way to Valencia. After that time, there are no later references to the cup in Rome. Early authors, going back to Ambrose (340–397 CE), note the tradition that Lawrence was responsible for hiding the Church's goods during the persecution. The first actual description of the cup in Spain is from a document dated December 14, 1134, CE, which mentions the cup and Lawrence.

Is this *the* cup? There is no way to be certain. Certainly the cup used by Jesus would have been a stone cup like this one, simple but elegant, not like the ornate chalices of Grail fame. Undoubtedly, after the Last Supper the cup would have been kept as an important item. It is small and easily hidden if needed. Such a cup would probably end up in the hands of the leadership and be used in early Eucharistic (that is, the re-enactment of the Last Supper covenant) occasions, replicating Jesus' example. It is also probable that it travelled to Rome and was in the hands of the early popes. And the whole Lawrence-Spain connection is plausible. Although likely the cup, there is no way of connecting this cup definitely to Jesus.

## THE SHROUD OF TURIN

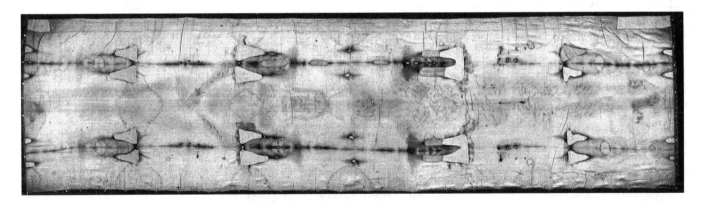

*Figure 53 **The Shroud of Turin***

*The image of a man can be seen in the centre of the cloth between the holes and scorch marks,*
*the upper view on the left and the rear view on the right.*

The Shroud of Turin is the most famous religious item in the world. Hundreds of books and thousands of research papers have been written about it; it has its own research tradition, called Sindonology. Scholars are of two opposing views: they either argue that it is the actual burial shroud of Jesus or point to the radio-carbon dating that puts its manufacture between 1260 and 1390 CE, making it a medieval forgery.

The shroud is rectangular, roughly 4.4 by 1.1 metres (14-feet-5-inches by 3-feet-7-inches, or 8 by 2 Assyrian cubits). The cloth is woven in a three-to-one herringbone twill composed of flax fibrils. It has been kept in the Cathedral of Turin since 1578. A fire in 1532 produced some burn holes and some scorching, but the damage was partially repaired with sewn-on patches.

Mark Antonacci[2] and Thomas de Wesselow[3] together give a comprehensive round-up of the current research on the shroud.

## THE IMAGE

There is a faint, brownish image of a naked man on the front and back of the shroud, with the two views meeting in the centre of the cloth and pointing in opposite directions. The image shows a man with a moustache, beard, and hair that falls to his shoulders with a central part; his physicality appears Middle Eastern. He seems muscular and of medium to tall height. According to various experts' calculations, he measured between 1.70 and 1.88 metres, or 5-feet-7-inches to 6-feet-2-inches.

A comprehensive scientific analysis of the Shroud was performed in 1978 by a team of scientists called the Shroud of Turin Research Group (STURP). The team concluded that:

"It was evident from the physical, mathematical, medical and chemical evidence that there must have been a crucified man in the Shroud."[4]

This statement is based on many observations. First, the man appears severely injured, and there are bloodstains on the cloth—over 130 injuries have been counted. He seems to have been beaten and whipped, has facial wounds, the crown of his head has small thorn-like piercings, he has wrist and feet piercings, was pierced in the side, and died before he came into contact with the cloth.[5] Next, there are scourge marks that match Roman whips. The man's arms were either elevated or bound, and he was whipped from behind, probably by two men. Also, the right-side wound was made post-mortem, and from which much blood and fluid flowed, so it probably pierced the heart. The shoulders show abrasions consistent with carrying a crossbar. Dirt and abrasions are visible on the knees, nose, and feet. The first two are compatible with falling forward while carrying a heavy weight. Moreover, it looks like a single nail was driven between the metatarsal bones of the feet, with the left foot placed on top of the right; neither leg was broken. Fluid flow patterns indicate first a vertical position, then a horizontal position, and correspond perfectly with the natural bleeding process. Nails driven into the wrists would cause the thumbs to contract into the palms, thus matching the lack of thumbs in the image. Blood and blood serum are present on the cloth; it is male blood, type AB, and the DNA is significantly degraded, indicating it is very old.

Additionally, there are no signs of decomposition, so the body would not have been in contact with the cloth for more than two or three days. The sharp blood stains are *not* due to natural staining, and the body in the image was not washed, in keeping with Jewish burial customs. The jaw appears to be tied up with a strip of linen, again keeping with Jewish burial customs. Finally, the cloth seems draped over the body and not tied in place, as would be expected in a normal burial, indicating a hasty burial with perhaps the finish of wrapping to be completed later.

## HOW WAS THE IMAGE FORMED?

STURP has determined that the image is a negative (just like a photographic negative) superficial to only the very top layer of fibres of the cloth. There is no directionality, such as brush strokes, in the image, which means that it was not painted on. Intensity is also inversely correlated with distance from the body; the image is darker the closer the shroud was to the body, such as the nose (darker) versus the eyes (lighter). Lastly, liquid blood blocked the image formation, and there is no image under direct bloodstains. The team was also able to establish that the image was formed in vertical straight-line paths to the cloth, which accounts for the distortions in the length of the legs and fingers, since the drape of the fabric was not parallel

2       (Antonacci 2000).

3       (Wesselow 2012).

4       (Heller 1983, 210).

5       For a detailed treatment of the image, see (Antonacci 2000, Chapter 2).

to the surface below it. The image exists as oxidized or degraded cellulose—by exposure to heat and/or light—in the fibres, making them appear slightly darker or older than the surrounding fibres (i.e. the image is encoded in accelerated aged cloth). Even today, it is impossible to see the image up close; centuries ago, the contrast would have been even weaker, so the earliest custodians may not even have seen the image. Parts of the man's skeleton closest to the surface appear: finger and hand bones, teeth, and part of the skull are visible, suggesting some form of X-ray-like effect.

## THE THEORY OF IMAGE FORMATION

The best explanation for image formation must explain the image characteristics while conforming to standard physics principles. STURP has determined that the image is not: a painting; a vapograph; an imprint due to body heat or bodily emissions or funeral anointing; made by any natural means of draping a cloth over a human body; a block print; a scorch; formed by draping the fabric over a statue or bas relief; or made from rubbing dry compounds on the cloth. Many experiments have been attempted to replicate the image's effect, and all have failed to produce an image like the Shroud's.

To date, the best theory that has been put forward is that some form of body dematerialization occurred and gave off light or radiation at low temperature; perhaps polarized gamma rays along with atomic particles emanated throughout the body with a range of about four centimetres. The shroud would fall through the body region, where protons and alpha particles would penetrate the topmost fibres of the cloth and encode the image vertically. Regions that have a longer path down would encode more heavily, for instance, the nose. This explains why it operated uniformly over the entire body independent of material, including skin, hair, and other inorganic material. It also explains the oddity of some blood marks, namely, a direct imprint of the bloodstain rather than a diluted blood mark from absorption, or even bloodstains that were never in contact with the cloth. A collapsing cloth would come into direct contact with all the blood wounds, encoding them as they were on the body. As the protons and alpha particles would not penetrate blood, the body image would not be encoded under the stain. Motion blurs can be seen from the collapsing jaw band in the beard area. This event could also alter the Carbon 14 balance, making the cloth appear much younger.

Interestingly, this theory helps to explain John's odd comment: "Finally the other disciple [John himself], who had reached the tomb first, also went inside. He saw and believed. (They still did not understand from Scripture that Jesus had to rise from the dead)" (John 20:8–9). John suddenly believed Jesus had risen. Why? If the image formation theory is correct, then the burial linen would have collapsed on itself and flattened out. It was not bundled up, re-folded, moved, or missing, had people removed the body. When John saw the linen undisturbed in the same place but flattened, the only explanation was that the body had simply vanished independently. That is why he suddenly believed.

## PHYSICAL PROPERTIES

The cloth itself is a very fine weave and would have been quite expensive. Limestone dust has been found on it that matches the environs of tombs around Jerusalem. Also, its physical dimensions conform almost precisely to eight by two Assyrian cubits, the Assyrian cubit being a standard measure of the marketplace in first-century Palestine.

Further scientific analyses have revealed other physical properties of the Shroud. Fifty-eight types of pollen have been found on the cloth; samples show a high correlation to pollen around Jerusalem and Palestine and Turkey, but not so much from France or Italy, the known locations of the Shroud. Furthermore, 45 of the 58 pollens found to grow in Jerusalem, while 13 grow (with one specific only to Constantinople) in Constantinople and 18 in (with two types of pollen specific to) Edessa, Turkey, reputed locations that the Shroud visited. During the traditional creation of flax, it is soaked first in natural water bodies and then new linen is laid out damp in the sun for extended periods to bleach the cloth, which would thus pick up much pollen from the area. A preponderance of pollen, therefore, would indicate the location of production. So the pollen evidence indicates Jerusalem as the origin for the cloth.

Another aspect of the Shroud lies in its fresh flower images, which are said to be visible. Of the 28 plants found, 27 grow around Jerusalem, with their blooming season being in March and April, when Jesus' death occurred. Twenty-five plants also have their pollen on the burial cloth. Interestingly, one type only blooms between 3:00 and 4:00 p.m., indicating when it was picked. The flowers on the cloth appear wilted as if after 24 to 36 hours. It is also possible that lettering on the shroud identifying the deceased and coins from Pontius Pilate's reign can be seen on the image of closed eyes printed on the cloth; putting coins on the eyes of the dead was common practice. However, in each case, the images are not clear and require subjective construction, so while fascinating, I am dubious of the flower, lettering, and coin claims.

## SPECIFIC TO JESUS

The image contains specifics related to the crucifixion of Jesus, namely, his beating, whipping, the crown of thorns, carrying, and falling with his cross piece, suggesting the reason why Simon of Cyrene was forced to carry it for him (Mark 15:21). He was also nailed (John 20:25), not tied up, as some crucifixions were done. His side was pierced, and the flow of fluids can be seen on the cloth, as witnessed by John (John 19:34–35). His legs were not broken, as was sometimes the practice to accelerate death, again witnessed by John (John 19:32–33). Finally, the body did not stay long enough with the cloth before decomposition could occur; the normal process would have stained the fabric. All these facts are attested in our eyewitness sources detailing the crucifixion.

## THE HISTORY OF THE SHROUD

If authentic, the Shroud's journey started in Jerusalem after Jesus' death. Its history until 944 CE is confusing, though, as there was another sacred image in the region, called the Mandylion, which purported to show just the face of Jesus on a cloth. According to a sermon by Gregory Referendarius, Archdeacon of Hagia Sophia in 944 CE, the Shroud, "an image of his [Christ] form," appears to have arrived in Constantinople on August 15, 944 CE.[6] Scholars argue that this Mandylion could have been the Shroud folded to display only the face. According to surviving records, "the burial shrouds of Jesus" were still in Constantinople in 1201.[7]

Antonacci explains that the image on the Shroud influenced reproductions of Jesus. Up until the 400s CE, Jesus was usually portrayed as young, clean-shaven, with short hair. In the 500s, this all changed radically, with Jesus being depicted in art and on coins in keeping with the image on the Shroud, that is, with a beard, moustache and long hair parted in the centre. Presumably, the Shroud was being displayed to artists from the 500s on, alluding to its existence before 944.

In 1204 CE, a primarily French army of crusaders sacked Constantinople and looted everything of value, and nothing is heard of the Shroud until 1356 CE. The most likely explanation is that the Knights Templar took it to France, but then the order was destroyed in 1307 by the French King. The Shroud re-surfaced at its first public showing in France during 1356; it was then in the possession of a knight called Geoffroi de Charny, thought to be related to a Geoffrey de Charnay, who was a high-ranking Templar. From 1390 onward, the Shroud is well attested and wound up in Turin, Italy.[8]

## CARBON DATING

In 1988, three independent carbon dating tests concluded with 95% confidence that the Shroud material dated to 1260–1390 CE. Hence, the Shroud was declared a medieval forgery. However, the debate has raged since then over these results. Supporters of the Shroud point out that carbon dating is not conclusive and can be subject to enormous error. Contamination of carbon dating samples has caused errors in the order of thousands of years in known instances. Supporters argue that the samples were contaminated, as proper protocols were not observed. Also, due to restrictions limiting physical damage of the Shroud put in place by the Catholic Church, only samples were taken away from the image, and these cannot be representative of the Shroud as a whole. Burn marks, repairs, human handling, and other contaminants were also present in the samples' area. Supporters also

6    (Guscin 2004).

7    (Mesarites n.d.).

8    For complete information on the history of the Shroud, please see (Antonacci 2000, Chapter 7).

argue that an earlier, unauthorized test took place in 1982 and placed the date at 200 CE, with a range of uncertainty well into the first century. Finally, they insist that if the image was formed somehow by a process that gave off neutrons or because of the fire of 1532, the Carbon 14 content, which carbon dating measures, would be altered to make the cloth appear much younger. All of this, supporters claim, would explain the late dating of the Shroud obtained from carbon dating.

*Figure 54 **The Manoppello Image***

*A cloth with an image claimed to be derived from contact with Jesus but widely acknowledged as being artificially made, probably in the 1400s. Stylistically it is like other images of Jesus painted in the Middle Ages or the Renaissance.*

According to the 1988 carbon dating process, the image on the Shroud is medieval artwork created before the first showing in 1356. But to art historian Thomas de Wesselow, this is highly unlikely. He says that "technically, conceptually and stylistically, the Shroud makes no sense as a medieval artwork."[9] He also explains that "The notion that such a physiologically and archaeologically accurate image could or would have been painted (in blood) by a medieval artist is patently absurd."[10] Tellingly other art historians have remained essentially silent on this masterpiece of medieval religious imagery.

A medieval artist is more likely to have produced a relic such as the Manoppello Image or the icon Mandylion of Edessa, both clearly man-made. Moreover, the image on the Shroud occurs from the accelerated ageing of the cloth; the initial image was almost invisible and only darkened through time, yet it is reported to have been visible in the 1300s, indicating an older history.

And if the image were created by contact with a crucified person, it would imply that it was made before the early 300s CE, when Roman Emperor Constantine the Great banned crucifixion in the Roman Empire.[11] A medieval forger would have to overcome a long list of technical problems to create the Shroud. As Antonacci put it: "To encode these features, our forger would not only have to have understood advanced scientific principles, but also have possessed a knowledge of anatomy and medicine that was centuries ahead of his time."[12] Indeed, as I shall show below, the same forger would have to have access to or must have created the Sudarium of Oviedo.

In sum, all the medical, scientific, archaeological, and historical evidence indicate that the shroud contains an image of a crucified man, specifically Jesus; that the cloth was manufactured in or near Jerusalem; that the image is due to accelerated oxidation of the top layer of the linen fibres; that the image formation seems to involve some form of a radiation event, in conjunction with the dematerialization of the body, the nature of which is currently unknown; and that the process of dating using carbon dating was flawed—the implied medieval forgery theory has been called "absurd."

Aside from the flawed carbon tests, though, all the empirical evidence from the study of the cloth supports its authenticity. The Shroud is hotly contested, of course. Still, a cursory examination of the arguments against authenticity, apart from citing the carbon dating results and some very early, now discredited, research produces no serious counterarguments to the more recent findings presented above. Based on the body of ongoing research, I am thus inclined to accept, pending other discoveries, that the Shroud is indeed the linen that John saw Jesus buried in. Some kind of yet to be explained "energy event" caused the body to disappear, and as the cloth was flattened out, the image was encoded.

---

9    (Wesselow 2012, 22).

10    Ibid. 131.

11    (The Editors of Encyclopaedia Britannica, Crucifixion 2018).

12    (Antonacci 2000, Appendix J).

# THE SUDARIUM OF OVIEDO

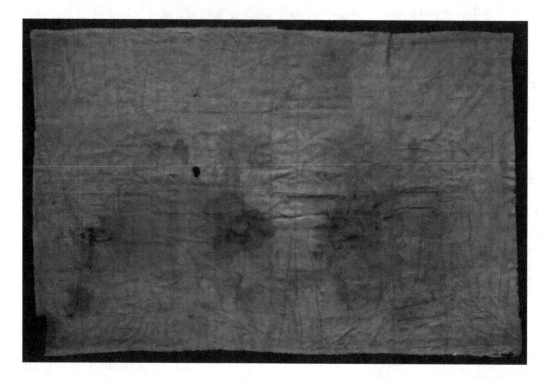

*Figure 56* ***The Sudarium of Oviedo***

*This is purported to be the cloth used to wrap Jesus' head after death. Image courtesy of Reinhard Dietrich via CC BY-SA 4.0.*

The Sudarium of Oviedo is the less well-known smaller cousin of the Shroud of Turin, and I follow Janice Bennett's information in this section.[13] It is a small cloth, kept in the Cámara Santa of the Cathedral of San Salvador, Oviedo in Spain. Initially, it was a white linen cloth with a taffeta texture, primarily rectangular and measuring about 33 by 21 inches (almost 1.5 by 1 in Assyrian cubits). It is now stained, dirty, and wrinkled, and it lacks any image, unlike the Shroud. It has bloodstains, light brown in the colour of varying intensity, in a mirror image along the axis of a still existing fold. It is called the "Sudarium" from the Latin word *sudarium*, a sweat cloth or face cloth used to wipe the face.

It is claimed that the Sudarium is the separate "head cloth" that John saw in the tomb. Here is the relevant passage:

"Then Simon Peter, who was behind him [John], arrived and went into the tomb. He saw the strips of linen lying there, as well as the burial cloth [sudarium] that had been around Jesus' head. The cloth was folded up by itself, separate from the linen." (John 20:6–7)

John also uses the term *sudarium* in connection with Lazarus' burial:

"The dead man came out, his hands and feet wrapped with strips of linen, and a cloth [sudarium] around his face." (John 11:44)

A more literal translation into English of John's description of his visit to the tomb has been proposed by Bennett and goes as follows:

> "[John] crouching down, sees that the linens are lying in the same position in which they had been placed, but didn't go in. Simon Peter arrives after him and entered the tomb, he contemplates the linens that are lying [or lying flat or smoothed out] in the original position in which they had been placed; and he contemplates the sudarium, that had covered His head, and that had not been placed with the linens, but separately,

---

13    (Bennett, Sacred Blood, Sacred Image 2001).

remaining rolled up in the same place it had been before. Then the other disciple [John], the one who had been the first to arrive at the tomb, also entered; he saw and believed."[14]

As we know, John was an eyewitness to the crucifixion and the initial wrapping of the body of Jesus. He also saw the final disposition of the clothes in the tomb, which seemed important to him. In addition, he uses the definite article "the" when referring to the face cloth, indicating his familiarity with it. This passage seems to contrast the "smoothed" state of the linens with that of the cloth, which remained rolled up.

## THE HISTORY OF THE SUDARIUM

If authentic, the history of the Sudarium would have started in Jerusalem, just after Jesus' death. It would have been one of the objects retained by Jesus' followers and the Early Church. A written account from a pilgrim mentions a relic called the Sudarium of Christ located in Jerusalem in the 500s, leaving Jerusalem in 614 CE due to invading Persians, and eventually going to Oviedo, Spain, where it remained from 761 CE.[15]

## ANALYSIS

Current research is ongoing and conducted by the Investigative Team of the Spanish Center of Sindonology (EDICES), using the same methods as used in criminal forensics. After ten years, apart from carbon dating, nothing has been found to disprove the claim that the Sudarium was indeed the headcloth of Jesus. It has been established that it is a coarse, inexpensive linen cloth made on a vertical loom. Also, 99% of the pollen and spores on the fabric are from Palestine, North Africa, and Spain, indicating the locations the Sudarium is reported to have visited. Finally, aloe and myrrh have been identified on the cloth; these would have been applied over the victim's bloodstains following Jewish burial customs.

According to forensic analysis, the cloth was placed on the head of an already dead man, whose body had been vertical for about two hours. Once rigor mortis set in, liquids would have started flowing again, post-mortem, from the wounds. The victim was upright for another hour, then horizontal for yet another based on the liquid flow. An attempt was made to stem the flow of blood from the nose during this time. Tiny dots of blood on the cloth are consistent with thorn wounds caused before death.

EDICES can confirm at present a series of conclusions. First, the Sudarium of Oviedo has a series of stains originating from human blood, type AB. The linen is also wrinkled and dirty, partially torn, and burned. It is stained and has a high degree of contamination but does not show fraudulent tampering or decay. It was undoubtedly placed on the head of the corpse of a normal adult male, who had a beard, moustache, and long hair tied at the back of the head. The subject was already dead because how the stains were formed is incompatible with any possible respiratory movement. Because of the composition of the stains, which have a proportion between blood and serum of one to six, the man certainly suffered a tremendous pulmonary oedema, that is, fluid in the lungs. Death would have been due to asphyxiation because of the dying process. The cloth was initially only wrapped partway around the vertical head, probably as the right cheek would have rested on the right upstretched arm. This implies that the body was suspended with both arms stretched out, and the feet were fastened. Otherwise, death would have occurred in 15 to 20 minutes, which does not allow enough time to generate the amount of liquid found on the cloth. His mouth was almost closed, and the nose was pressed to the right from the pressure of the mortuary linen. The mouth and nose have been perfectly identified on the linen and were the origin of the principal bloodstains. On the lower part of the left edge of the cloth are a series of stains that correspond to puncture wounds, produced while the man was still alive, and these bled approximately one hour before the linen was placed on them. Also, practically the entire head, neck, shoulders, and at least part of this man's back were bloody before being covered by this linen, because the stains observed in the hair, forehead, and on the upper part of the head are of vital blood. This man was undoubtedly mistreated before his death, with instruments that made him bleed from the scalp and produced wounds on the neck, shoulders, and upper part of the back.

---

14    (Bennett 2001, 2064). Translation by Luis Garcia.

15    For a complete history including manuscript evidence, see (Bennett, *Sacred Blood, Sacred Image* 2001 Chapter 1).

Like the Shroud, the cloth has been subjected to a series of confusing carbon dating tests. EDICES does not think that carbon dating could be relevant due to contamination; the tests conducted returned a series of vastly different dates, from 1 to 600 CE, 642 to 869, and 653 to 786. Aside from carbon dating being imperfect, it is susceptible to the methods used on "clean" samples, which were almost certainly severely contaminated. Therefore, the results obtained from such a method cannot be conclusive.

## THE SHROUD AND THE SUDARIUM

Both the Shroud and the Sudarium appear to have wrapped the head of the same victim, lending credence to the authenticity of both cloths. Stains on the Shroud and the Sudarium are very similar; they count 70 points of coincidence, indicating that they were in contact with the same object. Both blood types are AB, common in the Middle East but uncommon in Europe. Facial points and facial wounds match, including a probable broken nose. The bloodstains are very similar, including matches for before-death blood and after-death blood. Both cloths are consistent with a body that was scourged, crucified, and crowned with thorns. Along with other artefacts associated with Jesus, both cloths would undoubtedly have been gathered and kept by the Early Church. Finally, the correspondence with the Sudarium also casts doubt on the carbon dating of the Shroud, as the Sudarium's carbon dating is quite older than the Shroud's.

On its own, the Sudarium is interesting, but like the Chalice of Valencia, it does not have a complete history on which to assess it; we cannot be sure that it was the headcloth used after the crucifixion. But when taken together with evidence from the Shroud, the evidence for both becomes much more compelling, meaning that both are probably authentic. Indeed, we have scientific and physical evidence for the crucifixion that confirms the eyewitness Passion narratives. These facts cannot be reasonably ignored.

# APPENDIX 6.

# SUBSUMMATION

There are 25 remaining sources to be evaluated in terms of factual content related to Jesus against the richest sources of information, namely the Gospel of John, Q, and Peter-Mark. There are four entries to evaluate in my Source List, with Secret Mark being included in Peter-Mark.

I have sifted these sources and collected all the facts about Jesus they contain. Here are the titles along with estimated composition dates:[1]

Tacitus (115 CE), Josephus (93), *The Letter of Mara Bar-Serapion* (72), Quadratus of Athens (120–130), *Polycarp to the Philippians* (110–140), Papias (110–140), *1 Clement* (70), *Epistle of Barnabas* (75), 1 Peter (Spring 55), 2 Peter (61–62), 1 John (60–65), *The Fayyum Fragment* (70–200), *Oxyrhynchus 1224 Gospel* (50–140), 1 Thessalonians (Early 50), Philippians (Spring 58), Galatians (Late 56), 2 Corinthians (Early 56), Romans (Early 57), Colossians (Summer 58), 1 Timothy (Autumn 55), 2 Timothy (Autumn 58), Book of Hebrews (67), 1 Corinthians (Spring 55), the Corinthian Creed (33–39).

I list the facts mentioned by all these sources here, along with reference to that fact in an earlier work:

He ate (Mark 2:15) lived in "the flesh" (that is, was born a man, and he was not a spirit) (Mark 8:23), taught (Mark 4:2–9), collected followers (Mark 1:16–20), was arrested (Mark 14:46) due to the leading Jews (Mark 15:1) and was crucified (Mark 15:22–24) by order of Pontius Pilate (Mark 15:15). Jesus suffered (Mark 15:15–19, 34) outside the gate, was given wine vinegar (Mark 15:36) with gall to drink (Matthew 27:34), died on the cross (Mark 15:37), was buried (Mark 15:46), and was resurrected on the third day (Mark 16:14) and seen by Peter and the disciples (Mark 16:14). He performed miracles and wonders (Mark 3:1–5, 6:48–51, etc.), raised people from the dead (Mark 10:34b) and healed (Mark 1:34) and was known as the King of the Jews (Mark 15:26). He attracted followers (Mark 15:40–41), both Jewish (Mark 3:14–19) and non-Jewish (Q 7:1, 3:6b–9 ,10), and his movement survived his death (Mark 16:20). Jesus' brother, James, was killed in 62 CE.

All these facts, except two, can be found in the earlier works, so according to the Repetition Rule they can be set aside.[2] The two new facts are:

• Jesus suffered outside the gate from Hebrews 13:12.

• Jesus' brother, James, was killed in 62 CE reported by Josephus.

There are also some longer sequences and sayings of Jesus in these sources which can also be assessed using the Repetition Rule: *1 Clement* quotes Jesus as saying:

---

1    ECW's dates unless superseded by Robinson's dates or mine.

2    As noted, Peter-Mark (40 CE) and Q (early mid 30s CE) predate all the sources examined. The *Epistle of Barnabas* (85 CE), which mentions the gall added to the wine, is pre-dated by Matthew (58–61 CE), which contains that information.

"Be merciful, that you may obtain mercy; forgive, that you may be forgiven. What you do yourself, will be done to you; what you give, will be given you; as you judge, so you will be judged; as you show kindness, so it will be shown to you. Your portion will be weighted out for you in your own scales (*1 Clement* 13:2) … Woe to that man; it would have been a good thing if he had never been born, instead of upsetting one of my chosen ones. It would be better for him to be pitched into the sea with a millstone hung around him, than to lead a single one of my chosen astray." (*1 Clement* 46:8)

However, these are paraphrases of verses from earlier Q (Q 6:37–38, 17:1–2).

Polycarp has a single quote by Jesus:

"Judge not, that you be not judged; forgive, and you will be forgiven; be merciful, that you may obtain mercy; for whatever you measure out to other people will be measured back again to yourselves. Happy are the poor and they who are persecuted because they are righteous, for theirs is the kingdom of God."[3]

However, both quotes again paraphrase verses from early Q (Q 6:37–38, 6:20, 22–23).

1 John 1:5 has a short quote from Jesus: "God is light and in him is no darkness at all." This saying is otherwise unattested.

*The Fayyum Fragment* reports that Jesus predicted his disciples would desert him. Still, Peter insists he will not, but Jesus famously predicts Peter will deny him three times before the cock crows. This story fragment is a copy of the same story in Peter-Mark.[4]

*The Oxyrhynchus 1224 Gospel* fragment reports this incident: "The scribes, Pharisees and priests were angry with Jesus for eating with sinners. Jesus said, 'Those who are healthy have no need of a physician …'" This is a copy of the same story in Peter-Mark 2:16–17.

According to Paul's letter, 1 Corinthians 15:3–7:

"Jesus during the evening meal broke bread, and said, 'This is my body, which is for you; do this in remembrance of me.' After supper he took wine saying, 'This cup is the new covenant in my blood; do this, whenever you drink it, in remembrance of me.'" This short narrative is a restating of Peter-Mark's original version of the event (Mark 14:22–25).[5]

The only other unattested information from Paul's letters is the Corinthian Creed in 1 Corinthians. Given my assessment of Paul and his beliefs, I want to re-examine the Creed as it purports to offer new facts about Jesus. It starts well enough; we are told Jesus died, was buried, and was raised on the third day; he appeared to Peter and the disciples. So far, this agrees with facts from John's account. However, the Creed then says that Jesus appeared to 500 witnesses, then to James, and then to all the apostles. It is hard to know what to do with this sequence; perhaps 500 is just an arbitrarily large number, in the same way that the expression such as "a lot of people" is. Paul may also be speaking metaphorically, talking about all of Jesus' followers at some early stage. Maybe the number 500 even has some hidden numerology meaning. After all, John also used numerology in his Gospel. In any case, it is not clear who "the apostles" Paul is referring to are. But the answer to the usefulness of the Creed lies, I believe, within the final verse: "… and last of all he appeared to me also, as to one abnormally born" (1 Corinthians 15:8). This refers, of course, not to the resurrected physical Jesus reported by Peter-Mark and John, but rather Paul's experience of a heavenly and mystical Christ. I suspect the Creed originated with the events described by Peter-Mark and John, but that Paul interpreted the stories of seeing a physical resurrected Jesus as visions of Christ, like his. He then extended the Creed to encompass his and many of his own followers' (the "500" and "the apostles") ecstatic hallucinations. Therefore, I will set the Corinthian Creed aside, for it does not offer a reliable account.

Papias, in a surviving quote from his lost *Expositions of the Sayings of the Lord*, reported by Irenaeus, does provide us with a reliable teaching by Jesus:

"As the elders who saw John, the disciple of the Lord, related that they had heard from him how the Lord used to teach regarding these times, and say: 'The days will come, in which vines shall grow, each having ten thousand branches, and in each branch ten thousand twigs, and in each true twig ten thousand shoots, and in each one of the shoots ten thousand clusters, and on every one of the clusters ten thousand grapes, and every grape when pressed will give five and twenty *metres* of wine. And

---

3    (Polycrates of Ephesus n.d., 2:3).

4    Mark 14:27–30, except the rooster crows three times.

5    Interestingly, Paul's version includes the term "new covenant," implying a linkage to the original covenant in the JS. Peter reports "covenant" only, with no JS overtones

when any one of the saints shall lay hold of a cluster, another shall cry out, I am a better cluster, take me; bless the Lord through me. In like manner [the Lord declared] that a grain of wheat would produce ten thousand ears, and that every ear should have ten thousand grains, and every grain would yield ten pounds of clear, pure, fine flour; and that all other fruit-bearing trees, and seeds and grass, would produce in similar proportions; and that all animals feeding [only] on the productions of the earth, should [in those days] become peaceful and harmonious among each other, and be in perfect subjection to man.'

And these things are borne witness to in writing by Papias, the hearer of John [the Elder/Presbyter], and a companion of Polycarp, in his fourth book; for there were five books compiled by him. And he says in addition, now these things are credible to believers. And he says that, when the traitor Judas did not give credit to them, and put the question, 'How then can things about to bring forth so abundantly be wrought by the Lord.' the Lord declared, 'They who shall come to these [times] shall see.'"[6]

Although Irenaeus' reference is a little vague, this saying is a previously un-attested teaching of Jesus that was handed down by Papias. It will thus go into my Source List.

---

6    Irenaeus, *Against Heresies,* 5.33.3–4.

# APPENDIX 7.

# STARTING AND ENDING SOURCE LIST

The table below lists all the sources up for consideration. It consists of the ECW list with six additional sources at the top. The first two columns provide the original then revised composition date ranges. The fourth column lists the rule, if any, that disqualified the source from my Source List. The final column indicates my Source List.

| Original Consensus Composition Date Range (CE) | Revised Date Range (CE) | Source | Rule that ultimately eliminated source | In my Source List? |
|---|---|---|---|---|
| 600+ | | Muslim Sources | Date | |
| <1BCE | | Jewish Scriptures (JS) including the OT. | Date | |
| 0–100 | | 4 Maccabees | Facts | |
| 0–100 | | The Wisdom of Solomon | Facts | |
| | 33–99 | **Pericope Adulterae** | | Yes |
| | Summer-Fall 40 | Longer Ending of Mark | | Embedded in Peter-Mark |
| 30–60 | | Passion Narrative | | Embedded in John & Peter-Mark |
| 40–80 | Early 30s | **Lost Sayings Gospel Q** | | Yes |
| 50–60 | Early 50 | 1 Thessalonians | Repetition | |
| 50–60 | Spring 58 | Philippians | Repetition | |
| 50–60 | Late 56 | Galatians | Repetition | |
| 50–60 | Spring 55 | 1 Corinthians | Repetition | |
| 50–60 | Early 56 | 2 Corinthians | Repetition | |
| 50–60 | Early 57 | Romans | Repetition | |
| 50–60 | Summer 58 | Philemon | Repetition | |
| 50–80 | Summer 58 | Colossians | Repetition | |
| 50–90 | | Signs Gospel | | Embedded in John |

| 50–95 | 67 | **Book of Hebrews** | | Hebrews 13:12 |
|---|---|---|---|---|
| 50–120 | 40–60 | Didache | Facts | |
| 50–140 | 120–150 | Gospel of Thomas | Date | |
| 50–140 | | Oxyrhynchus 1224 Gospel | Repetition | |
| 50–150 | | Apocalypse of Adam | Facts | |
| 50–150 | | Eugnostos the Blessed | Facts | |
| 50–200 | | Sophia of Jesus Christ | Facts | |
| 65–80 | Summer-Fall 40 | **Gospel of Mark** | | Yes as Peter-Mark |
| 70–100 | 47–48 | Epistle of James | Facts | |
| 70–120 | 150–200 | Egerton Gospel | Date | |
| 70–160 | 150–200 | Gospel of Peter | Date | |
| 70–160 | 41–80s | Secret Mark | | Embedded in Peter-Mark |
| 70–200 | | Fayyum Fragment | Repetition | |
| 70–200 | | Testaments of the Twelve Patriarchs | Facts | |
| 73–200 | | Mara Bar Serapion | Repetition | |
| 80–100 | Early 50 or 51 | 2 Thessalonians | Repetition | |
| 80–100 | Late Summer 58 | Ephesians | Repetition | |
| 80–100 | 58–61 | Gospel of Matthew | Untrustworthy | |
| 80–110 | Spring 65 | 1 Peter | Repetition | |
| 80–120 | 75 | Epistle of Barnabas | Repetition | |
| 80–130 | 58–61 | Gospel of Luke | Untrustworthy | |
| 80–130 | 62 | Acts of the Apostles | Untrustworthy | |
| 80–140 | Early 70 | 1 Clement | Repetition | |
| 80–150 | 120–150 | Gospel of the Egyptians | Date | |
| 80–150 | 120–150 | Gospel of the Hebrews | Date | |
| 80–250 | | Christian Sibyllines | Facts | |
| 90–95 | Early 69 | Revelation | Facts | |

| | | | | |
|---|---|---|---|---|
| 90–120 | 64–65 | **Gospel of John** | | Yes |
| 90–120 | 60–65 | **1 John** | | 1 John 1:5 |
| 90–120 | 60–65 | 2 John | Facts | |
| 90–120 | 60–65 | 3 John | Facts | |
| 90–120 | 61–62 | Epistle of Jude | Facts | |
| 93 | | **Flavius Josephus** | Repetition (TF) | Antiquities 20.9.1 |
| 100–150 | Autumn 55 | 1 Timothy | Facts | |
| 100–150 | Autumn 58 | 2 Timothy | Facts | |
| 100–150 | Late Spring 57 | Titus | Facts | |
| 100–150 | | Apocalypse of Peter | Date | |
| 100–150 | | Secret Book of James | Date | |
| 100–150 | | Preaching of Peter | Date | |
| 100–160 | | Gospel of the Ebionites | Date | |
| 100–160 | | Gospel of the Nazoreans | Date | |
| 100–160 | 85 | Shepherd of Hermas | Facts | |
| 100–160 | 61–62 | 2 Peter | Facts | |
| 100–200 | | Odes of Solomon | Date | |
| 100–200 | | Gospel of Eve | Date | |
| 100–230 | | Thunder, Perfect Mind | Date | |
| 101–220 | | Book of Elchasai | Date | |
| 105–115 | | Ignatius of Antioch | Custody | |
| 110–140 | | Polycarp to the Philippians | Repetition | |
| 110–140 | | **Papias** | | Against Heresies, 5.33.3–4 |
| 110–160 | | Oxyrhynchus 840 Gospel | Date | |
| 110–160 | | Traditions of Matthias | Date | |
| 111–112 | | Pliny the Younger | Date | |
| 115 | | Suetonius | Date | |
| 115 | | Tacitus | Repetition | |
| 120–130 | | Quadratus of Athens | Facts | |
| 120–130 | | Apology of Aristides | Date | |
| 120–140 | | Basilides | Date | |
| 120–140 | | Naassene Fragment | Date | |
| 120–160 | | Valentinus | Date | |
| 120–180 | | Apocryphon of John | Date | |

| | | |
|---|---|---|
| 120–180 | Gospel of Mary | Date |
| 120–180 | Dialogue of the Savior | Date |
| 120–180 | Gospel of the Savior | Date |
| 120–180 | 2nd Apocalypse of James | Date |
| 120–180 | Trimorphic Protennoia | Date |
| 120–180 | Gospel of Perfection | Date |
| 120–200 | Genna Marias | Date |
| 130–140 | Marcion | Date |
| 130–150 | Aristo of Pella | Date |
| 130–160 | Epiphanes On Righteousness | Date |
| 130–160 | Ophite Diagrams | Date |
| 130–160 | 2 Clement | Date |
| 130–170 | Gospel of Judas | Date |
| 130–200 | Epistle of Mathetes to Diognetus | Date |
| 140–150 | Epistula Apostolorum | Date |
| 140–160 | Ptolemy | Date |
| 140–160 | Isidore | Date |
| 140–170 | Fronto | Date |
| 140–170 | Infancy Gospel of James | Date |
| 140–170 | Infancy Gospel of Thomas | Date |
| 140–180 | Gospel of Truth | Date |
| 150–160 | Martyrdom of Polycarp | Date |
| 150–160 | Justin Martyr | Date |
| 150–180 | Excerpts of Theodotus | Date |
| 150–180 | Heracleon | Date |
| 150–200 | Ascension of Isaiah | Date |
| 150–200 | Interpretation of Knowledge | Date |

| 150–200 | Testimony of Truth | Date |
| 150–200 | Acts of Peter | Date |
| 150–200 | Acts of John | Date |
| 150–200 | Acts of Paul | Date |
| 150–200 | Acts of Andrew | Date |
| 150–225 | Acts of Peter and the Twelve | Date |
| 150–225 | Book of Thomas the Contender | Date |
| 150–250 | Paraphrase of Shem | Date |
| 150–250 | Fifth and Sixth Books of Esra | Date |
| 150–300 | Authoritative Teaching | Date |
| 150–300 | Coptic Apocalypse of Paul | Date |
| 150–300 | Prayer of the Apostle Paul | Date |
| 150–300 | Discourse on the Eighth and Ninth | Date |
| 150–300 | Melchizedek | Date |
| 150–350 | Preaching of Paul | Date |
| 150–350 | Epistle to the Laodiceans | Date |
| 150–350 | Questions of Mary | Date |
| 150–350 | Allogenes, the Stranger | Date |
| 150–350 | Hypsiphrone | Date |
| 150–350 | Valentinian Exposition | Date |
| 150–350 | Act of Peter | Date |
| 150–360 | Concept of Our Great Power | Date |
| 150–400 | Acts of Pilate | Date |
| 150–400 | Anti-Marcionite Prologues | Date |
| 150–400 | Dialogue Between John and Jesus | Date |
| 160–170 | Tatian's Address to the Greeks | Date |
| 160–180 | Claudius Apollinaris | Date |
| 160–180 | Apelles | Date |
| 160–180 | Julius Cassianus | Date |
| 160–250 | Octavius of Minucius Felix | Date |
| 161–180 | Acts of Carpus | Date |

| | | |
|---|---|---|
| 165–175 | Melito of Sardis | Date |
| 165–175 | Hegesippus | Date |
| 165–175 | Dionysius of Corinth | Date |
| 165–175 | Lucian of Samosata | Date |
| 167 | Marcus Aurelius | Date |
| 170–175 | Diatessaron | Date |
| 170–200 | Dura-Europos Gospel Harmony | Date |
| 170–200 | Muratorian Canon | Date |
| 170–200 | Treatise on the Resurrection | Date |
| 170–220 | Letter of Peter to Philip | Date |
| 170–230 | Thought of Norea | Date |
| 175–180 | Athenagoras of Athens | Date |
| 175–185 | Irenaeus of Lyons | Date |
| 175–185 | Rhodon | Date |
| 175–185 | Theophilus of Caesarea | Date |
| 175–190 | Galen | Date |
| 178 | Celsus | Date |
| 178 | Letter from Vienna and Lyons | Date |
| 180 | Passion of the Scillitan Martyrs | Date |
| 180–185 | Theophilus of Antioch | Date |
| 180–185 | Acts of Apollonius | Date |
| 180–220 | Bardesanes | Date |
| 180–220 | Kerygmata Petrou | Date |
| 180–230 | Hippolytus of Rome | Date |
| 180–230 | Sentences of Sextus | Date |
| 180–250 | 1st Apocalypse of James | Date |
| 180–250 | Gospel of Philip | Date |
| 182–202 | Clement of Alexandria | Date |
| 185–195 | Maximus of Jerusalem | Date |
| 185–195 | Polycrates of Ephesus | Date |
| 188–217 | Talmud | Date |
| 189–199 | Victor I | Date |
| 190–210 | Pantaenus | Date |
| 190–230 | Second Discourse of Great Seth | Date |
| 193 | Anonymous Anti-Montanist | Date |
| 193–216 | Inscription of Abercius | Date |
| 197–220 | Tertullian | Date |

| | | |
|---|---|---|
| 200–210 | Serapion of Antioch | Date |
| 200–210 | Apollonius | Date |
| 200–220 | Caius | Date |
| 200–220 | Philostratus | Date |
| 200–225 | Acts of Thomas | Date |
| 200–230 | Ammonius of Alexandria | Date |
| 200–230 | Zostrianos | Date |
| 200–230 | Three Steles of Seth | Date |
| 200–230 | Exegesis on the Soul | Date |
| 200–250 | Didascalia | Date |
| 200–250 | Books of Jeu | Date |
| 200–300 | Pistis Sophia | Date |
| 200–300 | Tripartite Tractate | Date |
| 200–300 | Hypostasis of the Archons | Date |
| 200–300 | Prayer of Thanksgiving | Date |
| 200–300 | Coptic Apocalypse of Peter | Date |
| 200–330 | Apostolic Church Order | Date |
| 200–350 | Holy Book of the Great Invisible Spirit | Date |
| 200–450 | Monarchian Prologues | Date |
| 203 | Acts of Perpetua and Felicitas | Date |
| 203–250 | Origen | Date |
| 210–245 | Lucian of Antioch | Date |
| 217–222 | Callistus | Date |
| 230–265 | Dionysius of Alexandria | Date |
| 230–268 | Firmilian of Caesarea | Date |
| 240–260 | Commodian | Date |
| 246–258 | Cyprian | Date |
| 250–274 | Gospel of Mani | Date |

| | | |
|---|---|---|
| 250–300 | Teachings of Silvanus | Date |
| 250–300 | Excerpt from the Perfect Discourse | Date |
| 250–350 | Coptic Apocalypse of Elijah | Date |
| 250–400 | Apocalypse of Paul | Date |
| 251–253 | Pope Cornelius | Date |
| 251–258 | Novatian | Date |
| 254–257 | Pope Stephen | Date |
| 259–268 | Dionysius of Rome | Date |
| 260–280 | Theognostus | Date |
| 265–282 | Gregory Thaumaturgus | Date |
| 269–274 | Pope Felix | Date |
| 270–310 | Victorinus of Pettau | Date |
| 270–312 | Methodius | Date |
| 270–330 | Marsanes | Date |
| 270–330 | On the Origin of the World | Date |
| 270–350 | De Recta in Deum Fide | Date |
| 280–300 | Hesychius | Date |
| 280–310 | Pierius | Date |
| 280–310 | Pamphilus of Caesarea | Date |
| 297–310 | Arnobius of Sicca | Date |
| 300–311 | Peter of Alexandria | Date |
| 300–320 | Pseudo-Clementine Homilies | Date |
| 300–340 | Eusebius of Caesarea | Date |
| 300–350 | Manichean Acts of Leucius Charinus | Date |
| 300–390 | Letters of Paul and Seneca | Date |
| 300–400 | Apocalypse of Thomas | Date |

| | | |
|---|---|---|
| 300–400 | Freer Logion | Date |
| 300–600 | Gospel of Gamaliel | Date |
| 303–316 | Lactantius | Date |
| 310–334 | Reticius of Autun | Date |
| 320–380 | Pseudo-Clementine Recognitions | Date |

# BIBLIOGRAPHY

Adamnan. 1896. "Arculf's Narrative About the Holy Places, The library of the Palestine Pilgrims' Text Society." *Internet Archive*. Accessed October 29, 2020. https://archive.org/details/libraryofpalesti03paleuoft/page/n31/mode/2up.

Ali, Abdullah Yusuf, trans. 1998. *The Qur'an: Text, Translation & Commentary*. Tahrike Tarsile Qur'an, Inc.

Allison Jr., Dale C. 2010. *Constructing Jesus: Memory, Imagination, and History*. Grand Rapids: Baker Publishing Group.

Antonacci, Mark. 2000. *Resurrection of the Shroud*. M. Evans and Company.

Aslan, Reza. 2013. *Zealot: The Life and Times of Jesus of Nazareth*. New Yok: Random House.

Aurelius, Marcus. 2006. *Meditations*. Edited by Martin Hammond. Translated by Martin Hammond. Penguin Publishing Group.

Ayerbe, Carolina. 2012. "Is it really the Tomb of Saint Peter under Saint Peter's Basilica?" *Cultural Travel Guide*. 13 February. Accessed May 22, 2020. http://www.culturaltravelguide.com/real-tomb-saint-peter-under-saint-peters-basilica#lightbox[auto_group1]/32/.

Barnes, Tatum W. 1994. *John the Baptist and Jesus: a report from the Jesus Seminar*. Polebridge Press.

Bauckham, Richard. 2008. *Jesus and the Eyewitnesses; The Gospels as Eyewitness Testimony*. Grand Rapids: Wm. B. Eerdman's Publishing.

—. 2007. *The Testimony of the Beloved Disciple*. Grand Rapids: Baker Academic.

Bennett, Janice. 2001. *Sacred Blood, Sacred Image*. San Francisco : Ignatius Press.

—. 2002. *St. Laurence and The Holy Grail*. Littleton.

n.d. *Bible Gateway*. http://www.biblegateway.com.

Biblica. 1984. *The Holy Bible, New International Version*. Grand Rapids: Zondervan House.

Biblical Archaeology Society Staff. 2018. "The Bethesda Pool, Site of One of Jesus' Miracles." *Biblical Archaeology Society*. 24 April. Accessed August 14, 2019. https://www.biblicalarchaeology.org/daily/biblical-sites-places/jerusalem/the-bethesda-pool-site-of-one-of-jesus-miracles/.

—. 2021. "The Siloam Pool: Where Jesus Healed the Blind Man." *Biblical Archaeology Society*. 5 January. Accessed January 30, 2021. https://www.biblicalarchaeology.org/daily/biblical-sites-places/biblical-archaeology-sites/the-siloam-pool-where-jesus-healed-the-blind-man/.

Black, John. 2013. "Jerusalem Finds Validating Gospel of John." *International Christian Embassy Jerusalem*. 9 March. Accessed August 1, 2019. https://us.icej.org/news/special-reports/jerusalem-finds-validating-gospel-john.

Bockmuehl, Markus, ed. 2003. *The Cambridge Companion to Jesus*. Cambridge: Cambridge University Press.

Booth, R. P. 2012. ""We have a law ...": The Trials of Jesus of Nazareth." *The Denning Law Journal* 6 (1). Accessed April 9 2020. https://doi.org/10.5750/dlj.v6i1.199.

Bordeaux Pilgrim. 1885. "Itinerarium Burdigalense, The library of the Palestine Pilgrims' Text Society." *Internet Archive*. Accessed August 24, 2019. https://archive.org/details/cu31924028534158/page/n13/mode/2up.

Borg, Marcus. 1994. *Meeting Jesus Again for the First Time: the Historical Jesus & the Heart of Contemporary Faith.* San Francisco: HarperSanFrancisco.

Borschel-Dan, Amanda. 2018. "2,000-year-old 'Pilate' ring just might have belonged to notorious Jesus judge." *The Times of Israel*, 29 November. Accessed October 17, 2019. https://www.timesofisrael.com/2000-year-old-ring-engraved-with-pilate-may-have-belonged-to-notorious-ruler/.

Britannica, The Editors of Encyclopaedia. 2020. "Papias." *Encyclopædia Britannica*. 20 August. https://www.britannica.com/biography/Papias.

Brown, Raymond E. 1997. *An Introduction to the New Testament.* New York: Doubleday.

Bruce, F.F. 1983. *The Gospel of John; Introduction, Exposition and Notes.* Grand Rapids: Eerdmans Publishing.

Brug, John F. 2012. "A Mixture of Myrrh and Aloes - an Exegetical Brief on John 19:39." *WP Wartburg Project*. 1 August. Accessed April 9, 2020. http://wartburgproject.org/mdocs-posts/a-mixture-of-myrrh-and-aloes-an-exegetical-brief-on-john-1939.

Bushman, Richard L. 2020. "Joseph Smith." *Encyclopedia Britannica*. 19 December. Accessed February 27, 2021. https://www.britannica.com/biography/Joseph-Smith-American-religious-leader-1805-1844.

Capper, Brian J. 2002. "The Church as the New Covenant of Effective Economics: The Social Origins of Mutually Supportive Christian Community." *International Journal for the Study of the Christian Church* (2): 83-102.

Capper, Brian J. 2003. "The New Covenant Network in Southern Palestine at the Arrest of Jesus." Edited by James Davila. *The Dead Sea Scrolls as Background to Postbiblical Judaism and Early Christianity* (Brill) 90-116. Accessed April 4, 2020. https://brill.com/search?f_0=author&q_0=BRIAN+J.+CAPPER.

Carrier, Robert. 2014. *On the Historicity of Jesus: Why We Might Have Reason for Doubt. Kindle.* Sheffield Pheonix Press Ltd.

Carter, Charls E. n.d. In *The Wiley Blackwell Companion to Ancient Israel*, edited by Susan Nidtich. John Wiley & Sons.

Carter, Warren. 2006. *The Roman Empire and the New Testament; An Essential Guide.* Nashville: Abingdon Press.

Casey, Maurice. 2010. *Jesus of Nazareth : An Independent Historian's Account of his Life and Teaching.* London: T&T Clark.

Clement of Alexandria . n.d. "Letter of Clement of Alexandria on Secret Mark." *Early Christian Writings*. Edited by Peter Kirby. Accessed September 9, 2019. http://www.earlychristianwritings.com/text/secretmark.html.

Clement of Alexandria. n.d. "Fragments (Clement of Alexandria)." *New Advent*. Edited by Kevin Knight. Accessed March 4, 2020. http://www.newadvent.org/fathers/0211.htm.

—. n.d. "Who is the Rich Man That Shall Be Saved?" *New Advent*. Edited by Kevin Knight. Accessed March 28, 2020. www.newadvent.org/fathers/0207.htm.

Clement of Rome. 1885. "Clement of Rome, First Epistle." *Early Christian Writings*. Edited by Peter Kirby. http://www.earlychristianwritings.com/text/1clement-hoole.html.

Coakly, J. F. 1988. "The Anointing at Bethany and the Priority of John." *Journal of Biblical Literature* 107 (2): 241-256. Accessed January 20, 2020. https://www.jstor.org/stable/3267698.

Cornwall, Chris, Aaron Horiuchi, and Chris Lehman. n.d. *Sunrise/Sunset Calculator.* Accessed December 2, 2019. https://www.esrl.noaa.gov/gmd/grad/solcalc/sunrise.html.

Cragg, Albert Kenneth. 2020. "Hadith." *Encyclopedia Britannica.* 5 August. Accessed March 13, 2021. https://www.britannica.com/topic/Hadith.

Crossan, John Dominic. n.d. *The Historical Jesus; The Life of a Mediterranean Jewish Peasant.* 1991: HarperCollins e-books.

Crossley, James G. 2004. *The Date of Mark's Gospel.* London: T & T Clark International.

Cyril of Jerusalem. n.d. "Catechetical Lectures." *New Advent.* Edited by Kevin Knight. Accessed November 8, 2019. http://www.newadvent.org/fathers/3101.htm.

Dalby, Andrew. 2003. *Food in the Ancient World from A to Z.* Psychology Press.

Davidson, Paul. 2015. "Has the Q Source Been Under Our Noses All Along? Luke, Matthew, and the Didache." *Is That in the Bible?* 30 June. Accessed July 14, 2020. https://isthatinthebible.wordpress.com/2015/06/30/has-the-q-source-been-under-our-noses-all-along-luke-matthew-and-the-didache/.

Davis, Dr. Charles Patrick. 2020. "What Is Epilepsy? Symptoms, Causes, and Treatments." *OnHealth.* 22 10. https://www.onhealth.com/content/1/epilepsy_symptoms.

de Santillana, Giorgio. 1955. *The Crime of Galileo.* University of Chicago Press.

DeLashmutt, Gary. n.d. "Sejanus and the Chronology of Christ's Death." *Xenos Christian Fellowship.* Accessed June 9, 2020. https://www.xenos.org/essays/sejanus-and-chronology-christs-death.

Dickinson, Ian. n.d. "The Shroud and the Cubit Measure." *The British Society for the Turin Shroud* 24 (6). Accessed October 21, 2020. https://www.shroud.com/pdfs/n24part6.pdf.

Diogenes the Cynic. 2005. "Shredding the Gospels: Contradictions, Errors, Mistakes, Fictions." *Biblical Catholic.* 2 March. Accessed December 24, 2019. http://www.biblicalcatholic.com/apologetics/ShreddingTheGospels.htm.

Dospel, Marek. 2020. "Jesus Holding a Magic Wand?" *Biblical Archaeology Society.* 10 September. Accessed December 14, 2020. https://www.biblicalarchaeology.org/daily/people-cultures-in-the-bible/jesus-historical-jesus/jesus-holding-a-magic-wand.

Edwards, Mark J. 2018. "Origen." *Stanford Encyclopedia of Philosophy.* 18 April. Accessed April 9, 2020. https://plato.stanford.edu/entries/origen/.

Ehrman, Bart D. n.d. "After the New Testament: The Writings of the Apostolic Fathers." *Course 6537.* The Great Courses.

—. 2009. *Jesus Interrupted: Revealing the Hidden Contradictions in the Bible .* NY: Harper Collins.

—. n.d. "New Testament." *Course No. 656.* The Great Courses.

—. n.d. "The Greatest Controversies of Early Christian History." *Course No. 6410.* The Great Courses.

Ehrman, Bart J. 2012. *The New Testament; A historical introduction to the early Christian writings.* Oxford University Press.

EM. 2010. *Fin des Voies Rapides.* 16 June. Accessed July 9 2020. http://ifpeakoilwerenoobject.blogspot.com/2010/06/crucifixion-bodily-support-part-1.html.

Erskine, Andrew, ed. 2009. *A Companion to Ancient History.* Chichester: Wiley-Blackwell.

Estrin, Daniel. 2017. "Historic restoration of Jesus's burial shrine in Jerusalem completed." *The Times of Israel.* 20 March. Accessed September 27, 2020. https://www.timesofisrael.com/historic-restoration-of-jesuss-burial-shrine-in-jerusalem-completed/.

Eusebius. n.d. "Church History." *New Advent.* Edited by Kevin Knight. Accessed October 4, 2020. https://www.newadvent.org/fathers/2501.htm.

—. n.d. "Life Of Constantine." *New Advent.* Edited by Kevin Knight. Accessed July 30, 2020. https://www.newadvent.org/fathers/2502.htm.

Feldman, Louis. 2018. "The Mystery of the Testimonium Flavianum; A History from 93 CE to the Present." *The Flavius Josephus Home Page.* Edited by G.J. Goldberg. Accessed September 10, 2020. http://www.josephus.org/testhist.htm.

Finkelstein, Israel, and Neil Asher Silberman. 2002. *The Bible Unearthed; Archaeology's New Version of Ancient Israel and the Origin of the Sacred Texts.* NY: Touchestone.

Fraser, Paul. 2016. "Jewish War year 5 shekel expected to beat $125,000." *Paul Fraser Collectibles.* 21 January. Accessed November 19, 2020. https://www.paulfrasercollectibles.com/blogs/coins-banknotes/jewish-war-year-5-shekel-expected-to-beat-125-000.

Fredericksen, Linwood. 2020. "Saint Clement of Alexandria." *Encyclopædia Britannica.* 3 January. Accessed August 1, 2020. https://www.britannica.com/biography/Saint-Clement-of-Alexandria.

Fried, Bruce W. 2000. *Demography.* Vol. XI, in *The Cambridge Ancient History*, edited by Peter Garnsey, and Dominic Rathbone Alan K. Bowman. Cambridge: Cambridge University Press.

Friedman, Matti. 2012. "In a stone box, the only trace of crucifixion." *The Times of Israel*, 26 March. Accessed July 29, 2020. https://www.timesofisrael.com/in-a-stone-box-a-rare-trace-of-crucifixion/.

Friedman, Richard Elliot. 1997. *Who Wrote The Bible?* NY: HarperOne.

Fuller, Reginald. 1972. *The Formation of the Ressurection Narratives.* London.

Funk, Robert W. 1999. *The Gospel of Jesus according to the Jesus Seminar.* Santa Rosa: Polebridge Press.

Gafni, Isaiah M. n.d. "Beginnings of Judaism." *Course No. 6457.* The Great Courses.

Garrow, Alan. n.d. "An Extant Instance of 'Q'." Accessed March 18, 2020. https://www.alangarrow.com/extantq.html.

—. n.d. "The Apostolic Decree." *Alan Garrow.* Accessed March 2, 2019. https://www.alangarrow.com/texts.html.

—. n.d. "The Original Didache/Apostolic Decree." *Alan Garrow.* Accessed March 21, 2019. https://www.alangarrow.com/original.html.

generationword.com, Editors of, and The Editors of generationword.com. 2021. "Jerusalem 101." *Generation Word.* 14 March. http://www.generationword.com/jerusalem101/1-biblical-jerusalem.html#Jerusalem325AD.

Ghose, Tia. 2017. "The most famous solar eclipses in history, number 6." *CBS News.* 14 February. Accessed April 28, 2019. https://www.cbsnews.com/pictures/solar-eclipses-in-history/6/.

Gibson, Shimon. 2004. *The Cave of John the Baptist.* London: Arrow Books Limited.

Grivich, Matthew. 2011. "The Gospel According to Matthew and Q." *Christianity: A Systematic Defense.* 28 August. Accessed January 11, 2020. http://www.systematicchristianity.org/TheGospelAccordingtoMatthewandQ.htm.

Guarducci, Margherita. 1960. "The Tomb of St. Peter." *St. Peters Basilica.Info.* Hawthorn Books. Accessed October 28, 2019. http://stpetersbasilica.info/Necropolis/MG/TheTombofStPeter-8.htm.

—. 1960. *The Tomb of St. Peter: The New Discoveries in the Sacred Grottoes of the Vatican.* Translated by Joseph McLellan. New York: Hawthorn Books.

Guscin, Mark. 2004. "The Sermon of Gregory Referendarius." *The Shroud of Turin Website.* Accessed December 3, 2019. https://www.shroud.com/pdfs/guscin3.pdf.

Hall, Stuart G. 1979. *Melito of Sardis: On Pascha and Fragments.* Oxford: Clarendon. https://scholar.google.com/scholar_lookup?title=Melito+of+Sardis%3A+On+Pascha+and+Fragments&author=Hall+Stuart+G.&publication+year=1979.

Heller, J. H. 1983. *Report on the Shroud of Turin.* Houghton Mifflin Company.

Helms, Randel. 1988. *Gospel Fictions.* Amherst, NY: Prometheus Books.

Heroman, Bill. 2009. "A Common Error - Dating Herod's Temple." *NT/History Blog.* 29 October. Accessed October 4, 2019. http://www.billheroman.com/2009/10/common-error-dating-herods-temple.html?m=1.

History.com Editors. 2019. "The Reformation." *History.* 11 April. Accessed January 9, 2021. https://www.history.com/topics/reformation/reformation.

Hitchens, Christopher. 2009. *God Is Not Great: How Religion Poisons Everything.* Kindle. Enblem.

Holloway, R. Ross. 2004. *Constantine & Rome.* Yale University Press.

Holzapfel, Richard Neitzel, Jeffrey R Chadwick, Kent P Jackson, Frank F Judd, and Thomas A Wayment. 2008. "Jesus and the Ossuaries: First Century Jewish Burial Practices and the Lost Tomb of Jesus." *BYU Religious Studies Center.* Accessed January 30, 2020. https://rsc-legacy.byu.edu/archived/behold-lamb-god/jesus-and-ossuaries-first-century-jewish-burial-practices-and-lost-tomb.

Honore, A. M. 1968. "A statistical study of the synoptic problem." *Novum Testamentum* 10 (2/3): 95-147. Accessed April 26, 2019. www.jstor.org/stable/1560364.

Humphreys, Colin J. 1991. "The Star of Bethlehem, A Comet in 5 BC and the Date of Christ's Birth." *Quarterly Journal of the Royal Astronomical Society* 32 (4): 389-407. Accessed October 9, 2019. http://adsabs.harvard.edu/full/1991QJRAS..32..389H.

Hyland, Sean. n.d. "St. Irenaeus." *New Advent.* Edited by Kevin Knight. Accessed September 14, 2019. https://www.newadvent.org/cathen/08130b.htm.

Ilan, Tal. 2002. *Lexicon of Jewish Names in Late Antiquity: Part 1 Palestine 330BCE - 200CE.* Turbingen: Mohr Siebeck GmbH & Co.

Irenaeus. n.d. "Against Heresies." *New Advent.* Edited by Kevin Knight. Accessed 2019 November 29. https://www.newadvent.org/fathers/0103.htm.

Jefferson, Thomas. 1820. *From Thomas Jefferson to William Short, 13 April 1820.* Vol. Papers of Thomas Jefferson. National Achives. Accessed Jun 11, 2020. https://founders.archives.gov/documents/Jefferson/98-01-02-1218.

Johnson, Luke Timothy. n.d. "Early Christianity: The Experience of the Divine." *Course No. 647.* The Great Courses.

—. n.d. "Jesus and the Gospels." *Course No. 6240.* The Great Courses.

Josephus, Flavius. 2017. "The Antiquities of the Jews." *Project Gutenberg.* Edited by and David Widger David Reed. 9 August. Accessed October 3, 2019. https://www.gutenberg.org/files/2848/2848-h/2848-h.htm#link152H_4_0001.

—. n.d. "The Jewish War." *https://penelope.uchicago.edu/.* Accessed April 14, 2020. doi:https://penelope.uchicago.edu/josephus/war-5.html.

Just, Felix S. J. 2018. "Literary Features of the Fourth Gospel." *The Johannine Litearsture Web.* 5 June. Accessed August 17, 2019. https://catholic-resources.org/John/Themes-LiteraryFeatures.htm.

Keener, Craig S. 2009. *The Historical Jesus of the Gospels.* Wm. B. Eerdmans Publishing.

Keith, Chris, and Anthony Le Donne, . 2012. *Jesus, Criteria, and the Demise of Authenticity.* London: T&T Clark International.

Keller, Timothy. 2008. *The Reason for God.* Dutton.

Kirby, Peter. 2021. *Early Christian Writings.* Edited by Peter Kirby. 8 April. Accessed April 8, 2021. http://www.earlychristian-writings.com/.

—. n.d. "Historical Jesus Theories." *Early Christian Writings.* Accessed January 3, 2021. http://www.earlychristianwritings.com/theories.html.

—. n.d. "Josephus and Jesus: The Testimonium Flavianum Question." *Early Christian Writings.* Accessed January 9, 2020. http://www.earlychristianwritings.com/testimonium.html.

—. 2013. "Putting Papias in Order." *Peter Kirby.* 5 November. Accessed February 14, 2021. http://peterkirby.com/putting-papias-in-order.html.

Kirchhevel, Gordon D. 1999. "The "Son of Man" Passages in Mark." *Bulletin for Biblical Research* 9: 181-187. Accessed September 27, 2019.

Kisilevitz, Shua. 2016. "Terracotta Figurines from the Iron IIA Temple at Moza, Judah." *Les Carnets de l'ACoSt; Association for Coroplastic Studies* 15. Accessed August 8, 2020. https://journals.openedition.org/acost/980.

Klausner, Joseph. 2020. *Jesus of Nazareth. His Life, Times, and Teaching.* Translated by Herbert Danby. Eugene, OR: Wipf and Stock Publishers.

Kloppenborg, John S. 2008. *Q, the Earliest Gospel; An Introduction to the Original Stories and Sayings of Jesus.* Westminster John Know Press.

Knight, Kevin, ed. n.d. "Apostolic Constitutions (Book VII)." *New Advent.* Accessed April 25, 2020. www.newadvent.org/fathers/07157.htm.

Kostenberger, Andreas J., L. Scott Kellum, and Charles L. Quarles. 2009. *The Cradle, the Cross, and the Crown: An Introduction to the New Testament.* Nashville: B&H Academic.

Krosney, Hebert. 2006. *The Lost Gospel; The Quest for the Gospel of Judas Iscariot.* Krosney Productions Ltd.

Levine, Amy-Jill. n.d. "Great Figures of the New Testament." *Course No. 6206.* The Great Courses.

Library, The Editors of the World Library. n.d. "Codex Amiatinus." *World Digital Library*. Accessed October 20, 2020. https://www.wdl.org/en/item/20150/.

Lizorkin-Eyzenberg, Dr. Eli. 2014. "The Pool Of Bethesda As A Healing Center Of Asclepius." *Isreal Institute of Biblical Studies*. 1 December. Accessed August 7, 2019. https://blog.israelbiblicalstudies.com/jewish-studies/bethesda-pool-jerusalem-shrine-asclepius/.

Longenecker, Dwight. 2012. "The Early Date of Mark's Gospel." *Patheos*. 21 July. Accessed August 11, 2019. https://www.patheos.com/blogs/standingonmyhead/the-early-date-of-marks-gospel.

Lucian of Samosata. 2001. "Passing of Peregrinus." *The Tertullian Project*. Edited by Roger Pearse. 25 August. Accessed September 5, 2019. http://www.tertullian.org/rpearse/lucian/peregrinus.htm.

Lunn, Nicholas P. 2014. *The Original Ending of Mark: A new case for the Authenticity of Mark 16:9-20*. Eugene: Pickwick Publications.

Luther, Martin. 1960. *Luther's Works: Word and Sacrament 1*. Edited by E. Theodore Bachmann. Translated by Charles M. Jacobs. Vol. 35. Fortress Press.

Mara. n.d. "A Letter of Mara, Son of Serapion." *New Advent*. Edited by Kevin Knight. Accessed March 3, 2019. https://www.newadvent.org/fathers/0863.htm.

Martyr, Justin. n.d. "Dialogue With Trypho (Justin Martyr)." *New Advent*. Edited by Kevin Knight. Accessed November 12, 2019. http://www.newadvent.org/fathers/0128.htm.

Matson, Mark A. 200. "Luke's Rewritting of the Sermon on the Mount." *Society of Biblical Literature* (Miligan College) (39): 623-656. Accessed April 9, 2020. https://www.academia.edu/345010/Lukes_Rewriting_of_The_Sermon_on_The_Mount.

Mattis, Richard L. 1995. "First Jewish-Roman War." *HistoryNet*. December. Accessed March 22, 2020. https://www.historynet.com/first-jewish-roman-war.htm.

McCallum, Dennis. n.d. "A Chronological Study of Paul's Ministry." *Xenos*. Accessed May 26, 2020. https://www.xenos.org/essays/chronological-study-pauls-ministry.

McDonald, Alexander Hugh. 2021. "Tacitus, Roman historian." *Encyclopedia Britannica*. 10 February. Accessed March 3, 2021. https://www.britannica.com/biography/Tacitus-Roman-historian.

Meacham, William, James E Alcock, Robert Bucklin, K O L Burridge, John R Cole, Richard J Dent, P John Jackson, et al. 1983. "The Authentication of the Turin Shroud, An Issue in Archeological Epistemology." *Current Anthropology* 24 (3). Accessed August 1, 2019. https://www.journals.uchicago.edu/doi/abs/10.1086/202996#.

Meier, John P. 1991. *A Marginal Jew: Rethinking the Historical Jesus*. Vol. 1. Yale University Press.

Mellor, Robert. 1999. *The Roman Historians*. Routledge.

Mesarites, Nicholas. n.d. "Excerpts from The Palace Revolution of John Comnenus." *Shroud Spectrum International* (17 part 4). Accessed February 11, 2020. https://www.shroud.com/pdfs/ssi17part4.pdf.

Meyer, Madeleine Scopello and Marvin. 2009. *The Wisdom of Jesus Christ. The Nag Hammadi Sciptures: The Revised and Updated Translation of Sacred Gnostic Texts Complete in One Volume*. Harper One.

Meyer, Marvin. 2004. *The Gospel of Thomas; The Hidden Sayings of Jesus.* HarperCollins e-books.

—. n.d. *The Nag Hammadi Scriptures.* 2009: HarperCollins e-books.

Meyers, Robin R. 2010. *Saving Jesus from the Church.* NY: HarperOne.

Milavec, Aaron. 2003. *The Didache: Text, Translation, Analysis and Commentary.* Liturgical Press.

Miller, Arthur J. Dewey & Robert J. 2012. *The Complete Gospel Parallels.* Salem: Polebridge.

Miller, Robert J. 1994. *The Complete Gospels.* Sonoma: Polebridge.

Mitchell, Margaret M, and Francis M Young, . 2008. *The Cambridge History of Christianity; Origins to Constantine.* Cambridge: Cambridge University Press.

Moloney, Francis J. 2002. *The Gospel of Mark; A Commentary.* Grand Rapids: Baker Academic.

Morrison, Michael. n.d. "Old Testament Laws:Harvest Seasons of Ancient Israel." *Grace Communion International.* Accessed August 22, 2020. https://archive.gci.org/articles/harvest-seasons-of-ancient-israel/.

Mykytiuk, Lawrence. 2015. "Did Jesus Exist? Searching for Evidence Beyond the Bible." *Biblical Archaeology Review* 41 (1). Accessed February 9, 2020. https://www.baslibrary.org/biblical-archaeology-review/41/1/8.

—. n.d. "Necropolis (Scavi) Graffiti Wall G - The bones of St Peter." *St. Peters Basilica.Info.* Accessed January 9, 2019. http://stpetersbasilica.info/Necropolis/Wall%20G.htm.

Ngo, Robin. 2013. "Has Dalmanutha from the Bible Been Found?" *Biblical Archaeology Society.* 20 September. Accessed August 14, 2020. https://www.biblicalarchaeology.org/daily/biblical-sites-places/biblical-archaeology-sites/has-dalmanutha-from-the-bible-been-found/.

Ngo, Robin, Lawrence Mykytiuk, Phillip J King, Ken Dark, Birger A Pearson, and Jonathan Klawans. 2017. "Who Was Jesus? Exploring the History of Jesus' Life." *Bilical Archaeology Society.* Edited by Robin Ngo and Megan Sauter. Accessed February 24, 2020. https://www.biblicalarchaeology.org/free-ebooks/who-was-jesus-exploring-the-history-of-jesus-life/.

Noble, Thomas F. X. n.d. "Popes and the Papacy: A History." *Course No. 6672.* The Great Courses.

O'Connor, J.B. 1910. "St. Ignatius of Antioch." *New Advent.* The Catholic Encyclopedia. Accessed April 30, 2020. http://www.newadvent.org/cathen/07644a.htm.

O'Hare, Patrick. 1987. *The Facts About Luther.* TAN Books and Publishers.

Origen. n.d. "Commentary on the Gospel of Matthew (Book I)." *New Advent.* Edited by Kevin Knight. Accessed June 22, 2020. http://www.newadvent.org/fathers/101601.htm.

—. n.d. "Contra Celsum, Book I." *New Advent.* Edited by Kevin Knight. Accessed May 7, 2020. https://www.newadvent.org/fathers/04161.htm.

Palestine Exploration Fund. 1872. *Palestine Exploration Fund* (Quarterly Statement, New Series No. 1).

Parsons, John J. n.d. "Codex Sinaticus; Nomina Sacra and the Name." *hebrew4christians.com.* Accessed February 9, 2021. https://www.hebrew4christians.com/Names_of_G-d/Sinaticus/sinaticus.html.

Pellegrino, Simcha Jacobovici and Charles. 2007. "The Jesus Family Tomb: The Discovery, the Investigation, and the Evidence that Could Change History." *BYU Studies Review.* Edited by Kent P. Jackson. 1 April. Accessed March 30, 2020. https://web.archive.org/web/20070914025939/http://byustudies.byu.edu/Reviews/Pages/reviewdetail.aspx?reviewID=133.

Peppard, Michael. 2016. *The World's Oldest Church: Bible, Art, and Ritual at Dura-Europos, Syria.* New Haven: Yale University Press. Accessed May 13, 2020. https://www.jstor.org/stable/j.ctt1kft8j0.

Pfister, Samuel DeWitt. 2019. "Where Is Biblical Bethsaida?" *Biblical Archaeology Society.* 16 June. Accessed January 18, 2020. https://www.biblicalarchaeology.org/daily/biblical-sites-places/biblical-archaeology-sites/where-is-biblical-bethsaida/.

Philo of Alexanderia. n.d. "The Works of Philo: On The Embassy to Gaius." *Early Christian Writings.* Edited by Charles Duke Yonge. Accessed November 2, 2019. http://www.earlychristianwritings.com/yonge/index.html.

Pliny. 2016. "Letters of Pliny." *Project Gutenberg.* David Reed and David Widger. 13 May. Accessed September 29, 2019. https://www.gutenberg.org/files/2811/2811-h/2811-h.htm.

Polycrates of Ephesus. n.d. "Polycarp." *Early Christian Writings.* Edited by Peter Kirby. Accessed October 2, 2019. http://www.earlychristianwritings.com/text/polycrates.html.

Poole, Gary William. 2020. "Flavius Josephus." *Encyclopædia Britannica.* 19 June. Accessed October 8, 2020. https://www.britannica.com/biography/Flavius-Josephus.

Pope, Charles. 2017. "What Sort of Clothing Did People in Jesus' Time Wear?" *Community in Mission blog of the Archdiocese of Washington.* 17 March. Accessed February 1, 2020. http://blog.adw.org/2017/03/sort-clothing-people-jesus-time-wear/.

Powell, Mark Allan. 1998. *Fortress Intro To The Gospels.* Fortress Press.

Price, Christopher. 2004. "Did Josephus Refer to Jesus? A Thorough Review of the Testimonium Flavianum." *Bede's Library.* Accessed December 7, 2019. http://www.bede.org.uk/Josephus.htm.

Radwin, Danny Sadinoff and Michael J. n.d. *Jewish Holidays.* Accessed May 19, 2019. https://www.hebcal.com/.

Radwin, Danny Sadinoff and Michael J. n.d. *Jewish Calendar.* Accessed May 18, 2019. https://www.hebcal.com/hebcal.

Reich, Ronny. 1992. "Caiaphas Name Inscribed on Bone Boxes." *Biblical Archaeology Review*, 38-42, 44. Accessed March 25, 2020. https://www.baslibrary.org/biblical-archaeology-review/18/5/2.

Robinson, John A. T. 2000. *Redating the New Testament.* Wipf and Stock Publishers.

Rogers, Kevin. 2013. "Luke's Eye-witness Accounts in Acts." *Investigator* (153). http://ed5015.tripod.com/BActsWeSections153.html.

Sanders, E.P. 2021. "Jewish Palestine at the time of Jesus." *Encyclopedia Britannica.* 24 March. Accessed April 9, 2021. https://www.britannica.com/biography/Jesus/Jewish-Palestine-at-the-time-of-Jesus.

—. 2020. "St. Paul the Apostle." *Encyclopædia Britannica.* 30 April. Accessed January 21, 2021. https://www.britannica.com/biography/Saint-Paul-the-Apostle.

—. n.d. *The Historical Figure of Jesus.* Vol. New Edition. 1995: Penguin.

Epstein, I., ed. n.d. "Sanhedrin. Translated into English with Notes, Glossary and Indices." *Halakhah.* Accessed Mar 11, 2021. http://www.halakhah.com/sanhedrin/index.html.

Sardis, Melito of. 2001. "On Pascha; With the Fragments of Melito and Other Material Related to the Quartodecimans." *St. Anianus Coptic Orthodox Church.* Edited by Alistair Stewart-Sykes. St Vladimir's Seminary Press. http://sachurch.org/wp-content/uploads/2017/04/On-Pascha-Melito-of-Sardis.pdf.

Sauter, Megan. 2019. "How Was Jesus' Tomb Sealed?" *Biblical Archaeology.* 03 April. Accessed September 15, 2019. https://www.biblicalarchaeology.org/daily/archaeology-today/biblical-archaeology-topics/how-was-jesus-tomb-sealed/.

Schweitzer, Albert. 1998. *The Mysticism of Paul the Apostle.* Translated by William Montgomery. Baltimore, Maryland: Johns Hopkins University Press.

—. 1906. *The Quest of the Historical Jesus.* 2015. Translated by W. Montgomery. New York: Philosophical Library/Open Road Integrated Media, Inc.

Seminar, Robert W. Funk and The Jesus. 1998. *The Acts of Jesus.* NY: Harper Collins.

Serr, Marcel, and Dieter Vieweger. 2016. "Archaeological Views: Golgotha: Is the Holy Sepulchre Church Authentic?" *Biblical Archaeology Review* 42:3 (May/June). Accessed November 3, 2019. https://www.baslibrary.org/biblical-archaeology-review/42/3/11.

Shanks, Hershel. 2012. ""Brother of Jesus" Inscription Is Authentic!" *Biblical Archaeology Society.* July/August. Accessed April 3, 2021. https://www.baslibrary.org/biblical-archaeology-review/38/4/2.

—. 2021. "Ancient Jerusalem: The Village, the Town, the City." *Biblical Archaeology Society.* 30 April. Accessed May 3, 2021. https://www.biblicalarchaeology.org/daily/biblical-sites-places/jerusalem/ancient-jerusalem/.

Sheldon, Natasha. 2018. "Roman Solstice Celebrations." *History and Archaeology Online.* 21 December. Accessed September 7, 2019. https://historyandarchaeologyonline.com/roman-solstice-celebrations/.

Silberman, Lou Hackett, Haim Zalman Dimitrovsky, and The Editors of Encyclopedia Britannica. 2020. "Talmud and Midrash." *Encyclopedia Britannica.* 28 April. Accessed March 13, 2021. https://www.britannica.com/topic/Talmud.

Smith, Doug. 2000. "Buying Power of Ancient Coins." *Internet Archive Way Back Machine.* Accessed May 30, 2019. https://web.archive.org/web/20130210071801/http://dougsmith.ancients.info/worth.html.

Smith, Morton. 1973. *Clement of Alexandria and a Secret Gospel of Mark.* Cambridge: Harvard University Press. http://homes.chass.utoronto.ca/~browns/LGM.html.

Spriggs, Julian. n.d. "Unique passages found in the Synoptic Gospels." *Julian Spriggs.* Accessed May 19, 2019. http://www.julianspriggs.co.uk/Pages/UniquePassages.

Staniforth, Maxwell, trans. 1987. *Early Christian Writings: The Apostolic Fathers.* Hammondsworth: Penguin Books.

Stanton, Graham. 1997. *Gospel Truth? Today's Quest for Jesus of Nazareth.* London: Fount Paperbacks.

Strange, James F, and Hershel Shanks. 1983. "Synagogue Where Jesus Preached Found at Capernaum." *Bas Library.* November/December. Accessed November 27, 2019. https://www.baslibrary.org/biblical-archaeology-review/9/6/1.

Strange, James F., and Hershel Shanks. 1982. "Has the House Where Jesus Stayed in Capernaum Been Found?" *BAS Library.* November/December. Accessed December 18, 2019. https://www.baslibrary.org/biblical-archaeology-review/8/6/4.

Suetonius. 2007. *The Twelve Caesers.* Revised Edition. Edited by James Rives. Translated by Robert Graves. Penguin.

Tabor, James D. 2013. "Christianity Before Paul." *Huffpost.* 29 January. Accessed April 4, 2019. https://www.huffpost.com/entry/christianity-before-paul_b_2200409.

Tabor, James D. 2006. *The Jesus Dynasty: A New Historical Investigation of Jesus, His Royal Family, and the Birth of Christianity.* New York: Simon & Schuster.

Tacitus, Cornelius. 2013. *Annals.* Edited by Cynthia Damon. Penguin.

Taylor, Joan E. 2009. "Golgotha: A Reconsideration of the Evidence for the Sites of Jesus' Crucifixion and Burial." *Cambridge University Press.* 5 February. Accessed October 20, 2019. https://www.cambridge.org/core/journals/new-testament-studies/article/abs/golgotha-a-reconsideration-of-the-evidence-for-the-sites-of-jesus-crucifixion-and-burial/EBF49AC4C712692B1834307624C143F9.

Taylor, Joan. 2018. "What did Jesus wear?" *The Conversation.* 8 February. Accessed May 5, 2020. http://theconversation.com/what-did-jesus-wear-90783.

Tertullian. n.d. "The Prescription Against Heretics." *New Advent.* Edited by Kevin Knight. Accessed February 7, 2020. https://www.newadvent.org/fathers/0311.htm.

The Editorial Board of the International Q Project. 2001. "The Sayings Gospel Q in English Translation." *homes.chass.utoronto.ca.* Edited by John Kloppenborg. Accessed September 14, 2019. http://homes.chass.utoronto.ca/~kloppen/iqpqet.htm.

The Editors of Bible Hub. n.d. "Interlinear Bible." *Bible Hub.* Accessed October 9, 2020. https://biblehub.com/interlinear.

—. n.d. "Strong's Concordance." *Bible Hub.* Accessed October 26, 2020. https://biblehub.com/greek/3608.htm.

—. 2011. "Thayer's Greek Lexicon, Electronic Database by Biblesoft Inc." *Biblehub.* Accessed January 8, 2021. https://biblehub.com/greek/3027.htm.

The Editors of Cultural Travel Guide. 2012. "The Evolution of St Peter's Tomb under Saint Peter's Basilica." CulturalTravelGuide, 11 February. Accessed May 9, 2019. https://www.youtube.com/watch?v=5oJDbnDh7iA.

The Editors of Encyclopaedia Britannica. 2018. "Aramaic language." *Encyclopaedia Britannica.* 26 September. Accessed April 20, 2020. https://www.britannica.com/topic/Aramaic-language.

—. 2017. "Cargo cult." *Encyclopedia Britannica.* 19 Apr. Accessed Jan 13, 2021. https://www.britannica.com/topic/cargo-cult.

—. 2018. "Crucifixion." *Britannica.* Accessed December 3, 2020. https://www.britannica.com/topic/crucifixion-capital punishment.

—. 2019. "Eusebius of Caesarea." *Encyclopædia Britannica.* 30 December. Accessed November 19, 2020. https://www.britannica.com/biography/Eusebius-of-Caesarea.

—. 2020. "First Jewish Revolt." *Encyclopædia Britannica.* 4 February. Accessed November 21, 2020. https://www.britannica.com/event/First-Jewish-Revolt.

—. 2020. "Hebrew Bible." *Encyclopædia Britannica.* 20 May. Accessed October 28, 2020. https://www.britannica.com/topic/Hebrew-Bible.

—. 2020. "Messiah." *Encyclopædia Britannica.* 26 February. Accessed December 3, 2020. https://www.britannica.com/topic/messiah-religion.

—. 2020. "Nicene Creed." *Encyclopaedia Britannica*. 15 May. Accessed November 19, 2020. https://www.britannica.com/topic/Nicene-Creed.

—. 2020. "Papias." *Encyclopædia Britannica*. 20 August. Accessed December 4, 2020. https://www.britannica.com/biography/Papias.

—. 2020. "Philo Judaeus." *Encyclopedia Britannica*. 20 August. Accessed January 11, 2021. https://www.britannica.com/biography/Philo-Judaeus.

—. 2013. "Saint Clement I." *Encyclopædia Britannica*. 20 May. Accessed December 14, 2020. https://www.britannica.com/biography/Saint-Clement-I.

—. 2020. "Saint Polycarp." *Encyclopædia Britannica*. 19 May. Accessed November 20, 2020. https://www.britannica.com/biography/Saint-Polycarp.

—. 2020. "Saint Sarapion." *Encyclopædia Britannica*. 20 May. Accessed November 8, 2020. https://www.britannica.com/biography/Saint-Sarapion.

—. 2020. "Sibylline Oracles." *Encyclopedia Britannica*. 08 May. Accessed August 31, 2020. https://www.britannica.com/topic/Sibylline-Oracles.

—. n.d. "The prophecies of Deutero-Isaiah." *Encyclopedia Britannica*. Accessed December 2, 2020. https://www.britannica.com/topic/biblical-literature/The-prophecies-of-Deutero-Isaiah.

The Editors of halakhah.com. n.d. "Baylonian Talmud: Tractate Sanhedrin Folio 43a." *Halakhah*. Accessed December 1, 2019. http://www.halakhah.com/sanhedrin/sanhedrin_43.html.

The Editors of Loyola Press. n.d. "Paul's Journeys." *Loyola Press*. Accessed June 22, 2020. https://www.loyolapress.com/our-catholic-faith/scripture-and-tradition/jesus-and-the-new-testament/saint-paul-and-the-epistles/pauls-journeys.

The Editors of Sizes.com. n.d. *litra [Greek, λίτρα]*. Accessed November 28, 2020. https://www.sizes.com/units/litra.htm.

The Editors of studyjesus.com. n.d. "Johannine Studies: XIV. Archeology and the Origins of the Fourth Gospel: Gabbatha." *Study Jesus*. Accessed March 21, 2020. https://studyjesus.com/Religion_Library/Johannine_Studies/14_Archeology.htm.

The Editors of the Church of God Study Forum. 2019. *Calendar*. 2 October. Accessed January 14, 2021. http://www.cgsf.org/dbeattie/calendar/.

The Editors of the codexsinaiticus.org. n.d. "Codex Sinaiticus." *codexsinaiticus.org*. Accessed August 21, 2020. https://codexsinaiticus.org/en/.

The Editors of the New World Encyclopedia. 2017. "Gamaliel." *New World Encyclopedia*. 19 May. Accessed March 3, 2021. doi:https://www.newworldencyclopedia.org/entry/gamaliel.

—. 2016. "James the Just." *New World Encyclopedia*. 7 June. Accessed August 19, 2020. https://www.newworldencyclopedia.org/entry/James_the_Just.

—. 2018. "Justin Martyr." *New World Encyclopedia*. 15 June. Accessed March 3, 2021. https://www.newworldencyclopedia.org/entry/Justin_Martyr.

—. 2018. "Mesha Stele." *New World Encyclopedia.* 18 September. Accessed September 24, 2020. https://www.newworldencyclopedia.org/entry/Mesha_Stele.

The Editors of timeanddate.com. n.d. "https://www.timeanddate.com/sun/israel/jerusalem." *timeanddate.com.* Accessed October 11, 2019. https://www.timeanddate.com/sun/israel/jerusalem.

The Editors of TorahCalendar.com. n.d. "Determining the Hebrew Hour." *TorahCalendar.com.* Accessed March 9, 2020. https://torahcalendar.com/HOUR.asp.

The Jesus Seminar. 1994. *The Complete Gospels: Annotated Scholar's Version.* NY: HarperCollins.

The Staff of the AGES Digital Library. 1996. "New International Version Old Testament." *AGES Digital Library.* Accessed August 28, 2018.

Theissen, Gerd. 1991. *The Gospels in Context.* Minneapolis: Fortress Press.

—. 1986. *The Shadow of the Galilean.* SCM Press.

Theosophical Ruminator. 2011. "Biblical Archaeology 38: Peter's House in Capernaum." *Theo-sophical Ruminations.* 16 September. Accessed April 22, 2019. https://theosophical.wordpress.com/2011/09/16/biblical-archaeology-38-peter%E2%80%99s-house-in-capernaum/.

Tolstoy, Leo. 1893. *The Kingdom of God is Within You.* Edited by 2010. Translated by Constance Garnett. Watchmaker Publishing.

Tuccinardi, Enrico. 2016. "Christian Horrors in Pompeii: A New Proposal for the Christianos Graffito." *Journal of the Jesus Movement in its Jewish Setting,* 61-71. http://www.jjmjs.org/uploads/1/1/9/0/11908749/jjmjs-3_tuccinardi.pdf.

Twichell, David E. 2000. *The UFO-Jesus Connection.* Infinity Pub.

Tzaferis, Vassilios. 1989. "A Pilgrimage to the Site of the Swine Miracle." *Biblical Archaeology Review* (15:2). Accessed September 19, 2020. https://www.baslibrary.org/biblical-archaeology-review/15/2/1.

Valkanet, Richard. 2010. "Bible Timeline." *Bible Hub.* Accessed October 13, 2019. https://biblehub.com/timeline/.

Vermes, Geza. 2003. *Jesus in His Jewish Context.* London: Fortress Press.

Vermes, Geza. 2009. "Jesus in the Eyes of Josephus." *Standpoint Magazine.* Accessed March 28, 2020. https://standpointmag.co.uk/jesus-in-the-eyes-of-josephus-features-jan-10-geza-vermes/.

—. 1981. *Jesus the Jew; A Historian's Reading of the Gospels.* Philadelphia: Fortress Press.

—. 2001. *The Changing Faces of Jesus.* Penguin UK.

Vermeulen, Marian. 2020. "Year of the Four Emperors: A Complete Overview." *The Collector.* 27 September. Accessed February 11, 2021. https://www.thecollector.com/year-of-the-four-emperors-overview/.

Viklunds, Roger. 2011. "The Jesus Passages in Josephus – a Case Study, part 2a – "Testimonium Flavianum": Josephus' testimony and Witnessing." *rogerviklund.wordpress.com.* 27 February. Accessed March 2, 2020. https://rogerviklund.wordpress.com/2011/02/27/the-jesus-passages-in-josephus-%E2%80%93-a-case-study-part-2a-%E2%80%93-%E2%80%9Dtestimonium-flavianum%E2%80%9D-josephus%E2%80%99-testimony-and-witnessing/.

Waddington, W G, and C Humphreys. 1992. "The Jewish Calendar, A Lunar Eclipse and the Date of Christ's Crucifixion." *Tyndale Bulletin* (43.2): 331-351. https://legacy.tyndalehouse.com/tynbul/Library/TynBull_1992_43_2_06_Humphreys_DateChristsCrucifixion.pdf.

Waddington, W, and C Humphreys. 1983. "Dating the Crucifiction." *Nature*.

Wadholm Jr., Rick. 2015. "Greek Manuscripts, Mark 1 and Nomina Sacra." *W.onderful W.orld of W.adholms*. 12 September. Accessed February 4, 2021. https://rickwadholmjr.wordpress.com/2015/09/12/greek-manuscripts-mark-1-and-nomina-sacra/.

Walker, John. n.d. *Calendar Converter*. Accessed November 22, 2019. http://www.fourmilab.ch/documents/calendar/#juliancalendar.

Walker, Norman. 1960. "The Reckoning of Hours in the Fourth Gospel." *Novum Testamentum* (Brill) 4: 69-73. Accessed July 27, 2020. https://www.jstor.org/stable/pdf/1560330.pdf.

Walsh, John Evangelist. 1982. *The Bones of St. Peter; The First Full Account of the Search for the Apostle's Body*. Doubleday & Co.

Wesselow, Thomas de. 2012. *The Sign. The Shroud of Turin and the Birth of Christianity*. Penguin Random House.

Weyler, Rex. 2008. *The Jesus Sayings; The Quest for his Authentic Message*. Toronto: House of Anansi Press.

Whiteley, D.E.H. 1985. "Was John Written by a Sadducee?" Edited by W.de Gruyter. *WHANR 2.25.3*. Accessed February 12, 2020. https://www.degruyter.com/document/doi/10.1515/9783110855722-009/html.

Wilken, Robert L. 2020. "Tertullian." *Encyclopedia Britannica*. 28 April. Accessed November 21, 2020. https://www.britannica.com/biography/Tertullian.

Williams, Michael. 2019. "Gnosticism." *Encyclopedia Britannica*. 19 Mar. Accessed October 17, 2019. https://www.britannica.com/topic/gnosticism.

Windle, Bryan. 2019. "Biblical Sites: Is el-Araj Bethsaida?" *Bible Archaology Report*. 11 September. Accessed February 26, 2021. https://biblearchaeologyreport.com/2019/09/11/biblical-sites-is-el-araj-bethsaida/.

Witherington III, Ben. 2017. "The Most Dangerous Thing Luther Did." *Christianity Today*. 17 October. Accessed March 14, 2021. https://www.christianitytoday.com/history/2017/october/most-dangerous-thing-luther-did.html.

Wright, N.T. 1999. *The Challenge of Jesus, Rediscovering Who Jesus Was and Is*. Downers Grove: IVP Academic.

Young, Francis, Lewis Ayres, and Andrew Louth, . 2008. *The Cambridge History of Early Christian Literature*. Cambridge University Press.

Zardoni, Raffaella. 2012. "Holy Sepulchre, a 3D-journey back in time." Associazione pro Terra Sancta, 2 Feb. Accessed August 20, 2019. https://www.youtube.com/watch?v=7JrtcvNUK6Y.

` information can be obtained
w.ICGtesting.com
d in the USA
W051059090323
1270LV00010B/169